THE

NATURE

OF

PHILOSOPHY

THE
NATURE
OF
PHILOSOPHY

An Introduction

Samuel M. Thompson
MONMOUTH COLLEGE

Holt, Rinehart and Winston
New York

To
Margaret Jean
and
Roberta Grace

PREFACE

This book is written in the conviction that the most effective introduction to philosophy is an encounter with the problems as they arise out of common human experience. The aim of this book is not to introduce the student to the various philosophies but to introduce him to the kind of thinking from which philosophy comes. At this stage the student needs not so much an acquaintance with the writings of important technical philosophers of the past and present as to be confronted by the problems which will make those writings significant to him. Instead of being launched into the technical controversies of contemporary philosophy he needs to concern himself first with what most contemporary philosophical discussion takes for granted or has passed beyond. Many of the masterworks of philosophy are products of highly sophisticated thought developed about technical problems; and even where this is not the case they often reflect the more immediate concerns of a different time and a different place. An introduction to philosophy which involves first level reflection will prepare the student to appreciate the importance of the problems which arise at more advanced stages of philosophical inquiry.

Since philosophy is unfamiliar territory to most beginning students it is important to enter the field slowly and to give much attention at the outset to the question of what philosophy is about, its place in the intellectual realm, and its methods of inquiry. As they begin the study of a new field students of this generation are anxious to know what they are doing and to have some awareness of the relation of this to other and more familiar fields of knowledge. As the book proceeds the pace is increased and the level of difficulty rises. At every stage, however, an attempt is made to show how the problems discussed arise out of ordinary experience or from special fields of inquiry with which it may be supposed that students already have some acquaintance.

The problems discussed here are so presented that the student is exposed to a definite point of view. This is not because of a desire to indoctrinate but because of a conviction that such problems cannot be discussed profitably from a neutral standpoint. If this book may be said to have a thesis, however, it is that conflicts between philosophers and philosophies are not simply issues between what is true and what is false. The very fact of conflict shows that something is neglected by one or both sides. This book therefore is written in a spirit of reconciliation. Views which are rejected are rejected because of inadequacy, not because they are merely false or perverse. An attempt is made to present them with genuine appreciation of their contributions to the progress of thought, and attention is frequently called to the fact that points of view which have to be superseded are what make possible a more adequate understanding.

In the same spirit of reconciliation there is much stress upon both the autonomy and the complementary relationship of different fields of inquiry. Particular attention is given to the relationships between the sciences and the humanities, a matter of increasing importance and urgency today. The whole approach here is an attempt to take human experience seriously in its cognitive function, including not only mathematics and the natural sciences but also ethical evaluations, art, and religion. In all human experience there is, in addition to preoccupation with immediate and pressing needs, a constant search for meaning and for intelligibility. As no other discipline, philosophy draws its sustenance from the whole range of experience and knowledge. Each problem discusssed is presented as a focal point or perspective from which wide areas of meaning can be seen in terms of a pattern of mutual relevance.

The questions for study and discussion at the end of each chapter are intended primarily to provoke thought and to test comprehension. At the beginning of each set of questions is a list of terms which are important for an understanding of the chapter and are introduced for the first time in that chapter. Those terms will all be found in the Glossary.

I wish to express my thanks to Professor Howard D. Roelofs of the University of Cincinnati and to the administrators of the Charles Phelps Taft Memorial Fund for their invitation to give the Taft Lectures at the University of Cincinnati in March 1959. This provided an occasion for working out the theory of art and of the relation of art and religion which is presented here in the last two chapters. I am under special obligation to Mr. Charles E. Lee and to others who read extensive parts of earlier versions of the manuscript. Their criticisms and suggestions have been most helpful, although of course they bear no responsibility for the outcome. I am grateful also to Monmouth College for a grant from the Faculty Development Fund which greatly lightened the burden of preparing the manuscript, and to Mrs. H. A. Loya for her expert and expeditious help as a typist.

S. M. T.

Monmouth, Illinois
January, 1961

CONTENTS

PART II. PHILOSOPHY OF SCIENCE
AND MATHEMATICS

PART III. PHILOSOPHY OF
NATURE AND MAN

PART IV. THE WORLD OF VALUES

PART I

The Nature
and Method
of Philosophy

CHAPTER 1

What Is Philosophy?

THE APPEAL OF PHILOSOPHY

It is through wonder that men begin to philosophize, whether in olden times or today. First their wonder is stirred by difficulties of an obvious sort, and then gradually they proceed to inquire about weightier matters. . . . Now the result of wonderment and perplexity is to feel oneself ignorant; if, then, it was to escape ignorance that men began to philosophize, it is evident that they were pursuing this sort of study in order to know and not from any motive of utility.[1]

"Philosophy," combining two words meaning *love* and *wisdom*, is from the Greek language, and is the name given by some early Greek thinkers to the search for truth for its own sake. Thus the source of philosophy is intellectual curiosity, the desire to know the truth about existence and to understand the significance of that truth for man. In this desire, and man's attempt to satisfy it, is the source of all theoretical inquiry; and out of philosophy have come the sciences of nature and man and society, critical history, the criticism of literature and art, and theology. Philosophy itself has

[1] Aristotle, *The Metaphysics*, 928b 11-21, translated by Philip Wheelwright, in *Aristotle* (New York, The Odyssey Press, 1951), p. 72. By permission.

3

lived on, side by side with its offspring, doing its own work; learning from the work of other disciplines, and considering the bearing of their findings on its own problems.

Philosophy springs from wonder, and wonder is aroused by the awareness of difficulties; by the need to understand. The difficulties which not infrequently lead men and women into the province of philosophy are the problems they meet in the attempt to live their own lives intelligently and with discrimination. What makes life worth living? What goals shall I choose? What is the meaning of failure and evil and suffering? What is my place in the scheme of things, if indeed there be a scheme of things? What is the nature of knowledge, and how can I identify truth and distinguish it from what is false? These and many other questions face all of us who take our own existence seriously and are not content to live by other people's rules and to carry out other people's wishes; who believe that life is not merely to be accepted and lived blindly, but is to be examined and its possibilities compared and tested.

According to Plato's account of Socrates' trial, a trial which resulted in his conviction and sentence of death, Socrates based his defense on the proposition that the unexamined life is not worth living. The examination of life is first of all reflection upon whatever it is that we are doing, and it is out of such reflection that many of the problems of philosophy arise. If we are scientists we investigate some aspect of the world of nature, but if we are philosophers of science we turn our attention back upon the process of scientific investigation. As philosophers of science we do not so much study the world of nature directly as we study the study of the world of nature. We seek to understand what scientific knowledge is, its significance and its relation to other modes of knowledge and belief. As the pursuit of scientific knowledge is a part of life, so the examination of that pursuit is a part of the examination of life. The same principle applies to all areas of life: philosophy of religion, philosophy of history, philosophy of the state, philosophy of education, philosophy of art, all include some kind of examination of life.

The more special and limited problems of philosophy lead into inquiries of more general scope. In its broader aspects philosophy examines the various kinds of existence and their interrelationships, in ontology; the general features of the universe as a whole, in cosmology; the nature of knowledge, in epistemology and logic;

and the nature of value, in ethics and esthetics. Philosophy may reach very abstract levels and some of its problems may seem far removed from the immediate concerns of life. Yet the most abstruse and technical of philosophical problems arise out of the attempt to understand what we are, what kind of a world we live in; how we know ourselves and our world, and on what basis we select the goals for which we strive.

Why is it important to live an examined life? This itself is a philosophical problem, but we may say here that examination is essential to understanding. Without an attempt to understand we do not live our lives at their full human stretch; we are only half alive, or worse. Without understanding we do not know what we are doing or why; we are like leaves blown about by shifting winds. Without understanding our choices tend to center on the immediate issues that arise as we pursue goals and carry out purposes of which we are only dimly aware. To act as human agents in the fullest sense, to be capable of responsible self-direction, we must be able to choose our final goals and our means of reaching these goals. If we wish to make such choices in the light of knowledge and under the guidance of reason we need as adequate an understanding of ourselves and our place in existence as we can obtain. But to know our goals and how to reach them is not enough for responsible self-direction, nor is it all we need for the examination of life. To live an examined life we need to know why the goals we seek are desirable and why the means we use to reach those goals are appropriate. There are three kinds of people in the world: those who do not know what they are doing, those who do know what they are doing but do not know why they are doing it, and those who know what they are doing and know why they are doing it.

Is there not danger in this that we shall substitute thought for action? On this theme Hamlet soliloquizes:

> And thus the native hue of resolution
> Is sicklied o'er with the pale cast of thought,
> And enterprises of great pith and moment
> With this regard their currents turn away,
> And lose the name of action.

Certainly it is possible and often tempting to substitute thought for action, and the result can be disastrous. But it is also true that we sometimes act impulsively in order to avoid the painful struggle of thinking through our problems—a task we must carry out if we are to arrive at a reasoned conclusion concerning what we ought to do. When a person does not think but acts on impulse, is the act truly his own? If he does not know what he is doing he may not be even legally responsible for his act. Suppose he knows what he is doing but does not know why, or for what end, or how this action accords with the basic policies he accepts for himself. May we not say that the act is only partly his own act? When the time for action comes, when it is too late for reflection, when the pale cast of thought would now turn away the currents of enterprises of great pith and moment, then truly it is too late for thought. But unless thought has already done its work, unless the path of action has been set by thought and confirmed by reflection, we shall find ourselves acting under the control of whatever outside influences happen to be working upon us; and we shall surely be the puppets of circumstance.

Most young people of college age in our culture have lived their lives thus far almost entirely under the control of other people. Most young people are eager for independence, for the opportunity to make their own decisions and to control their own lives. But if they think that this desirable state can be achieved merely by becoming independent of parents and teachers and others who have directed their activities in the past, they are surely deceiving themselves. Merely to escape from earlier controls means only the substitution of new controls. Many who think they are living their own lives are actually the victims of social and psychological pressures of various kinds; and the chief difference between their present and past situations is that now they are pulled this way and that by forces they are not aware of, by anonymous agencies which have no genuine concern for persons. If young people are to attain to personal independence, to a true freedom of choice and decision, they need an understanding of what they are and of what values of life are available to them; they must understand something of the way in which effective decision can be made, and they must have the knowledge and insight which enables them to discover and compare and judge the alternatives open to them. Without philosophy life either is lived blindly or else is lived on trust alone.

WHAT IS PHILOSOPHY ABOUT?

> Philosophical inquiry [says Professor Philip Wheelwright] may be directed toward anything whatever, but its aim will always be to behold and understand the object of inquiry (1) in its whole character and (2) in relation to man's most enduring and most deep-rooted interests.[2]

The special sciences advance by the progressive isolation of the objects of their investigations. Chemists and physicists study the various kinds of materials we find in nature by breaking them down into their molecular components. A molecule is analyzed into its atomic structure; and atoms are understood in terms of electrons, protons, neutrons, and other sub-atomic particles and processes. Even the study of the interrelationships of the parts of a complex structure is pursued scientifically by considering each distinguishable relation in isolation. The very heart of the experimental method is in its techniques of varying one factor while holding others constant, and this is a technique of isolation.

Similar strategy is used in other special disciplines. Advances in historical knowledge have come from the intense concentration by specialists upon limited areas and problems. Instead of on the history of a period or place, professional historians often concentrate on such specific aspects as the political or economic or cultural or military. In the social sciences, in the study of literature and art, in every field of investigation which carries knowledge into hitherto unknown areas of fact and value, the same method of isolation and specialization is used.

In contrast with such specialization, one basic aim of philosophy is to bring things together in thought and to try to understand them in their broadest relationships. This aim at wholeness appears in two forms. In the first place it is an attempt to see each object studied in its own unity rather than to study its various parts in isolation from each other. In the second place it is an attempt to see each object in its relations with other objects—an attempt which may lead finally to a consideration of that object in its cosmic setting.

In addition to the concern for wholes and the trend toward

[2] *The Way of Philosophy*, Revised Edition (New York, The Odyssey Press, 1960), p. 7.

synthesis, philosophy has also its analytical side. Preoccupation with synthesis is exposed to the dangers of becoming careless of detail, uncritical of assumptions, and of confusing wishes for reasons. So philosophy needs for its own protection constant and vigorous critical analysis of the process of thinking in terms of wholes, in the attempt to see more clearly the things that may have been distorted or obscure from the perspective of the whole.

> All philosophy [said Alfred North Whitehead] is an endeavor to obtain a self-consistent understanding of things observed. Thus its development is guided in two ways, one is the demand for a coherent self-consistency, and the other is the elucidation of things observed.[3]

These two ways of thinking do not always go along together. Some thinkers aim at synthesis, others are concerned mainly with analysis. Some periods are periods mainly of synthesis, others are periods of analysis. For the late Bernard Bosanquet, for example, philosophy is concerned with totality:

> The essence of philosophy lies in the connected vision of the totality of things, maintaining in every point the subordination of every element and factor to every other element and factor as conditioned by the totality. . . . It includes the direct contemplation—the valuation— of the whole spectacle of life.[4]

Much of the emphasis in present day philosophy is in the contrary direction, upon analysis alone. But there are indications of a renewed interest in problems of wider scope, and it is likely that concern for integration will become stronger. Each aspect of philosophical inquiry leads naturally to its opposite. The more ambitious and inclusive is the attempt at synthesis, the greater is the need for careful analysis of the structure and method of that philosophy; and the further we go in analysis, the more pressing becomes the need to find some unity and meaning in the scattered results of that method of inquiry.

The entire development of modern science has been in the direction of analysis, and illustrates very well the general principle that analysis without integration leads to specialization. Of course specialization is necessary, for knowledge cannot advance very far

[3] *Modes of Thought* (New York, The Macmillan Company, 1938), p. 208. By permission.
[4] *Science and Philosophy* (New York, The Macmillan Company, 1927), pp. 25-26. By permission.

without the concentrated pursuit of localized inquiry. But the very success of a limited inquiry often invites uncritical generalizations beyond the area to which the new knowledge properly applies. To overcome this we have to turn again and again to the central organization of our beliefs and to the basic structure of our knowledge, and the problems which face us there are among the chief concerns of philosophy.

Intellectual analysis and integration are the tasks of the philosopher [says Professor Lewis White Beck]. Philosophy has been defined as "a persistent attempt to think things through." The characteristic attitude of the philosopher is, or ought to be, patient and open-minded inquiry in a serious, disciplined, and ambitious effort to find the general traits of reality, the significance of human experience, and the place of man in the universe as a whole. Philosophy is a vigorous attempt to think about the ultimate questions that are usually "answered" by our emotions and vague hopes and fears. It is a reasoned effort to see facts and ideals, emotions and truths, man and the universe, in such a way that they will, when taken together, make more "sense" than when taken piecemeal.[5]

This suggests that in both its aspects of synthesis and analysis, philosophy is a search for meaning. We discover the meaning of the part when we find its relations with other parts and its place in the whole. To do this we need some degree of analysis, to see the part as a part in its own nature; and we need to see it also in its setting. As Susanne K. Langer has said, the guiding principle which gives to philosophy "a working basis as well as an ultimate aim . . . is the pursuit of meaning."[6]

The pursuit of meaning leads us to inquire concerning the relevance of knowledge for man. What is all this to us, to our enduring interests and basic needs? What is the human situation in relation to the world as we know it? In considering such problems, philosophy can help to open up to us also the meaning of other disciplines. As Erwin Schrödinger, the distinguished physicist, has said:

It seems plain and self-evident, yet it needs to be said: the isolated knowledge obtained by a group of specialists in a narrow field has in

[5] *Philosophic Inquiry: An Introduction to Philosophy* (New York, Prentice-Hall, Inc., 1952), p. 4. By permission.
[6] *The Practice of Philosophy* (New York, Henry Holt and Company, 1930), p. 21.

itself no value whatsoever, but only in its synthesis with all the rest of knowledge and only inasmuch as it really contributes in this synthesis something toward answering the demand . . . "Who are we?" [7]

THE SEARCH FOR MEANING

Philosophy is an attempt to grasp in thought the forms of existence disclosed in human experience, the search by thought for the rational structure of existence. It is true that philosophy is not the only kind of search for the rational structure of existence, for the sciences also engage in such a search. But philosophy differs from the natural sciences partly in that its search is by reflective thought alone. Knowledge of existence which requires experiment or the use of mathematical forms as instruments of inquiry belongs to the natural sciences and not to philosophy.

As Susanne Langer insists, philosophy is also a search for the meaning of existence, and in this, like the arts and literature, philosophy belongs with the humanities. As a search for the meaning of existence, philosophy differs from other humanistic disciplines in concerning itself with the meaning that existence has for thought. What do we mean, in our thought about existence? and What meaning has existence for thought? are two sides of the same question. Any attempt to answer this question by means of reflective thinking which is subjected to logical tests of validity and truth is philosophy.

Because of the importance of the search for meaning as a part of philosophy's task, philosophers have usually given considerable attention to language. Some contemporary philosophers, indeed, consider that the main task of philosophy is the analysis of language. The current emphasis upon language analysis is an understandable and a salutary reaction against claims made by many philosophers that they are giving a direct and final report of the ultimate nature of existence and knowledge. The analysis of language is a part of what Whitehead calls "the elucidation of things observed." Language is an expression of thought, and thought that claims to have obtained truth is thought about something. Thus the analysis of language contributes to our understanding of how we think about

[7] *Science and Humanism* (Cambridge, Cambridge University Press, 1953), p. 5.

the things and events we find in experience. As it is a reflection upon the concepts we use in our efforts to understand existence, philosophy is also an examination of the basic structures or forms we find in existence.

A serious philosopher, however, needs assistance from others who are engaged in the same kind of task. To read a philosopher who thinks differently from us about existence is to expose our own thoughts to contact with forms of existence we had missed before. Philosophers may be expected to differ about what forms of existence are basic; for this is a matter of interpretation founded on the individual thinker's own unique pattern of experience. A philosophy is a conceptual interpretation of existence in terms most meaningful to the interpreter, and by discovering what interpretations are significant for other thinkers we expand and transform our own understanding. The process by which this takes place, and its contribution to the discovery of truth, we shall consider later in our study of the method of philosophy.

In human anatomy we study the various structures of the body; and in physiology we study the functions which those structures perform. In psychology we study man's behavior and his modes of experience and adjustment; and in the social sciences we study the various relationships men have with one another in society. The physiologist is concerned with anatomy, but only so far as it has a bearing on physiology; the psychologist takes account of anatomy and physiology, but only so far as those sciences are pertinent to the study of human behavior. Each discipline makes whatever use it can of the results achieved in other disciplines; but no special science studies man as man in an attempt to understand the meaning of human existence.

Sociology and anthropology and psychology give us valuable information concerning human motives and the methods by which men live together; they show us the differences and contrasts among human cultures; they help us understand why some societies have been strong and long-lived while others have been weak and ineffective. But no such studies, so long as they are concerned with discovering and reporting the facts as those facts are observed, can answer the question of what kinds of human life and society are desirable for man. They may be able to tell us much about what man *does* desire but they cannot tell us what man *ought* to desire. To inquire what man ought to desire is to inquire into his place in the whole scheme of things, and this requires some conception of what that scheme is.

To say that philosophy aims at wholeness is to say that philosophy seeks to understand an object not only in terms of its own internal unity but also in terms of its relations to other things. Just as the significance of man's physical make-up can be understood only as we see it in its relations with other aspects of man's nature, so the significance of man's existence can be grasped only by considering man's relations to other existences. In this way alone thought can hope to find the meaning of human life, for the question of the meaning of something is the question of its place in a whole to which it belongs.

Whenever we ask the question of what is the meaning of this or that, we ask the question of how this or that exists in relation to other things. If we wish to understand the meaning of a man's position as an officer of a corporation, for example, we try to discover the relationships he has in that office to other officers and departments. In order to understand this, in turn, we need to know something of the pattern of organization, the kind of business in which the corporation is engaged, and the various relations it has to other industrial and financial organizations. This, in turn, can be understood only in the light of our knowledge of the economy as a whole and even of the world economy together with its historical setting and development.

Even when the pursuit of meaning requires that we break something up into its parts, the attempt to discover the meaning of each part leads into a study of the relation of that part to other things. The search for meaning thus may not always proceed as if in a straight line from the lesser to the more inclusive. It may require frequent steps of analysis, and new attempts which take their point of departure from the products of analysis; but as we push the search for meaning in any single direction we are driven on to wider and wider wholes. If we do not stop short at some point, the search for meaning inevitably leads to questions about the whole of existence, about the various modes of being and their relations with each other. Thus when pursued relentlessly the search for meaning leads to the attempt to find out what is ultimate and final in existence and to understand other things in terms of their relations with these ultimates. Various systems of philosophy are theories concerning ultimates. They are attempts to push our explanations back until we come to something that explains other things but cannot itself be explained in terms of anything else.

If, as some ancient philosophers supposed, the cosmos is ultimately a plurality of material particles ("atoms") in motion in empty space so that everything that happens is understandable as a complex of atomic motions and collisions; then the moving atoms and the empty space in which they move are the ultimates for that philosophy. The existence of these ultimates explains the events of the world, but nothing accounts for the atoms and empty space. If, as some other philosophers have held, the world of nature is the expression or manifestation of a universal mind, then no part of nature accounts for the existence of that mind. The existence of the universal mind is what accounts for the existence of nature; and the universal mind is the ultimate for that philosophy. If the world is the creation of a self-existent God, as Hebrew, Christian, and Muslim versions of theism contend; then God is the ultimate and everything else is dependent on God. The existence of the world is explained by the creative activity of God, but the world in no way accounts for God.

Even those philosophies which deny that there is any ultimate in existence, or deny that we can know such ultimates if they do exist, or deny that the very question of ultimates has any meaning, are setting forth theories of ultimates. The denial of ultimates is itself an ultimate of a sort, for although it denies that there is anything in existence that is ultimate, yet this knowledge is taken to be final. The denial that we can know ultimates is a claim to have a kind of ultimate knowledge. The contention that the questions of philosophy, as traditionally understood, are meaningless is itself a claim to finality in our knowledge of the significance of the traditional questions of philosophy. They turn out to have a meaning after all, even if only as expressions of human misunderstanding and confusion.

When we begin to ask why certain actions are required of us and why certain other things are denied to us we have begun an inquiry which raises philosophical questions if followed out far enough. In this sense most of us are engaged to some degree in philosophical inquiry. Our philosophizing may be well or poorly done, but is a kind of philosophizing nevertheless. The practical importance of the study of philosophy is found in the fact that it is better to do our philosophical thinking with some competence and awareness of what we are doing and of how we are doing it than to do such thinking blindly and incompetently. Any conscious control which a person exerts over his life is exerted with reference to some framework of existence and value. Surely it is worth our while to become familiar with some of the important possible frameworks of life.

PHILOSOPHY AS REFLECTIVE INQUIRY

As the search for the meaning that existence has for thought, philosophy is a *reflective* inquiry. We are directly aware of clouds in the sky, of fields and trees and houses, of living things, of other people and of what they say and do. To increase our knowledge of the nature of any of these things we turn to a special science or special factual discipline. But our awareness that some of the things we think about really exist while others do not is almost sure to be a reflective awareness. We ordinarily judge that the things we see are things that really exist, but we do not in a strict sense *see* their existence as we see, say, their colors and shapes. The distinction between what exists and what does not is a distinction based on experience but made explicit only by thought. We accept as true or reject as false the statements we hear from the lips of others; but only as we turn our attention from the statements themselves and reflect on our way of judging do we become aware of that distinction between truth and falsity we actually use when we agree or disagree with what others say. In our political society we try to establish justice in human relations; but as philosophers we ask, "What is justice?" and "What is the distinction between justice and injustice?" Such reflective inquiries are not pursued primarily by seeking new information but trying to discover the meaning of the facts we already know.

Of course every inquiry is in some sense a search for meaning. Philosophy's search for meaning, however, is in a framework of ultimates. As soon as any inquiry begins to raise questions about ultimates it begins to be concerned with philosophical problems. But the distinction between what is proximate and what is ultimate, between what can be explained by something else and what cannot be explained at all or else is its own explanation, is a distinction that comes into explicit awareness only as we reflect on what we already know. We may *act* in terms of a distinction between the proximate and the ultimate, we may even *feel* such a distinction, but it becomes explicit in our awareness so that we know *what* it is only when we examine it in reflection.

From this we may formulate a brief statement of what is distinctive about a philosophical problem. In the first place, philosophy is concerned with the kind of question which can be investigated by thought alone. This does not mean that we can depend on thought alone for knowledge. In order to learn something by thinking we must already have something to think about. We learn about our world and about ourselves from sense perception, from scientific observation and experiment, and by the use of imagination in art and literary creation. Whatever additional well-grounded knowledge we can obtain by thought alone is philosophical knowledge. We can see what people look like, we can observe their behavior, and we can examine their physical constitution. From such sources we get our common sense and scientific knowledge of man. But if we ask whether man is capable of free choice or is controlled in all his actions entirely by causes beyond his reach, we ask a question that can be investigated only by reflective thought. What we need in order to answer this question is not further factual accounts of how people act but an understanding of the import of the acts we already know about.

Philosophy, like any serious inquiry, is a search for truth. But philosophy differs from other kinds of inquiry in its concern not only to discover what the truth is but also to inquire into the method by which we attempt to find the truth. Philosophy's search for *what* we know always involves the problem of *how* we know. This is the second distinctive character of philosophy. At the point when the question of how we know is raised in any other discipline —such as in a science or mathematics, or history—inquiry becomes philosophical and only the methods of philosophy can be used. The problem of whether or not the method used in a scientific inquiry is a sound one is not a scientific question; the question is one of logic and the philosophy of science. The tests of truth used in historical investigation cannot be examined by the methods of historical inquiry. The problem is one for the philosophy of history. As we shall see later, philosophical inquiry is always unformalized inquiry. As soon as a definite formal procedure is established in any field of inquiry, then investigations can be carried on in that area independently of philosophy.

The third distinctive character of philosophy is its concern with ultimates. We reflect on many questions that face us from day to day, in our work and in our other activities. Someone wants to buy a property I own. Shall I accept his offer or not? A college student must decide upon his major field; a medical student considers whether to specialize or go into general practice; a lawyer is offered appointment as a judge. These are matters of serious concern, and anyone faced with such choices will surely reflect carefully before he decides. But these as they stand are not philosophical questions. Although they may all lead into philosophical questions, each one is limited in scope. Each is limited in scope because it is a question about what is to be done rather than primarily an attempt to discover truth for the sake of knowing what the truth is. When we ask what the truth is and how we know what it is, we are raising the kind of question which remains a problem until our inquiry has taken us to the foundations of our knowledge. We are not through with such a question until we have discovered and recognized our basic assumptions, until we are satisfied that our thinking has reached its ultimate foundations. When our practical problems lead us into such questions as What is the best kind of life for man to live? and Are the values by which I make my choices genuine or counterfeit values? we are seeking not only to decide but to know. We are seeking the kind of knowledge which makes wise decision possible.

Practical questions lead into theoretical questions if we press those practical questions far enough. Of course we seldom have to do so in the ordinary affairs of life, but the affairs of life are not always ordinary. In time of crisis we find ourselves facing questions which can be dealt with adequately only by examining our assumptions concerning what life is about, what goals are truly desirable, and what limits upon our own power and knowledge we need to respect. The question of what the government needs to do when an industrial conflict threatens the national economy may lead into the question of how far the powers of government ought to be used to bring about the settlement of such a conflict. This is a question of political philosophy. Any practical question concerning which is the better course to follow, whether it arises in our personal lives or in business or in politics, can lead into questions concerning what the difference is between the better and the worse, the difference between good and evil, and the basis upon which we can make these distinctions.

Theoretical questions in other fields may also involve philosophical problems. A physicist who is concerned with problems about atomic structure may be forced to reflect on the question of just what a structure is. The scientific search for truth about matter and energy and life may lead into questions of what we mean by truth and how we distinguish what is true from what is not true. These are not scientific questions, and they cannot be investigated by the methods of science. These are philosophical questions and we can get on with them only by using methods appropriate to philosophical questions. Reflection is often philosophical, in the sense that it concerns matters of philosophical import, without reaching to the level of philosophical inquiry. It arrives at some conclusion but neglects the question of how we know the conclusion is sound. Such thinking may be quite revealing; it may communicate discoveries which have far-reaching influence. The sayings of great religious teachers are usually of this character; and the writings of philosophers often contain material of this kind. For example, the following passage from Epictetus is philosophical but not by itself a philosophical inquiry:

> What disturbs men's minds is not events but their judgments on events. For instance, death is nothing dreadful, or else Socrates would have thought it so. No, the only dreadful thing about it is men's judgment that it is dreadful. And so when we are hindered, or disturbed, or distressed, let us never lay the blame on others, but on ourselves, that is, on our own judgments. To accuse others for one's own misfortunes is a sign of want of education; to accuse onself shows that one's education has begun; to accuse neither oneself nor others shows that one's education is complete.[8]

Here we have perhaps some conclusions reached as the result of philosophical inquiry; or perhaps they are insights which were somehow suddenly recognized by Epictetus as worth recording and communicating. At only one point in this passage does Epictetus give a reason in support of anything he says: "Death is nothing

[8] "The Manual of Epictetus," #5, *Arrian's Discourses of Epictetus*, translated by P. E. Matheson, in *The Stoic and Epicurean Philosophers*, edited by Whitney J. Oates (New York, Random House, 1940), p. 469. By permission of Oxford University Press.

dreadful, or else Socrates would have thought it so." Everything else is either an announcement of what he sees to be true or a recommendation concerning its application to conduct. We are convinced that some statements are true merely by having our attention called to them. Where this happens to us, we are not aware of being confronted by a problem; and inquiry is at an end. Such insights may contribute to the solution of philosophical problems, and they may well be a part of philosophical inquiry; but by themselves alone, merely as something announced, they constitute a philosophy only in part.

To say that this pronouncement by Epictetus is philosophy only in an incomplete sense is not to deny that it is philosophy at all. We here see what a great and discerning mind, reflecting upon his and other men's experience, has discovered to be implicit in that experience. Epictetus gives us one interpretation of the significance of our failures and anxieties, an interpretation which must be understood and taken into account in any serious attempt to evaluate this aspect of life.

Literature is full of philosophical reflection, in this limited sense of "philosophical." Consider the following passage by Joseph Conrad:

> I need not tell you what it is to be knocking about in an open boat. I remember nights and days of calm, when we pulled, we pulled, and the boat seemed to stand still, as if bewitched within the circle of the sea horizon. I remember the heat, the deluge of rain-squalls that kept us baling for dear life (but filled our water-cask), and I remember sixteen hours on end with a mouth dry as a cinder and a steering-oar over the stern to keep my first command head on to a breaking sea. *I did not know how good a man I was till then.* I remember the drawn faces, the dejected figures of my two men, and I remember my youth and the feeling that will never come back any more—the feeling that I could last for ever, outlast the sea, the earth, and all men; *the deceitful feeling that lures us on to joys, to perils, to love, to vain effort—to death;* the triumphant conviction of strength, the heat of life in the handful of dust, the glow in the heart that with every year grows dim, grows cold, grows small, and expires—*and expires, too soon—before life itself.*[9]

Much of what Joseph Conrad has to say here is a direct report from experience. But in the three passages which have been printed

[9] From Joseph Conrad's story, "Youth."

here in italics, Conrad is not merely reporting the facts about an experience; he is either reflecting upon the experience or reporting an earlier reflection. "I did not know how good a man I was till then," is an order of knowledge quite different from: ". . . the heat, the deluge of rain-squalls that kept us baling for dear life(but filled our water-cask). . . ." We perceive rain-squalls as we perceive clouds and trees, but by no such perception does a man discover how good a man he is. To discover this required reflection upon experience and the discovery in that reflection of the meaning of his strength and endurance. In his reference to the feeling of power as "the deceitful feeling that lures us on to joys, to perils, to love, to vain effort—to death . . . and expires, too soon—before life itself," Conrad is reporting something that can be learned only by reflection. Here is judgment upon that feeling; a statement of its significance and import.

In both of these examples, the one from Epictetus and the one from Joseph Conrad, we see how reflection contributes to our understanding of experience. In both instances reflection brings a grasp of the meaning of certain experiences—the fear of death, and the challenge of a harsh nature to a man's strength and will. In neither of these passages, however, do we have an instance of philosophical thinking as it actually goes on. Each reports what may have been a result of reflective inquiry or, in contrast, may have been nothing more than an intuitive estimate or the expression of a mood. We engage in philosophy only when our reflection leads to inquiry in which we state explicitly the reasons for our conclusions and examine critically their logical relationship to the reasons we give for them. Much thinking is philosophical, in the sense that it concerns problems of philosophical import; but that does not constitute philosophy if it takes no account of the way in which its conclusions are reached, or fails to examine the logical basis for the claim of truth.

THE KIND OF TRUTH PHILOSOPHY SEEKS

Philosophy's search for the meaning existence has for thought is a search for this meaning as knowledge and not merely as satisfactory belief. A philosophy may be interesting or stimulating or inspiring, but its primary concern as philosophy is for truth.

Since he uses thought alone as his instrument, the philosopher's test of truth must be a test which can be applied by thought alone. This would be a logical test, and so philosophical thinking is guided and evaluated in terms of its logical soundness.

Whenever we reach a conclusion by thinking alone and base its truth claim on thought, there is only one way to defend that conclusion without appealing to some kind of evidence other than that presented in thought. The only defense open to us is to show that admitting the basic assumptions upon which our thought is operating, what we claim to be true is true because it *has* to be true. We defend such a truth claim by showing that the conclusion is undeniable without contradiction.

In such cases the standard by which we distinguish between what is true and what is false is a logical standard, and the use of logical standards of course is not confined by any means to philosophy. If I already know that a man prominent in national politics is a naturalized citizen of the United States, and if I know that no one but a native born citizen can be elected President of the United States, then I know also by thought alone that this man is not eligible for the Presidency. The conclusion I draw has such a relation to my other knowledge that it *cannot* be false if the other assertions are true. Its truth follows by necessity from the truth of the other statements. The conclusion is not a new truth generated by a blending of the other statements, as if by some mysterious synthesis, a new item is added to previous knowledge. On the contrary, what thought does here is to bring into the open, where it can be seen directly, some aspect or relationship within the facts already known. Reasoning exhibits something already implicit in what we were aware of before; although what reasoning does thus bring into the open may not have been recognized by us previously as involved in what we knew. We have not seen it before, perhaps, because we have not before organized our knowledge in such a way as to make this further aspect of it apparent.

I may know that the left guard of the football team at Belmont College is to be the captain of the team next year. I may know that Harry Brown, a business acquaintance, has a son on the Belmont team. These are two apparently unrelated, or at best only remotely related, bits of information I happen to have picked up in casual contacts. If, however, someone tells me that young Brown plays left guard, then I see these other facts in a new relationship—a relationship which brings out what before had not been apparent to me, that young Brown is to be the new football captain. I may say to myself, "I wish I had known that when I saw Brown yesterday; I'd have said something about it." I did not know it because I was not aware of the additional fact—that young Brown plays left guard—the fact needed to show the mutual relevance of the facts I already knew.

The process of thinking by which a conclusion is obtained, and its necessary relation with its premises is shown, is *reasoning*. Not all rational knowledge, however, is obtained by this form of reasoning. Some statements we know to be true, and true necessarily, when we become aware of the meanings of the words used to express thought. We have certain *concepts*, and from our understanding of the concepts we can recognize that certain assertions involving those concepts are necessarily true and that certain other assertions cannot be true. If we understand the way in which an ordinary map is constructed we know that there *cannot* be two places on that map with the same latitude and longitude. Our ordinary concept of time *requires* us to deny that the past can be repeated.

There is a further consequence of the fact that truth claims of thought are defended by showing their necessity. These truth claims are also claims of universality. To defend our thinking as true by showing its logical necessity is also to claim that any other person who thinks logically and who uses the same concepts and makes the same assumptions will have to agree with the assertions we contend are involved in those concepts or implicit in those premises. This does not mean that another's disagreement with our assertions is an indication that those assertions are false; for the disagreement may be based on misunderstanding or may result from unrecognized differences in our concepts. It does mean that disagreement cannot survive mutual understanding except as an indication that at least one position is false.

The kind of truth philosophy seeks is the truth which can be obtained only by the sustained application of such standards as rational necessity and universality, an application carried through to the end. We do not reach the end of a philosophical inquiry until we have found the ultimate reasons for our conclusions and have given careful consideration to the kinds of reasons we are appealing to and their relevance to our problem. We may be quite confident that some of the ultimate principles of any philosophy will be found to be assumptions. Some assumptions are arbitrary, and are assented to because a thinker has chosen to make a commitment. Sometimes reasons are offered not in support of the truth of an assumption but in defense of making the assumption, in the same way that a person might offer reasons for assuming the veracity of a witness although he had no evidence to support the truth of what the witness had said. That a philosopher makes assumptions is not to his discredit, for it is a considerable achievement to bring basic assumptions into the open to see what they are, and to see also what conclusions follow from them. A systematic philosophy puts such relationships upon public exhibition.

PHILOSOPHY AND OTHER FIELDS OF KNOWLEDGE

Although various fields of inquiry have close relations with each other, and students in one field use results obtained in other fields, yet each discipline has a certain autonomy. Only confusion can result from failure to respect that autonomy. Indeed the consequence is often much more serious than mere confusion; bitter intellectual controversies, violent political conflicts, and even bloody wars have come from failure to respect the difference between the questions appropriate to one field of inquiry and those appropriate to another. As a condition of clarity in our thinking and in the organization of our knowledge we must respect the autonomy of each field of knowledge.

Before the emergence of the natural sciences, as we now know them, philosophers often attempted to solve scientific problems by the use of thought alone. In the following quotation, note how Lucretius appeals to what "must" be and what "ought" to be in his discussion of the motions of atoms:

> Again things which look to us hard and dense must consist of particles more hooked together, and be held in union because welded all through with branch-like elements. . . . Those things which are liquid and of fluid body ought to consist more of smooth and round elements; for the several drops have no mutual cohesion and their onward course too has a ready flow downwards. All things lastly which you see disperse themselves in an instant, as smoke mists and flames, if

they do not consist entirely of smooth and round, must yet not be held fast by closely tangled elements.[10]

In contrast with the passage from Lucretius, the following by Marcus Aurelius is at least the beginning of a genuinely philosophical reflection concerning the cosmos:

> Either it is a well-arranged universe or a chaos huddled together, but still a universe. But can a certain order subsist in thee, and disorder in the All? [11]

The rhetorical question is, of course, an appeal to what we must think. Whether the implicit conclusion is true or false, nevertheless the quesion is one that can be investigated only by reflective thought directed upon what we already know and not by collecting further factual evidence.

In spite of the autonomy of each science and intellectual discipline, philosophy is in a unique position in its relation to other fields of inquiry. For every kind of intellectual inquiry makes its own philosophical assumptions and raises its own philosophical problems. Every inquiry makes assumptions about what exists and what does not exist, about the nature of knowledge and the tests of truth, and about the worth of its own existence as an inquiry. If questions are raised concerning the philosophical assumptions or implications of a discipline, those questions can be properly investigated only by the methods of philosophy.

It is easy to see how the very existence of a field of inquiry can lead to important philosophical problems. Although a philosopher does not investigate the problems of a natural science, such as physics, unless he is a physicist as well as a philosopher, he may consider what significance physics has for man. To pursue the problem of the human significance of a science he may ask such questions as how scientific knowledge exists and what is its structure, what are its assumptions and implications for human welfare. Such questions about physics cannot be investigated by the methods used in a physics laboratory any more than we can look at the science of biology through a microscope or examine astronomy with a telescope.

[10] *On the Nature of Things*, Book II, translated by H. A. J. Munro, in Oates, *op. cit.*, pp. 99-100. By permission of Oxford University Press.

[11] *The Meditations of Marcus Aurelius Antoninus*, IV, 27, translated by G. Long, in Oates, *op. cit.*, p. 512. By permission of Oxford University Press.

Philosophy differs from the special sciences and disciplines in another respect. The methods and techniques of a special science are governed by the desire to know and understand the object of investigation solely for what it is. The scientist attempts to be completely objective and impersonal. Whatever other desires and interests he may have, his personal likes and dislikes or even his ambitions as a scientist, are kept out of the picture. One basic aim of philosophy, however, is to understand the objects of its inquiry "in relation to man's most enduring and most deep-rooted interests."

This is not to say that a philosopher solves his problems by expressing his preferences and feelings concerning the objects he studies. He may confuse the expression of personal preference with logical thinking, but when he does so he fails as a philosopher; the process of philosophizing is a strictly intellectual activity. But the intellectual problem itself, when it is a philosophical problem, requires the philosopher to take intellectual account of man's wishes and desires in relation to his enduring and deep-rooted interests.

It is very easy, of course, to say that we must respect the autonomy of each discipline and refrain from trying to solve problems that belong to one by use of the methods of another. In practice this principle is sometimes difficult to apply. As human knowledge pushes back its borders and opens up new problems we do not always know in the early stages just where the new problems belong. It is important, however, to be on guard constantly against the danger of such confusion and to avoid it whenever and as soon as possible. But if we are to err on one side or the other it may be better for a worker in one field of study to trespass on another rather than to be held back by any strictures concerning the danger of confusion and the importance of autonomy. If he goes too far, that error can be corrected later by his critics; but if he holds back, the world may lose something important. This applies of course primarily to those who have something important to say and, as in the arts, to those who know the rules well enough to understand what they are doing when they violate those rules.

PHILOSOPHY AND OTHER QUESTS FOR MEANING

As we have seen, the questions of philosophy are not questions which lead us to push further the frontiers of factual knowledge; they are rather questions which require reflection upon what we already know. Reflection upon what we already know leads to an important extension of our knowledge, but it might well be considered an extension in depth rather than a widening of the field of knowledge. We discover by other methods what the things in our world are like, but philosophy's primary question is what these things mean to thought.

The question of meaning, in the sense in which we have discussed it, is usually a question of special personal interest to the individual thinker. His primary concern is often the meaning of his own existence. What am I? Who am I? What is my place in the scheme of things? These are the questions that perhaps most often lead to philosophical reflection. A scientist's intellectual curiosity as he exercises it in his field of study is objective and impersonal. The first thing he has to learn is to exclude his own wishes and hopes from his inquiry. He presents the results of his study to other scientists, and they undertake to consider those results with the same impersonality and objectivity. The philosopher's intellectual curiosity, however, is more likely to have a deep personal involvement. The knowledge he seeks may be personal in the sense of revealing to him his own existence and the meaning of other existence in relation to himself and to human values. Even if a philosopher attempts no more than the clarification of thought by the analysis of language and concepts, the thought which he analyzes may have a very personal significance and the desire for clarity may be so intense as to be a passion.

Since the search for meaning is likely to be a personal thing, one which involves our attitudes and our deepest concerns, it is not strange that man seeks meaning by other than philosophical methods. Because of this it is important for us to see clearly the difference between philosophy and such other approaches as literature, music, art, and religion. These differ from philosophy in that they are discoveries of what existence means in terms of feeling and imagination and personal encounter. Philosophy is the discovery of what experience and existence mean to thought. It seeks not appreciation or encounter, but understanding; and its tools are concepts. Philosophy will not reveal the meaning of existence for feeling or for imagination, nor will it place us in our proper personal relation to God or to the ground of being; but neither in literature or art or religion can we ever discover the meaning of existence for thought. We may obtain important and even indispensable data from them, data for the reflective inquiries of philosophy, but only by the method of philosophy can that inquiry be pursued.

No one waits until he becomes a philosopher to find some meaning in life. In the very process of growing up we get ideas of what we are and of where we stand in relation to others and to the world. We get these ideas from the beliefs and attitudes we encounter in our families and friends and neighborhood and school. The great difference between philosophy and the schemes of interpretation we find in common sense and popular religion is that philosophy is a conscious search for truth under the control of logical standards. As soon as we question the truth of the beliefs we have acquired in childhood we are beyond the reach of those beliefs to help us. At this point belief is not enough; we need a different kind of assurance of truth. When we begin to think we express the need not merely for something to accept but for intellectual understanding and insight.

SUMMARY

Philosophy arises out of intellectual curiosity, from the need to understand ourselves and our world. The examination of life leads us into the examination not only of our beliefs but also of the ways by which we arrive at our beliefs. Philosophy is not a substitute for action, but philosophy is an essential preparation for self-directed action which is undertaken with some assurance that the course to be followed is wise and sound.

Philosophical inquiry views its object, whatever that object may be, in its whole character and in its relation to man's most basic interests. To accomplish its aim philosophy needs to use the methods of intellectual analysis as well as those of synthesis, and to keep them in proper relation with each other. Philosophical inquiry, however, involves more than merely a point of view or a set of answers to questions. It includes also an explicit presentation and examination of the reasons for the conclusions reached, together with a critical consideration of the method by which thought proceeds. Philosophy is reflective inquiry which includes a concern with the problem of *how* we know as well as an attempt to find *what* we know, and which has no stopping place short of an explicit exposure of the basic assumptions and the ultimate considerations which enter into our thinking.

Inquiry which views its objects in relation to man's basic interests becomes a search for meaning. Philosophy's search for meaning is a search for the meaning which existence has for thought. This cannot be carried very far without an analysis of language, for language is the indispensable instrument of thought. Philosophy's task is a cooperative task; for although thinking is something that goes on only in the individual, yet the individual's own thinking, if it is to achieve results of any importance, needs the help it can get from the work of others. The search for meaning involves us in the search for relations and for wholes; for to discover the meaning of something is to discover its place and its function in the whole to which it belongs. This leads us naturally into a consideration of ultimates.

Philosophical inquiry is reflective inquiry, but not all reflection is philosophy. First of all, philosophical reflection involves, directly or indirectly, a concern with ultimates. Secondly, it is reasoned inquiry in which we examine evidence, become aware of our assumptions, and evaluate our inferences under the control of logical standards. The logical standards which thought employs are necessity and universality, and the kind of truth which philosophy seeks is the kind we obtain by applying those standards rigorously to the very end. One of the important achievements of philosophy is to bring out into the open the basic assumptions we have been making in our thinking.

Each kind of inquiry has its own problems, its own methods, and its own assumptions. Philosophy, science, mathematics, history, and theology are autonomous disciplines, and the problems of one cannot be solved by the methods of another. The position of philosophy, however, is unique in this way: every field of inquiry makes philosophical assumptions and raises philosophical problems, but philosophy alone is in a position to subject such assumptions and problems to rational examination and inquiry. Recognition of this fact thus requires us to distinguish philosophy from other ways by which we seek to find the meaning of things in relation to our fundamental interests. Philosophy differs from literature, music, art, and religion in that it seeks to discover the meaning of life and existence for thought.

QUESTIONS FOR STUDY AND DISCUSSION

1. *Terms:* esthetics, analysis, assumption, atom, concept, contradiction, cosmology, epistemology, ethics, existence, form, God, knowledge, logic, meaning, ontology, philosophy, reasoning, reflection, synthesis, truth, ultimate, value.

2. Compare Aristotle's distinction between the desire to know and motives of utility, with the distinction between a concern about the ends or goals of life and a concern about the means of reaching those goals. Illustrate both distinctions.

3. When the time for action has come in any important situation does this mean that the time for thought is past, or does it mean that the time has come for a different kind of thinking? If the latter, just what is this difference?

4. Are there any questions at all which can be answered "successfully by our emotions and vague hopes and fears"?

5. Identify some of the ultimates in your own thought and action. Can you justify your dependence upon them?

6. Show how the following illustrate the difference between reflective and non-reflective questions:

    (a) What grade will I make in this course?
    (b) What difference does it make what my grade is?
    (c) What is the honest thing to do in this situation?
    (d) Why be honest?

7. Distinguish between reflecting, guessing, and speculating.

8. Examine: "Every inquiry is in some sense a search for meaning."

9. In what does the *compulsion* of logical necessity consist?

10. Illustrate the difference between a defense of the truth of a belief and a justification for holding a belief.

CHAPTER 2

The
Study
of
Philosophy

OUR INTRODUCTION TO PHILOSOPHY

Long before any of us ever began to study philosophy we were introduced to ideas from which have come some of its most important and most persistent problems. Our introduction to these ideas goes back further than our memories take us, and our use of them will continue whether we study philosophy or not. To be introduced to some of the subject matter of philosophy is, in a sense, to be introduced to philosophy; and to use ideas which belong to the subject matter of philosophy may be said, perhaps, to be a use of philosophy. It is in this broad sense of contact with philosophy and the use of philosophy that we shall begin our discussion of the study of philosophy.

It is not surprising that we are for the most part quite unaware of our contact with philosophy and our own personal use of it, for we begin to use some of the ideas that concern philosophy in much the same way we begin to use the grammar of our native language. We cannot study grammar or even be aware that there is such a thing until we have learned to use it, for if we could not use grammar we could not understand any statement about grammar. So it is with philosophy. We cannot study philosophy unless we can think in terms of such ideas as *existence, knowledge, true* and *false, good* and *bad,* and the like. But just such ideas as these are an important part of the special subject matter of philosophy.

We use these ideas constantly, and often with little thought about their meanings. Perhaps most people who hear rumors about a house being haunted, or are told a story of thought transference, believe or disbelieve largely on the basis of their ideas about what does and what does not exist. A person who disbelieves in ghosts will not go looking for them, although indeed he might look for a credible explanation of someone's report of seeing a ghost. One who is quite ready to say he does not believe that ghosts exist might have difficulty in telling us just what he understands to be the difference between existence and non-existence. In spite of his inability to formulate it, he nevertheless is making and using such a distinction in accepting or rejecting a ghost story. Broadly speaking, this is a kind of use of philosophy. Even though it cannot be clearly specified, some idea of the distinction between what exists and what does not exist is implicit in such a specific judgment as the one about ghosts. Persistent questioning might very well bring to awareness the standards which operate unrecognized in our thinking, just as Socrates was able to show that the slave boy who had received no mathematical instruction was actually using certain important mathematical ideas.[1]

There are those who might object to this use of "philosophy," who might complain that we are giving to the word a meaning which is too wide and loose to tell us anything very definite. We shall have to be more specific and more restrictive in our use of the term, it is true; but at this stage of our study we need to recognize that the concerns of philosophy, in the stricter meanings of the word, have their roots in these ideas which are active in our thoughts and desires and decisions long before we attempt to formulate them explicitly and to determine what precisely we mean by them.

In order to use a philosophy we must have one, but to have a philosophy is not enough to give us knowledge about philosophy.

[1] See Plato's *Meno.*

There is a difference between *having* a philosophy, *using* a philosophy, and *engaging in* philosophical thinking and inquiry. In a sense we *have* a philosophy just as soon as we have some idea of what is real, of the difference between things that exist and things that do not exist, of the difference between the true and the false and between good and bad. We *use* a philosophy whenever we use such ideas to guide our action. But we do not *participate in* the work of philosophy until we try to think these things out for ourselves.

To think *for* ourselves, however, does not mean to think *by* ourselves. If we try to think by ourselves we shall not get very far. If we could not benefit from the work of other thinkers each of us would have to start from the beginning. To try to think by ourselves hardly seems sensible in the face of the fact that we have available the results of twenty-five hundred years of philosophical inquiry. On the other hand, if we are to engage in philosophy we do not go to other philosophers merely to pick out for ourselves a philosophy that suits us, as we might select a coat or an automobile or a house. Other philosophers can help us only as we think their thoughts after them, only as we follow the paths they have taken from starting point to conclusion. They guide our thinking, they remind us of what we would not think of by ourselves; but they cannot do our thinking for us. No matter how well other thinkers have done their work we cannot benefit from it except by the active participation of our own thinking. Every great philosophy is an important intellectual experiment, and if we are to benefit from the results of these experiments we must first trace through them in our own thinking.

Let us now look a little more carefully at what it means to have a philosophy and to use a philosophy. We shall then consider some preliminary questions about the study of philosophy.

HAVING A PHILOSOPHY

We begin to have a philosophy just as soon as we begin to get the idea that there is a world of real things and begin to distinguish between those real things and imaginary things. A child's early awareness of the difference between a fairy story and a story of something that "really happened" is a part of his introduction to philosophy. His discovery that a dream is not real, that sometimes his wishes do not fit fact, that things have their own stubborn natures and that we have to deal with them in terms of what they are if we are to use them successfully—these are his introduction to philosophy, punctuated by burned fingers, bumped knees, laughter, and tears. These early lessons are learned painfully, for the child's idea of what the world is like includes little recognition of its stubborn indifference to our wishes. As Walter Lippmann has said:

> The discovery that our wishes have little or no authority in the world brings with it experience of the necessity that is in the nature of things. . . . The world of the child is a kind of enchanted island. The labor that went into procuring his food, his clothes, his toys, is wholly invisible at first. . . . Only gradually does the truth come home to him how much effort it costs to satisfy his wants. It takes even longer for him to understand that not only does he not get what he wants by asking for it but he cannot be sure to get what he wants by working for it.[2]

Unless we have some knowledge of ourselves and our world, or at least unless we have some beliefs which we take to be true, we have no occasion to distinguish between what is of primary importance and what is secondary. On the other hand, if we do know anything, or think we know something, we also have some attitude toward it. We treat the things we know as important and unimportant, and we relate them to ourselves and to our own interests in our thought about them. To avoid having a philosophy we should have to avoid having any knowledge or beliefs in which we had any consistent personal interest.

"To have a philosophy" in this sense of the phrase, however, is not to have it *as* a philosophy. As we have already seen, many of our most important concepts are in active use in our thinking long before we begin to examine them. Concepts are ordinarily what we think *with*, not what we think *about;* and until we have been thinking with a concept for some time we are not in a position profitably to think about it. To understand why this is so, and why the examination of our concepts is so difficult, we need to consider briefly some of the distinctive features of the kind of knowledge we have as human beings and the part which concepts play in that knowledge.

[2] *A Preface to Morals* (New York, The Macmillan Company, 1929), p. 187. By permission.

We do not begin life with knowledge already in our possession. Even if we begin our conscious life by noting and responding to the things in our environment, this is not the kind of awareness which can properly be called knowledge. Before we can be said to know a thing or an object we have to know it as the kind of thing it is. The hungry infant sees his bottle of milk and reaches out for it; he is aware of the bottle and he responds to its presence. But we do not say that he knows what the bottle is until he is aware of it *as* a bottle. At this point we have arrived at one of the distinctive features of human awareness, that human awareness is conceptual.

Knowing, in this latter sense, is more than habitual response or conditioned behavior. There is, in the thought, something which pertains to the nature of the object known rather than to the nature of the thought about the object. When a child does become aware of the shape of a bottle he sees, it is the shape of the bottle he is aware of, not the shape of his thought. This is the difference, for example, between the mere experience of heat as a nameless and inarticulate awareness which may lead to a change in body position or to the loosening of the collar, and the awareness that *this*, the room or the outdoor surroundings or one's clothing, is *hot*. It is the difference between an awareness which does not, and one which does include an assent or denial in thought. It is the difference between an awareness that merely *is*, and a thought that not only *is* but is *true* or is *false* about something other than the thought itself. In the latter case I recognize the heat I feel as the heat *of* something —of the air or of my body or of an oven; or I may think of it simply as heat itself—as a condition which actually exists—without associating it with any specific cause or other object. Thus the heat is, in a sense, present to my awareness and yet what is present to my awareness is not itself a feature of my awareness; it is rather what I am aware *of*. My awareness is an awareness of heat, not a heated awareness. Any awareness which we can call knowledge in this sense is an awareness that refers to something beyond itself.

This reference of what is in awareness to objects which exist beyond that awareness becomes explicit in concepts. We see and hear and touch and smell and taste, but we do more than sense. Some at least of the things we sense, we also think. Our seeing is more than just the experience of red or blue or green or some other color; we see a red sunset, or a brown hat, or a blue sky, or green grass. Besides an awareness of color we have an awareness of something that is colored.

A concept is an awareness of *what* something is. A concept is an idea of some kind of definite nature. We build up a stock of concepts as we discover similarities and differences among the things we perceive. Patterns of qualities and quantities and relations become relatively fixed in our minds and ready for use in identifying the things we encounter later in our experience. A certain sound, for example, leads me to recognize immediately the presence of another person, for that sound is the sound of a human voice. Unless I had some idea of what human voices are like I could not recognize this as that kind of sound. To become vividly aware of the part that concepts play in our experience we need only take note of the importance of recognition. What kind of awareness would we have without recognition? But recognition is *re*-cognition; and recognition cannot occur unless we have already in our possession, in idea and concept, the *what* or *nature* we are to find in whatever thing we can be said to recognize. I cannot recognize this or that tree *as a tree* unless I already have an idea of *what a tree is*.

We have a philosophy, in the broader sense of the word, as soon as we have a stock of concepts by means of which we try to grasp in thought the nature of the things we encounter in our experience. Our ideas may be inadequate, much of what we take to be knowledge may actually be false, but in so far as we have a set of ideas by means of which we identify and recognize things we have a philosophy. For once we have such a stock of ideas we have secured for ourselves a basis upon which to distinguish between real and unreal and between the true and the false. No such distinctions can be made except in terms of some idea of the world, of the world as a field of reference within which our experience acquires meaning in terms of some notion of what really is. We may change our notion, and this is to change our philosophy. But at any moment when we do make a distinction between real and unreal, between true and false, or between good and evil, we accept as true, for that moment at least, some conception of the nature of things.

More is involved in our awareness, however, than merely our ideas of *what* things are. Every such idea includes also an awareness *that* those things are. In all our thinking we are thinking in terms of *being.* Even in saying that something is not, that it does not exist, we attribute some mode of being to it. If I wish to say meaningfully that ghosts do not exist I must refer to something in my use of the word "ghost." Obviously I do not mean that a ghost is just pure nothingness, for if I did I could not answer your question of what it is that I think does not exist. I may as well say "X does not exist"; and in answer to the question, "What is X?" reply, "Nothing." When I say that ghosts do not exist I mean that they are fictions or imaginary beings, not real and actual things. But a fiction is *something;* to be a fiction or to be imaginary is *to be,* in that way at least. Thus I can exclude ghosts from the realm of real existence, and give some meaning to the word "ghosts," only by including them in some other realm of being. The exposure of the treachery of Hamlet's uncle, Claudius, for example, is not an event, so far as we know, which belongs to actual history as does Napoleon's exile to St. Helena. But it is not just nothing; it is something that happens in the play.

Traditionally such distinctions have been a prime concern of philosophy, for philosophy's interest in *what* things are is an interest in what things *are;* it is a concern with their modes of being, with *how* they are. To ask whether something is real or unreal is one of the obvious forms of a philosophical question. To ask how to tell the difference between the true and the false and between the good and the bad are also philosophical questions, as is every other question which involves these questions.

USING A PHILOSOPHY

We have to have a philosophy, in the broad sense of a set of basic beliefs about ourselves and our world, before we can use it; but as we have already seen, the philosophy we have may be quite inarticulate. A philosophy comes to us first as a set of unrecognized assumptions and attitudes. We absorb the beliefs and judgments of family and neighborhood; then, as we grow up, we are led into ways of thinking and believing that are generally accepted in our cultural tradition. By the time we are ready to make decisions for ourselves about what is real or unreal and true or false and good or bad we have a set of basic ideas and beliefs to which we turn. Our decisions are usually based on those answers which seem to fit best into the context of our basic beliefs.

In this sense we *have* a philosophy before we have it *as* a philosophy. Here we repeat the experience of the race, for man had philosophies long before he recognized them as philosophies or engaged in any explicit philosophical thinking. Philosophy is no different in this respect from other basic concerns of human life. Man had religions before he recognized anything as a religion; he had societies before he ever had the idea of a society; he had governments long before he formulated any theory of the political state. Man had philosophies and religions and governments even before he had the slightest glimmerings of any one of these in distinction from the others.

We begin to use philosophy long before we know that we are doing so. In decisions about our personal conduct, for example, we are early influenced by the attitudes and ideas concerning right and wrong which have come from those close to us. Many people carry through life the political and religious loyalties of their parents. How people vote and their attitudes toward religious and social conflicts may be influenced more by those loyalties than by anything else. But the act of making a decision, no matter what the source of the ideas on which the act is based, is the use of philosophy.

In the beginning we always have to get our ideas from someone else, and even the conflicts of thought that lead us to try to think for ourselves almost always come from our exposure to conflicting beliefs held by others. Thus if we come to repudiate the attitudes and standards that governed our early lives at home we are able to do so only because we come into contact with people or with the writings of people who have different ideas of what is worthwhile and of how life should be lived. The conflict of philosophies is one of the most potent of social forces.

Every culture contains inconsistencies and conflicts within itself, and we sometimes encounter problems which bring these conflicts into the open. The discovery that different and conflicting answers are given to the questions that face us is also the discovery that not all the answers offered us can be true. This is the kind of experience which so often prepares us to think for ourselves. We may now come to be aware of a new kind of problem. We now no longer ask merely what is the accepted belief or action in this situation, the "right" one, or what is the "true" answer to our question; we begin to ask *how we can tell* where the truth lies. When we have asked this question, and really have been troubled by it personally, we are ready for the study of philosophy.

It is not enough just to ask where the truth lies, for we can get all sorts of answers to this question without doing any thinking for ourselves. The conflicting answers that made us aware of our original problem may represent conflicting loyalties or emotional attachments. We may be quite able to accept one and reject the others not because we apprehend the truth of the one and the falsity of the others, but merely because of our attitudes toward those who hold to the different positions. Sometimes we may even avoid trying to think for ourselves for fear we shall find a weakness in the position we are determined to support.

We may get our philosophy without thinking for ourselves, but we actively engage in philosophy only as we work out for ourselves some idea of what our important beliefs mean, and only as we examine them on their merits. In so far as we take our ideas and their applications ready-made from others and do not weave them into the texture of our own understanding, our use of those ideas will be largely ineffectual. John Locke said, in a celebrated passage in his *Essay Concerning Human Understanding:*

> The floating of other men's opinions in our brains, makes us not one jot the more knowing, though they happen to be true. . . . In the sciences, every one has so much as he really knows and comprehends. What he believes only, and takes upon trust, are but shreds; which, however well in the whole piece, makes no considerable addition to his stock who gathers them. Such borrowed wealth, like fairy money, though it were gold in the hand from which he received it, will be but leaves and dust when it comes to use.[3]

On the other hand, we cannot think in a vacuum; and, as we have already seen, to think for ourselves is not to think by ourselves in complete isolation from the thought of others. In order to grasp the thought of another and to use it in the solution of my own problems I have to think it through; merely to be informed about the other's conclusions is not enough. If we are to find the meaning of another's philosophical conclusions we have to reconstruct in our

[3] Book I, Chapter III, Section 24, Alexander Campbell Fraser edition (Oxford at the Clarendon Press, 1894), Volume I, pp. 115-16.

own thought the process by which those conclusions were reached. Even to choose among different philosophies, if the choice is to be an informed one, requires a re-thinking of each of those philosophies in its own terms. To try to think for ourselves in philosophy assuredly involves something more than merely the attempt to be original.

FROM WORDS TO IDEAS

Since the most important ideas we use are abstract, many of them are almost complete strangers to us. The ideas of mathematics, the sciences, law and politics are abstract ideas; but so are the ideas of right and wrong, success and failure, and the concepts of human relationships that govern our lives day by day and hour by hour. We seldom originate our abstract ideas for ourselves; we absorb them from our parents, from our neighbors, from our teachers, from books and magazines and newspapers. It is significant that when we acquire abstract ideas from others the first step usually is to learn the names of those ideas. Then if we use the names as others around us use them, we may not have to think very much about what the names mean. We begin to use such words by imitation; and as long as we continue to imitate their use by others, our own use of them is not likely to be called into question.

Thus many words change their meanings as a direct result of lack of precision in their use. People now say, for example, that "John Smith graduated from college" instead of "John Smith was graduated from college." Of course they do not really mean that John Smith conferred his degree upon himself; they simply ignore the distinction. They ignore in speech a distinction which, if it could be ignored in practice, would simplify the problems of many college students. It is quite acceptable to say that a convicted murderer "was executed" where a stricter usage would have us say that "a sentence of death was executed upon the murderer." It is possible to detect a grisly logic in this popular and accepted use of "execute": to execute a sentence is to carry it out, so to execute the sentence of death may be also to "execute" the murderer; for presumably he does not walk out of the execution chamber after the ceremony has been performed. In both these examples, as in most of our ordinary speech and thought, the use of words is governed not by a clear awareness of precise meanings but by a vague recognition of the appropriateness of the word to the context in which it is used. In such cases as "graduate" and "execute," vagueness of thought may be of no importance; but in some of our thinking its effect can be serious indeed.

If we were to take a poll to find out how many people in this country favor democracy, the verdict likely would be an overwhelming majority in its support. But just what do people mean by "democracy"? Do they mean majority rule? Or do they mean a political system that protects individual rights? Or do they mean both? If they mean both, do they see any conflict between the two? The citizens of the free nations may believe that "democracy" means popular self-government, yet in Communist ideology "democracy" refers to a dictatorship which supposedly governs in the interests of the proletariat. In Communist usage, "democracy" is quite consistent both with minority rule and with the most extreme suppression of individual freedom.

In our political campaigns of the past few generations people of many different and conflicting political views have called themselves "liberals." How can a socialist and one who wishes to restrict the functions of government to a minimum both be liberals? Does a liberal advocate freedom of the individual from external control, or does he advocate greater and more extensive governmental authority for the sake of increasing the individual's freedom from want and disaster?

When we use such words as "democracy" and "liberal" without thinking through for ourselves their meanings and applications, we solve no problems and clarify no issues. We may be worse off than if we had never heard the words at all; for if their use as mere words gives us the impression that we have been thinking with those concepts, then we are only fooling ourselves. This holds true even more significantly when we use without comprehension such words as "true," "real," "exist," "good," "right," "substance," "cause," "purpose," "freedom," "beauty," "belief," and "knowledge." For these terms refer to ideas that are basic to our thinking.[4]

[4] For a number of helpful examples of such examination, see *Philosophical Analysis*, edited by Max Black (Cornell, Cornell University Press, 1950), especially the articles: "Obligation and Ability," by William K. Frankena, and "Substratum," by Morris Lazerowitz.

As was pointed out earlier, the fact that we do not engage in philosophy until we begin to think for ourselves does not mean that we have to free ourselves from the influence of the ideas of other people. Such "freedom" would only impoverish our thought. We do not become philosophers by freeing ourselves from the ideas of others but by appropriating those ideas with understanding and critical examination. We have to turn from words to what the words mean, and this is to say that we have to think about the things and events to which the words refer. When we do this under the guidance of those who have already developed such inquiries, their ideas become available for our own use.

The careful analysis of our concepts is of great practical importance. How can a course of action succeed except by accident if we operate at one time on the basis of one theory concerning the kind of world this is, and at another time on the basis of a contrary theory? Suppose a physician thought of the human body part of the time in terms of scientific concepts, and the rest of the time in terms of animistic ideas. How could he tell whether to use chemical therapy or incantations in the treatment of an illness?

Not only is it important for us to understand the general ideas we follow in our action, but we need to understand also the ones we do not follow. Presumably our use of a philosophy means that we consider it more adequate than its alternatives. But unless we understand the issues dividing different philosophies we cannot make these intellectual distinctions with any competence, and if we are to understand the issues we need to understand the different and competing philosophies.

THE DIFFERENCE PHILOSOPHY CAN MAKE

Decision or choice is often what shows a basic idea in action. Suppose someone picks up a wallet from the sidewalk. No one sees him pick it up, and there is nothing to associate him with it. Suppose also that the wallet contains a considerable sum of money, that the name and address of the owner is shown on a card, and that the finder has an urgent need for money. What will he do?

He may keep the wallet, rightly confident that he will not be found out. The other man's bad luck, he may reflect, is his own good luck. Careless people ought to have to take the consequences of their own carelessness. Or he may say to himself that the money is not his and that it is his duty to restore it to its owner.

Here we have two different basic ideas of what is right and wrong in handling of other people's property. The action followed in each case is governed by such an idea, and in this sense each is an instance of the practice of philosophy.

Although we may practice a philosophy in such a situation, it does not follow that we shall. For we may act without using any conception of what is right or wrong; we may merely act on impulse without thinking of what we are doing. Or we may act only after a hard and bitter struggle with our thoughts and yet not be governed in action at all by the conclusion we have arrived at in our thinking. The person who finds a wallet may be fully convinced intellectually that the wallet with its contents intact should be returned to its owner, and yet the temptation to keep it for himself may be so strong that he acts not in accordance with what he judges to be right but in accordance with what he so strongly desires at the moment.

Two people may differ in what they take to be real. One may believe that what he sees or hears or touches is real, and that these realities have all the qualities and characteristics they seem to have. Another may believe that the things we see or hear or touch do not exist with the qualities we seem to find in them, but that they in truth are only extremely complex systems of unit particles and vibratory patterns of energy. He may conclude, then, that the sounds and colors we attribute to things are only ideas in our minds, and that the world as it appears to us is a mental construction.

If the world as we find it is only a sham world then none of our primary activities, such as eating and walking and dealing with things in terms of their appearances, are what they seem to be. If we are of this opinion and are not to be in a condition of perpetual deception, we need constantly to remind ourselves that the real world has no colors or sounds or beauty or ugliness or good or evil, that all these are merely ideas in our minds. On the other hand, if we insist that the world is essentially as it appears to be, then are we to conclude that the scientist's picture of the world is either a falsification or is composed of arbitrary conventions which he uses in order to carry out certain operations and manipulations? A third possibility is that these perspectives can be reconciled, and a fourth possibility is that the question itself is meaningless. What our problem requires, however, if we wish to reach a satisfactory conception of the situation, is not that we examine our world further but that we examine further our ideas of the distinction between real and unreal.

We use philosophy also in our political thinking and action. Our ideas of justice and right, for example, may be the chief influences on our political attitudes. Those who interpret justice to mean conformity with the views of the majority may well approve of anything a government does provided it has majority support. If the majority should decide, for example, that the provisions of the Bill of Rights cause wasteful delay in the prosecution of crime and so should be abolished, then those who understand justice as conformity with majority preference would approve the abandonment of the Bill of Rights.

Some believe, on the other hand, that justice includes a respect for certain unalienable rights of the individual, and that nothing except an immediate and overwhelming threat to the public safety can warrant even a temporary suspension of these provisions. Those who have such beliefs will oppose any action that interferes with individual rights in order to facilitate the prosecution of crime. They consider such action to be usurpation; to be the exercise by a government, of functions which do not properly belong to it.

The general ideas by which we live may make the difference between a system of freedom and a totalitarianism. Fascism, Hitler's National Socialism, and Soviet Russia's Communism are all systems of ideas in action. The important differences between these and the free societies of our world is a difference in the basic ideas of man and society and of good and evil, ideas which are acted out in those various societies and are embodied in their institutions. Ideas do have consequences.[5] Nothing that man does makes so much and such far-reaching difference to what happens to him as does his thinking. The difference between human and animal life is the difference between action in accordance with ideas and action by instinct and habit and sensori-motor adjustment. The whole difference between primitive and civilized man is a difference in ideas—ideas in practice; and all the differences between man's various civilizations are rooted in differences in ideas.

The differences that count the most are differences in our most

[5] Some of these are pointed out by Richard M. Weaver in *Ideas Have Consequences* (Chicago, The University of Chicago Press, 1948).

general and basic ideas. That we prefer our meat cooked and that people of another society prefer their meat raw is a difference of slight significance. But the difference is important if in one society a man is judged by his success in promoting the welfare of others and by the kindness and consideration he shows, and if in another society a man is judged by the number of his enemies' heads he can display or by the extent of the power he can exercise over others. One person may believe that the action of the moment is, as soon as it is done, as if it had not been done at all. He may believe that his life is only a brief localized eddy in an all-inclusive stream of energy—a temporary pattern which has no more significance than the fact that a cloud in the sky has one shape rather than another. His attitude toward himself and others, his choices and decisions, will surely be very different from the attitude and actions of one who believes that his every act makes a difference to the cosmos itself and that his responsibility is for eternity.

All of our initiative, all of our plans, all of our freedom, all of our purposes are based on ideas. In so far as we act for ourselves with freedom and responsibility, our action is governed by what we think is true and by what we think is valuable. Human nature is everywhere much the same in basic biological and psychological capacities. Some individuals may have more or less of certain native powers, but we know of few if any such inherent differences separating human groups or races or cultures. Yet there are great differences in the achievements of different human groups, and those differences are differences in their ideas. The difference between the primitive witch-doctor and the product of our most advanced medical schools is not primarily a difference in original ability and capacity; it is a difference of ideas. The difference between the accomplishments of a hut builder in a jungle village and those of a professional architect or engineer is first of all a difference of ideas. Just so far as these differences involve basic ideas, or are influenced by differences in basic ideas, they are different ways of understanding the meaning of existence for human experience.

The importance of our ideas comes home to us when those ideas and the actions they inspire bring us up against the facts of existence. Advertisers and salesmen may help us build castles in the air, but if those "castles" do not have a solid foundation on the hard facts of the relation of expenditure to income they are truly "in the air." Certain political and economic policies may seem very attractive when we think about the results they are intended to bring, yet they are nothing but pleasant daydreams if they do not reckon with the hard facts of human nature and human society. Similar considerations apply to all our important personal policies and decisions. The difference between our success or failure as human beings will not be a matter of fate, or even the result primarily of differences in opportunity; the important difference will be the difference in our thinking. The important differences in our thinking are not so much differences in acuity or cleverness, or even differences in intelligence. The important differences are differences in the ideas we use. They are differences in aspirations and in evaluations, and these in turn are rooted in our notion of what is true, what is real, and what is of value.

The qualities of human life and human society depend on the ideas by which life is lived and on which society is founded. It makes a difference to an individual whether he lives his life under the guidance of concepts which he has examined or submits his life to the control of prejudice, hearsay, and popular beliefs. It makes a difference to a society whether it contains an appreciable number of individuals of influence whose judgments and decisions are enlightened by knowledge and understanding. These are some of the differences philosophy can make, and among them are differences on which may depend the issue of the survival or the destruction of that society. It may very well be that incompetence in philosophy is today a greater threat to a society than the threat of military attack.

WHY STUDY PHILOSOPHY?

For most of us the question is not *whether* or not we shall philosophize, but *how* we shall philosophize. Shall we try to understand what we are doing when we philosophize? Shall we be naïve and gullible, or shall we do our philosophizing with some competence? He who begins the formal study of philosophy, however, should be warned at the outset that even a modest success in his study will make it impossible any longer to be content with many of the confusions and ambiguities which have marked his thinking thus far. The outcome of his study will surely be more questions and fewer answers than he had when he began.

If the effect of the study of philosophy is to discontent us, then would we not better be left to our confusions and ambiguities? If the study of philosophy leaves us with more questions and fewer answers than we had before, then is not the outcome a net loss? These are specious objections. We may as well argue that it is inadvisable for a person to have a medical examination for fear it might disclose something wrong and thus impair his peace of mind. Such an attitude reminds us of the saying that "what we don't know won't hurt us." The facts are otherwise. The things we do not know about, and so cannot deal with before they hurt us, are more often than not the things that make us suffer.

To believe what is false, to distinguish falsely between the real and the unreal and between the important and the trivial, is to suffer from a deformity of the self. Just as the body cannot perform its functions successfully in disease, so too our thought and power of decision cannot do their proper work when we suffer from basic ignorance. For basic ignorance is not merely lack of information; it is that lack of understanding which makes it impossible for us to interpret successfully the information we do have. When the framework in which we interpret the facts is distorted the facts are bound to be misinterpreted. A correctly reported fact understood in the wrong context is just as serious an error as an incorrect factual report. If we want to protect ourselves against the kind of ignorance which compromises the very foundation of knowledge and thought and action, we have no place to turn except to philosophy. Philosophy can furnish this protection, however, not in the form of fixed answers but only as a persistent and systematic inquiry into the assumptions, methods, and criteria by which we distinguish between what is true and what is false, and between what is desirable and what is undesirable.

The relation of fact and theory is closer than we often recognize. "I am not interested in theories," we hear over and over again, "just give me the facts." But fact and theory cannot thus be separated. When we try to formulate statements of fact with no mixture of theory we only fool ourselves by ignoring the theory which our statements of fact assume.

Just as statements of fact involve theory so the more narrow facts involve wider and more inclusive perspectives. A narrow fact, taken by itself, shows little of its meaning. It is like a single piece of a jig-saw puzzle. An officer in battle may receive information about the disposition of enemy troops. If he does not know what is expected of his own command in that engagement he does not know how to evaluate the information he has received. A person may have reports of his medical tests, but what can such data mean to him if he has no knowledge of the medical sciences? A tourist may have accurate information about road conditions, but what can he do with that information if he does not know where he is going?

These, of course, are not examples of philosophical understanding. A battle plan is a military matter, the medical sciences are not a part of philosophy, and a plan for a trip is a matter of business or pleasure. But these non-philosophical questions may quickly lead to philosophical ones. The question of whether wars should be fought, or whether human life should be saved, or whether a certain trip is justified may well involve philosophical questions. The pacifist and those government officials who make the decision to go to war, for example, may differ concerning the more effective means of promoting the welfare of their country; but they differ also concerning ends—concerning what values are absolute and what are relative, or concerning what values take precedence over others. The pacifist may believe that no political policy should be implemented by measures which require the taking of human life, while others may believe that it is permissible to sacrifice human lives in order to preserve the conditions which make human life tolerable. An issue that may seem to be only a question of technique or of relative values may take us into the more fundamental questions of the nature of existence and of intrinsic value.

How can we use the information we acquire unless we have some way to distinguish between what pertains to fact and what to fancy? How can we think critically if we do not know on what basis we draw a distinction between the true and the false? How can we hope to accomplish anything, to live our lives in anything but blindness, if we have no awareness of how we distinguish between the valuable and the worthless?

There is only one place to look for answers to these questions, provided we wish to seek for answers strictly on their merits and in the light of our own powers of knowing and understanding. For this we can look only to philosophy. We find answers to many important questions in ordinary experience, in the sciences, in art and literature, and in religion. But if we seek to understand what these answers mean for thought, the methods by which we arrive at them, and the assumptions on which they rest, we have to participate in philosophical inquiry. We find in the study of philosophy the answers that have been attempted, we find the methods by which those answers were obtained, and we prepare ourselves to pursue the search further in our own thinking.

In so far as it is an aim of education to help the individual make himself at home in his world, to understand what his world is like, and to develop some critical control of evaluation and purposeful thinking, the study of philosophy is of paramount importance. Philosophy is not co-extensive with knowledge, but philosophy is concerned with what other knowledge presupposes. In the sciences and other non-philosophical disciplines we investigate certain specific areas of existence and human activity; philosophy cuts beneath all other studies and disciplines and concerns itself with what they take for granted.

Let us be quite clear about this. Any program of higher education which takes the student into advanced study of mathematics or the natural sciences or the social sciences or history or literature or art is incomplete without philosophy. The objects studied in mathematics and those studied in the natural sciences are there studied in abstraction from their modes of existence, without examination of their assumptions as ways of knowing or of their relationships to other kinds of knowledge. These are questions for the philosophy of mathematics and the philosophy of science. These questions cannot be investigated by the methods of mathematics and science, and yet they must be considered if the attempt to understand the human significance of our mathematical and scientific knowledge is to have any success.

In our study of history we make assumptions concerning the way in which individual human agents exist and act, concerning their freedom or lack of freedom, concerning the nature of time and the relation of past and present. All of these raise philosophical problems. As historians we do not discuss such problems, or, if we do, we have to use the methods of philosophy rather than the methods of history. When we investigate and write as historians we deal with history in abstraction from these other questions; and so any history is incomplete without a philosophy of history—not incomplete as history, but incomplete as knowledge.

In the social sciences, in so far as they are constructed on the model of the natural sciences, we limit our study to the factual.

But there are few significant facts about human activity and human interests which are not intertwined with judgments of moral value. Surely we cannot pretend to any kind of adequate knowledge of a human society if we ignore such questions as concern the soundness of the moral evaluations which are at the foundation of that society and are reflected in its institutions and customs. But the examination of the soundness of moral judgments cannot be carried out by the methods of the social sciences. In literature and art the importance of value theory is obvious. We cannot get very far in these fields without the use of critical standards, and our critical standards are arbitrary and without rational support apart from a philosophy of art.

We can avoid the critical examination of our ultimate beliefs and basic assumptions, but we cannot avoid having ultimate beliefs and basic assumptions unless we manage somehow to stop thinking. The alternatives are not those of having or not having such beliefs; they are those of having examined or unexamined beliefs. Socrates' statement that the unexamined life is not worth living is the case for philosophy. As human beings we are aware of ourselves and of what we take to be our world. Philosophy is the attempt to stretch that awareness, in its rational dimension, to the very foundation of human experience and existence. Is this worth a trial? We may not reach our final goal; yet if we try, we may bring our intellectual awareness to a level of comprehension we could not even dream of reaching without philosophy.

SUMMARY

Our earliest contacts with the subject matter of philosophy begin as soon as we are aware of such distinctions as those between the actual and imaginary, the true and the false, the good and the bad. As soon as we begin to use language we begin to acquire concepts and beliefs in terms of which we make these distinctions. But concepts are primarily instruments of awareness rather than objects of which we are aware; consequently we use them for a long time without being aware of what they are. Since those concepts and assumptions provide us with the basic organization of our experience and of our world we may say that their use is, in a sense, the use of a philosophy. We do not engage in philosophy, however, until we turn our attention directly toward those concepts and assumptions and begin our own inquiry into the problems which they involve.

We first make our acquaintance with abstract ideas by learning the words which stand for those ideas, and ordinarily we encounter no great obstacles in our use of those words so long as our use conforms to the practices of others with whom we communicate. This means that the ideas themselves are often vague and ambiguous. The result is that not only is our thinking confused and often incoherent, but the practical decisions we base on our thinking carry confusion and incoherence into our actions. The important differences among people and among human groups are not differences in innate abilities, but differences in ideas; and the need for philosophy is the need for the critical examination of basic ideas and assumptions. This includes the need not only to think about our own beliefs but also to become acquainted with the thinking that has been done by others. Along with this will come an enriching extension of our awareness, both in breadth and depth; and this is valuable for its own sake as well as for the practical consequences it will have for decision and action.

Questions for Study and Discussion

1. *Terms:* abstraction, being, belief, evil, fiction, good, idea, ideology, mode of being, presupposition, quality, quantity, real, relation, theory.

2. What is the concept of *fairness* as the word is used in the following: "To charge different customers of a store different prices for the same item is not fair."? Compare the meaning of the word "fair" in the above sentence with its meaning in the following: "The weather today will be fair." "The State Fair will be held next week." "He has a fair chance of winning the election."

3. Bring out the different kinds of answers required in each of the following pairs of questions:
   (a) What is a molecule? and How does a molecule exist?
   (b) What is a metaphor? and How does a metaphor exist?
   (c) What is a perception? and How does a perception exist?
   (d) What is a corporation? and How does a corporation exist?

4. Consider some of your own beliefs which are most important to you. What can you say concerning the way by which you acquired those beliefs? How would you test their truth? Are there any beliefs of your own that you would not be willing to examine? Are there some beliefs you consider it inappropriate or irrelevant to examine?

5. Compare the advantages of precision in the use of language with the advantage of imprecision.

6. Can you find any inconsistencies in the meanings you give to "democracy," "liberal," or "justice"?

7. Examine: There are no differences between a convicted criminal and the judge who hears his case which cannot be understood eventually in terms of differences in their ideas and their ways of thinking. Could you compare two such people as examples of "different ways of understanding the meaning of existence for human experience"?

8. On what grounds did Socrates assert that the unexamined life is not worth living? (See Plato, *Apology*.)

CHAPTER 3

The Origin
and Growth
of Philosophy

THE PROBLEM OF THE ORIGIN OF PHILOSOPHY

If we ask what *was* the origin of philosophy we ask an historical question, a question to be answered by the methods of the historian. If we ask what *is* the origin of philosophy we may be asking about the circumstances and motives that lead an individual into the study of philosophy. If we ask this about some particular person the question is biographical; if we ask it about people in general, in an attempt to find the patterns of motivation and interest that lead people into the consideration of philosophical problems, the question is psychological. To answer the one question we should have to use the methods of the biographer and to answer the other, the methods of the psychologist. There is, however, a philosophical problem involved in the question of the origin of philosophy, and indeed this is more fundamental than the historical or biographical or psychological problem.

The origin of philosophy, considered as a philosophical problem, concerns the relation of philosophy as a way of thinking and as a kind of knowing, to pre-philosophical thinking and knowing. Our problem here is not to identify and reconstruct a sequence of events either in the history of a civilization or in the lives of particular individuals; nor is it the investigation of modes of human behavior. Our problem is to try to see what it is in pre-philosophical thought and belief which makes that level of understanding incomplete and leads logically into philosophical inquiry.

In some ways this is similar to the question of how the study of arithmetic leads into algebra. In arithmetic we study the relations of numbers with special concern for combinations of numbers that are equivalent. Two plus two is numerically equivalent to four; eight minus three, to five; three times two, to six; and twelve divided by four, to three. Now if we ask *why* these relations hold good of numbers we find that we have to study the relations at a different level of generality. Instead of examining the relation of two to four, which might lead us to note that both numbers are even numbers, we have to consider numbers in terms of what would apply to all numbers. So we may use a sign such as the letter *a* to stand for any one number, and *b* to stand for any other number. Thus in considering the relation of *a* and *b* in *a plus b*, we are studying every plus relation of two numbers. Whatever understanding of this we obtain will apply to any particular plus relation—such as two plus three, or twenty-six plus eighty-four. In this sense, algebra is a logical development from arithmetic, and it helps to make intelligible what we have already found to be the case in arithmetic.

To say that the emergence of philosophy is a logical development from pre-philosophical thought does not mean that the intellectual development of an individual or of a society is the inevitable result of some inexorable law which brings into being a train of events laid down ahead of time in the structure of existence. A logical necessity is not an historical or a psychological one. Not all people who study arithmetic go on to study algebra; and although every human culture has had its pre-philosophical stage, only a few cultures have produced philosophers. If there is a necessary connection between the conditions that lead to philosophy and its emergence in practice, it does not follow that there is another law of necessity which requires all these conditions to be fulfilled. Where they are fulfilled, we have philosophy; where they are not, philosophy does not appear. This means simply that under certain conditions the emergence of philosophy makes sense; it is intelligible, and our grasp of its intelligibility is our grasp of a rational relationship.

In our discussion of the origin of philosophy we shall refer to the prephilosophical stage as "common sense." Our problem will be to try to understand the relation between common sense and philosophical thinking in order to see how, under certain conditions, the difficulties and limitations of common-sense belief lead logically into philosophy. In examining the relation of common sense to philosophy, however, we are not setting them up as rivals, and in pointing out the limitations of common-sense knowledge there is no intention to disparage it. On the contrary, philosophy without common sense is the breeding ground of intellectual monstrosities. There are cogent reasons to consider that philosophy supplements common sense, and that sound philosophy does not destroy but finds its confirmation in common sense. For one thing, common sense and philosophical thinking use the same logical processes and are about the same world. If the human mind were so perverted that its common-sense beliefs had no truth, then that same perversion would infect its philosophical and scientific thinking as well. Further, we shall find that in so far as philosophy is successful, it makes intelligible much of the basic knowledge we have at the common-sense level. Not all common-sense belief is true; but, as we shall see presently, there is a hard core of common-sense knowledge which is seldom if ever challenged, and which is never challenged successfully.

COMMON-SENSE BELIEF

By *common sense* we mean those beliefs which are accepted without question as true. Some beliefs are accepted by many and are doubted by others. For those who do accept them without question those beliefs are a part of common sense; for others they are not. Thus whether a certain belief is a common-sense belief is a relative matter; it depends on what group we are talking about. Common sense undergoes changes within the same group. As soon as a belief previously accepted as obviously true begins to be questioned, it ceases to be a part of that body of common sense; so also common sense includes beliefs today that were never dreamed of or would have been regarded as fantastic in an earlier generation. In a society as fluid as ours the common-sense beliefs of an individual often change as his relationships with social groups change, and what one reads may be a more important influence than where one lives.

The very phrase, "common sense," suggests that the beliefs included within its scope of reference in any instance are beliefs not of an individual alone but are common to those who belong to a group. This suggestion seems, on the whole, to be correct. If some individuals arrived at their beliefs largely on their own, with a minimum of influence from others, we should rightly hesitate to speak of those beliefs as common sense. Common sense seems to be a consensus; but more than this, it seems also to include the idea that the group is the important source from which the individual derives his ideas.

Most of those who belong to our society today accept as plainly true the belief that if we were to go far enough in any direction on the earth's surface we should eventually go around the earth. In an earlier time it seemed just as obvious that if a person were to go far enough in any direction he would eventually fall off the earth. Today we take it for granted that there are immense distances between the earth and other parts of the universe, distances of millions and billions of light years. Yet not many centuries ago it seemed just as obvious that the heavenly bodies were only a short distance away from an immovable earth.

The chief difference between those beliefs which are accepted and those which are rejected by common sense seems to be a difference in familiarity. For common sense the plausible is the familiar; the unfamiliar is implausible, and on the common-sense level the unfamiliar may be incredible because of its strangeness. Basic to the formation of common sense is the well-established psychological principle that what is repeated over and over without challenge tends to be believed. In hypnosis, during which the subject's critical powers are temporarily suspended, a mere assertion by the hypnotist is sufficient to make the subject believe he sees or hears or feels whatever the hypnotist suggests. In our dreams, with sleep blocking our perceptual contact with the environment, we take images and idea associations to be genuine perceptions and logical relations. So in his early years the individual takes to himself the beliefs accepted and unchallenged by those around him, not because he is hypnotized or dreaming but because he is in no position to apply his critical powers to those beliefs. He is unable to examine them because he is yet unaware that there are other ways of thinking.

Since common-sense beliefs are accepted without question there may be many unnoticed difficulties and even contradictions among those beliefs which do not attract attention until something more reliable than familiarity is used as a test of truth. Common sense now says that the fall of a body to the ground is a matter of gravitation; but in another age common sense said that the body was seeking its natural habitat, returning to the earth where terrestial things belong. In the earlier age the difficulties involved in attributing purposive action to inanimate objects escaped notice. But how many people today, who accept without question the idea that the earth exerts an attractive force on the falling body (as does the sun on the earth), are disturbed by any difficulties involved in the idea of action at a distance? The common-sense version of gravitation seems plausible enough, but its plausibility to common sense does not consist in a perception of its obvious truth; it is rather only an indication of the degree of familiarity the idea has acquired. Few of us have tried to think through that relationship of bodies which we call "gravitation." To a man like Albert Einstein, however, familiarity was not a satisfactory test of truth, and when Einstein took a straight look at some of our familiar ideas about motion and gravitation many of them seemed anything but plausible to him.

The familiar exerts a strong hold on the thinking even of those who attempt to apply the standards of truth of rational thought and experimental inquiry. In the early period of modern science, for example, it was quite difficult for some of the greatest scientists of the time to accept the Copernican theory that the earth moves. What force in the universe, they asked, was strong enough to set into motion this immense body, the earth, and to keep it moving? It seemed utterly incredible that a body of such tremendous weight and huge size could be pushed into motion. Today the idea that the earth moves does not seem incredible to most of us, not because we are better thinkers but because we were born into a society in which the accepted ideas about motion have changed.

To say that familiarity is the test of truth of common sense is to say that the test here is agreement with the beliefs of our associates. We tend to accept uncritically the beliefs prevalent in those circles in which we have our intimate contacts. Such uncritical acceptance is a kind of intellectual provincialism, and one of the primary aims of higher education is to overcome our provincialism by introducing us to unfamiliar knowledge and unfamiliar points of view.

We must not suppose, however, that all common-sense belief is on the same level. Some of our beliefs that seem obviously true not only are true but are obviously true. We seldom have any trouble, for example, in distinguishing between a dream and a waking perception. When we find someone who has this difficulty we do not give him special instruction about the differences between dreams and perceptions; we examine his mental condition instead. Except under the influence of certain theoretical considerations, or because of some abnormal mental condition, people do not question their sense perceptions or their immediate memories. We do make mistakes in perception and memory, and recognize them as mistakes; but this does not lead us to challenge the soundness of perception and memory as such.

When, at twilight, I think I see a man standing off in the distance and then find later that what I saw was a post, I do not explain the error in terms of some supposed inherent deceptiveness of sense perception. This would be absurd, for it is by a true perception that I correct the erroneous one. I explain the error rather as the result of the poor light and my distance from the object. We also make mistakes in memory, not because memory is inherently false but because of the time lapse and our inattention and the confusion of the details of one experience with those of another. To question my immediate memory in the sense of doubting its soundness in principle would be pure nonsense, for if I cannot rely on my memory I cannot know from moment to moment what I am talking about, even when I talk about doubting my memory.

Thus it seems that common-sense claims of truth do not all have the same significance; some deserve more respect than others. The dependability of common-sense belief seems to vary with the extent to which it includes assumptions and inferences, for one of the distinctive features of common sense is the absence of critical examination. Since it is our assumptions and inferences which stand most in need of critical examination in any serious search for truth, the less part these have in common-sense belief, the more dependable is that belief. The closer our common-sense beliefs are to immediate experience, therefore, the better we can rely on their claims of truth. The test of truth that common-sense uses, the test of familiarity, thus is dependable only within narrow limits. Within those limits it gives us genuine knowledge of fact, but if we are to extend our knowledge beyond those limits we can do so with confidence only under the control of some special discipline such as philosophy or mathematics or the sciences or history. The further a common-sense belief takes us from what can be confirmed in direct experience and the harder it tries to reach an explanation for what direct experience discloses, the weaker common sense becomes. In its generalizations and theories, popular thought is almost always wrong, just as popular taste in painting, music, architecture, and literature is sound only with respect to the most obvious and superficial.

This weakness of common sense comes from the fact that although common sense is always ready to theorize it does so without knowing what it is doing and without the tools for testing its theory. Professor Howard D. Roelofs points out that

> the virtue of common sense is neither its correctness nor its error, but that it is the source of data unbiased by interest in a theory. Common sense may be mistaken or correct, it may have prejudices; but it is, as regards philosophic theories, disinterested. This is not because common-sense has no theories, in fact it uses many, but because it is not aware of them.[1]

In reflecting upon the relation of common-sense belief and knowledge it is important to remember that the formal disciplines and all rational inquiry depend for their possibility on the existence of some genuine knowledge at the common-sense level. Here we have a philosophical principle fundamental to rational inquiry of any kind. Inquiry cannot begin unless we already have some knowledge relevant to that inquiry. I cannot seek for something unless I have some knowledge about the object I seek, since without such knowledge I would not know what to look for or how to recognize it if I encountered it. Unless I already have knowledge I cannot apply any rational test of truth to a belief or knowledge claim, for I should be unable to recognize a rational test or know how to use it.

An important consequence follows from this principle. If the conclusions reached in an inquiry are in conflict with the supposed

[1] "A Case for Dualism and Interaction," *Philosophy and Phenomenological Research*, Volume XV, No. 4, June, 1955, p. 454.

knowledge upon which that inquiry rested, then something is wrong. Either some error has been committed in the course of the inquiry or else what was supposed to be known at the start was false. But in either case something else assumed to be true must really be true if we are to discover our error. Thus no inquiry can impeach all inquiry; no inquiry can establish the conclusion that nothing is known.

In this principle we have an example of philosophical knowledge. We have not here uncovered a new fact to add to other facts already known. Rather we have brought to light, by a process of reasoning, something involved in the knowledge we already have. The principle that no inquiry can impeach all inquiry is not an arbitrary rule to be followed, like a rule of a game, only because we agree to follow it. The principle pertains to the very possibility of knowledge; we discover its truth when we reflect on what knowledge actually *is*, when we become aware of what is involved in the fact that there is knowledge. To deny this principle is not merely to deny that this or that claim of knowledge is sound. To deny it is to deny the very possibility of any knowledge, including the knowledge claimed by the denial itself. Here we have an ultimate principle of knowledge, ultimate because without it knowledge could not *be*.

PHILOSOPHY AND COMMON SENSE

In contrast to common sense, philosophy tries to appraise every truth claim concerning basic beliefs in the light of the most nearly final knowledge available. Philosophy is the persistent attempt to get as close to the last word as rational inquiry can come. Even when the results of philosophy are in agreement with common-sense belief, the way by which philosophy reaches those results is quite different from the method of common sense. Philosophical beliefs are intended to be reasoned beliefs, and whether or not they are accepted as true by one philosopher should not depend on their familiarity or on their acceptance by others. We may agree with Gilbert Chesterton that "philosophy is merely thought that has been thought out," [2] and this characteristic of being thought out

[2] G. K. Chesterton, *The Common Man* (New York, Sheed and Ward, 1950), p. 176.

is the very thing that sets philosophy apart from common sense. For to the extent that common sense begins to think out its thought it becomes something other than common sense. When thinking begins to take charge of belief the test of truth is shifted from familiarity to the reliability of evidence and to the logical relation of a conclusion to its evidence.

The relation of a conclusion to its evidence is *logically valid* in so far as the truth of the conclusion is required by the truth of the evidence. When the relation between evidence and conclusion is logically valid we cannot assert the evidence as true and deny the truth of the conclusion without contradicting ourselves. If I assert as premises that John is taller than Charles and that Charles is taller than Harry, there is the logically valid conclusion that John is taller than Harry. To assert the premises as true and deny the conclusion would be to say that what is true is not true. Thus a logical relation of a conclusion to premises or evidence should be distinguished from relations based on such psychological factors as familiarity, preference, prejudice, aversion, desire, and hope.

In the light of the distinction between philosophy and common sense we may see how philosophy began and how it emerged from a common-sense view of the world. Any dissatisfaction with the ordinary beliefs of common sense is almost sure to lead to the abandonment of that particular common-sense standpoint. Dissatisfaction with ordinary beliefs may come with the discovery that some of those beliefs are in conflict with others equally familiar. If dissatisfaction persists, and cannot be removed merely by choosing one or the other of the conflicting beliefs, then an attempt may be made to get at the truth in some other way. When equally familiar beliefs are in conflict, familiarity is no longer a satisfactory test of truth.

Philosophy and science are needed to supplement common sense because things are not merely what they appear to be. Things are what they appear to be, else we could make no contact with them in knowledge and so could have no world of real things directly accessible to us to raise questions about. But things are not *only* what they appear to be. The activities and sequences and relations of things as we find them in experience cannot be understood entirely in terms of what we see of things on the surface.

Man's earlier attempts to understand things in their inner nature were awkward enough. The only effective cause of action he knew at first hand was what he found in himself. He saw himself bringing about effects on other things by means of his own choices and decisions. He recognized that his own actions came from hate and love, anger and forgiveness, pride and humility. So he supposed that other things as well—the growth of plants, the changes of wind and rain, the attacks of wild animals, and even the rising of the sun—were governed by like forces.

Here we find the characteristic approach of common sense in which things are made understandable by an appeal to the familiar. Philosophical inquiry did not begin until there was an attempt to explain things in terms of causes which have a *logical* relation with what they are intended to explain. Thales, who was called the first philosopher, apparently thought he had found an explanation of the changes and complexities of nature in the principle that all things are water. Water takes on such varied forms—vapor and liquid and solid—that if things really were water (Thales may have thought), the changes and differences we see among them might be intelligibly explained in terms of the nature of water itself. Thales is important, however, not because of his peculiar theory but because of the kind of question he asked and because of one special feature of the way in which he tried to answer it. Instead of trying to understand other things in terms of his own nature, or of the actions of divinities conceived in man's likeness, he tried to understand things in terms of what he took to be *their* own nature. The attempt itself was so important that it gave Thales a unique place in history.

Of course philosophy does not come into existence with an adequate understanding of the difference between good evidence and poor evidence and between correct and incorrect reasoning. These are themselves philosophical problems. But philosophy did come into existence with a new and distinctive attitude; the desire to discover the truth about things in the nature of things themselves.

At the common-sense level we assume that the truth is already known. Philosophy begins with the attitude that truth is something to be found, that the answers to our questions are not already known, and that just to *have* a right answer without understanding why it is true is not to *know* that it is true.

Here you see the beginning of philosophy [Epictetus said] in the discovery of the conflict of men's minds with one another, and the attempt to seek for the reason of this conflict, and the condemnation of mere opinion, as a thing not to be trusted; and a search to determine whether your opinion is true, and an attempt to discover a standard, just as we discover the balance to deal with weights and the rule to deal with things straight and crooked. This is the beginning of philosophy.[3]

The need for rational understanding is the condition which, perhaps more than any other, makes the difference between those who go beyond common sense and those who do not. Rational understanding is awareness not only of what a thing is but also of why it is what it is. Rational understanding is awareness of causes or reasons, and of logical patterns and relationships. I may be *aware* that a person's skin is flushed and is unusually warm to the touch; I *understand* this when I know its causes, when I discover, for example, that he suffers from an infection or that he has been playing tennis in the hot sun. This is rational understanding in so far as the relation between what I see and what I consider its cause is a relation I can be aware of only by thought. It is rational understanding in so far as the relation between the fact to be explained and the statement of the reason for it involves a logical relation.

Some have the desire for rational understanding in larger measure than others, and those who have little of it are likely to remain satisfied with common sense. Some are drawn by a deep and moving desire not only to know what the facts are but to understand why the facts are what they are. The need to understand constantly prods them into inquiry and leads them to break the bounds of common-sense belief. One of the chief tasks of higher education in a society such as our own is to discover and identify those who have this need for understanding. Once they are found, the next step is to bring them to a recognition of their own need and to the discovery of the direction in which its satisfaction will be the more meaningful to them, and finally to prepare them to become competent and responsible inquirers and interpreters in their own right. These minds have been the well-springs of our civilization; they and minds like them will continue to be our only protection against relapse into savagery.

The desire for understanding does not begin with philosophy,

[3] *Arrian's Discourses of Epictetus*, Book II, Chapter XI, translated by P. E. Matheson, in *The Stoic and Epicurean Philosophers*, edited by Whitney J. Oates (New York, Random House, Inc., 1940), p. 301. By permission of Oxford University Press.

for the desire to understand is the life of the mind. But common sense does not know where to go for understanding or how to find it. Common sense does not even know how to recognize a genuine explanation when such is found. The reason why something is believed, at the level of common sense, is only by accident the reason why it is true; and common-sense belief can be relied on only as it concerns matters about which no one in his right mind can for very long be mistaken. At this point, however, we can and must rely on common sense; for from this level of common sense theoretical inquiry arises, and then returns to it again for confirmation.

PHILOSOPHY AS THE SEARCH FOR ULTIMATES

In any act of thinking we take something for granted, something not called into question or given expression. If we wish to make explicit or to question what we take for granted in one act of thinking we can do so only in another act of thinking. The difference between the two acts is not the difference between taking something for granted and not taking something for granted; it is a difference in *what* is taken for granted. If I ask a friend, "Are you going to the meeting?" my question leaves unexplained and unexpressed what meeting I refer to, what time it is to be held, and what connection either I or my friend has with the affair. It also assumes without explanation that the form of my question and the words used in it make sense. If he asks, in reply, "What meeting?" then a new statement has to be made, and this statement in turn has its own unexpressed assumptions.

A thought or an assertion or a question also assumes the existence of a world in terms of which it makes sense. If I ask, "Will it rain today?" my question assumes the existence of an atmospheric system in which rain is not only possible but something to be expected from time to time. One would not be likely to ask this question in a locality where either it never rained or else rained every day. Suppose now the question evokes not a direct answer but a comment about what my question takes for granted: "Rain? How absurd! The wind is not right; there is not a cloud in the sky; the barometer is rising!" But here again something is taken for granted, a relation between the likelihood of rain and certain weather signs.

It still would be possible to raise a question about these and then to have that question answered in terms of the causes of rain—with a description of the process of the evaporation of surface water, its absorption by the air, and the conditions under which the moisture held by the air is precipitated. We could then push our analysis a step further and raise a question about the existence of the causal connections assumed in the first explanation. But if we do raise such a question we shall raise it because we think the world may not be the kind of world assumed in the account given of the causes of rain.

An important part of the work of philosophy is to bring our unexpressed assumptions to light and to subject them to examination. It is plain that we cannot depend entirely on logical proof in the examination of our assumptions; for logical proof supports the truth of one proposition, the conclusion, by showing its logical relation to other propositions which are taken to be true. If we try to require proof of all premises we find ourselves in an endless regression. If such a regression is to be avoided, either we have to find some premises that are known to be true without proof, that are self-evident, or we have to find some premises we are justified in assuming to be true. In either instance we reach a final stage of our search for the grounds of our beliefs. If we claim that a proposition is self-evident we claim for it a truth we ourselves cannot demonstrate to anyone else; and so we cannot carry the examination further. All we can do now is to help another see what we see in the way we see it, and so grasp its self-evidence. If we claim that we are justified in assuming the truth of a proposition that is neither proved nor self-evident, then we no longer engage in the examination of that proposition; for now we are concerned with the question of the soundness of our justification for assuming that the proposition is true.

If I am asked, "How do you know that John is out of the hospital?" I may reply, "I saw him on the street this morning." The evidence here is in the seeing itself. If my statement is believed, it will be because others suppose that what I saw they too would have seen for themselves if they had been where I was. Ordinarily we accept sense perception as self-certifying. We also accept elementary thinking and calculating processes. There is little that can be said to a person who does not recognize that two plus three add up to five. Even our mistakes in addition can be discovered to be mistakes and corrected only by operations which are not in error. If challenged to prove that our direct perception is true or that our basic thought processes are valid we would find ourselves quickly at a standstill, for the examination of one perception requires us to assume the reliability of other perceptions, and an error in thinking can be discovered only by thinking which is not in error. To bring out into the open these features of perception and of thinking is not to offer proof, evidence of the truth of what we are assuming, but to show why we are justified in making such assumptions.

We have no choice whether or not we shall make assumptions, but we can choose whether or not we shall examine those assumptions. This is the choice of whether or not we shall engage in philosophy. When we stop that examination we either give up philosophy at that point or else we have reached a stage beyond which we cannot go. When we go as far as we can, and are stopped because we can go no further, we have reached the ultimates of our own thinking.

What do we gain from philosophy? To the extent that we are successful we discover the foundations upon which our theories and evaluations rest, the foundations of our hopes and fears, the source of whatever coherent policy our lives may have, and we discover the meaning that these basic ideas have for thought. Still more important, the discovery of our ultimate assumptions opens the way for their examination and reconstruction, to the discovery of still more adequate foundations—to foundations that are more adequate because they survive the critical examination to which the earlier ones had succumbed.

Professor Marten Ten Hoor has called attention to three levels of ultimates which philosophy seeks.

On . . . the lowest level of philosophical inquiry, the philosopher seeks concepts which are ultimate within the realm of a particular science. On the next higher level he seeks concepts which interconnect and interrelate the special sciences. . . . The concepts of gravitation and evolution are good examples. . . . By means of this type of ultimates the mind seeks to bridge the intellectual gaps which have appeared as a result of the differentiation and diffusion of the special sciences. Some of the ultimates on this level are concepts of substance, some are concepts of process. . . .

On the third and highest level of philosophic inquiry the quest is for concepts which are ultimates from the standpoint of a synthesis of all the sciences, for ideal terms which are cosmic in scope of reference.[4]

We may supplement Professor Ten Hoor's analysis by recognizing levels of depth as well as levels of generality. Philosophy is also an inquiry into the methods of inquiry; an attempt to disclose the ultimate assumptions upon which knowledge rests, and to discover the final standards by which a knowledge claim is to be judged.

Whether we know it or not, we all have ultimate beliefs. Thus far we have discussed ultimates as relative. My ultimate beliefs are ultimate in relation to my other beliefs, those which are not called into question by my other beliefs and to which other beliefs must conform. But are there ultimates, to which other beliefs, whether mine or those of anyone else, have to conform if they are to be true? This is one of the perennial problems of philosophy. However it is answered it would seem at least, as we shall see later, that there are basic assumptions which are absolute for any inquiry; assumptions which cannot be challenged without challenging the possibility of inquiry.

THE VALUE OF FALSE PHILOSOPHIES

Once a person is convinced of the inevitability of philosophy he is likely to want to know immediately which philosophy is true, so that he will not waste his time with inadequate or false accounts of ultimates. But when he sees the great number of different philosophies and the apparent confusions and disagreements among them he may become discouraged. If even those from whom he is to learn cannot agree among themselves then how, he wonders, can they guide his thought and lead him to something better than he already has.

Few things are more discouraging and exasperating to the beginner than his discovery of the conflicts and controversies that have been characteristic of philosophy throughout its long history. He quite naturally sees all this as evidence of weakness and failure. He does not yet see that the very life-blood of philosophy is controversy, and that genuine philosophical conviction—as distinguished from credal conviction or party allegiance—can come only

[4] "The Philistines Over Philosophy," *The Journal of Philosophy*, Volume XXXV, No. 20, September 29, 1938, pp. 538-39.

to those who have met every plausible alternative on its own ground and are satisfied that they have found and exposed its weakness. In philosophy we can discover truth only by thinking through what is false, for in no other way can we learn how to recognize the difference between the true and the false as reflective thought grasps this difference. If by some magic the ability to think only what is true were given to a person, he would never be able to apprehend that truth *as truth*. To recognize the falsity of even the simplest assertion we have to understand its meaning, and to understand its meaning we have to think it as if it were true. Without this we could not discover its conflict with what is true, and without the discovery of such conflict we could not be aware of anything from which being true is to be distinguished.

Of course there is no simple and easy way of classifying philosophies as true or false. Some philosophies are more successful than others in bringing to light the complex factors which need to be considered in dealing with a problem and in making explicit the ambiguities and conflicts of previous attempts, and in this sense are truer. It would be rash indeed, however, for one to suppose that he can reach finality merely by exposing the confusions and misunderstandings of others. What reason has he to think himself an exception to human fallibility? His thinking will have its own confusions, and it can hardly be expected that those confusions can be uncovered by the very thinking of which they are characteristic. Still his grasp of the problem and his discovery of fresh approaches may be a significant contribution to thought and may never have come about if he had not encountered other points of view which seemed unsatisfactory.

One reason we have to go through the false in order to reach whatever truth is accessible to us lies deep in the contrast between the nature of philosophy's task and the limitations under which we labor to accomplish that task. Philosophy seeks a knowledge of ultimates, of that which is final, and yet it has to work through human minds that are limited both in their powers and in their contacts with existence. The false starts and wrong turns of one philosopher have to be corrected by others. These others also make their own mistakes, to be discovered and exposed by still others.

To do his work well a philosopher first of all has to think straight. As one has said: "Philosophy is bound by two main requisitions: It ought to be true, and it ought to be reasoned. It is more important that philosophy be reasoned than that it be true." [5] A philosophy that is true without being reasoned is true only by accident. Since it cannot show why it is true, no one can know that it is true. If a philosophy is reasoned, however, then even its errors are a contribution to knowledge. For a reasoned but false conclusion shows that something is wrong with the evidence from which the conclusion was drawn. We often do not know that we have taken a wrong road until we find ourselves at the wrong destination. A wrong road may look every bit as good while we are on it as the right road would look if we were on it instead. Those who have followed wrong roads to the end have performed the great service of showing the rest of us where not to go; if their philosophies are reasoned they have shown us also where not to begin. As Jacques Maritain has said:

A great philosopher in the wrong is like a beacon on the reefs, which says to seamen: steer clear of me; he enables men (at least those who have not been seduced by him) to *identify* the errors from which they suffer, and to become clearly aware of them, and to struggle against them.[6]

A false philosophy, however, is not merely a warning against error. As was suggested earlier, it is a positive contribution to the search for truth. In fact a false philosophy may serve as an important communication of truth at just that point where it is seen to be erroneous. For in so far as a false philosophy is reasoned it shows what would have to be true of real existence if the premises and assumptions of that philosophy were true. Thus it is not merely false but contains, as it were, a kind of truth in showing at least one of the credible possibilities. To know the possibilities that are not also actualities is an essential part of the discovery of the actual, for the intellectual vision of the real is won only as the real is seen in its differentiation from the unreal.

As the will cannot desire evil except under the aspects of good, so intelligence by its very nature assents to error because it dimly per-

[5] From the account of the philosophy of James Frederick Ferrier in *The Idealistic Argument in Recent British and American Philosophy*, by G. Watts Cunningham (Copyright, 1933, G. Watts Cunningham), p. 23. By permission of Appleton-Century-Crofts, Inc.

[6] "The Philosopher in Society," *Report of the Third Conference of the Association of Princeton Graduate Alumni*, January 1-3, 1953 (Princeton, Princeton University Press, 1953), p. 61.

ceives, in however distorted a fashion, some truth to be involved. Thus error, in spite of itself, reveals the contrasting truth more clearly.[7]

Perhaps it is a mark of our human frailty that few of us are able to summon the strength of purpose to investigate rigorously the consequences of a philosophy we already believe to be false. The errors of a false philosophy can best be brought to light in the work of one who believes them not to be errors but truths.

THE COMPETENCE OF PHILOSOPHY

Some have seen the apparent disparity between philosophy's goal and the tools it must use to reach that goal as proof of the absurdity of philosophy itself. The attempt by fallible human minds to grasp the ultimate may seem like an attempt to capture the absolute in terms of the relative or the infinite in terms of the finite. It may seem to be a project as ridiculous as a plan to count all the numbers. And yet this very criticism is itself possible only as the mind grasps something of the nature of an ultimate, and grasps this in terms of ideas that are not themselves ultimate. Even if we grant that no finite mind can grasp the ultimate in its finality, and this would depend on our notion of what is ultimate, still a finite mind in all its finitude might know that there *is* an ultimate. To deny on the grounds of our minds' limitations that this is possible would be like saying that we cannot know that the number series is infinite *until* we count all the numbers.

If we take philosophy to be a search for ultimates, what shall we say about philosophies which deny that there are ultimates? A philosophy may insist that all things are relative, that nothing is absolute and nothing final. Skeptical philosophies may be so far from admitting a knowledge of ultimates as to deny that it is possible for us to know anything at all. Positivism argues that the traditional problems concerning what is ultimate and final in existence stem from misunderstandings and confusions in the use of language and devotes itself largely to the study of language structure and function. There is a sense, however, in which a denial of ultimates may itself involve another kind of ultimate. Relativism's

[7] Journet Kahn, "The Threat to Academic Freedom," reprinted from *The Proceedings of the American Catholic Philosophical Association* (Washington, D. C., The Catholic University of America, 1957), p. 13. By permission.

denial of ultimates in existence is presented as the best we can do with the ways of knowing which we possess. The denial by skepticism of the possibility of knowledge is presented as something beyond which we cannot go. Positivism's interpretation of some traditional problems of existence as the consequence of a misuse of language is not offered as something provisional and conditional.

Although it seems that every philosophy has a concern with ultimates, it still remains true that some philosophies recognize the philosopher's own limitations and insist that whatever is presented as ultimate should be accepted only tentatively. Yet how can we say that a philosophy seeks for the last word if it recognizes its own inadequacy to reach that goal? Can we be said to seek something which we know is unattainable? Perhaps we should say that every philosophy tries to get as close as it can to the last word, and while recognizing that it can never reach the ultimate and grasp it in its finality philosophy can still seek a closer and closer approximation. Thus philosophy might recognize the inevitable incompleteness of its own accomplishment while still able to make and note its progress. But this is like saying that philosophy's last word is that it cannot have a last word, and we scarcely can rest with this.

So the question remains. If philosophy is the search for ultimates then how can a philosophy claim to be successful without at the same time implying that it is the one true philosophy and all others are failures? Such claims have been made, but the arrogance they seem to express repels us. Does not modesty and the honest recognition of our limitations require us to admit that one philosophy is as good as another? No extension of relative knowledge can reach ultimate truth. The absolute is not a degree of the relative; we cannot pile on more and more of the relative and by this means reach something absolute. Nor is the infinite a degree of the finite; stretch a finite as far as you please and it is no closer to infinity. As all finites, no matter how much greater one is than another, are equally noninfinite, so all relativities are equally nonabsolute.

Perhaps the best reply to this attack on the competence of philosophy, an attack based on a supposed fatal disparity between man's instruments of knowledge and the goal of philosophy, is to point out that it involves a misunderstanding concerning the relation of thought to thought's objects. There seems here to be a confusion of two quite different ideas, the idea of *a knowledge of ultimates* and the idea of *an ultimate knowledge*. The former, which is the true aim of philosophy, is confused with the latter. Once we see that a knowledge of ultimates does not itself have to be ultimate we discover the weakness of this line of attack upon the competence of philosophy. To confuse a knowledge of ultimates with an ultimate knowledge is like saying, when we see green grass, that we have a green perception of grass; or that we have an even thought of a number or a square concept of a plane figure.

The main tradition of philosophy has not been a search for finality of formula but for an awareness of the real being to which the formulas refer. The formula, or statement of principle, is an instrument of knowledge rather than the object known. To understand how philosophy can make sense as a search for finality we must carefully distinguish any supposed finality of statement and knowledge from the finality of the existence which we hope to apprehend by means of that statement and in terms of that knowledge. An ordinary photograph of a house, for example, is not itself three-dimensional as a photograph. Of course the paper on which the photograph is printed is three-dimensional, and so is the coating in which the color contrasts have been chemically fixed; but the arrangement of the colors is two-dimensional. This two-dimensional picture shows us something of the nature of the three-dimensional house; we are not restricted to taking pictures of two-dimensional houses. *The limitations of the instruments of knowledge and communication do not themselves pertain to the thing known by their means.* So a philosophy can be about ultimates, and communicate something of the nature of those ultimates, without being itself an ultimate philosophy. There may be better ways of communicating, and more adequate knowledge, waiting for further investigation to discover.

An attack upon the competence of philosophy as such can hardly be significant, for the attack itself would be an instance of philosophizing. The question of competence arises with respect to specific philosophies and philosophers. If a charge of incompetence is based on prejudice or ideology or upon a disagreement in some other area of inquiry, it has no philosophical significance. To warrant the attention of philosophers such a charge must be argued upon the basis of evidence which is philosophical in nature.

THE PROGRESS OF PHILOSOPHY

As we have suggested before, philosophy is able to progress because the work of past philosophers provides us with starting points in advance of their own. We do not have to go back and begin again. Yet when we first recognize that this is the case we may wonder why philosophers keep going back to the work of earlier philosophers instead of forging ahead on their own. Scientists do not do this; it would be rare indeed for a physicist who is working on a current research problem to have any need to study or repeat the experiments of Galileo. Why should philosophers, and those who wish to philosophize with competence, have to study again the philosophies of the past?

This difference in the attitudes of philosophers and scientists toward earlier work in their own fields is not hard to understand. In so far as the results of Galileo's or Newton's work are recognized today as sound physics those results are incorporated into today's physics texts. The student today does not have to repeat for himself the mistakes and follow out the false clues which earlier physicists had to work through before arriving at their solid achievements. He needs only to understand the results of the earlier work and to see how the evidence supports those results.

The situation is different in the case of philosophy. The philosopher simply cannot take over the results, say, of Plato's work. He cannot be made acquainted with Plato's conclusions and his reasons for those conclusions unless he repeats in his own mind the thought processes of Plato. A report of the results of an earlier philosopher's work and a statement of the evidence supporting those results are not sufficient in philosophy. The thought process itself must be reconstructed in our minds. As we shall see later in our discussion of the differences between philosophy and science, philosophic thought always takes us beyond standardized concepts and formally defined symbols. Its symbols are forged in the process of thinking and not merely taken over from others and used in senses that are quite plain to anyone who knows the vocabulary of the field. This is why the attempt to summarize the work of the great philosophers in verbal capsules is so misleading. The great philosophers do not use neatly defined concepts; the work that made them great was their discovery of new concepts. To understand what their thinking ends with we have to repeat in our own minds something of the same process of thinking by which they reached their conclusions.

The scientific discovery that air is a mixture of gases and not itself a chemical element took a long time and followed devious paths. The inquiry was complicated by deep-seated assumptions and long established misunderstandings about the process of combustion. But today's student of elementary physics does not have to follow in his own mind the tortuous course of thought which led to the discovery of the composition of the air. In contrast with this, we cannot grasp Plato's philosophical theory of the relationships of various levels of knowledge unless we traverse his argument in his own version or in an exposition which reconstructs the journey of Plato's mind from starting point to conclusion.

That we have to retrace the thought of earlier thinkers does not mean that we have to do their work over again. It is true that we have to think their thoughts if we ourselves are to reach the point at which they stopped; but we do this with one stupendous advantage, we think their thoughts *after them.* The records they have left of their thinking guide our own efforts to follow them. We do not solve their problems, but when we follow their thinking in our own thought processes we reach a comprehension of the solutions they themselves had reached.

The progress of philosophy is not simply a matter of adding new answers to take the place of the old answers we reject; progress here requires an understanding of the philosophical achievements of the past and the reinterpretation and assimilation of insights already reached. It would not be too far wrong to say that all the broad alternative philosophies were worked out, in principle at least, during the first three or four centuries of philosophical inquiry. Of course change takes place, and no philosopher today would simply identify his point of view with that of any of the early philosophers; but there are no competent philosophers today whose work has not been influenced directly by the achievements of earlier philosophers. New work in this field is a matter of carrying earlier work further, of making underlying assumptions more explicit and bringing to light the less obvious implications. New insights in philosophy come from seeing other philosophies in new relationships with each other and from perspectives not available to earlier thinkers. Much of philosophy's progress comes from persistent attempts to reconcile conflicting views and to bring them together in a synthesis which does justice to all the different sides of what before appeared to be irreconcilable opposition.

Progress in philosophy cannot be brought about by committees. Organization and regimentation are always obstacles to progress in this field. The insights of many thinkers can meet, marry, and multiply only in the mind of an individual thinker. To make this possible the individual must appropriate to himself the thoughts of others and allow these ideas free play in his own mind. Premature decision as to what he will accept or reject interferes with the generation of new insights.

The thing of importance for the student in the study of a technical philosophy is to find how a philosopher obtained his technical concepts and what he meant by them. The philosophical significance of a philosophy, as distinguished from its personal significance, is not in the application and use of its concepts. As soon as we adopt a concept for use in our own thinking we announce in effect that so far as we are concerned the important philosophical work in the formation of that concept is complete. What we get as philosophers from those more competent than ourselves is not a set of concepts to employ in our own thinking; it is rather the discovery of a different perspective or interpretation of experience and existence. We may use another's concepts to solve our own problems; but then we are using his philosophy, and we are not engaged in philosophical inquiry. The life of philosophy is in the thinking process itself, not in the products of that process.

SUMMARY

The problem of the origin of philosophy is not only a problem for the historian but involves a philosophical problem as well. What is there about the prephilosophical level of thinking, the level of common-sense belief, which leads the human mind into philosophical inquiry? The distinctive character of the common-sense belief of a group is the unquestioned acceptance of those beliefs by the members of that group. The basis of common-sense belief is familiarity, and this means in practice that the test of truth we use in our common-sense thinking is whether or not our beliefs are in agreement with those of our associates.

Although agreement with others is a shaky foundation upon which to rest our claims of truth, yet there are levels of common-sense belief upon which we can rely. The security of common-sense belief varies inversely with its distance from direct experience. The more extensively involved in common sense are assumptions and inferences, the less we can trust it. The test of truth used by common sense, familiarity, is dependable only within such narrow limits of direct experience as sense perception, immediate memory, and our awareness of the intellectual processes in which we are engaged at the moment. All rational inquiry and all the formal disciplines by which we seek to extend our knowledge of the world and of ourselves depend for their possibility upon the existence of dependable knowledge at the common-sense level. No inquiry can start at the beginning; every inquiry assumes that we know something to start with. Consequently no inquiry can cast doubt on all inquiry without destroying the foundation of its own claim to truth.

Philosophy differs from common sense primarily in its substitution of reliable evidence and logical validity for familiarity as the test of truth. This usually comes about as the result of the discovery of conflicts between different beliefs held at the common-sense level. At this point the test of familiarity breaks down. In early Greece the outcome of this, on the part of the few men whose thinking provided the first steps forward in Western philosophy and science, was the attempt to understand the things of our world in terms of the nature of those things themselves.

All inquiry involves assumptions, and one of the chief tasks of philosophy is to try to bring our assumptions to light and to examine their truth. We may try to *prove* the truth of an assumption by showing that it follows logically from more basic beliefs, and this is to turn it into a conclusion. We may try to *justify* an assumption by showing that the denial would involve unacceptable consequences. Or we may simply exhibit an assumption as a basic element in our thinking. In all of these we are working toward something more basic than what we had to start with; we are working toward the discovery of ultimates.

The value of philosophy as a search for ultimates is not restricted to those which happen to be true. A philosophy may be known to be false and yet represent a positive contribution of a higher order. For a false philosophy spells out for us many of the implications of its own assumptions. Frequently we do not discover the weakness of an assumption until we discover some of its implications. Likewise we are unable to understand truth *as truth* until we have come to understand the difficulties involved in all of the plausible alternative possibilities. We have to go through the false in order to reach the true. Although this may suggest a challenge to the competence of philosophy, yet such a challenge is bound to fail; for the challenge itself is an exercise in philosophy. Progress in philosophy goes through, not around, the thought of those who have worked earlier with its problems; progress here comes from seeing the work of other philosophers in new relationships and from new perspectives. In this we cannot merely take the results of other thinkers' labor and build upon those conclusions; on the contrary we have to follow their thought processes in our own thinking.

Questions for Study and Discussion

1. *Terms:* common sense, conclusion, evidence, necessity, premise, proof, self-evidence, validity.

2. Do you see any parallels between common sense belief, with its independence of critical examination, and gossip? What is it in each case that relaxes our critical powers and promotes gullibility?

3. Formulate your own example of common sense belief which you think no competent person could doubt.

4. "In its generalizations and theories, popular thought is almost always wrong. . . ." Can you think of any exceptions to this?

5. Which of the following statements would you defend or attack by appealing to the evidence and which by an attempt to justify them as assumptions?
   (a) The sun will rise tomorrow.
   (b) I shall never meet myself coming toward me.
   (c) My father and mother are interested in me for myself and not for some advantages they hope sometime to obtain from me.
   (d) Freedom is better than slavery.
   (e) Knowledge is better than ignorance.

6. Illustrate the principle: We have to go through the false in order to reach the true.

7. Does the discussion in this chapter of the progress of philosophy imply that one basic difference between philosophy and science is that philosophy is personal while science is impersonal? Examine critically the contrast expressed in this statement.

CHAPTER 4

The Method of Philosophy

RATIONAL THOUGHT AS THE METHOD OF PHILOSOPHY

Our discussion in this chapter can be no more than an introduction to some of the main features of the method of philosophy, for we can describe the method of philosophy effectively only by using it. Our presentation of that method includes what has gone before and all that comes after this chapter. Here we can only identify and illustrate its broader features.

Once we understand the nature of philosophy's task the question arises as to how philosophy is to perform its task. The scientist works in field and laboratory, examining specimens and performing experiments. The philosopher sits in his study and reflects. The scientist looks at and listens to and feels and tastes the things he studies; he makes records and charts, and analyzes his data mathematically. The philosopher thinks about things and about the process of thinking. Thus the scientist seems to have the advantage over the philosopher; for the scientist goes to the facts and reports what he finds, while the philosopher would appear merely to "make up" his theories in his own mind and not even to test them by experiment or mathematical analysis. How can the philosopher expect to get any information about the actual facts by the use of his methods?

Questions like this have often been asked, and sometimes still are; but they reflect a serious misunderstanding about the kind of knowledge philosophy seeks. The difference between the tasks of philosophy and science will be explored in later chapters; we need to understand here, however, that philosophy seeks a knowledge different from scientific knowledge, and that philosophy and science are not rivals but each supplements the other. It is quite true that the problems of a science cannot be solved by the methods of philosophy; the philosopher in his study cannot do the work of the scientist in his laboratory. But it is also true that the problems of philosophy cannot be investigated by the methods of the sciences, and to turn philosophical problems over to scientists for scientific investigation is to insure at the outset that no progress toward their solution will be made. Scientists sometimes have made important contributions to philosophy, but only as they have reflected philosophically.

What we have said so far suggests that philosophy is concerned with the investigation of those aspects of things which do not require us to observe their qualities under special conditions or to experiment with them in the laboratory. Philosophy is concerned with aspects of things which can be known and investigated by rational thinking. By this we do not intend to suggest that thought is sufficient by itself to produce knowledge. Unless we already know something we have nothing to apply our thought to; without experience thought is empty. When we ask what we can know about things by rational thinking we mean to ask what we can in this way add to the knowledge we already have. There are many ways of extending our knowledge. We may extend it by means of new experiences and by learning what others have found out, and we may extend it by use of the methods of the sciences. We may extend our knowledge also by reflecting on what we already know, and this is the kind of extension of knowledge which philosophy provides.

Not all thinking is philosophical thinking; scientists and mathematicians, lawyers and physicians, business men and politicians have to think and to think with some expertness in order to do their work successfully. The aim of philosophical thinking is knowledge while the thinking which is done by lawyers, physicians, business men, and politicians is for the solution of practical problems. The distinction is not always sharp, but we recognize here a basic difference in purpose between the theoretical and the practical. But scientists and mathematicians are also engaged in theoretical inquiry. Although the differentiation of philosophical inquiry from scientific and mathematical inquiry will be discussed in detail in Part II, we may say here that philosophy, like mathematics and unlike the special sciences, is concerned with inquiry which makes use of unaided reflection alone. Unlike mathematics, philosophical thinking is unformalized: mathematics begins with precisely defined concepts and specified operations and seeks to discover their logical consequences; philosophy works toward more and more adequate concepts, trying this and that, revising and discarding until no further progress can be made at the time.

Every other theoretical discipline operates on the basis of and within the scope of certain assumptions which are not open to examination by the methods of that discipline. Our discussion of philosophy in earlier chapters has suggested that philosophical thinking is, directly or indirectly, about ultimates. Philosophy is, in large part, the examination of assumptions, the assumptions of other disciplines and its own assumptions as well; and this is of course a concern with ultimates. As we shall see later, when we think about ultimates our thinking cannot be formalized, for the very forms we would use must themselves undergo scrutiny if philosophy is to do its proper work.

THE METHOD OF DISCOVERY

The method of philosophy, like any method of inquiry, has two main phases: the phase of *discovery*, and the phase of *proof*. If we are to have philosophical ideas there must be some way in which they come to us, and if they are to be a source of knowledge we must have some way of demonstrating and testing the conclusions we reach when we use these ideas in our thinking. In philosophy the method of discovery is *abstraction*, and the method of proof is *argument*. Philosophical argument includes *logical deduction* and *dialectic*.

We saw earlier that philosophy is concerned with what can be known about things by means of rational thinking, and we saw also that thinking does not take place without something to think about. If we exclude all kinds of supposed supersensuous intuition and divine revelation and restrict ourselves to the knowledge we get by the ordinary use of our natural faculties, we must conclude that the only original source of material to think about is sense experience. After we begin to think about what we discover by sense experience we become aware of the thinking processes themselves and we can think about them by further acts of reflection. Our concern at this point, however, is to get some idea of what we can come to know by rational thinking alone concerning the things we find in sense experience.

Instead of illustrating the method of discovery in philosophy by means of an example drawn from the technical literature of the subject, it may be more helpful here to scrutinize some very ordinary experiences. The purpose of our analysis here is to show what we can find in the way of basic ideas and assumptions which are involved in perfectly familiar ways of looking at things, ideas and assumptions which are there but are hidden from ordinary awareness unless we make an effort to find them. Our examples may not be especially philosophical, in a technical sense; but technical philosophy usually operates at a level which takes for granted much previous analysis. The three examples at which we shall look briefly here are taken from ordinary observation and are intended to show how reflection can bring to light much that is assumed in direct experience. Some of these assumptions are crucial; for although we are seldom aware of them explicitly, their denial would radically change our interpretation of the experience itself.

Suppose I plant a vegetable garden. Under a warm sun the seeds sprout and soon I see the plants as they have pushed through the surface of the soil. The plants grow in size, more and more leaves appear, then blossoms, and finally peas and beans and tomatoes are ready to pick. I am confident that each of these growing plants is the same plant that it was yesterday and the day before. It does not even occur to me to wonder if the appearance of growth is not the result of someone slipping out to the garden each night, digging up the plants already there, and substituting slightly larger ones in their places. I have no doubt that I have observed the actual growth of these plants, watching them day by day as they passed through the growth cycle. As I reflect on what I have observed I may recognize that here is an instance of a principle that applies to all changing things, that a changing thing retains its identity through the process of change. Thus I recognize that each of these growing plants has a unity of existence in spite of the fact that it is in process of change; each is *one* thing, not a series of replacements. The discovery we make here by reflection upon what we have observed, the presence of both change and unity, is the source of one of the earliest of philosophical problems: How can a thing change and yet be the same thing?

I pound a nail into a board. With each blow of the hammer the nail sinks further into the wood. I reflect on this and recognize that the hammer blows are causes and that each increase of penetration of the wood by the nail is an effect. I see and hear the hammer strike, I notice that less of the nail is exposed than before the blow was struck, and I feel in my hand the recoil of the hammer as it strikes the nail. But I do not *see* or *feel* the cause and effect relation with my eyes and hands as I see the nail lengths and feel the recoil of the hammer. My recognition that these things are in causal relation is the product of *reflection about* what I see and feel and hear. It can be observed, but not by eyes or ears or hands; awareness of a causal relation is awareness of a feature of the event which can be observed only in reflective thought.

Here is a silver coin stamped with a design. As I look at it I recognize its shape and compare its size with other coins. I read the words stamped upon it and recognize what the design represents. As I reflect upon what I see I become aware of a distinction between the material of which the coin is made, the silver alloy, and the form or shape of the coin. Two dimes that lie side by side in my hand have the same form and shape and design, but they are made of different bits of metal. The bit of silver alloy from which one coin is made is not the same bit of metal from which the other is made. This is not something about the coins that I can see or hear or taste or smell or feel. To know that there is a distinction between form and material is true knowledge, but I can become aware of that distinction only by thinking it.

Each of these three examples illustrates a different aspect of the knowledge we get by reflecting on our sense experience, and so each is an example of elementary philosophical knowledge. We discover by reflection that changing things have unity, that an event involves the relation of cause and effect, and that a physical thing combines a distinguishable form with material. In each instance we have discovered something about the objects of sense experience not by adding more sense experience but by reflecting on what already was known.

When we consider the question of the source of such ideas it is evident that we do not get them directly from the stimulation of our sense organs; we are not aware of them until we think about the things we sense. What thought discovers cannot be sensed, and yet without the use of the senses we would have nothing to think about. How is it that there is anything except sensation in our experience for thought to discover?

This in itself is a formidable philosophical problem and it has been dealt with in many different ways by different philosophers. In order to illustrate some of the complexities into which reflection can lead us as we consider such problems, we shall now develop in some detail one possible answer to this question.

Sense experience is not only sensory response to stimulus, it is also perceptual; and as perception it is awareness *of* something. The distinction can be grasped quite readily if we compare sense perception with sense experience that is not perceptual. Whenever my attention is called to it I can feel my clothing touch my skin, but those moments of perception are few and far between in comparison with the moments when I am not directly conscious of the contact of my clothes. Yet the sensory stimulation is continuous. As I walk along the street my steps are guided by what I see, but little of this involves perception. As I cross the street and step over the curbing the precise time and place and distance I raise my foot are controlled by what I see. Without long practice I could not do this with my eyes shut. Even so, I do not have to *perceive* the curbing in order not to stumble, even though my eyes must be open. I can be carrying on a conversation or be thinking about something far removed from where I am and from what I am doing.

If, when we attend to a sense experience, we find that we are aware not merely of the quality *red* but of *something that is red*, why should we not conclude that the sense experience communicates to our minds not only *red* but the *being of something red?* We have no reason to deny this unless we insist that our sensory and intellectual processes are entirely separate from each other. If sense and intellect do cooperate in cognition then we have every reason to regard a sensory response, merely as sensory, as incomplete. For some activities nothing more is needed, but for minds endowed with intellect as well as sense there is more to be found in what is given in sense experience than the senses alone are able to report.

The senses by themselves, acting apart from the cooperation of the intellect, are incapable of grasping all that is presented to us in sense experience. But when intellect co-operates in awareness, as it does in sense perception, we grasp what the senses by themselves would have missed. As Professor Veatch so well expressed it:

> To be sure, there is no denying that all that we see with our eyes are mere colors, or that all that we hear with our ears are mere sounds, etc. And yet, does it follow from this that nothing more is given or presented in sense experience than colors, sounds, odors, etc.? Quite the contrary; it is quite possible that a great deal more might be given in sensation than the senses themselves are liable to discern. In such a case, while what would be presented to us through the senses would really be so presented, it would still not be through the senses alone that we would come to apprehend what was so presented.[1]

To avoid this conclusion we should have to insist that we sense one thing and perceive another, as if we had not a thing that is red but two things, a red that is not the red of a thing and a thing that is not red. In the words of Professor Veatch again,

> it is *the very same object* that is presented to sense, and whose properly sensible qualities are apprehended by the senses, that comes to be recognized by the intellect as existing substantially in itself and not as a mere accident of something else.[2]

We may conclude, then, that the presence of *something* colored is just as much a "given" in sense experience as is the color. What is given is given in its being and unity and in various relationships to other things. It is true that we can analyze our sense experience and attend to the colors of things, for example, in abstraction from the things themselves. I may compare two shades of blue which I see in sky and water without attending to anything else involved in the experience. This does not alter the fact that there are other features given, to be attended to if I wish to concern myself with them.

When I see a tree I see it as something that *is*, and so I can turn my attention upon the fact of its existence and ignore for the mo-

[1] Henry Babcock Veatch, *Intentional Logic* (New Haven, Yale University Press, 1952), p. 88. By permission.
[2] *Ibid*, p. 90.

ment its shape and color and other sense qualities. I see it also in a *place* and in spatial relationship with other things; and I see it *now*. I see it as a distinct entity, as having *unity*, so that it is quite meaningful to refer to *this* tree in distinction from *that* tree. I see its branches bend under the wind that I hear and feel against my face, and so I perceive the tree as one whose branches are moved by the wind. As I look at the tree I remember how it has grown in the past years. Thus in the same way that I think of its being I can think, by abstraction from what is presented, of its place and time, its unity, its causal relations with other things, and its becoming.

If this analysis is convincing it may lead us to reflect further that the intellect has its own activity. It sorts out similarities and differences, isolates certain relationships, and ties together in experience aspects of things that are separate in their own existence. But in all of this the intellect has nothing to work with except what it finds. It contributes nothing to the content of what is known except where the intellect itself is the object known. As the intellect gets all of its material from experience so it gets all its patterns from experience; thus whatever it constructs it constructs with materials and patterns derived originally from experience. The basic activity in knowing is abstraction. All differentiations and identifications and comparisons are instances of abstraction; and without these activities we could not become aware of the structure and relationships of the objects we find in experience.

PHILOSOPHICAL ARGUMENT

As abstraction is the method of discovery in philosophy, so argument is the method of proof. In its broadest sense, argument is the presentation of a case for or against some belief or proposal. It is a way of contending for the acceptance or rejection of something. The appeal may be emotional; it may use threats, ridicule, appeals to pity, to pride, to prejudice, or to jealousy or hate or any other emotion. On the other hand, argument may be reasoned discourse, composed of logically related statements which present evidence in support of a conclusion. In logically valid arguments, reasons and conclusions are so related that if the reasons given for a conclusion are true then the conclusion has to be true. Philosophical argument always claims to be reasoned argument. As argument, philosophical argument is always *for* or *against* something; it is always contention for a point of view.

The description of philosophical argument as defense of a point of view may suggest that philosophy is a kind of prejudiced inquiry, pursued with a closed mind and incapable of impartial examination of evidence. Although philosophical argument should not show prejudice, in the ordinary sense of the term, yet it does involve a kind of prejudgment. Until we have formulated for ourselves some kind of a point of view concerning a problem we cannot think about it philosophically. No one can think philosophically about any problem if he has a completely neutral attitude toward it. He may study the view of others without having a view of his own, but until that study leads him to take a position of his own he will not be investigating the problem. He will be investigating only the arguments of others concerning the problem.

This does not mean that philosophical thinking requires a closed mind or that a philosopher is incapable of a fair and balanced examination of the evidence. Although he must have a position to defend, the goal of his thinking is truth. If he finds, in his attempt to defend his position against other views, that his own is in any way defective he will change his position. This is the only way a beginner can become a learner in philosophy, and it is the only way a philosopher can progress in his study of the problems of his field.

To some it may seem a serious or even fatal weakness of philosophy, as a method of reaching true conclusions, that the philosopher does not consider different proposed solutions of a problem impartially, examining and comparing them *before* he accepts any particular view as his own. Strange as it may seem to some at first thought, however, such a proposal fails to distinguish between a serious inquiry into philosophical problems and merely verbal play. We are not ready for serious philosophical investigation of a problem until we have arrived at some point of view regarding it. Philosophical discussion may change a point of view, but not unless there is one to change.

In this respect philosophy differs from the sciences. In a scientific investigation of a problem we can consider competing hypotheses without accepting any one and even without having any preference. In philosophy we cannot do this. We can come no closer to doing it than to ignore the point of view which we unconsciously assume. The more competent a philosopher is, the more clearly aware he is of his own presuppositions and commitments. The difference between philosopher and scientist, however, is not that the scientist lacks a point of view and has no commitments about ultimates. It is rather that such commitments *are not at issue* in a scientific investigation. The method of science, when properly followed, insures that they will not be at issue; and at the moment a scientist's commitments do become an issue in a scientific investigation, at that moment he becomes incompetent to proceed with his inquiry. A philosopher's commitments, on the other hand, are involved directly or indirectly in any properly philosophical inquiry and should be given explicit statement.

It must be emphasized that any search for knowledge involves assumptions. If we were informed at the outset that an inquirer had no point of view about anything and believed in nothing, that his mind was completely open about everything, we certainly should not take his "inquiry" seriously. For this would mean that he had no commitment even to try to find the truth, and no standards by which to distinguish the true from the false. Of course a scientist can be impartial about competing hypotheses under investigation; if he cannot, he is incompetent as a scientist. But he cannot be impartial concerning the question of whether the methods of science are valid. He cannot even raise the question without abandoning, at least temporarily, his role as a scientist. A scientist has his basic commitments just as does a philosopher; but since the problems which they involve are philosophic, the methods of philosophy are the appropriate ones to use in their investigation.

The contention that we cannot investigate a philosophical problem from a neutral position is itself a theory concerning the nature of philosophical inquiry; but it is a theory very difficult to avoid accepting. An attempt to be neutral in philosophical inquiry would compel us to avoid committing ourselves to any definite positions concerning the nature and limits of knowledge and concerning the mode of existence of the knowing mind and its objects. We should have to be careful not to take the position of neutrality as itself as an ultimate, for that would not be a neutral position. The only easy way to be neutral about philosophical problems is to ignore them.

This does not mean that the only requirement for competence in philosophy is to have a point of view. To have a point of view is a necessary but not a sufficient condition of competence. Nor does it mean that one who is competent cannot change his point of view, although it is likely that a philosopher who does change his position considers himself more competent after the change than before. Competence requires an understanding of all the known alternatives and of their relations with each other. Thus there may be different levels of competence; and a claim of absolute competence would be arrogant indeed. Competence varies with the extent to which a philosopher understands and is able to appreciate the plausibility of the different possible positions and with the degree of success with which he supports his own position.

If philosophical inquiry proceeds on the basis of an already accepted point of view, how can a philosopher investigate new problems? In answer to this question we may say that problems may be new to him *as philosophical problems* and still not be unfamiliar. I may recognize that there are problems of philosophical significance for others which I am not in a position to investigate philosophically, for I do not yet see the bearing of these issues upon my own conceptions of existence and value. Since I do not see whatever issues they may raise about my own position I cannot deal with them philosophically. I may be quite aware that views concerning ultimates are at stake for those who discuss these issues, and so I may suspect that it is because of my own imperfect insight into these problems that I do not see their bearing on my position. But until I do see their relevance to my own thinking I am not in a position to begin a philosophical inquiry into them. As I read and reflect on others' discussions of these problems I may come to see their import for my own point of view. Until this happens I am not engaged in philosophical inquiry in the sense that I am trying to solve a philosophical problem. I am engaged rather in learning something about another's philosophical inquiries. At this stage I am not even in a position to decide which of the various views I encounter I shall accept or reject; not until I raise the question under inquiry for myself have I any business attempting to evaluate the solutions offered for consideration. Professor John E. Smith has called attention to this:

> We earn the right to criticize . . . attempts at solution only when we are seeking to answer the same questions. To refuse to raise a question is to forfeit the right to assess the answers offered by others.[3]

[3] "John Dewey: Philosopher of Experience," *The Review of Metaphysics,* Volume XIII, No. 1, September, 1959, p. 76. By permission.

There is still the question of why a philosopher should be interested in investigating new problems or care to reopen old ones. If he has already reached his own conclusions why does he not simply rest with those conclusions? The answer to this question brings us back again to what distinguishes a philosopher from other people. Even though a philosopher does have a definite position of his own concerning a problem about ultimates he does not have a closed mind on the matter. *The willingness and desire to examine the rational foundation of his basic beliefs is the philosopher's distinctive characteristic.* A person becomes a philosopher in spirit even if not in achievement as soon as he becomes genuinely concerned about the rational grounds of those beliefs. He wants not merely beliefs about ultimates, no matter how satisfying those beliefs may be, but knowledge. No matter how plausible a philosopher considers his own view to be concerning a problem, he never considers his view immune from rational and critical examination. The philosopher should be more clearly aware than any one else of the limitations of such knowledge. Since he desires knowledge, he welcomes every reasoned attack upon his own basic beliefs, for only as a result of such attack is he likely to discover weaknesses he has hitherto overlooked.

Because philosophy is reflective it cannot merely look and see and report what the truth is. Reflection is an activity, not a condition of passive receptivity. Since it involves abstraction, reflection is especially liable to distortion, for abstraction itself is a process by which other features are ignored in order to examine an abstracted feature. When what is ignored is relevant to the problem, the act of abstraction in which that relevant feature was ignored must be supplemented by other acts of abstraction.

The more completely convinced a philosopher is of the importance of showing the truth of a position he has arrived at, the more eagerly he should encourage the formulation and expression of arguments against that position. For its truth can be shown only *against* the arguments to the contrary.

Professor Arthur O. Lovejoy has pointed out:

> Effective cooperation among philosophers consists . . . primarily in disagreement. For, given a sufficiently well defined problem, philosophy can really get forward with it only by bringing together in their logical interconnection all the considerations which have occurred, or are likely to occur, to acute and philosophically initiated minds as

significantly pertinent to that problem. These considerations will always be numerous, they will always, during the progress of any philosophical inquiry, be conflicting, and they must be contributed by many minds of diverse types and different training and preconceptions. . . . The true procedure of philosophy . . . is thus that of a Platonic dialogue on a grand scale, in which the theses, proposed proofs, objections, rejoinders, of numerous interlocutors are focused upon a given question, and the argument gradually shapes itself, through its own immanent dialectic, to a conclusion.[4]

The "solution" of a philosophical problem is seldom if ever a definitive conclusion capable of statement in a formula. Philosophers offer us the conclusions they have reached in their thinking, but we miss entirely the meaning of a philosophical conclusion unless we understand it in the light of the reasons which have been given in its support and see its relationship to other positions. Merely to offer a definitive answer in a fixed formula is to tell us in effect that there is no problem; to suggest that where we differ we are simply mistaken. To get answers we do not need to think; we need only to be informed. Errors detected in reports of observed fact can be corrected and eliminated from further consideration; but in philosophy, errors are comprehended, and through their comprehension, advance is made. Perhaps the most important difference among philosophers is the extent to which they try to do justice to the insights of other philosophers. We need to remember, however, that responsible inquiry in philosophy is in support of one point of view as over against the known alternatives. A philosopher can be satisfied he has made genuine progress toward the solution of his problem only where he can give cogent reasons to support his contention that one way of understanding the matter is more fruitful and adequate than others.

THE TEST OF PHILOSOPHICAL ARGUMENT

How can we estimate the success of a philosophical argument? Is there any point at which philosophical dialectic can reach finality? The contention that finality has been reached in a particular philosophical argument is itself not necessarily final; it is

[4] *The Revolt Against Dualism* (Chicago, The Open Court Publishing Company, 1930), p. ix. By permission.

always open to critical scrutiny. But philosophers do attempt to reach finality, and in this section we shall look at a limited and modest version of the view that at some points finality is possible.

As was mentioned earlier in this chapter, a final proof requires more than logical validity alone. If an argument is valid, its conclusion has to be true provided its premises are true. But what about the premises themselves? Suppose the reasons that are given for a conclusion do not hold. In that case the argument is still valid, for it is still the case that if the premises *were* true the conclusion would have to be true. But in spite of its validity the argument fails to establish the truth of the conclusion. Any time I have my head cut off I shall die. The conclusion follows from the premise whether I have my head cut off or not. My knowledge that this so so leads me to try to avoid having my head cut off. But no assurance of the validity of this reasoning will assure me that I shall not have my head cut off.

If we depend only on formal logic in our search for truth we shall have to bring forward additional premises for each of the original ones, and so on indefinitely. So long as we stay on this path we never escape the *if* which qualifies our claim to have established the truth of a conclusion. So long as the *if* remains our thought is separated from the existence of the thing we are thinking about; we have no bridge from validity to truth. The problem of proof in philosophy is the problem of getting from thought to existence without the *if*. Abstraction leads our thought away from existence: the problem is to return to existence again with the results of that thought. Our contact with existence is in experience. So our problem here is to link thought to experience in such a way that the truth of the premises of our thinking is guaranteed by existence itself.

We get some light on this problem when we see that our thought about something always involves existence in two different ways. There is first the existence or non-existence of the thing we are thinking about. Thought alone may not be able to settle this issue. But there is always also the existence of the thought itself. The thought is something that happens. Any thought of any kind, no matter what it is about, is a direct presentation of existence, that is, of its own existence. Thus *any line of reasoning that leads us to a conclusion whose truth would be in conflict with its own existence as an act of thought is false.* Philosophical proof would seem to reach a quite stable position wherever we can show that a denial of the conclusion reached would be in conflict with the existence of that denial itself. We may call this method of proof, *existential dialectic;* and its test of truth, *existential self-evidence.*

There are at least two kinds of self-evident truths. There are those which assert of a subject something already contained in the meaning of the subject-term itself. The statement, "All men are human beings," is an example. The subject term, *men,* already includes in its meaning that of the predicate term, *human beings.* Such self-evident propositions have a certain importance in spite of their appearance of triviality, for to be caught in the denial of such a statement is proof that something is wrong. It can be a truly relevant observation to make concerning certain views about mankind and the things that people sometimes propose to do with men to say, "But after all, men are human beings." We may call these propositions *essentially self-evident,* for to deny such a proposition is to attribute a self-contradictory *nature* or *essence* to something.

Rationalistic philosophies appeal to what we here call "essential self-evidence." They attempt to establish certain conclusions concerning existence by means of an appeal to reason or logic alone. The difficulty is that although the presence of logical contradiction shows that something is wrong in our thinking the absence of logical contradiction does not establish truth. Self-consistency is a necessary but not a sufficient condition of knowledge. A common mistake of rationalistic philosophies is to suppose that this necessary condition is also a sufficient condition.

The conflict involved in the denial of an existentially self-evident proposition, however, is not the merely logical contradiction of subject with predicate, as is the case if we say that some men are not human. The conflict rather is between what the proposition says, and the fact of its own occurrence. For example, if I make the statement, "I cannot speak a word of English," the meaning of what I say is in conflict with the fact that I say it. If it is true that I cannot speak a word of English, then it simply is a fact that I cannot say "I cannot speak a word of English"; for this statement itself is in English. This is not a conflict merely of thought with thought but of thought with fact.

We can be sure, for example, that knowledge is possible, for to deny this is to claim to know something. "Nothing can be known," is not an essential contradiction, for some things may be unknowable in some sense or under some conditions. But the statement that hing can be known is itself a claim to know something, so that what it *means* is in conflict with the fact that it purports to *be*. Such a conflict is the point of a story told during World War I about a detail of soldiers engaged in burying enemy casualties. Some of the casualties protested, "But we are not dead!" The work went on, however, as one of the soldiers said, "Bah! They are such liars: why should we believe them?"[5]

AN APPLICATION OF THE METHOD OF PHILOSOPHY

The relation of abstraction and argument and their cooperation in philosophical inquiry may be better understood if we use them in a more extended analysis of a quite ordinary case of observation and thought. Here again our illustration is quite elementary and perhaps of too little technical interest for the working philosopher. But as some of the work of contemporary philosophy in the analysis of ordinary language has shown, much more is involved in the meaning of a familiar statement than is obvious to casual inspection. The following extended analysis is intended to show some of the assumptions involved in this statement when understood in the usual sense and to bring out something of the relationship of these assumptions to the traditional themes of philosophy. Our analysis will illustrate the use of both abstraction and argument. It is not itself, however, a philosophical inquiry; it is merely an illustration of the use of some of the techniques of philosophical inquiry to uncover basic ideas and assumptions.

Suppose I say: "The sky has become dark with clouds; I think it will rain." Here I am saying something about the sky and about what I think will happen in the future. This is the report of an observation and a guess or prediction based on that observation; thus it is a report both of my experience of the sky and of my experience of my own mental processes. Its truth claim is based on the direct perception of the moment together with the background of knowledge and information by means of which I interpret this perception. This background includes factual knowledge: it is an awareness of a certain state of affairs and of the relation of this state of affairs to

---

[5] Told by Albert Guérard in *Fossils and Presences* (Stanford, California, Stanford University Press, 1957), p. 101.

a future one. But the statement expresses more than factual knowledge. It also involves philosophical concepts and ideas, and these are such that unless they are sound our supposed factual knowledge is not knowledge at all.

To say, "The sky has become dark with clouds," and to mean by this what we ordinarily do mean, I have to think of the sky and the clouds as *being* something. The sky is something to which my statement refers; it is that about which the statement is made. My concept of *sky* may be quite vague, so that I may not be able to say precisely what I include as a part of the sky and what I do not include. But this is a question of fact and perhaps of word usage. No matter how vague may be my concept of *what* the sky is, I have here no question whatever about *whether* the sky is. I may question *what* it is but I do not question *that* it is. Even to be aware that there might be a question of *what* it is, constitutes a recognition *that* it is. To ask about the nature of something is to suppose that there is something to ask about.

In the kind of situation we are discussing here, I am not likely to be in any doubt about *how* the sky exists, for I take it without question to be some sort of physical being. It is conceivable that someone might raise a question about how the sky exists, perhaps as a result of confusion of thought or perhaps as a result of certain theories concerning what is real and what is unreal. The sky is sometimes referred to in poetic language as "the heavens"; as where the Psalmist says, "The heavens declare the glory of God." If the expression, "the heavens," were to be confused with the theological concept of *Heaven*, then one result might be to raise the question of *how* the heavens (that is, the sky) exist. No doubt children sometimes confuse the idea of Heaven they get from religious instruction with the idea of the sky and may even think of Heaven as a place in the sky. Even such confusion as this, however, involves no doubt of the being of the sky; it is a confusion of two modes of being. Or a person may be mentally confused, not sure whether he is seeing the real sky or having a dream. But even in the awareness of such an uncertainty, no question is raised about the real existence of the sky. The only question is whether the present experience is a perception of that real sky or is a dream.

A philosophical subjectivist, who believes that the things he sees and hears and feels are but ideas in his mind, has a different understanding of how the sky exists. In Berkeley's words, "all the choir of heaven and furniture of the earth . . . have not any subsistence without a mind . . ." [6] Even so, Berkeley does not in any sense deny the *being* of the sky; and if he is right in contending that it has only mental being, he still is asserting something ultimate and final about the sky.

As we ordinarily understand the statement that the sky "has become dark with clouds," three additional basic ideas are involved. First, in making this statement, I distinguish between the *sky*, which has its own existence, and a *quality* or *state* or *condition* of the sky. The sky exists in its own right, but *dark* does not. The sky is *substance;* its color is *accident*, existing only as the color *of* something. This is no mere distinction of language; it is a distinction of thought. If I say something like, "Darkness covers the sky," I do not take the fact that "darkness" is a noun to mean that it is a substance, that darkness is something that has its own existence as does the sky or a cloud in the sky. Few of us would share, for example, the primitive superstition that darkness is in itself a real force which is a menace to those caught in it.

Secondly, the statement that the sky has *become* dark involves the idea of change. It states not merely that the sky *is* dark, although this is included in its meaning, but that the present condition of darkness differs from an earlier condition. The same sky is there now that was there before it became dark, but it has undergone a change in its condition. If I did not think in these terms I would not understand the meaning of the statement itself. The idea of change is an ultimate, for we cannot raise the question of whether there is change without assuming, in asking the question, that there is. Once we reflect on what it means to ask a question we recognize that a question is a request for an answer or clarification we did not have before. The existence of inquiry itself does not make sense unless there is change.

The third basic idea involved in this part of the statement is *time* or *duration*. That the sky is a temporal thing is not just something that happens to be the case, such as the fact that the sky is blue or that it is hazy. As something which involves change in its very exist-

6 "A Treatise Concerning the Principles of Human Knowledge," Part I, Section VI, in *A New Theory of Vision and Other Select Philosophical Writings by George Berkeley* (Everyman's Library, New York, E. P. Dutton and Company, Inc., 1910), p. 115. This passage is quoted in its context below, in Chapter 10.

ence, the distinction between *before* and *after* applies to it necessarily. Without such distinction the idea of change is unintelligible.

In the second clause, "I think it will rain," the word "I" of course refers to something that exists and has unity. The *I* who thinks it will rain is the same *I* who notes that the sky has become dark with clouds. In making this statement to another person there is also an awareness that the *I* who makes the statement is not the one to whom the statement is made. Unless I recognize the being of another self when I make this statement, I am merely talking to myself. That this is of some significance in ordinary experience is apparent when we recall the momentary shock we experience when we discover that someone we thought to be in the next room, and to whom we thought we were talking, is not there at all. Certainly the existence of the *I* who thinks and speaks and intends something is a condition without which the very occurrence of the statement would not make sense, whether the speaker is talking to himself or to another.

In saying I *think* it will rain, not only do I say that this case of thinking takes place, and has being and unity, but I say something which involves the idea of *truth*. The idea of truth is included in two ways. First, in saying that I think it will rain I am reporting something about my state of mind; I am distinguishing the state of mind I actually have from other states, such as *knowing* or *wishing* or *doubting* it will rain. Such a distinction, if made meaningfully and intelligibly, involves some idea of truth. In the second place, the idea of truth is a condition without which the statement as a whole could not be made and could not be supposed to have the kind of existence it purports to have. For the assertion *is* a truth claim. The claim of truth is not a part of the statement, as is a clause or a phrase, nor is it a fact reported by the statement; it is rather a way in which the statement has to *be* in order to serve as a report of fact. Unless this were a truth claim I might say these same words as the quotation of another's statement; but even so I should be making a different truth claim: the claim that it is true that the other person did say these words. To say the words without some truth claim would be only to make sounds or express an emotion or perhaps to practice the enunciation of words.

The verb, *will rain*, is in future tense, and so again the statement involves the idea of duration. The idea of *rain* is here the idea of a happening or event, and requires some awareness of the distinction between something that *is* in the sense that it is taking place, and something that has another mode of being. We recognize also that the statement can be thought of not only with reference to a certain time, but also with reference to a certain *place*. Involved in this is the concept of *space*. Furthermore, the relation of the two main clauses is such that we could not understand the full meaning of the statement without an awareness of causal relations. A causal relation is quite different from the relation signified by such a statement, say, as: "The sky has become dark with clouds; the leaves on the trees are beginning to turn." We could not see an important difference between this and the original sentence if we had no idea of causality, and the difference we do see would not have the significance it seems to have if it were not true that causes exist. This is no mere difference of sentence structure, for the two sentences are identical in structure. The difference is in the actually existing relationships of real things which the two statements are intended to indicate.

Thus far our analysis has concerned the basic ideas involved in the meaning of the original assertion. If successful, it has revealed some basic assumptions concerning the situation to which the statement refers, such as something of the mode of being of various things and events and of the properties of those things, and the distinction of substance and accident. It has shown also that what we are talking about involves time and place, and is an order of existence in which causal relations are found. We found also that the idea of truth is a condition without which no such assertion can be made. Thus there is much more in even the commonest observation or most casual comment than we ordinarily recognize. All these things are a part of what we mean, and they all are taken to be ultimate characteristics of the realm of being to which they refer. Our analysis thus far, however, is far from complete. By pushing it further we can uncover in this same statement another dimension, as it were, of philosophical knowledge. We have been concerned with how this complex of fact exists; we need to consider now how our *knowledge* of it exists. The fact that the statement involves a truth claim serves as a bridge between the being of the thing known and the being of the knowing of the thing.

In the first place, my statement about the sky and the rain expresses an awareness. An awareness is something mental; it may exist as a concept which I express in a word or phrase, or as a judgment which I express in an assertion or denial, or as an argument which I express in a combination of assertions some of which purport to be reasons why others are true or false.[7] These are not the only modes of mental existence but they are the ones we are directly concerned with when we make claims of truth.

If I can make a statement about a physical thing or event and make any sense of the claim that my statement is true, there must be some way in which the thing I am talking about can have a mental existence as well as its own physical existence. I recognize implicitly some such distinction every time I distinguish between my idea of the sky and the actual sky. If I am to be aware of the sky I must have an idea of it, and yet unless I am a subjectivist I do not consider that the sky I am aware of is merely an idea. The awareness exists in my mind, but the sky I am aware of does not. Although the two are not identical, it seems that there has to be some kind of identity involved in their relation with each other if the one can possibly be an awareness of the other. There have been many theories about this, and some stand has to be taken if the claim of truth is to have a meaning that will survive the slightest examination.

The answer to this question with perhaps the longest history is based on the distinction between essence and existence. We distinguish between *what* the sky is, its *essence;* and the fact *that* the sky is, its *existence.* This is not a distinction between parts of the sky, nor does it mean that the sky is formed by the coming together of an essence and an existence to constitute a combination of things which before were separate. The distinction is one made by the intellect as a distinction of aspects, as in somewhat the same way we distinguish between the sides of a board. (No one thinks that a board is made by taking six one-sided things and putting them together to make one six-sided thing!) By means of a distinction between the essence and existence of the sky, for example, we can admit an identity in knowing without blurring the distinction between the sky itself and our idea of the sky as existences. The *content* or *what* of the idea is identical with something in the real nature of the sky, but idea and sky are quite separate in their respective existences. This is one way, at least, to attempt to make the truth claim intelligible.

[7] See Francis H. Parker and Henry B. Veatch, *Logic as a Human Instrument* (New York, Harper and Brothers, 1959), Chapter 1.

On this interpretation our statement involves a reality which is physical, and a reality which is cognitive; one that exists as spatial and temporal substances with properties and in causal relationships, and one that exists as an awareness of something other than itself. There is also a third mode of being, the being of the statement itself as a statement. The statement is not only about something and the expression of an awareness, but it *is* something. It must *be* something in its own right else we could not make statements about *it*. We may say of our statement that it is a single sentence, composed of two clauses, made up of twelve words, etc. As we can say of the sky that it has become dark with clouds, so we can say of "the sky" that it is composed of two words of three letters each. Thus in addition to physical being, the nature or essence of which may have also mental being, and in addition to the existence of the process of knowing, there is *verbal* being. Such a distinction as this, the distinction of one mode of being from another, is sometimes called *supposition*. The supposition of a term or assertion is the mode of being which that term or assertion *designates*. Thus the original statement has *real* supposition; a reference to a thought or concept has *mental* supposition where the reference is not to the thought as an actually occurring event, but to what can *be* only in thought— such as a classification; and a reference to the statement itself has *verbal* supposition.

One step of our analysis remains, one which involves very difficult problems and which can be only briefly referred to at this point. The statement would not have been made unless there had been some point in making it. The fact that it was made cannot be completely understood without some notion of *value*. If I make the statement in the service of some purpose then of course I am assuming that it is good to carry out the purpose. I may be engaged only in idle conversation, but the conversation is not wholly worthless even if only an attempt to fill a void with something more than silence. At times, of course, silence would be the valuable part. Whenever we do anything as a conscious and deliberate act we do it for the sake of something we consider desirable, or because we consider it desirable for its own sake. But the idea of value involves the relation of *possible* and *actual*, and the relations of various possibilities to each other. To be fully explicit, the awareness of value requires also the recognition of a *standard*. Values, possibilities, and standards all have some kind of being, else we could not meaningfully refer to them. What kind or kinds of being they have is one of the central and most difficult of philosophical problems, and we shall leave it for later discussion.

The illustrations of philosophical abstraction and argument we have developed in this section are only a beginning of inquiries which, if followed out in their various ramifications, would take us into almost every corner of the history of philosophy. Some of these themes we shall follow further in chapters to come.

SUMMARY

Philosophy is limited to the kind of inquiry which can be undertaken by unaided rational thought alone. As distinguished from the sciences philosophy is assisted neither by special instruments of observation nor by the use of physical experiments. As distinguished from mathematics philosophy is not confined in its operations to formal patterns or precisely defined concepts or abstract intellectual constructs. Philosophy is the only discipline which can examine its own assumptions, and the examination of the assumptions of each special science and discipline requires the methods of philosophy.

The method of philosophy has two phases: the phase of discovery that makes use of abstraction, and the phase of proof that employs argument. Philosophical argument is either deductive, in which the implications of basic assumptions are made explicit for examination, or dialectical, in which the assumptions themselves are subject to examination. The possibility of discovery by the use of abstraction may be understood as dependent upon the fact that sense perception, which is the basis of our knowledge of existence beyond ourselves, makes available to intellectual discrimination much more than is grasped in sense perception alone.

The use of argument as the method of philosophical inquiry always involves the defense of a thesis or hypothesis. Unlike scientific inquiry philosophical inquiry cannot be neutral, for whereas a scientist can exclude his commitments as a scientist and as a person from the scope of his inquiry, such exclusion is impossible for a philosopher since his basic assumptions are themselves the objects of his inquiry. All inquiry rests upon basic commitments; only in philosophy are basic commitments the subject matter of inquiry.

As a consequence we have to distinguish philosophical inquiry itself from inquiry about philosophy, and to recognize that only in the context of philosophical inquiry can we examine and evaluate significantly the work of other philosophers. The solution of a philosophical problem is not the establishment of the "right" conclusion which from then on may stand by itself, but rather the understanding of the kind of situation out of which the problem arises, the discovery of the available alternative ways of understanding that situation and the issues it involves, the discovery of the assumptions and logical implications of each of these alternatives, and the formulations of the reasons why one alternative provides a more adequate and fruitful understanding than do the others.

The tests of philosophical argument include logical validity as the test of proof. This, however, cannot stand alone, for every formal proof which claims to establish the truth of a conclusion assumes the truth of its own premises. If the examination of the premises of a proof proceeds by additional formal demonstration, then the premises of each such demonstration are left unproved. Logic alone is insufficient; we must carry our thought to existence if we are to reach conclusions which apply to existence. Our direct contact with existence is in experience, and the truth of a thesis becomes existentially self-evident at the point where the meaning of its denial is seen to be in conflict with the existence of that denial as something which actually occurs.

An application of the method of philosophy to even a familiar and commonplace statement shows that the statement involves basic assumptions and ideas which are not expressed as parts of the statement. These were found to include ideas of being and modes of existence, of quality, change, duration, self, act of thought, truth, cause, value, and the distinction between the possible and the actual.

QUESTIONS FOR STUDY AND DISCUSSION

1. *Terms:* accident, actual, argument, attribute, cause, deduction, designation, dialectic, doubt, duration, essence, essential self-evidence, existential dialectic, existential self-evidence, formalized thinking, identity, intellect, intuition, matter, possible and potential, prejudice, sense, standard, subjectivism, substance, supposition, thought, time, unity.

2. Give some examples, from ordinary experience, of the extension of knowledge by thinking alone. Are any of these which occur to you, examples of philosophical thinking? Which of these examples represent thinking which is primarily practical, and which represent thinking that is primarily theoretical?

3. Work out a differentiation between theoretical and practical inquiry which holds good of every kind of situation you can think of to which such a distinction might apply.

4. Is the thinking in which politicians engage, primarily formalized or unformalized? Compare the thinking of a lawyer. What about such studies as economics and sociology?

5. How can the same thing be the same in spite of the fact that it changes? Is the word "same" completely unambiguous here?

6. ". . . it is quite possible that a great deal more might be given in sensation than the senses themselves are able to discern." Is there an instructive parallel between this and a case in which a message contains more than the messenger may be able to understand? What about the case of the words of a poem and some aspects of their meaning? Try to think of other parallels.

7. In what way is the process of abstraction used in evaluating a play or an actor's performance? In deciding what career to follow? In designing a house?

8. Examine a political speech or a newspaper editorial. How much reasoned argument do you find? What other kinds of appeal are present.

9. Compare a philosophical argument in support of a position with a lawyer's advocacy of his client's case. What is the essential difference between the two?

10. Should a person have an open mind about everything?

11. Distinguish between solutions of problems and answers to questions.

12. Apply the distinction of existence and essence to the following: Mount Everest, George Washington, Apollo, a triangle, the Republican Party, General Motors Corporation, the United States of America, mermaids, the present King of France.

PART II

Philosophy
of Science
and Mathematics

CHAPTER 5

The
Nature
of
Science

BEFORE PHILOSOPHY AND SCIENCE

In this and the next two chapters our primary concern will be to see how philosophy and science and mathematics are related to each other. In the present chapter we shall try to reach an understanding of some of the distinctive features of science. Our question here is: What kind of knowledge is scientific knowledge? This is plainly not itself a scientific question, and whatever answers there may be are not to be found by the use of the methods of science nor will they be additions to our scientific knowledge. If we are successful we shall obtain some knowledge *about* scientific knowledge.

The attempt to understand the nature of scientific knowledge will lead to an inquiry into the nature of mathematics, and then into the use of mathematics in scientific investigation. The study of mathematics will be in no sense a mathematical study. We shall be seeking knowledge *about* mathematics, not an extension of our technical competence as mathematicians. The result of our inquiry in these three chapters should be a better understanding of what science and mathematics are. The point of view which will be developed here is by no means the only way in which the nature of science and of mathematics may be understood, but it is a helpful approach because it brings out problems which the student should face early in his study.

Although philosophy and science are both fairly recent developments in human affairs, in comparison with man's long existence upon the earth, yet philosophy is the oldest kind of intellectual search for truth. Man had long looked to divination, revelation, tradition, and authority for his knowledge of himself and his destiny. But it was in philosophy that he first attempted to reach *rational* knowledge of himself and his world. In contrast with philosophy the natural sciences, as we understand them today, are young. While philosophy has existed for some twenty-five centuries the modern natural sciences, with the exception perhaps of astronomy, do not reach back more than five.

Man has thought about the world longer than he has tried to understand it philosophically, and he has explored nature far longer than he has been in possession of the methods of the natural sciences. Our records of human civilization take us back several times as far as philosophy goes; and we may infer that man began to have ideas about himself and the world, and to express them and to hand them down through the generations in song and story and ritual, long before he began to keep written records or to build enduring monuments.

The predecessor of philosophy was myth. Man first tried to understand his world in terms of the dramatic conflicts and symbols of the stories he told of his past. Fire and water and blood, mountains and rivers and trees and animals, and sun and moon and stars were identified with legendary heroes and mysterious divinities, and played their parts in a cosmic drama. Man made himself and his world intelligible by telling a story of good and evil, of fate and destiny, and by setting familiar scenes in the framework of stupendous and mysterious forces. Day by day events, birth and death, coming of age and mating, planting and harvesting, found their meaning in the context of that drama.

Before the appearance of the sciences and scientific technology there were the arts and crafts. The earliest human records and relics show us something of man's earlier methods of dealing with nature, as do also contemporary primitive societies. He learned to measure and count, to take the raw materials of nature and adapt them to his needs. He made weapons for the hunt and for war; he shaped vessels of clay and baked them in the sun and in fire; he wove fiber into cloth and dressed the skins of animals; and he built himself dwellings and temples and tombs. In all this, he had to work with his materials in accordance with their true qualities. In making pots out of clay he had to respect the properties of clay: he could not fit clay to his purposes by the methods he used to make things of wood. Thus the arts and crafts from earliest times required a kind of knowledge, not scientific knowledge but a practical "know-how" composed of skills.

The arts and crafts were predecessors of the sciences; but the sciences, although influenced by some of their techniques, did not grow out of them. Nowhere in the history of human culture do we have any evidence of the unassisted transformation of a craft into a science. All peoples of the world have had their techniques of production but no science has appeared except under the influence of pure theory. All science had its origin in philosophy and mathematics.

Before philosophy, myth and technology were the two fundamental expressions of human intelligence. The one was a way of satisfying the need to understand—for when seen in terms of his myths man's world seemed to make sense. The other was a response to practical needs, to man's need to make his world habitable and secure.

Myth and technology, however, were not entirely separate activities, for in practice they came together in religion and magic. In religion man performed the rituals which celebrated the meaning of his myths and which brought him, his family, and his tribe, into effective relation with the cosmic forces that seemed to shape human life. In magic he used these forces for his own immediate needs. In so far as he depended on religious ceremony to make his technology successful the ritual itself tended to become the more important part of the technique. But magic was more than the application of religious ritual to practical purposes; it included also many secret and cunning ways to take advantage of the likes and dislikes and individual propensities of the gods and other unseen powers.

The coming of philosophy is one of the great dividing lines of history, for it marks the beginning of a new approach to the most important and fundamental problems of human life. When man began to seek knowledge and understanding of truth for its own sake and not merely as a means to some other end, when he attacked the problems of his own nature and destiny and place in the scheme of existence not in terms of his wishes but in terms of what he thought he could *prove* to be true, the human mind began to fulfill the highest of its potentialities.

Man's mind has always sought intelligibility, but the beginning of philosophy brought a distinction between two entirely different ways of trying to discover how existence makes sense. One approach, the only one available before the advent of philosophy, is to construct a scheme of ideas and supposed events that seems intelligible and which, if true, would satisfy the need to understand; and then to interpret the facts to fit that scheme. Mythologies and cosmogonies are products of this approach. The other method, the method of abstraction, is to go to existence itself to try to discover in the facts some intelligible pattern in terms of which those facts may be truly understood. The one approach is to devise a pattern of interpretation which seems to make sense and then to impose this upon existence. The other way is to seek for intelligibility in existence itself.

So far as the truth we seek is truth about things, then even as rational truth it must in some sense be found in things themselves; it cannot be *found* if it is first merely imposed upon things by the mind that seeks it. Thus in the search for rational truth about existence the method of abstraction would seem to be the proper method to follow. To construct a pattern for existence rather than to find that pattern in existence makes our knowledge of that pattern a knowledge of our own creation. Some philosophers have been led in this direction, and in so far as they use a method of construction rather than abstraction they may be said to be using the method of myth, even though their "myths" are myths of reason rather than of imagination.

This is not intended to suggest that myth is simply false. The method of construction and creation may be the appropriate one for some kinds of knowledge or understanding, and myth may express important and profound truths. The stories that serve to communicate religious truth and to pass on from one generation to another the wisdom of our ancestors may give us something of great importance concerning the meaning of life and existence. They may even contain, as the higher religions insist, revelations of truth inaccessible to rational inquiry alone. But they do not constitute rational or demonstrable knowledge, and to confuse the two leads only to the distortion of both.

THE BIRTH OF MODERN SCIENCE

Philosophy appeared much earlier than the sciences, and there are several reasons for this. For one thing, the techniques of philosophy are all within the reach of unassisted thought; they do not require measuring instruments or special tools or apparatus of any kind. Of greater importance, the method of philosophy is more basic and less contrived than are the methods of the sciences. Most important of all, however, philosophy came into existence ahead of the sciences because a certain stage of philosophical achievement had to be reached before the sciences could appear; indeed, each basic science came into the world by separating itself off from philosophy and assuming an independent existence of its own.

Every basic natural science began as a specialized inquiry into problems and areas of fact with which philosophy had long been concerned. Astronomy and physics were the first of the modern sciences to become independent, and both of these had been fields of philosophical speculation as long as there had been any philosophy. Medicine, which was the chief inspiration of prescientific biological studies, had separated from philosophy even in ancient times; and it is quite significant in this connection that the biological studies were slow to adopt scientific methods and to become genuine sciences in their own right. Medicine did not make biology scientific; it was rather the development of biology as a science that helped to make medicine scientific. Until very recently much of medicine was still a matter of tradition and esoteric lore. The requirement of genuine scientific training in preparation for the practice of medicine is quite new, and a great part of the truly scientific development in modern biology has been independent of medicine. Until recently, psychology was a branch of philosophy, and sociology was invented by the nineteenth century philosopher, Auguste Comte. Economics and political science originated as specialized areas within the fields of ethics and political philosophy and are only barely beginning to use distinctively scientific methods.

It did not just happen that the basic sciences came out of philosophy. They could have come from no other source. For the sciences originated as attempts to solve theoretical problems. Their early efforts were devoted not to the exploration of new ranges of fact but to the attempt to discover the precise structures and relationships of already known fact. The theoretical problems had to be posed before there was any recognition of the applicability of what we now understand as scientific methods. Only in the context of a previously existing theoretical study could such questions as led to the establishment of the special sciences be raised. Of course once the sciences began to take their places as independent areas of inquiry their further subdivision naturally followed. No science begins with strictly practical problems. Theoretical problems may be suggested by practical problems, but without the theoretical there is no science. The method of science, as we shall see later, always involves a formalization of rational inquiry, and if there is to be any rational inquiry to undergo formalization there must already have been unformalized rational inquiry. *Unformalized rational inquiry is philosophy.*

As a consequence of this, the sciences could not appear in their own right until there had been an adequate development of mathematics as an instrument of formalization. It is not too much to say that without mathematics no area of investigation is fully scientific. We may describe and classify, but until we are able to formulate our descriptions and classifications mathematically we are still at best only at the outer doorway to science. Mathematics, and mathematics alone, made it possible for modern astronomy and physics to differentiate themselves from philosophy and to work out their own independent roles.

The reason for this can be stated, in principle, very briefly, and this statement may well be considered the theme of our argument in this and the succeeding two chapters: *Mathematics provides rational structures which constitute autonomous patterns of proof, with the result that mathematics frees inquiry from the need to return at every step to the method of philosophy to justify each claim of truth.* Here we have a necessary condition for building a body of established knowledge concerning the uniform structures of any area of existence; a body with common principles and methods, the acceptance of which permits a continuous extension of inquiry as a result of the efforts of many different investigators, and provides complete freedom in the use of the results of one person's inquiry by any other qualified person.

We must not conclude from this that the interdependence of mathematics and the sciences is in one direction only. Although it is true that a new field of scientific investigation cannot develop without mathematical techniques, yet it is true also that the need for mathematical techniques in a certain field of inquiry may be the occasion for turning the interest of mathematicians in that direction. To say, for example, that the social studies will not be sciences until they are mathematical does not mean that they must find some use for already known mathematical techniques. On the contrary, the need for mathematics on the part of the social studies may be the very thing which will stimulate new mathematical developments.[1]

A further requirement for the original appearance and cultivation of scientific inquiry is a genuine curiosity concerning nature, a curiosity which seeks knowledge of nature for its own sake. This can come only as attention is directed from the ideal to the actual, from the other-worldly to the this-worldly, from speculative theories about nature to what can be seen and heard and touched and smelled and tasted. Such an interest in nature emerged in the Renaissance first in art and literature; and it is not surprising that this is so, for nature has to be appreciated if an interest in observing her is to be aroused.

We may think of philosophy as the mother of the sciences and of mathematics as their father. The birth of a science takes place when it reaches the point where it can use direct experience, such as sense perception, as its test of truth. The availability of mathematical techniques was not sufficient of itself to bring about the separation of the sciences from philosophy. The first influence of mathematics is to intensify and stimulate activity within certain areas of investigation; but a new science does not appear until the use of mathematics has completely reorganized the terms in which the problems are stated and understood. In short, the birth of a science is its separation from philosophy and its emergence as an independent discipline with its own test of truth. This occurs when

---

[1] See Raymond L. Wilder, *Introduction to the Foundations of Mathematics* (New York, John Wiley and Sons, Inc., 1952), p. 283. An example of this may be found in the techniques developed by John Von Neumann and Oskar Morgenstern in their *Theory of Games and Economic Behavior* (Princeton, Princeton University Press, 1944).

those working in the field have succeeded in formulating its problems in such a way that observation can be used to distinguish true from false hypotheses.

The acceptance of actual observation as its test of truth limits the field of scientific inquiry. If there are things which exist but the existence of which cannot be confirmed directly or indirectly by observation, then those things are beyond the reach of scientific inquiry. Scientific method is a powerful tool of investigation and its practical effects upon man and society are incalculable. But the power of scientific method is bought at a price, the price of its limitations. Once we accept observation as the test of truth in natural science, and the acceptance of this test is one secret of the mighty scientific progress of modern times, we do by the same act renounce the use of science as a mode of inquiry into any problem which concerns things not accessible to observation.

OBSERVATION IN SCIENCE

The requirement that the test of truth in science shall rest on observation is so important that we need to consider what observation includes. Here we have our most direct contact with the world which the sciences investigate, and although there are many individual variations in the ways in which we observe things yet such variations are fewer and of less importance than in any other way of knowing.

Our best and most familiar example of observation is sense perception. We see and hear and touch and taste and smell; in these experiences we come into direct contact with the physical world. Such direct contact is the last step in the confirmation of hypotheses and the final test of truth in the natural sciences.

The only exception to this rule, and even this exception is not admitted by some scientists, is in the field of psychology. In addition to the study of activities and behavior which can be observed by means of sense perception, some psychologists also study such things as sensations and feelings and emotions and volitions and processes of reasoning. These are all private mental activities, not open to public inspection. Many psychologists believe, however, that even this kind of observation, called "introspection," is sufficiently public for scientific study in so far as it is possible for one observer to follow the directions of another and have an awareness that fits the description that the other observer has given of his experience. If a psychologist is studying after-images, for example, it is desirable that other psychologists will be able to follow his directions and produce for themselves after-images that fit the description he has given of his own. Ordinarily a report of a private experience which cannot be confirmed in the experience of others is not accepted, as it stands, as scientific observation. This does not mean that such reports are false, or that those who report such experiences are lying. It means only that it is difficult to use unrepeatable experiences as the factual basis of scientific study.

There is a sense, of course, in which every experience is unrepeatable; each experience has its own particular occasion at a particular time and place, and has its unique relationships to other experiences of the person concerned. But unless the relevant features of one experience can be found also in the experiences of others, it would be ordinarily of little significance as a scientific observation. As an exception to this, we can imagine a situation in which the first observation of the other side of the moon is reported by a scientist from a space ship. His observation would be unrepeatable by others until they, too, could take such a journey into space. Yet it is likely that they would accept his report, and might even recognize it as confirming or eliminating some scientific hypothesis. In this they would be accepting it as a report of what they themselves would observe under similar conditions. Thus they would be accepting the report in its potentially repeatable features. A like attitude may be taken toward observations physically impossible to repeat where others are confident that if repetition were possible the report would be confirmed. Much depends here upon the general confidence in the competence of the observer and upon what aspects of his experience are the ones he appeals to as evidence. These and other questions concerning the proper subject matter of scientific inquiry make it important for us to examine the distinctive nature of observation as a mental act. The distinction between the natural sciences and non-scientific inquiries depends in part on the nature of observation.

Whether perceptual or introspective, observation is a kind of awareness in which we have direct contact with actual fact. What we are aware of is directly present to us, either by virtue of its contact with our senses or as an act of mind observed in the course of its actual occurrence. Thus the house I see now as I look out of my window is observed, but when I remember something I saw yesterday I do not call my remembrance a case of observation. In memory the event I am aware of is past. I am aware of it, not in the sense that I am observing what happened, but only in the sense that I remember it. In introspective reflection, however, I can now observe my present memory of yesterday's event. My present act of introspection, of observing my own memory process, is an awareness of something going on now. Observation then is a direct awareness of something as actual and present.

It is a distinctive character of observation that it makes us aware of a kind of fact which can be known for what it is only by being *found*. To observe is to find; it is to discover what something is by means of, and only by means of, an encounter with it. Thus the confirmation of a scientific hypothesis is in an encounter with fact, with fact as it is found.

Here is one of the significant distinctions between modern and premodern science. Ancient and medieval scientists did observe; and some of their observations were keen and discriminating. It is true also that many of them welcomed the results of observation in support of their theories; they recorded and collected records of facts. But, except for the few who partially anticipated the modern approach, they did not consciously and explicitly place the whole burden of the difference between the proved and the not proved upon the outcome of direct observation of the facts themselves.

Modern scientific method is a technique for placing the burden of proof on the facts. Its success in working out devices to accomplish this is the source of that impersonal objectivity which is the secret of the great advances of modern science. We must never forget, however, that the strength and success of modern science is the product of the self-imposed limitation which restricts scientific inquiry to those things which are open directly or indirectly to observation.

DESCRIPTION AND EXPLANATION IN SCIENCE

We may say that the natural sciences are investigations of the facts of nature and of the underlying relationships of those facts. We may say further that the sciences classify those facts systematically and try to bring them under general laws. Up to this point we have been concerned in a preliminary way with the nature of scientific method and its dependence on direct contact with natural fact in experience. We need now to look more closely at these topics and to formulate more specifically the relation of scientific inquiry to the facts of nature as we find them in our experience.

The statement that the sciences systematically classify the facts they are concerned with and try to bring them under general laws, suggests a distinction often made between two apparently different kinds of scientific study: description and explanation. The beginning of scientific inquiry in any area would seem to require an examination of the relevant facts and an attempt to put those facts into some meaningful order. At later stages the goal of inquiry seems to change, and we pass into the stage where we attempt to discover general laws or principles and to establish their truth by means of scientific proof.

This distinction of levels of scientific inquiry is useful, and it applies not only to the historical development of a particular science but also may characterize different sciences in comparison with each other. Thus we should expect to find that the less advanced sciences are closer to the descriptive level while the more developed sciences are concerned primarily with the discovery of general principles and only indirectly with problems of description and classification. On the other hand, we must not take this distinction to be one that separates the sciences into two mutually exclusive groups. Although the distinction has some use, it is only a relative one and the differences it calls attention to are only differences of degree. Every science contains both description and explanation.

Mere description without any attempt at explanation is not so much science as it is exploration or natural history. Suppose, for example, that a person who has no technical knowledge of anthropology stumbles upon a flint knife. Although this knife may turn out to be the first bit of evidence that will lead to a significant advance in scientific knowledge, the person who found the knife did not himself make a scientific discovery. If he gives the knife to an anthropologist the latter may recognize it as belonging to a certain prehistoric culture not hitherto known to have penetrated the area where the knife was found. The scientific discovery in this case is not in finding the knife but in its identification and in the recognition of the significance of its presence in that place. Such discovery could not be made with assurance except by one who has scientific competence in the appropriate field. Only one with that competence can recognize the need to explain the presence of the object in the locality where it was found. Only such a scientist can identify the object accurately and thus in a sense explain why it has the shape and design it has. Only one who has the requisite knowledge can think of plausible explanations of the presence of the object in that place.

At first thought this kind of scientific knowledge may not seem to include anything mathematical, such as formulas and geometric diagrams. Yet if we went into the study of scientific anthropology we should find that such study does involve elaborate timetables, maps and diagrams showing geographical relationships, and careful measurements of artifacts. Without some such methods of establishing precise relationships, anthropology would not be a science but only a collection of observations and folklore.

The same is true of those scientific investigations which consist entirely of classification. A significant classification is based on a pattern or arrangement which shows important relationships among the things classified, relationships which are not at all apparent to direct observation. These features become apparent only when we arrange our specimens in accordance with a formal scheme or table which the inquiring mind itself constructs for the purpose of bringing out into the open what cannot be directly observed. Classifications of plants and animals, for example, reveal significant anatomical similarities and differences between groups and among the members of any one group. The arrangement of geological strata in accordance with a time-chart may throw light on events of the distant past. In all such description and classification there is an explanatory factor. For in so far as the formal schemes we use, the tables and charts and patterns of arrangement, are relevant to the inquiry, the location of a specimen in terms of that scheme makes intelligible to some degree its own characteristics and its relations to other specimens.

At the other extreme we may take an example of a discovery that is primarily explanatory, such as Galileo's discovery of the law of uniform acceleration of falling bodies. Anyone who watches bodies fall can see that the further they fall the greater is their velocity. This is not a fact which Galileo discovered. His discovery, on the other hand, was the precise pattern of the acceleration of a falling body. He saw that if the principle of inertia applies to freely falling bodies then it is not true, as had been assumed, that a falling body would stop falling unless some force continued to keep it moving. For according to the law of inertia, a body does not change its state of motion by itself; acceleration or deceleration must be the result of forces from outside the body. If no force were applied from outside, a moving body would continue to move in a straight line at the same velocity. The application of force to a falling body would make it move faster if that force were applied in the direction of its motion. So, Galileo reasoned, the fact that falling bodies do increase in velocity can be explained by the hypothesis that some force is being applied to them. If this force is uniform then the acceleration will be uniform, for the force affecting the motion of the body will have a cumulative effect. By means of a diagram we can measure the increase in velocity against equal time intervals. This shows a uniform cumulation and thus proves that the acceleration of the body is uniform.[2]

In one sense Galileo did not in this case discover a hitherto unknown fact; for the kind of event which concerned him had been known as long as men had noticed that an object hit harder when dropped from a higher point than when dropped from a lower. Much of the important and basic work in such a fundamental science as physics has concerned the explanation of similarly familiar facts. On the other hand, the explanation of a familiar fact does involve the discovery of other facts not precisely known before. Galileo's accomplishment here was twofold. First, it occurred to him to apply an already familiar concept, that of inertia, to a situation to which it had not been applied before, namely, to freely falling bodies. In the second place, he devised a diagram by which the increases in velocity during equal time intervals could be shown graphically and from which a mathematical proof of the conclusion could be constructed. Thus he discovered the precise space and time relationships of the motion of a falling body, and the knowledge of these relations was new factual knowledge.

This brings us to a point of the utmost importance in under-

[2] See A. Wolf, *A History of Science, Technology, and Philosophy in the Sixteenth and Seventeenth Centuries,* Second Edition (London, George Allen and Unwin, Ltd., 1950), pp. 39-42.

standing the nature of scientific investigation. No matter whether a scientist is describing new areas of fact or explaining why familiar facts are as they are, he is dealing with facts beyond the reach of *ordinary* observation. Anyone who finds a flint knife in the desert is able to observe that knife, to see its shape and heft its weight and feel its edge. But unless he is trained in the appropriate scientific discipline he cannot recognize its place in the culture which produced it. We all observe that falling bodies fall faster as they fall further, but none of us is able to observe directly the mathematical relation between the velocity of the body at one point in its fall and its velocity at another.

Scientific observation takes place only under conditions of technical control instituted by the observer. The scientific observer uses methods and devices of observation which the situation itself does not provide. It is *he* who has to provide them and to introduce them into the situation. This is the case whether his aids to observation are such instruments as telescopes or microscopes or delicate balances or chemical solutions, or whether they are geometric diagrams and algebraic equations. This means that scientific observation is never random but always planned. Not only is it planned, but the plan is governed by some explanatory hypothesis which the observation is intended to help to test.

THE NATURE OF SCIENTIFIC EXPLANATION

We need now to look more closely at what we mean by explanation, and at the difference between scientific explanation and other kinds. To explain something is, first of all, to make it intelligible. I reach for the telephone directory and find it missing. This puzzles me until I remember taking it into another room to look up some street addresses. Thus I account for, make intelligible, its absence from its usual place; for if it is somewhere else it cannot be here too.

Usually we do not feel the need for explanation unless we find some of our expectations unfulfilled or something unexpected happens. In ordinary experience understanding and intelligibility are pretty much matters of familiarity. We say we "understand" something when it is what we are accustomed to. In this sense a person may say he understands why his automobile engine started, and he may "explain" it by saying that he turned on the ignition and the starter. If the engine does not start, a familiar sequence is broken. This, in turn, becomes intelligible if he discovers that there is no gasoline in the tank or that the battery is dead. Explanation in such cases as these is nothing more than the substitution of one familiar sequence for another.

The demand for explanation raises genuine problems and leads to inquiry when we are not content merely to substitute one familiar sequence for another but turn our attention to the sequence itself. A child asks, "Why did the car start?" and I answer, "Because I turned on the ignition and connected the starter." But suppose this does not satisfy him, and he asks, "How does turning on the ignition and connecting the starter make the car start?" To answer this I must fill in the gaps in the familiar sequence. So I may tell him that when I turn on the ignition and the starter an electric contact is made which allows current from the battery to flow through an electric motor and make it turn, and that the electric motor turns the crankshaft of the car engine. This motion of the crankshaft pulls down the pistons in the cylinders, sucks in and compresses the gasoline vapor and then, at the point of maximum compression in each cylinder, a spark is produced which explodes the mixture of gasoline and air. The explosion forces the piston down again, and the continuous sequence of such explosions keeps the crankshaft turning.

Such an explanation would contribute little to a child's understanding until each step of the process was described and illustrated. Even so, there may still be questions to ask. "How does an electric current flow through wires?" he may want to know. "How does electricity flowing through a motor make it turn? What is a spark, and how does electricity make a spark?"

These questions all concern matters that are unfamiliar to the child and which cannot be made familiar merely by pointing to something. The only way I can answer the first of these questions, for example, without putting him through a technical study of electricity, is to try to explain the mysterious process in terms of something that is already familiar. I may tell him that electricity "flows" through copper wires as water flows through a pipe. If he is familiar with the flow of water through pipes, and if he is not too curious a child, this inadequate and misleading answer may quiet him. But if he is curious and not easily put off with superficial answers, he will look at the end of a wire and ask where the hole is. Or he may ask whether, if we hold the end of the wire over a cup, the electricity will run into the cup as water does. The "explanation" in such case is a failure, as it deserves to be, for the similarities are hidden by the differences.

The inadequacy of "explanations" like these is in their confusion of intelligibility with familiarity, of logical with psychological understanding. For familiarity is not itself a true test of intelligibility, and merely to remove a feeling of mystery is no assurance that intelligibility has been achieved. What is sufficiently familiar to common-sense experience is accepted whether it is understood or not. Familiarity tends to stifle curiosity and to inhibit the asking of questions. Everyone knows that the moon looks larger near the horizon. How many understand why? How many even wonder? This is simply a fact accepted without understanding; it is familiar enough that it does not need to be intelligible. The true genius of many of the great pioneers in scientific discovery is shown most plainly in their ability to wonder about the familiar things of ordinary experience and to look at them in unfamiliar ways. They refuse to be satisfied with the kind of explanation which merely directs attention away from the thing itself toward something else, something we are so familiar with that it does not occur to us to ask questions about it. In fact we may go so far as to say that modern science actually began with a persistent refusal to accept those explanations which had long been psychologically satisfying and with a demand for explanations that satisfy the reason.

Scientific explanation is logical rather than psychological; it is the representation of facts in terms of a formal scheme or model which has an intrinsic intelligibility in its own right. Once such understanding is achieved the explanation is psychologically satisfying as well. Thus Galileo's explanation of the behavior of falling bodies was in terms of the mathematical scheme by which he showed the relations of the velocities at different points of the fall. Kepler's discovery that the planets sweep equal areas of the figures described by their orbits in equal times was made only as the result of a persistent search for mathematical uniformities. Simple observation of the planets in motion would never have disclosed this law. In each of these instances *facts become rationally intelligible because they come to be understood in terms of something which is rationally in-*

telligible in itself, in terms of formal mathematical relationships. Explanation in terms of mathematics is quite independent of familiarity. Understanding is achieved by anyone who understands the mathematical pattern and the way in which it is applied to the facts in question. Whether the pattern is familiar or not to begin with, it provides psychological as well as logical intelligibility for anyone who will go to the trouble to reach an understanding of it.

Those who seek truth for its own sake have one thing in common: they refuse to be satisfied with explanations that are merely psychological, that do no more than remove the feeling of unfamiliarity; and they demand explanations in terms of something intelligible in itself. Since this is true of philosophers as well as scientists we need to develop a closer comparison of philosophy, science, mathematics, and other forms of knowledge. Only thus can we find what kinds of problems belong to each field and what kinds of answers each mode of inquiry is and is not capable of giving.

We must not think that the distinction between logical and psychological intelligibility is itself an adequate account of the distinguishing characteristics of scientific knowledge. Scientific knowledge is not the only kind of knowledge we have; and whatever the area in which we come to know, our knowledge always rests on logical intelligibility. What is distinctive of scientific inquiry is the level of logical explanation at which it operates.

EXPLANATION AND INTELLIGIBILITY

The dependence of the sciences on mathematics suggests that the objects of scientific study are not self-explanatory. This does not mean that they are inherently unintelligible, for if they were then the scientific explanations we are able to construct with the aid of mathematics would have no relevance to the things they are supposed to explain. Such "explanations" would be spurious. This is precisely the predicament in which we find every theory of the nature of science which holds that because the things the sciences investigate are not self-explanatory they are therefore unintelligible. To avoid this difficulty we have to understand how explanation and intelligibility stand in relation to each other.

To be intelligible is to be *open to explanation*. The explanation may be obvious or it may be hidden. If it is obvious no question arises. I find my car in my garage just where I left it the evening before. I have no question in my mind why it is there. If I find the garage empty then there will be a question and I shall seek an explanation. I may find that someone else in the family has taken the car for an early errand; thus its absence is explained. If this does not turn out to be the case I look for another explanation. In looking for an explanation I suppose that there is an explanation to be found, and this is what we mean by saying that the fact is intelligible even where we do not actually understand it.

The illustration used above is from the common-sense level. Scientific investigation does not begin until we seek the explanation of facts which are not explainable in terms of common-sense knowledge. Everyone knows that if we throw a piece of wood and a piece of iron on an ordinary bonfire the wood burns and the iron does not. Few of us, however, would find it easy to explain this in common-sense terms. So far as ordinary observation goes this difference is simply a brute fact we have to recognize but cannot explain. To explain this fact we have to push our inquiry beyond the reach of mere inspection and observation; we have to find out something about the inner structure of these things.

But this is not the whole story. Suppose that when we analyze these substances we do find certain differences in structure that seem to be linked with the ones already observed. Here again we have something that calls for explanation. We then should have to push the same process further; and so on without end. At each stage we come up against a set of encountered facts which, no matter how much they help us understand other facts, do not explain themselves. Each step involves something not explained, and so the scientific goal of *revealing* the intelligibility of actual fact can never be reached along this line.

We can discover the intelligibility of facts only as we understand them in terms of something that is intelligible in itself. Mathematics, as we shall see later, is a field of knowledge in which what is known is intelligible in itself, and so the escape from our difficulty is found in the use of mathematics as an instrument of explanation. In so far as any set of facts satisfies the conditions of a mathematical relation or function those facts are capable of mathematical explanation. To this extent their own intelligibility is revealed to us. If I have twenty dollars in my pocket and spend ten of it I shall have ten dollars left. This is a relation of facts that I experience over and over again. But it is not made intelligible to me by my repeated experience of it, for if I had only my experience to depend on I might still hope that the next time I could spend ten of my twenty dollars and have fifteen left. How many fairy tales and castles in the air have been built on this theme! The true explanation of these facts is to be found in the mathematical relation of twenty to ten, and once this is understood no further explanation is needed or relevant to this particular situation.

We need now to consider why the facts which the sciences investigate are not self-explanatory.

THE CONTINGENCY OF SCIENTIFIC FACT

The things and processes and relations which the scientist tries to understand and explain are not self-explanatory but contingent. By "contingent fact" we mean that which happens to be the case but which might not have been. In our decimal number system the sum of two and two is four; it has to be four and can be nothing else. This is non-contingent fact; it is a necessary truth. There are no conceivable circumstances in which it could be different. But the existence of that tree I see growing yonder is a contingent fact. The seed from which that tree grew might have fallen at some other place, or its first sprout might have been destroyed, or any one of countless other things might have occurred to prevent the growth of that tree in precisely its present form and condition.

We cannot discover the nature of a contingent thing without observation. Since it did not have to be what it is no matter what the circumstances, but could have been something else under other conditions, we cannot come to a knowledge of its nature merely by reasoning. We have to look and listen and touch and taste and smell, for we are trying to discover what it *happens* to be, not what is *has* to be. Here is a plant with certain distinctive characteristics of leaf and blossom. What those characteristics are we can find only by studying the plant. There is no knowledge we have or could have, except knowledge communicated by someone else who has already examined the plant, that would enable us to know before we looked just what we should see. When we do look we find nothing about the actual characteristics of the plant to suggest that they are necessary and inevitable. So far as the plant itself is concerned it might never have existed at all. Its germination and growth depended not only on its own potentialities but also on accidental circumstances over which it had no control whatever. Even the evolution of its kind in the plant world depended on causes outside the plant world. The plant we see here happens to be; it might have not been. If what we find is a ragweed, that does not surprise us; if it is a dandelion, that fact does not seem paradoxical or contradictory.

Someone may object that if all the conditions for the existence of just this ragweed plant at this spot are fulfilled, if the seed from which this plant grew had fallen at this spot and germinated and grown to maturity, it surely would be surprising to find the plant to be a dandelion. This is true. In fact it would be more than surprising; it would challenge a whole body of carefully authenticated factual knowledge. Yet even the belief that if certain conditions are fulfilled there are certain necessary consequences, does not preclude the recognition of contingency; at most it only pushes contingency back a step. Still, no matter how fully determined we find such a fact to be, the causes that account for it include many conditions outside the plant itself. The plant is dependent for what it is and for its existence on things other than itself. From a wider perspective it depends on the basic physical structures and processes that are characteristic of our world. This is not the case with the fact that in our ordinary number system the sum of two plus two is four.

But so far as we can see the world itself is a contingent fact. The earth and its composition, the atmosphere with which it is surrounded and the water which covers so much of it, depend on the way in which our solar system developed. The solar system in turn would not be what it is but for the fact that the cosmos developed as it did. The physical universe seems to be a world of four dimensions, three of space and one of time. Why these four? Why not six, or thirteen? One of the so far basic and irreducible facts of our world is that light travels at 186,000-odd miles per second. Why just this velocity? Is there anything inconceivable about a light velocity of 200,000 miles per second? This is not like the suggestion that two plus two, as we understand them in terms of our number system, might make five. Every unit of radiant energy is a multiple of h, Planck's constant, and h is 0.000,000,000,000,000,000,000,000,-006,55. Is there anything inconceivable about the existence of a world in which the constant of radiant energy would be greater or less than this?

For every scientific fact there are conceivable alternatives. We do not reject the alternatives because they are in themselves absurd or because they are self-contradictory. We reject them only because we have found that they happen not to be the case, and we know that they are not the case only because we have *found* that something else is the case. Every scientific truth is one among a number of conceivable possibilities, and every scientific truth excludes the other possibilities. Whatever is actual in this contingent world happens to be what it is because other things happen to be what they are. In our ordinary thinking we account for one fact by appealing to other facts we call its "causes."

At ordinary levels of explanation this is quite sufficient, for our common-sense knowledge of causal relations is fairly dependable. Usually it enables us to form reliable expectations and to deal with things intelligently. We know that certain wounds are usually fatal, that plants need water and animals need food. We depend on such knowledge as this, and its various details, for the management of our lives. Without some knowledge of causes there could be no management; we could only wait for what might happen. But our ordinary knowledge of causes seldom includes any understanding of why just those specific causal relations hold. Everyone knows that we must have air to live, that without air we would quickly suffocate. But to understand *why* air is essential we have to go beyond this level of knowledge to the results of technical scientific studies. The facts of nature taken simply as we find them do not show why they have the causal relations they seem to have.

The great eighteenth-century philosopher, David Hume, inferred from this that we have no rational justification for believing that there are causal relations at all. Such belief, he argued, rests on purely psychological factors. The reason he took that position was his belief that the final analysis of any observed fact reduces to something completely arbitrary and unconnected with anything else. Whatever may be our final estimate of his analysis, we need to recognize that his argument does bring out and emphasize a very important point. Unless our examination of the facts with which we begin does lead us to something we can understand in terms of a rational necessity, we can never get beyond the arbitrary, and the events that make up our world will remain unintelligible to us. Hume was right to this extent at least, that if we do find explanations that are rationally intelligible we shall not find them in, or be able to construct them from, the mere appearances of the facts themselves. To grasp the rational connections of things we shall have to understand them in terms of something that is intelligible in itself. Factual existence does not wear its intelligibility on the surface or yield it to any mere inspection. The intelligibility of facts is in their rational structure, and their rational structure can be discovered only by the use of rational instruments.

In our ordinary experience of things and in our common-sense knowledge about them, we are confident that each thing or happening can be explained by other things and happenings. We do not believe that things just come to be with nothing to account for what they are or for the fact that they are. And so we suppose that the things and events of our world are intelligible. On the other hand, we do not and cannot, by any mere inspection of things just as we find them, come to an understanding of *why* they have the causal connections they do have. However great our confidence in the intelligibility of those relations, we cannot discover at the level of ordinary experience in what their intelligibility consists. In order to account for the connections and dependencies we find, we have to interpret them in terms of something that is intelligible on its face, and so we interpret them in terms of mathematical relations.

Now the question arises: How can the rational intelligibility of mathematics apply to things which are not themselves mathematical entities? What right have we to interpret actual existents in terms of a rational structure which is mathematical? Before we can deal with these questions we shall have to pay careful attention to the nature of mathematics, and this will be the subject of the next chapter.

SUMMARY

The earliest philosophy was man's first attempt to obtain rational knowledge concerning his world and himself. Long before the natural sciences, as we now know them, appeared, man had acquired advanced technical skills, but the sciences themselves did not grow out of technology. Each basic science had its origin within philosophy, and became an independent discipline as it developed formal structures of proof which set it free from the need to justify each of its conclusions by the methods of philosophy. Unformalized rational inquiry is philosophy; each field of formalized rational inquiry is a special science. The formalization of inquiry in any field is made possible by the use of mathematics.

Although mathematics makes it possible for a special field of inquiry to exist in independence of philosophy, yet mathematics does not provide the sciences with a test of truth. The concern for objectivity has led to the acceptance of observation as the test of truth to which a scientific hypothesis must be subjected. Observation is a direct awareness of something as actual and present, and is the way by which we become aware of the kind of fact which can be known for what it is only by being found. Since the methods of modern science are techniques for placing the burden of proof on observation those methods are applicable only to inquiry concerning objects which are accessible, directly or indirectly, to sense perception.

Every science is both descriptive and explanatory. Description alone, without some scheme of explanation, is natural history rather than science. Since scientific observation is for the sake of explanation, it is never merely random but under the control of the hypothesis under investigation. Scientific explanation is logical rather than psychological, and is a search for intelligibility. To explain the facts of nature in this sense is to understand those facts and their mutual relationships in terms of formal mathematical relations; that is, in terms of something which has an intrinsic rational intelligibility. Since the facts investigated by the sciences are contingent facts and since mathematical relationships have the character of logical necessity, so that they have to be just what they are, we are faced with the questions of how mathematics can be relevant to the contingent objects of nature and what right we have to interpret the actually existing things of our world in terms of the abstract formal relationships of mathematics.

Questions for Study and Discussion

1. *Terms:* after-image, art, classification, contingent, divination, explanation, hypothesis, intelligibility, introspection, mathematics, myth, natural history, religion, revelation, ritual, science, self-contradictory, technology.

2. How does scientific technology differ from pre-scientific technology?

3. In what important areas of life today do we still use the method of construction in seeking answers to our questions? (Consider especially the methods used in law, theology, economics, and history.)

4. Why has not all unformalized inquiry become formalized and thus transformed into separate special sciences so that nothing remains for philosophy itself?

5. Illustrate from the history of physics or chemistry, the part which mathematics plays in bringing a science into existence as a special field of inquiry and knowledge.

6. Are there some problems which are beyond the reach of scientific inquiry? If so, are there any of these to which scientific inquiry could make no contribution whatever?

7. What is the difference between "public" and "private" observation? In what way, if any, is an observer's experience of the color of a chemical solution less private than his experience of the color of an after-image?

8. Examine a technical scientific report or study and distinguish carefully between the descriptive and explanatory parts. (See the *Harvard Case-Books*.)

9. What is there that is mathematical about a telephone directory? A schedule of classes? A road map?

10. Some important scientific discoveries were accidental, such as the discovery of X-rays. Does this fact in any way conflict with the statement that "scientific observation is never random but always planned"? In the case of the discovery of X-rays, did Roentgen's accidental observation establish anything scientifically? At what point did scientific observation begin in this case?

11. How would you explain to a child the fact that water runs downhill? That a pump can raise the level of water?

CHAPTER 6

The
Nature
of
Mathematics

MATHEMATICAL ABSTRACTION

Our discussion of scientific knowledge has left us with the problem of how mathematics can provide the rational connections required for scientific explanation. Before we can deal with this problem directly we must examine the nature of mathematics. We need to ask what mathematics is about and how its objects differ from those of the natural sciences. We need to consider what kind of knowledge mathematics provides and how it differs from scientific knowledge. These questions are difficult and complex, and we cannot hope to do full justice to them in this study. But we shall try to go far enough to clarify, on an introductory level, some important aspects of the relation of mathematics to the natural sciences.

The first major difference to note between mathematics and the natural sciences is that the objects of mathematics are abstract while the objects of the sciences are actually existing things. No one ever saw a mathematical point or the number seven. We see marks on paper which stand for points and numbers; but the pencil dot is not a point, it is a bit of graphite which has rubbed off the pencil. The lines on paper which stand for seven, 7, or VII, have their own shapes; but these are shapes of the marks, not shapes of the number. We do not see, hear, or touch mathematical objects although by means of things we can see or hear or touch we may be brought to think the objects with which mathematics is concerned. In contrast, the bacteria a biologist examines through his microscope, the molecules whose structure a chemist may be studying, the atoms of physics are all objects which exist in the actual world. It makes no sense to say that a number is here or there, or moves about; it does make sense to say that bacteria or molecules or atoms are somewhere and that they move about.

We become aware of the objects of science first of all by observation, but this is not true in the same sense of the objects and relations we study in mathematics. Although our awareness of mathematical objects has a basis in observation, we do not observe mathematical objects as such. To become aware of numbers and geometrical figures, for example, we have to attend to the things we perceive, and to this extent we depend on observation. But this is only the first step. Before we reached an awareness of anything properly mathematical we have to hold in thought, and attend to, some of the *features* of those things *without reference to the actually existing things themselves*. I look at a door and note its shape. I can then think of that shape not as the shape of this door but simply as the kind of shape it is, such as a rectangle with sides in the relation of 5:2. Then whatever I discover about the shape itself will be true of that shape wherever it is found, whether it is the shape of a door or of a farmer's field or the floor of a building or whatever it may be. The angles formed by the diagonal, for example, will be the same number of degrees in all these cases no matter what may be the size of the rectangle.

This process of distinguishing various features of the things we perceive, isolating some of those features in thought, and attending to them without reference to the things in which we found them, is a mode of *abstraction*. *To abstract* is, literally, *to take away from*. The shoplifter abstracts merchandise, and this is a kind of *physical* abstraction; an entirely honorable variety of physical abstraction occurs in the isolation of various materials in scientific experiment. *Mental* abstraction is the separation of something in thought, and this is the kind of abstraction we perform when we think mathematically. As Aristotle put it long ago, "The mind when it is thinking the objects of Mathematics thinks as separate, elements which do not exist separate." [1] In a scientific experiment we separate the material to be studied from influences and relationships which are not relevant to the problem under investigation. Mathematical abstraction, however, is solely intellectual, and it extends further than the mere isolation in thought of what exists actually in relationship with other things. In mathematical abstraction *what we hold apart in thought could not exist in its own right under any conditions.*

We would never become aware of numbers if we did not find things in groups. But to think the number *two*, for example, *as a number*, we have to think it in abstraction from all actual groups of two things. We learn to count two apples and two trees and two people, but we do not think *two* as such until we think it apart from apples and trees and people. When we think of it not as two of this or two of that but only as a number, in its relations as a number to other numbers, we are thinking in a way that is exclusively mathematical. For example, we are thinking of *two* mathematically, when we are aware of it as an even number, or as a prime number, or as the square root of *four*. But *two*, as an object that we think about in this way, is something that can have no existence of its own. Man formed his concepts of numbers originally out of his experience with real things, but the number he thinks about mathematically and uses in his scientific thinking about real things is not itself one of those real things.

Mathematical objects thus are not presented to us as such in our perception of things in the real world. In order to become aware of mathematical objects we have to reflect on what we perceive. If we are to think as separate those things which do not exist in separation and which can be separate only in thought, then it is our thought itself which has to do the separating. The door I see before me is rectangular. I do not see a rectangle before me; I see a rectangular door. Suppose I wish to think about the shape apart from the door. I cannot physically separate the shape from the door so that I have two physical bodies lying side by side, the door over here and its shape over there. I can change the shape of the door, but I

[1] *De Anima* 431b 16-17, translated by J. A. Smith, in *The Basic Works of Aristotle*, edited by Richard McKeon (New York, Random House, Inc., 1941), p. 595. By permission of Oxford University Press.

cannot remove the shape from the door as I can remove, say, by saw-ing it off, a part of the wood of which the door is made. If I wish to think about the shape of the door apart from the door I can take it apart only in thought.

This, however, is only the first step of mathematical abstraction. To think about the shape apart from the door requires more than the simple abstraction by which, for example, we can think of the door apart from its present surroundings. Mathematical abstraction does not consist solely of dropping off this or that item from what is given in experience, but requires the further step of making some aspect or relation of real things into an object in its own right. The mind abstracts such aspect or relationship from what exists and *sets it up as an entity* to be examined in and for itself. When I count the number of people in a room and find that there are twelve peo-ple there, I have found out something about the people and about the contents of the room. Those things are the objects I am thinking *about*. Although I am here using the idea of a number in my think-ing about the people in the room, I am not yet thinking about the number itself. But if I reflect that *twelve* is divisible by two, three, four, and six, then the number itself becomes the object I am think-ing *about*.

Since we do not just find numbers lying about here and there, as we find sticks and stones, there is a sense in which we may say that they are formed by the mind that knows them. This does not mean that mathematical objects are made out of nothing, that they have no basis in what exists in itself. It means that the mind makes these to be its objects. Unless what is found is set apart as an object in abstraction from real existence it cannot be an object of mathematical thought; in this sense the mind constructs mathemati-cal objects. But unless there is something, in what we find in our experience, to be set apart then there is nothing to abstract and noth-ing for the mind to set before itself as an object to be examined in and for itself. The truly constructive activity of the mind in mathe-matical thinking is in what the mind does with these mathematical objects as it discovers new relationships among them.

Thus mathematics is abstract in a double sense. Not only is mathematical thinking abstract, but the very things we think about when we engage in mathematical thinking are themselves abstract. I use abstractions when I try to find out the size and the shape of the door, but the object I am thinking about is still the door. The door is not something abstract, as I painfully discover if I bump into it in the dark. However, when I think of the shape not as the shape of this door, or as the shape *of* anything else, but simply as the kind of shape it is, then not only is my thinking abstract but so also is the object I am thinking about. In philosophy and science we think abstractly about real things; in mathematics we think abstractly about abstract things.

The level of abstraction necessary for mathematical thinking was difficult for man to reach. The doubly abstract nature of geometry, for example, was not fully recognized until after the discovery, about 1825, of non-Euclidean geometries by Bolyai and Lobachevsky. Until then geometry was generally supposed to be the science of real space, and its theorems were thought to be true because the definitions and axioms from which those theorems are derived were thought to be self-evidently true of real space. Sir Edmund Taylor Whittaker points out:

> When it was realized that the parallel axiom is not universally and eternally true, opinion changed about the place of axioms in mathematics. It now came to be accepted that the business of the mathematician is to deduce the logical consequences of the axioms he assumes at the basis of his work, *without regard to whether these axioms are true or not;* their truth or falsehood is the concern of another type of man of science—a physicist or a philosopher.[2]

We know now that no geometry, simply as geometry, has any inherently privileged position with respect to real space. Some geometries hold good of the space properties of the objects of experience and some do not. Which do and which do not is a question that can be answered only by checking the theorems of a geometry against actually observed space properties and relationships. This is a question not for geometry but for physics or astronomy.

The abstractness of numbers was learned slowly, although not so slowly as that of geometry. Some of the early Greek philosophers confused numbers with geometric shapes. The Pythagoreans, for example, spoke of *square* and *oblong* numbers. Even today we speak of the square of a number, and in this there may be a relic of Pythagorean influence. But when the Pythagoreans spoke of a square number they meant that the number actually has a square shape.

---

[2] "Mathematics and Logic," in *What Is Science?* edited by James R. Newman (copyright 1955, by James R. Newman), p. 37. Reprinted by permission of Simon and Schuster, Inc., New York.

They used a number notation composed of arrangements of dots, and this made it easy to confuse the number with its sign and to attribute the shape of its sign to the number itself. The Pythagoreans went still further and took these shapes to be the actual building blocks of the universe, and from this came their basic teaching that all things are numbers. There is a close connection between these confusions in Pythagorean thought and the later Greek atomism of Leucippus and Democritus whose atoms were, strictly speaking, the treatment of abstract shapes as if those shapes were real things in their own right.

> Although numbers have been in use since the earliest ages [Whittaker tells us], it was not until the last quarter of the nineteenth century that any satisfactory philosophical explanation was given of what they are.
>
> Number is a property not of physical objects in themselves, but of collections or *classes* of objects.[3]

Our own language preserves many echoes of the confusion of numbers with things. Our many ways of designating duality, for example, differ according to the kind of thing to which duality is applied, such as deuce, couple, doublet, brace, pair, span, yoke, dyad, and distich. It is as if these were many different kinds of *two-ness*. Many superstitions, some still prevalent, are based on the attribution of certain nonmathematical properties, properties that belong to real things, to numbers. No one who understands the abstract character of numbers can find any significance, for example, in the idea that certain numbers are lucky or unlucky. A lucky number would not be an abstract entity; to be lucky or unlucky, a number would have to have physical or moral qualities or powers.

The objects of mathematics are abstractions and they do not have the properties or powers of real things. When we think about a number or a triangle or a sine or cosine we are thinking about something, but these objects do not exist in the way that trees or people or stars exist. On the other hand, the objects of mathematics are not fictitious things, for they have a relation to real existence quite different from that of fictions. A fiction is something which does not exist but which we think of *as if* it did. We do not think of numbers and geometric shapes as if they were real existences, as we may think of the characters and events of a novel. There may be

---

[3] *Ibid.*, pp. 40-41.

mathematical fictions, but a mathematical fiction would be something thought of and treated *as if* it were a mathematical entity; some have considered $\sqrt{2}$ to be such.

MATHEMATICAL ENTITIES

Our discussion of mathematical abstraction is still incomplete. We have not yet seen just how an abstracted characteristic of existing things is made to be itself an abstract entity. In order to understand how this is done we have to be clear as to just what the mind leaves out in this further step of abstraction by which mathematical entities are formed. Our discussion is incomplete in a further respect, for we have not yet identified those aspects of things which can be abstracted and formed into mathematical entities. All knowledge is knowledge *of* something, and our questions are: What do we know *about* when we know mathematically? and: How are the objects of mathematical knowledge related to real objects? Before taking up these two questions, however, we must look more carefully at the distinction between mathematical and nonmathematical abstraction by examining some specific examples of the difference. We shall then return to the question of the formation of mathematical entities and the question of what our mathematical knowledge is knowledge about.

Suppose I look at a rosebush in my garden and notice that it has three open buds. This is not what we would call "abstract thinking." It is thought about a present actual thing and contains something I observe here and now to be true of that actual entity. In my observation of the rosebush I use concepts, such as *three* and *open* and *bud*, and concepts are abstractions. But my thought at this point is not about the nature of *three* or about what it means for something to be *open* or about what constitutes a *bud;* my thought is about the actual bush and about something I observe as I look at it. If, however, I now turn my attention from the bush to the ideas I have used in thinking about the bush I shall be engaged in abstract thinking. When I think about *three* and about *open* I am not thinking about things that really exist in their own right; and although buds are real things yet when I think about the nature of a bud as such I am not thinking specifically of this or any other actual bud but of what may be true of *any* bud. In my nonabstract thinking I *use* the concepts to think about the actual rosebush; in the abstract thinking which may be prompted by my observation of the bush I turn my attention away from the actual bush before me and think about *three* and *open* and *bud*.

All mathematical thinking is abstract, but not all abstract thinking is mathematical; let us recall first what this difference is. Our thinking about actual things may make use of mathematics and yet not be itself mathematical thinking. When I think, "This bush has three open buds," I am not thinking mathematically even though I use the mathematical concept of *three*. Of course I am applying my knowledge of what *three* is as a number, but I am not thinking about *three;* I am thinking about this bush that I see before me. Even my count of the buds, although it is a mathematical operation in a sense, is not a case of mathematical thinking. Of course something may turn my attention away from the buds I am counting, toward the act of counting. It is plain, however, that if I begin to think about the act of counting the buds on the bush, I am no longer counting the buds. In other words, when I think about the bush I use the mathematical concept of *three* to think about something nonmathematical, but when I think about *three* my thinking is mathematical. I think about *three* in such terms as: "Three is between two and four in the number series," or "Three is a prime number," or "The square of three is nine." Here I am not using the idea of *three* to think about some actual entity; I am thinking about *three*, and about its properties *as* a mathematical entity.

Just as I can think about *three*, so I can think about *open*, and this too is abstract thinking. I may ask myself what I mean by "open" in the statement that the bush has three open buds. How do I distinguish an open rosebud from one that is not open? In reflecting on this I may conclude that an open rosebud is one in which the tips of the petals have parted, while to the extent that any petal tips are still in contact with each other the bud is closed. This is abstract thinking; I am thinking about *open*, and there is no such actual entity in real existence. There are real things that are open but there is no such thing as *an open*. Now the question is whether we can find the significant difference between the kind of abstract thinking we do about *three* and the kind we do about *open*.

We may suppose at first thought that the difference between these is one of generality. In thinking about *open* we have tied our thinking to the nature of a bud, specifically a rosebud. But in thinking about *three* there was no such restriction. What we thought about *three* in the examples given concerns any case of three whatever. But what we thought about *open* does not apply to every case. It does not apply to an open field, or an open society, an open hand, or an open house. In other words, we do not know what is meant by "open" unless we know to what it refers. We have to specify the kind of thing we are talking about before we can understand what we mean by saying it is open. In fact each of the above phrases is itself ambiguous. Do I mean by "open hand" that the fingers of a hand are extended, or do I refer to someone's generosity? Is an "open house" one with the doors unlocked or ajar, or is it a social occasion where all who wish to come are invited? Does "open field" mean an unfenced plot of land, or does it refer to a political campaign? Is an "open society" one in which there is freedom of action for the individual and flexibility of institutional forms, or is it a club which excludes no group or class of people from membership? In contrast with the indefiniteness of *open* taken by itself without any indication of its specific context, we know what we mean by three without waiting to find out anything else. We do not have to specify the kind of things we are talking about before we understand what we mean when we say there are three of them.

Perhaps we can eliminate this difference by constructing a more general concept of *open*. What is common to the various meanings of "open"? Even a small dictionary will give a dozen meanings, such as free, not closed or clogged, unrestricted, disengaged, empty, not secret or disguised, expanded or spread out, frank, not yet decided, and so on. Let us suppose that all these may be brought under four main meanings: free, exposed, empty, not concluded. More thorough analysis might find some overlapping among these but for our present purpose we may take them provisionally as the basic meanings. What happens now if we try to carry our generalization further? It is difficult to find much more that these have in common than the idea of being not not-open. But wherever we stop short of this our meaning is still restricted by the nature of the things to which the term is applied descriptively; unless we do stop short of this, no meaning is left. Our knowledge of the meaning of "three" does not involve a tie with any kinds of objects or situations. It is true we could not learn the meaning of "three" unless we were acquainted with something, but any kind of thing at all will do provided there are more than two of them.

We shall be mistaken, however, if we conclude from this comparison that there is only a difference of degree between mathematical and nonmathematical abstraction. It is true that *three* has an incomparably wider reference than *open*, but still its reference is restricted to pluralities. *Three* does not apply to the earth's moon, or the nation's capital city, or to any other unique thing. Thus although there is a difference of generality in the application of the concepts *open* and *three* it is a difference of degree only and thus does not furnish an explanation of what is distinctive about the objects of mathematics.

It becomes apparent that the place to look for the important difference between these two concepts is in the second step of mathematical abstraction. When we think about *three* mathematically, as a prime number or as between two and four in the number series or as the square root of nine, we are thinking of it as an entity rather than as a property of something else. *To be third* may be, in a sense, a property; but *to be three*, in the sense of being the number three, is to be something that has properties but is not itself a property of anything else. On the other hand, when I think about *open* I am not thinking of it as an entity at all (unless I am thinking of the *word* "open") but as a character or quality of something. Even when I use the verbal form of a substantive, such as "openness," I cannot turn the object of my thought into an entity that has properties of its own. *Openness* is always an openness *of* something; and unless this is the case the concept is empty.

Here we find the important difference between nonmathematical and mathematical abstractions. Apart from the nature of the situations to which it refers, *open* has no meaning by itself. If reference to things is lost in the use of such concepts, the concepts themselves lose their meanings. The properties of *three*, however, do not refer to the special characteristics of the things we find in groups of three. There is no real thing, or group of real things, of which we can say that it is between two and four in the number series or that its square is nine. Unlike *open*, *three* does have a meaning by itself which can be thought about without considering what any particular kind of actual thing is like.

This distinction may be illustrated further by reference to relations, such as, "John is the father of Peter." In its strict sense, *father of* is a relation between people. Sociologists and anthropologists may study this relation as one of the important aspects of the structure of human society. Psychologists are interested in the relation of father and child as an influence in the development of a child's personality. All of this nonmathematical knowledge of the relation comes from the study of fathers and children. On the other hand, if a mathematician turns his attention to this relation as a mathematician and not as a sociologist or anthropologist or psychologist, he will be concerned with its properties *as a relation;* he will not be interested in what it tells us of people and of their societies. He will examine the relation not as a characteristic of something else but as itself something that has characteristics of its own.

When a mathematician looks at the characteristics of *father of* as a relation, he finds two obvious properties. First he will note that if the order of terms is reversed the relation does not hold. If A is the father of B then it is plain that B cannot be the father of A. Even if this is suggested to us by our knowledge of human beings, we have here knowledge about a relation as such. The relation is *asymmetrical.* Our mathematician finds further that if A is the father of B and B is the father of C, it is not the case that A is the father of C. A is the grandfather of C. The relation is *intransitive.* If we compare this with the relation, John is *taller than* Peter, we find that while the latter is also asymmetrical, it differs from the former in being transitive. For if John is taller than Peter and if Peter is taller than Charles, then John is taller than Charles.

Of course to know that *father of* is intransitive and that *taller than* is transitive we have to know something about the real situations in which there are fathers and differences in height; but to be transitive or intransitive is a property of the relation, not of the things to which the relation pertains. Neither John nor Peter nor Charles is transitive or intransitive; and although each may be said to be symmetrical or not in a different sense of the term, no person may be said to be symmetrical in the sense that a relation is.

THE FORMATION OF MATHEMATICAL ENTITIES

Since the objects of mathematics are abstract they exist, as entities, only in and for thought. This means that they must have their origin somehow in concepts. A concept, as we have already seen, is an awareness *of* something. It is *intentional;* it refers to something other than itself, and it gets its content wholly from what it refers to. The question of the formation of a mathematical entity is thus the question of how we transform a concept, which has its entire nature in what it refers to, into an entity which has its own nature and properties. There are, of course, mathematical concepts, and like any concept a mathematical concept is an awareness of something other than itself and gets its whole meaning from the nature of its object. But if there are to be mathematical concepts then there must be mathematical objects for the concepts to refer to. The concepts of odd and even as applied to numbers are mathematical, and their meanings are to be found in the nature of those numbers to which they refer. But how do we obtain the mathematical entities themselves as objects to be thought about and known?

The key to the solution of this problem is in the contrast between a concept as referring to something beyond itself and a mathematical entity as something to which concepts may refer. In nonmathematical abstract thinking, it will be recalled, we think about our concepts. But in our thought about those concepts we find nothing in them except what is derived from the objects to which they refer. In mathematical abstraction there are certain meanings which we cut loose from the objects to which those meanings originally pertained. We suppress and ignore whatever reference they may have had to things. We not only exclude from our attention the things they refer to but *we exclude also the fact of reference itself*. By this act a concept ceases to function as a concept, as an awareness of something other than itself, and becomes instead something to which other concepts refer.

To recapitulate and restate this very important distinction: All logical concepts are about something. Our thinking is always about something, and of course this includes our mathematical thinking. But when we think *about* a concept, in reflection, then that concept itself becomes the object of our awareness. If the concept we think about can be thought about without taking account of what *it* refers to when used as a concept, then our thinking can become mathematical. A concept is formed by abstraction; but as a concept it remains an awareness *of* something or other, for it has been formed by abstraction *from* something or other. A concept becomes a mathematical object at the point where the concept's reference to things is ignored and the content of the concept is considered for itself. *Three*, as a mathematical object, is not the concept *of* anything. It is the terminus and not the instrument of a thought. Mathematicians as mathematicians, says Raymond L. Wilder,

> seem to be dealing with, or studying, abstract forms or structures and relations between them. . . .
>
> It would seem, then, that present day mathematics is properly characterized as a living, growing element of culture embodying concepts about abstract structures and relations between those structures.[4]

The suppression of all reference to actual things in the formation of mathematical entities means that a mathematical calculation or set of equations does not in any way specify the actual situations to which it may apply. We are free to use it wherever it may be pertinent. This is strikingly illustrated by Sir Edmund Whittaker:

> . . . the vibrations of a membrane which has the shape of an ellipse can be calculated by means of a differential equation known as Matthieu's equation: but this same equation is also arrived at when we study the dynamics of a circus performer, who holds an assistant balanced on a pole while he himself stands on a spherical ball rolling on the ground. If now we imagine an observer who discovers that the future course of a certain phenomenon can be predicted by Matthieu's equation, but who is unable for some reason to perceive the system which generates the phenomenon, then evidently he would be unable to tell whether the system in question is an elliptic membrane or a variety artiste.[5]

The question of what can be included among the objects of mathematics is nothing more or less than the question of what abstractions can be carried through the second step and thought about in complete independence of any explicit or latent reference to other things. Such concepts as *man, state* or *nation*, and *molecule* cannot be thought about apart from reference to some possible or actual situation, for it is only in such reference that they have any meaning. But our ideas of the number of men, or certain of the relations of men in society, or certain aspects of the structure of a

[4] Reprinted with permission from Raymond L. Wilder, *Introduction to the Foundations of Mathematics* (New York, John Wiley and Sons, Inc., 1952), pp. 274, 275.

[5] Edmund Taylor Whittaker, *Beginning and End of the World* (London, Oxford University Press, 1942), p. 17. By permission.

molecule have content which remains after we cut away all reference to actual or possible existence. The potential range of mathematical thinking can be discovered only as we see what we have left when we eliminate all reference to existence and try to consider the content of a concept by itself. To specify what concepts will be found in the future to have content apart from reference to existence would be to determine ahead of time the limits of all future developments in mathematics. The abstractive ingenuity of the human mind has not yet revealed the limits of its capacity.

MATHEMATICS AND EXISTENCE

Although we cannot specify ahead of time the future developments in mathematics we may still be able to reach some understanding of the kind of knowledge mathematics provides. Knowledge is always knowledge *of* something, and we have seen that mathematics is first of all knowledge of the abstract entities formed by leaving entirely out of account the reference beyond themselves of certain of our concepts. But to leave this reference out of account is not to abolish it. Mathematical entities always have potential reference to existence even though that reference is suppressed in their status as mathematical entities; to suppress reference to existence is not to abolish it, and this is the case even though its reference to existence is not something of which mathematics itself can take any account.

It follows that mathematics cannot stand alone as a mode of knowing existence. The question of the relation of mathematical objects to existence is not a mathematical question at all. One reason for this is that the very possibility of mathematics as a form of knowledge requires that we suppress all consideration of the relation of the abstract entities which are its objects to anything except other such abstract entities. Otherwise we would have nothing mathematical for our knowledge to be about.

When we consider this now in the light of the preceding section, the problem appears to be that of determining just what aspects of things can be abstracted and investigated apart from their connection with those things themselves. The traditional answer to this is that mathematics is the science of quantity, and although this is now recognized as too narrow a concept, yet quantities and their relations are certainly an important part of the mathematical. The quantitative nature of existence, even when abstracted from existence, still has a nature of its own to be studied. The mathematical study of quantity, however, has led to a broadened concept of the subject matter of mathematics to include all abstract forms, relationships, and types of order. Any abstraction which has a meaning that survives its complete separation from the objects from which it has been abstracted can be itself an object of mathematical investigation.

When men turned their attention to the systematic study of quantity they were in a peculiar situation, for they were studying something that has no existence of its own. Any actual quantity is always a quantity *of* something. But in order to study quantity as such, and not just this or that actual instance of a quantity, it was necessary to transform quantities into abstract entities. In a way the mathematician's intellectual abstraction parallels the anatomist's physical abstraction when he removes and dissects an organ of the body in order to study its structure. So the mathematician isolates in thought and dissects logically very important aspects of real existence, namely, quantity, order, and certain relationships. There is an important difference, however, between the mathematician's intellectual abstraction and the anatomist's physical removal and dissection of an organ from an animal's body. The dissected organ cannot be put back again, but there is a sense in which the intellectual return of the mathematical object to existence is possible. As we shall see, some such return is essential if we are to justify the claim that mathematics is significant as a field of knowledge in its own right in addition to its practical applications.

MATHEMATICAL CERTAINTY

The second step of abstraction in the formation of mathematical entities brings its own special reward. As a consequence of our separation of the objects of mathematics from actual existence we are able to obtain knowledge about those objects which is certain and necessary. In this respect mathematics differs from the natural sciences. The sciences are concerned directly with actual existence; mathematics is not. The sciences can claim only a hypothetical finality and certainty, for the truth of the conclusions of a scientific inquiry depends in part on the truth of it assumptions. In mathematics our conclusions follow from postulates instead of from assumptions concerning the nature of real existence. In an assumption we accept something as true without offering or asking for evidence in its support. I *assume*, for example, that the sun will rise tomorrow; I *assume* that the evening paper will be delivered. A postulate, on the other hand, is simply asserted or "posed" without reference to whether it is true or false of anything actual. It is asserted in order to find what other propositions follow from it when we examine its logical relations with other propositions.

The postulates of a mathematical system are basic premises; they are the propositions which set forth the nature of the abstract entities that compose the subject matter of the system. Postulates, along with definitions, are the means by which mathematical objects are formed, and are the premises from which additional knowledge about those objects in their interrelationships can be obtained by logical deduction. Consequently the question of the truth or falsity of postulates with respect to any matters of fact cannot be a mathematical question, for the question of truth concerns their relation to actual existence rather than to other mathematical objects. Mathematical postulates *have* to hold good of their objects, for the postulates fix the nature of those objects; the objects can be nothing other than what the postulates specify.

The question in mathematics is whether the work of thought is consistent with itself, whether our thinking about the objects of mathematics is consistent with the thinking by which those objects were formed. Thus mathematics is concerned only with validity. Whether certain mathematical propositions hold true of some actual situation is a question which arises not in mathematics itself but in the applications of mathematics. The question in a natural science, however, is whether the assumptions upon which the inquiry proceeds and the reports of fact which it uses are true of the nature of things which have their existence in themselves and are not the products of abstraction on the part of the thought which knows them.

To say that every valid mathematical conclusion has finality and certainty does not mean that a conclusion may not be superseded by later work that is in some way preferable to the earlier. Techniques may be improved and new fields opened up. It does mean that any valid mathematical conclusion stands against any attempt to deny its claim. The thinking which established it may have lacked elegance and technical polish, but in so far as the conclusion is a valid deduction it has been established once and for all. Scientific conclusions, on the other hand, are reached tentatively and held to be true with varying degrees of probability. Our scientific knowledge is admittedly incomplete at any particular stage. Although we have a high degree of assurance of the truth of established scientific doctrine, yet there always remains a theoretical incompleteness of proof.

In this way our mathematical knowledge differs from our knowledge of matters of fact. That two and two are four cannot be intelligibly questioned; to try to deny it is to assert a contradiction. The only way such a denial might be defended against the charge that it is meaningless jargon is to suppose that either the word "two" or the word "four" is used in a sense different from its meaning in ordinary arithmetic. On the other hand, if someone denies that there are four ten-dollar bills in the cash drawer, I cannot charge him with uttering a contradiction on the ground that I twice put two such bills in a drawer that before had none. Nor would I regard his statement as meaningless, particularly if the money belonged to me. In such a situation I surely would look to see whether he was right, and if he was, I would try to find out what had happened to the missing money.

If, however, someone says that two and two are three we do not set out to find whether or not there are some cases in which this is true. A person who proposed to do this would not be raising a mathematical question; the real question would be that of his competence, or sanity. In the case of the missing money, it is only because I know for sure that two and two are four that I know something is wrong if I find only three bills in the drawer; and it is because we know for sure that two and two are four that we question the competence or sanity of anyone who says they are three.

Why can I reasonably be mistaken about the number of bills in the drawer and not about the sum of two and two? In principle the answer is that my knowledge of matters of actual fact is governed by the fact. If I am right about the contents of a cash drawer, the contents of the cash drawer are what made me right. If I am right in my statement that Napoleon died on St. Helena, it is

Napoleon's death on St. Helena that makes my statement true. I have control over my thought, to a degree at least, but I do not by my thought control fact. Of course I can manipulate and change things, but I cannot do this merely by an act of thought in which I determine what they shall be.

In mathematical knowledge the situation is different. The process of abstraction by which mathematical entities are formed brings its objects within the control of thought in a way that is impossible in the case of actually existing things. Of course I cannot change the mathematical fact that the sum of two and two is four; this follows necessarily from the nature of two and of four and from their relation to each other in the number series. Just as if I am right about the cash drawer it is the content of the drawer that makes me right, so if I am right about the sum of two and two it is the nature of the numbers that makes me right. But two and four and the number system in which we use them are entities whose being *as entities* is the result of the abstractive processes of thought. These entities have precisely those properties which thought assigns to them in their formation as objects, they have whatever other properties are logically implied by those assigned to them in their formation, and they have nothing else. There is nothing to find in them except what thought *can* find, for they have nothing in their nature except what thought has given them. They do not change, they do not act; they have no history and they have no future. Our thinking about mathematical objects has a history and has a future, but the objects themselves do not.

What we discover about mathematical entities, and some of our discoveries may be surprising indeed, are what we find must be asserted because a denial would deny to those entities themselves the very nature we have assigned to them in thought. Any difference here is a difference of identity; the admission of a difference *is* the formation of *another* abstract entity. Actual things change without losing their identities—I am the same person today I was yesterday in spite of the fact that I have changed somewhat; but an abstract entity has no existence of its own. Since, as that entity, it has only the existence that thought gives it, then to try to think it as different is only to put a different entity in its place. One abstract entity may be replaced by another but it cannot change into the other. Because it has no existence of its own it cannot act or be acted upon.

Genuine discovery and progress is possible in mathematics because mathematical objects have relationships with each other of which thought cannot be aware when it considers one object in isolation from others. We cannot see from the nature of a straight line alone the relationships we shall find if that line is cut by two parallel lines. It is not surprising that many of the great advances in mathematics have come from the discovery of relationships between previously separate and independent mathematical disciplines. Analytical geometry, for example, was the result of Descartes's discovery of a way of formulating geometric relations in algebraic terms.

Although mathematical entities are abstractions, they have a foundation in real things. We form them by setting up *as entities* certain aspects of real existence which abstract thought finds there and discovers to be separable in thought from the existence in which it is found. Removed by thought from their original setting, the relationships of these abstract entities can be discovered only by thought. Our thinking isolates intelligible quantity and order; and so only by thought can its intelligible nature be explored. Deliberately severing their links with existence in order to form the objects of mathematics, thought cannot go back to experience to discover new facts about those same abstract entities. On the other hand, the discoveries thought does make, carry with them a unique certainty, for neither can experience intrude into the realm of abstraction and modify the objects that compose that realm. We may add new objects, and these may enrich our knowledge of the old; but the addition of new objects can never invalidate our earlier knowledge of those previously included.

SUMMARY

Unlike the objects of the natural sciences, the objects of mathematics are abstract and thus have no existence in their own right. Mathematical abstraction has two stages: (1) Some characteristics or relationships of existing things or groups of existing things are identified and separated in thought from the things themselves. (2) These characteristics or relationships are set before the mind as entities and objects to be examined in and for themselves. While in philosophy and science we think abstractly about real things, in mathematics we think abstractly about abstract things. The second step of abstraction occurs when the content of a concept is thought about without consideration of any reference to existence it may have had in its original formation. In the formation of a mathematical entity from a concept we abstract not only from the things to which the concept referred originally but also from the very fact of reference itself. As the concept loses its function of referring to something else it becomes instead the object of thought. Whether a concept can be made into a mathematical entity is entirely a question of whether any content is left after its reference to existence is suppressed.

To suppress reference to existence, however, is not to abolish it, but only to remove it from consideration. What has been taken from existence can be returned to existence, and this makes possible the use of mathematics in science and technology. Yet the restoration of a reference to existence is in no respect a mathematical operation.

Knowledge of the objects of mathematics has a finality and certainty which our scientific knowledge of real existence lacks. The objects we know in mathematics have their being as objects by virtue of the acts of abstraction by which they were formed, consequently they have only the properties which thought assigns to them in their formation. Discovery and originality is possible in mathematics because mathematical entities have relationships with each other of which we are not aware when we consider those objects apart from each other.

QUESTIONS FOR STUDY AND DISCUSSION

1. *Terms:* atomism, axiom, postulate, property, intentional, symmetrical-asymmetrical, theorem, transitive-intransitive.

2. Does abstraction play any part in sense perception? In memory?

3. Construct new abstractions for yourself and think of names you might give to them.

4. Can you think abstractly without the use of words?

5. Which of the following are mathematical statements?
   (a) Thirteen is a prime.

(b) Thirteen is too large a number of people to entertain in this house.

(c) Thirteen is an unlucky number.

(d) Thirteen minus seven leaves six.

(e) If seven of these people get off at the next stop only six will be left on the bus.

(f) This polygon has six sides.

(g) This building has six sides.

6. Illustrate mathematical and non-mathematical uses of the following: reciprocal, infinite, converging, square, continuous, even, equality.

7. Can any of the following concepts be transformed into abstract entities by suppressing their intentionality? Maturity, preliminary stage, irregularity, complexity, ending.

8. What are some mathematical properties of the following relations?

(a) A is employed by B.   (e) A is a classmate of B.
(b) A is a brother of B.   (f) A is an agent of B.
(c) A is a cousin of B.   (g) A is next to B.
(d) A is east of B.   (h) A is further away than B.

9. Invent a new mathematical entity. (Obviously you are not expected to invent a useful or significant mathematical entity, but only to form a concept which has some content left after all reference to existence is suppressed.)

10. How does mathematical certainty differ from your own assurance that you are alive? That you existed yesterday? That you are not someone else? That you have a brain within your skull?

CHAPTER 7

The Scientific Use of Mathematics

THE RELEVANCE OF MATHEMATICS TO EXISTENCE

We return now to the question left at the close of our earlier discussion of the nature of science. How can mathematics reveal to us the intelligible nature of the objects of scientific investigation? Mathematical knowledge is knowledge of abstract entities and scientific knowledge is knowledge of real existence. As we have already seen, a number may have a square root, but no actual existent has; a triangle is bounded by three intersecting straight lines, but no real object is. Actual objects are numerable and some of them are triangular, but none of them are numbers or triangles. Yet if objects are not numbers, how can they be numerable? If they are not triangles, how can they be triangular? That the results of mathematical reasoning can hold good of real things no one doubts, and it is only because they do that our scientific knowledge reveals the intelligible nature of things. But how is this possible? How can our knowledge about mathematical objects, which owe their being as entities to their abstraction from real existence, reveal the nature of the objects of science?

The answer has already been suggested, in principle at least. No matter how elaborate and complex are the abstract entities of mathematics, and no matter how far removed from direct experience, the material out of which we form them is obtained originally from our experience of real things. So, in principle, our answer is that *what is taken from the actual by thought in abstraction can be returned by thought to the actual.* Since the act of taking is not real but mental, what is taken can be returned by the mind to its source. Because the material for mathematical objects is abstracted from real things, and not produced by the mind from itself or obtained from any other source, such as the feelings and emotions, the reality to which it is returned by thought is that to which it belongs.

Although this is the answer in principle, there are certain possible difficulties which must be considered. If what the mind abstracts, in its formation of mathematical objects, is quantity or order then what can it return to existence, according to this principle, except that quantity or order in the form in which it was originally abstracted? At first sight it would seem that the results of a strictly mathematical investigation could apply only to quantity and order conceived apart from existence, not to quantity as a property of real existence. When, in thought, we return to real existence what was previously abstracted, have we not abolished the very condition which makes possible a *mathematical* knowledge of quantity and order? So it might seem that although our mathematical knowledge does hold good of mathematical objects, it has no relevance to real existence. Mathematics would, on this view, be relevant to certain features of actual existence when considered apart from existence; but how can it be relevant to them as properties of things themselves?

I count five houses on one side of the street in a certain block, or I estimate the lengths of two sides of a field and calculate the number of acres it contains. But the number series I use in counting the houses is not composed of houses, and the field I measure by use of the relations of the lengths of the sides of a rectangle to its area is not a rectangle and its sides are not lines. How can I count houses or estimate mathematically the surface of a field? How can the complex and abstruse formulas of higher mathematics have any relevance to actual things? That they do, no informed person is likely to question. But what makes this possible?

One answer might be that since mathematical properties pertain to mathematical objects they can be applied to actual things just to the extent that those actual things can be treated *as if* they were mathematical objects. For example, we can count the chairs standing in a classroom provided we think of them *as if* they were units, each identical with every other. To that extent the relations which pertain to a plurality of units pertain also to the chairs. Of course neither the chairs nor the people who sit in them are genuine units, for this chair and that one and that one are not identical. We can count them but the results of our counting will hold true of them only so far as we can, for this purpose, ignore their differences. On this supposition, then, we can refer the relations of mathematical entities to real things only in so far as we can ignore the respects in which real things differ from mathematical entities.

In counting chairs, we treat the chairs *as if* they were identical when in fact they are different chairs. Does this mean that we have to falsify the true nature of things, or pretend they are what they are not, if the results of mathematical calculation are to apply to them? Not at all. Our difficulty comes from failure to keep in mind a basic difference between abstract entities and actual things. Although abstract entities may be identical, the things which have real existence in a world of change and process are only partially identical. Two things, we say, have the same shape; this does not mean that they are the same thing but that, in respect to the shape, they are the same *kind* of thing. No actual existence can be *only* a shape, and in order to form an idea of the shape of something we have to leave out of that idea all its other characteristics.

The way out of our difficulty may be found in recognizing that although real things do differ from each other, and although no two actual things are identical as such, yet *in certain respects* they may be identical. Our mathematical thinking can never exhaust the nature of any real thing; but this in no way implies that what mathematics is *about*, namely quantity, structure, and order, does not belong to real things. The door I see before me is not a geometrical figure, and we do not say that the door *is* a shape. But we do say that it *has* a shape. In so far as the shape it has satisfies the conditions of a rectangle, that is, so far as its opposite sides are parallel and equal in length and the four angles made by the intersections of those sides are right angles, then to that extent the geometric properties of a rectangle hold good of the shape of this door. As the shape of the door approximates a rectangle we can expect the properties of a rectangle to be found in our measurements of the door. Since no physical measurement is absolute, the determination of the geometric properties of the shape of the door is not absolute but approximate. We must remember, also, that in applying our knowledge of geometry to any physical object we apply it, strictly speaking, to the geometric properties of that object taken in abstraction from the object itself. It is the *shape* of the door we determine, and the *length* of a boundary of a field we measure. We calculate the *number* of chairs; we do not calculate chairs. To add and subtract chairs is not to calculate but to move actual chairs from one place to another.

This is the case not only in mathematical thinking but is true of all our conceptual knowledge. To recognize that this flower is red I have to use the concept *red*. Now of course it is false that this flower is red in the sense that it is redness. So also when I say that John is a man I use the concept *man*, but I do not mean that John is man. I use concepts in my thinking about the flower and about John, in my recognition of *what* they are, but I do not mean that these things are concepts. There is no such real thing as *man*, although there are and have been and will be *men*; there is no such real thing as *red* or *redness*, but there are *red things*.

When I say that this flower is red or that John is a man I am attributing to the flower and to John a certain property or a certain nature I have learned to recognize. The concepts which enable me to recognize these were formed by abstraction; and in most cases the formation of a concept depends on the experience of many different things. This flower is neither the first nor the only red thing I have seen; I recognize a host of things as red. Recognition is re-cognition. It is the awareness that in this or that, there is some character already encountered in other things or on other occasions. How do we know that the things we think about must have identical features? Because, for one thing, it is only in terms of their identical features that thought can grasp something of what they are; without identities recognition would be impossible.

No real thing is one or two or a square root or a prime. But real things can be numbered. We can number them because we can think of their quantitative identities in abstraction from their differences. I see in a basket, a red apple, an orange, a peach, a yellow apple, and a pear. How many are there? The question cannot be answered without specifying *how many what*. How many pieces of fruit? Five. How many peaches? One. How many apples? Two. How many red apples? One. How many things? It depends on what you take as one thing; *the mathematical process does not govern its own application*. Is the basket one thing, or are we to count each strip of material of which it is woven as one thing? How about the specks of dust on the basket, the seeds in the apples, the molecules of which these are composed, the units of energy they are radiating and absorbing? But if we do specify, we specify something in the nature of the things which is identical in each. If there are two apples, each is an apple in the very same sense as the other, no matter how they may differ in color or shape or size or in any other property.

To recognize identities among things is to render them numerable, for in so far as our concern is with the respect in which they are identical we can leave their differences out of account. This does not mean that we deny the fact of differences; it means only that we ignore differences because reference to them is not relevant to our purpose. To whatever things are numerable we can attribute the results we reach in our knowledge of numbers. In the same way mathematical formulations may hold good of actual things in so far as those actual things exemplify quantitative, structured, or ordered existence.

Mathematical thinking applies to things in the same way that any thinking does. Our thinking uses concepts and we form those concepts by abstraction. Mathematical abstractions differ from others in that they have content that can be known apart from any consideration of the things from which abstraction originally was made. Nevertheless, quantity and order do belong to the nature of real things, and what is true of quantity and order is true of something that belongs to the nature of real things. What we can discover about quantity and order only when we consider them apart from all reference to real things must pertain to them also as a part of the nature of things. We have to take quantity and order apart from things in order *to discover* their properties, but the properties of quantity and order which we do discover truly belong to them whether we consider them in the form of abstract entities or as the properties of something else.

FROM GENERALIZATION TO EXPLANATION

We may distinguish two phases of scientific inquiry: the preliminary phase of generalization, and the phase of mathematical explanation. As we take note of a uniformity or identity among the objects of experience we may formulate it as a generalization, such as: "All bodies gravitate." If this statement is true then all bodies without exception have this characteristic, and some will call it a "law of nature." But if there are exceptions then what is stated to be a law of nature and understood as a generalization is false. If we are to use such a generalization as the basis for further conclusions then we shall have to examine each case separately in order to make sure that it holds good. If we have to do this, however, there would seem little point in formulating the law or generalization in the first place. This is why generalization alone is insufficient for scientific inquiry. It is merely the entrance to science. Generalization does not provide the solution of a scientific problem; on the contrary, generalization is what *poses* such a problem. We discover uniformities, but we do not begin the really important work of science until we seek a rational understanding of those uniformities. In the words of Stephen Toulmin's differentiation between natural history and science: "Natural historians . . . look for regularities of given forms; but physicists seek the form of given regularities." [1]

If a generalization is to be of use as a basis for further inquiry we cannot very well include within it all the qualifications and state all the conditions under which it holds, for there would be no place to stop. If we include in the statement of a generalization the admission that there may be unknown exceptions which, if found, would show the law to be false then we are saying only that it is true where it is true. Suppose we propose to use the generalization that all bodies gravitate as the basis for further work in physics, and someone objects by asking, "What about the possibility that somewhere some bodies exist that do not gravitate?" Now we would not be likely to allow a question like this to divert us from our investigation, so we should perhaps reply to the effect that if there are

---

[1] *The Philosophy of Science* (London, Hutchinson's University Library, 1953), p. 53.

such bodies they are not the ones we are interested in at the moment. To make this quite definite, so that no misunderstanding can arise, we might say, "We know that all bodies gravitate because that is what the word 'body' means as we use it in this area of study. So far as we are concerned here, whatever does not gravitate is not a body."

In this way generalizations may be turned into propositions which are true by stipulation and acquire a certain usefulness for scientific inquiry. In so far as there are actual things to which the stipulated meaning applies then all its implications will hold good of those things. There may well be other things to which it does not apply, but the scientist need not specify what they are. Of course he could not, for he cannot exhaust the range of possibility. *The definitions and assumptions of his science are also specifications of the scope of its conclusions.* Where his definitions and assumptions apply, his conclusions also apply. If the results of his inquiry have little application then they simply will not be much used. The tests come to be relevance and utility rather than universal truth.

Once this is recognized, however, it also becomes evident that such a statement as "All bodies gravitate" has a very limited usefulness for scientific work. It may be meaningful in summing up the results of an inquiry, and thus be significant if true. But its final truth as a generalization is just what we are unable to discover with any theoretical assurance. On the other hand, if we turn this generalization into a statement which is true by specification then its usefulness as a guide to action or further inquiry is no greater than that of the statement that all poisons are harmful to the body, that is, that all poisons are poisonous. If such statements are to be significant for knowledge *they must have content which is fruitful material for rational inference.*

What has happened in the modern development of the methods of science can now perhaps be seen more plainly. When we turn a generalization into a statement which is true by definition we thereby remove all significant reference to existence, and as a result the proposition loses all its meaningful nonmathematical content. This is why modern science has found its fruitful developments in the direction of mathematical formulation.

Since only mathematical abstractions have content apart from their reference to existence, the scientific statements which take the place of factual generalizations have to be formulated in mathematical terms if they are to provide a basis for inference. If instead of saying that all bodies gravitate, we say that any two bodies attract each other with a force which is directly proportional to the product of their masses and inversely to the distance which separates them, we can state this in the form of an equation and thus open the way for actual measurements. Such a formulation makes accessible to us all the mathematical consequences which follow from it in relation to other mathematical formulas.

If scientific investigation were merely a matter of looking at things, even of looking at them with the aid of elaborate instruments, and reporting what was found, then there would be nothing rational about it. Whatever idea of proof it might use, its "proof" would not be rational proof; it would consist of nothing more than the confirmation of one observer's report by another observer. On the basis of observation alone we could raise no question of why things have the characteristics they have; we could only report that they do have such characteristics. No conflict or contradiction could exist. If water suddenly turned into a solid as we looked at it, with no change of temperature or anything else to account for that change, and then became a column of vapor which all at once disappeared without a trace, all we could do on the basis of observation alone would be to report what we had seen. To insist that such things cannot happen, that those who reported their occurrence must have been having illusions or hallucinations, would be to leave behind the standpoint of observation and to introduce a theory concerning what can and what cannot happen in nature.

Since the more highly developed sciences depend on proof for the development of their theories and principles, it is plain that those sciences must have a rational structure. Mathematics provides that rational structure. Only by the use of mathematics does a science get beyond the stage of observation and generalization and begin to establish its conclusions by rational demonstration. Only then does science have any truly cognitive significance by providing explanations which show us something of the intrinsic intelligibility of actual fact. Progress in mathematics is the condition on which progress in science depends for its possibility. As Professor John G. Kemeny says:

> When we find some Physics problem as yet unanswered, we assume that it is because no one has yet found the right "trick" to solve

it. Actually it is possible that this problem needs an entirely new branch of Mathematics.[2]

MATHEMATICAL INTELLIGIBILITY

In Chapter 5 we considered briefly some examples of scientific explanation to illustrate the part played by mathematics in scientific inquiry. It will be helpful now to look at another example of scientific explanation in somewhat more detail and in contrast with an attempt to make the same facts intelligible without the use of mathematics.

Everyone who has played baseball knows that the strength of impact of a hard-hit or hard-thrown baseball on the hands of one who catches it depends partly on the way the ball is caught. If the hands are held rigid in a fixed position the ball may hit them hard enough to sting or bruise. But if, in catching the ball, the hands "give" a bit, that is, if they move a short distance in the direction of the motion of the ball, the ball can be caught without discomfort. How can we interpret this fact so that we can understand *why* it is the case?

First let us try to understand this fact without the use of mathematical ideas. I hold my hands still and I feel the sting of the impact. I move my hands in the direction of the motion of the ball and I feel no sting as my hand follows through with the motion of the ball. With the hand held rigid, there is the sensation of a blow struck, a stinging sensation in the palm and inside surface of the fingers, and an aching sensation through the muscles and bones of the hand. With the hand in motion as the ball strikes, there is the sensation of contact and pressure against the palm and closing fingers, and the feeling that the hand and arm are being pushed in the direction of their motion. How do we account for this difference without the use of mathematics? We cannot differentiate the two in terms of intensity or force, for these involve quantitative distinctions.

The only other kind of rational explanation seems to be one in terms of the relation of cause and effect. The ball striking the hand is the cause, and the jar of the hand and the sting and the ache are

[2] *A Philosopher Looks at Science* (Princeton, D. Van Nostrand Company, Inc., 1959), p. 194. By permission.

the effect. The ball, we may say, has the power when in motion to jar and sting a hand and make it ache. This is because, as it strikes the hand, the tissue of the hand is compressed. The compression of tissue, when severe enough, stimulates sense organs of pain. The blow also brings pressure against the bones of the hand so that tendons and ligaments are pulled and the joints are slightly stretched. These effects also are registered by sense organs. In the second instance the movement of the hand in catching the ball changes the conditions under which the cause operated and so a different effect is produced. In this case the effect consists of two kinds of sensation of pressure: compression of the tissue of the hand, and the pressure which gives the hand and arm a push in the direction of the motion of the ball.

What have we accomplished in this explanation? We have done two things. We have recognized the presence of causal relationships in which the effect varies with a difference in certain of the circumstances, and we have described the events in greater detail. Both of these are important. It surely would be a handicap to be unable to link causally the impact of the ball with what we feel in our hands and arms. A more detailed description is also of advantage, for it does greater justice to the complexity of the event and enables us to see the causal connections of some of the less obvious processes. Thus we are better able to identify a specific factor which is the cause of a specific variation in the effect. Then, too, the intermediate links in the causal sequences may become accessible to our control and thus we may be able to exert a more effective direction of our activities.

Such an explanation, however, takes us no nearer an understanding of why there is this difference. We have made intelligible the fact that it does exist, for we understand it as a variation of effect linked with a variation of the cause; but in this we have nothing more than a set of facts in causal relation with each other. If we are to discover the intelligibility of these facts we must analyze them in terms of relationships which exhibit an intrinsic intelligibility. This means that we must analyze our facts in terms of mathematical relationships. Since we do not have the space to do this exhaustively we shall confine our explanation to the difference in the force of impact of the ball on the hands in the two instances.

We may now interpret the facts, in terms of the concepts of physics, as follows: The moving ball has momentum and to stop the ball requires force, the force opposed to the ball by the hands when the ball strikes them. We know that if the ball is to be stopped the force applied to it by the hands must be equal to the momentum. But we find that the impact of the ball is less when the hands move with it as it is caught than when they are held in a rigid position. What is the significant difference between these two cases? We assume that the velocity of the ball is the same. The same hands, with the same flesh and bones and nerves and skin, catch the ball in the two cases; but in one case the hands receive the impact of the ball all at once while in the other the hands are moving as the ball strikes them so that a longer time is taken to catch the ball. In the latter case the hands slow down the ball gradually while in the former they stop the ball abruptly. We conclude that the time it takes to catch the ball makes a difference in the amount of force required at any moment during the time the hands are stopping the ball.

We can see why this is so, that is, we can bring to light its intelligible nature, if we can find the mathematical relationships of the units of force, time, velocity, and mass. Since we assume that the velocity is the same and the mass is the same in the two instances, we are left with time and force as the two variables. What we need to find, therefore, is the mathematical relation of the difference in the force of impact with the difference in the time required to stop the ball.

If now we consider momentum (mass and velocity), force of impact, and time in terms of their quantitative nature, the relation we have found to hold between them becomes intelligible. Since the same amount of momentum is present in both cases it seems plain that the smaller force must be applied over a longer period of time if it is to stop the ball. Or, the shorter the time taken to stop the ball the greater the force of impact. In one case the momentum is countered quickly, and if this could be done in a minimal interval of time the force applied to stop the ball would, at that moment, almost equal the momentum of the ball. At the other extreme, if the ball struck something that offered minimal resistance to its motion its momentum would be affected hardly at all. Such resistance would have to be present for a comparatively long time before the ball would be stopped. An example of resistance which is small in comparison with that offered by the human hand is the resistance of the air, or of gravity.

What makes this factual situation intelligible is the mathematical relation of these various factors. We can now see this in a vague fashion, but in order to see it precisely and explicitly we must give it a formal statement and show its rational necessity.[3] The relation of the force (F), mass (m), and acceleration (a) of a moving body is shown by the equation

$$F = ma \tag{1}$$

The acceleration is a relation between two velocities (v) at the beginning and end of a given time interval (t):

$$a = \frac{v_2 - v_1}{t} \tag{2}$$

Substituting (2) for a in (1), we have

$$F = m \left(\frac{v_2 - v_1}{t} \right) \tag{3}$$

This is mathematically equivalent to

$$Ft = mv_2 - mv_1 \tag{4}$$

Thus the force times the time during which it acts is equal to the change in momentum. So long as the values for the momentum side of the equation remain constant any decrease in F requires an increase in t, for the same reason that if we substitute a larger number for one of two factors of a product, the other factor must be smaller by the same proportion. If we substitute 6 for the 3 in 3 x 4 = 12, then we must substitute 2 for the 4; that is, if we double one of the two factors we must halve the other.

Steps (1) and (2) of the proof are assumed, and, so far as this proof taken by itself is concerned, can be regarded as definitions of F and a. Steps (3) and (4) are obtained by exclusively mathematical operations, and the conclusions we draw concerning the relation of F and t in (4) are based entirely on the mathematical relations of the factors of a product. The validity of the mathematical operations does not have to be shown here; such a question would be one for mathematics and not for physics. These operations rather are *used;* they are the instruments of proof. Whether the proof pertains to the actual situation is the question simply of whether there is anything

[3] The following analysis is adapted from Oscar M. Stewart, *Physics*, Fifth Edition by Newell S. Gingrich (Boston, Ginn and Company, 1950), pp. 75, 80.

in the events themselves to which these symbols apply. In other words, the question is whether or not there is a measurable force of impact in each case, a measurable change in volocity, a measurable mass, and measurable time intervals.

Now we can understand why a ball stopped by something that does not yield with the impact hits with greater force than when stopped by something that is moving in the direction of the motion of the ball. What makes this understandable is the mathematical relation between the factors of a product. This relation is such that a change of one factor, by increase or decrease, requires a change of the other factor in the opposite direction and in the same proportion. So in the relation of F and t, which are factors of $mv_2 - mv_1$ in (4), we have an intelligible explanation of the observed fact that a ball hits harder when stopped suddenly than when stopped gradually. The intelligibility of the fact is shown by the relation of F and t, *as quantities*. As quantities they are factors of another quantity, their product, which we assume in the present case to be constant, namely, $mv_2 - mv_1$. In so far as we can consider force and time and momentum in their quantitative nature, to that extent *the inherent intelligibility of the mathematical relationship of varying factors of a fixed product belongs to these actual events.*

We must emphasize that an understanding of the facts of nature can never be obtained merely by observing those facts. Such a relationship as F $= ma$, Jacob Bronowski observes,

> does not arrive from nature ready-made. On the contrary, it has to be puzzled out from an apparently meaningless multiplicity of everyday observations and experiments, and the puzzle is to find the units which matter within these.[4]

To *understand* the facts of nature scientifically, we must discover some mathematical structure which those facts exemplify. The intelligibility of the facts themselves is then found not in any observed relationship of the facts to each other but in the relationships which obtain within the mathematical scheme itself. When, for example, an understanding of the relationship of certain events in nature is reached by use of a diagram, the intelligibility of those factual relations is found in the geometric relationships of the parts of

[4] "Science as Foresight," in *What Is Science?* edited by James R. Newman (copyright 1955, by James R. Newman), p. 429. Reprinted by permission of Simon and Schuster, Inc., New York.

the diagram. If we use a parallelogram to exemplify the relationships of certain physical forces, we reach an understanding of the relationships of those forces from the properties of the parallelogram.

Before we leave our illustration it may be well to point out that our earlier attempt to explain these facts without the use of mathematical ideas was not only a failure to explain but also a failure to exclude the mathematical. The direction of motion and, indeed, the very idea of motion itself involve the concepts of extension and direction in space. The idea of before and after is impossible to have without the idea of order, and the distinction between the inside and outside surfaces of the fingers requires some concept of structure. The idea of closing fingers and of something being pushed in a certain direction also involve motion in space. What we did succeed in doing was not to exclude the mathematical but to avoid any measurement or examination of these mathematical relationships.

SCIENTIFIC TRUTH

As a science becomes more and more mathematical it tends to formulate its laws and principles without including in those formulas any reference to things. With this has come a new conception of the nature and role of scientific law. We are not so much inclined to ask, "Is this law true?" as to ask, "Is this or that case an instance to which the law applies?" If the answer to the second question is in the negative, it does not follow that the law has been shown to be false. We have shown only that the case in question is one for which the law does not hold. *The question of whether a scientific law is true or false does not arise in connection with the statement of the law itself.*

But may we not say that a law is true in so far as it holds and false in so far as it does not hold? If we try to take this position we are forced to conclude that every law is false; for no scientific law holds of everything. What do we mean when we say that a law is true in so far as it holds and false in so far as it does not? Does this mean anything more than that it is true or false that the law holds? If not, then it is not to the law itself that truth or falsity is to be attributed. Thus a scientific law is true *under certain conditions*, if it can be said to be true at all. But the conditions are not stated as a part of the law, and so we do not say that the law as such is either true or false. The law statement is in terms of elements within the postulate system; it asserts certain relations among those elements. But neither the law statement nor the system itself says anything about its own applicability to fact.

We said earlier that the sciences differ from mathematics in claiming to be true of matters of fact, while mathematics neglects and ignores the original reference to existence of its basic concepts. Have we not now destroyed this distinction and made the sciences branches of mathematics? This might be suggested by our discussion so far in this section, and it is important now to bring out clearly the distinction in this respect between the sciences of nature and mathematics.

In the first place the sciences use mathematics but no natural science, not even the most "mathematical" of them, is a part of mathematics. The sciences may suggest and inspire certain developments in mathematical fields, but such developments are not themselves part of the work of the sciences. For example, certain important mathematical concepts which made possible the development of the theory of relativity were much neglected by mathematicians until Einstein found them useful. Although its application to physics stimulated interest in an area of mathematics, still mathematics is not physics and physics is not mathematics. For mathematics is about mathematical entities, and mathematical entities have content and meaning in themselves. Although scientific statements do not themselves include assertions concerning their reference to existence, *those statements are formulated in terms of concepts that have no meaning apart from such reference*. Although modern physics understands by means of mathematics the relationships of mass and force and velocity and time, of atoms and electrons and positrons and neutrons; these are not themselves mathematical concepts. They are physical concepts, and they have no meaning apart from the situations and processes in nature to which they refer.

From this we may draw a very important distinction. A mathematical system has meaning and is of mathematical interest whether or not any application to fact is ever found for it. It may not have the practical importance of other branches, but many mathematicians are unconcerned about the practical importance of their work. For some the satisfaction is intellectual, or even aesthetic. The physicist, on the other hand, would find it difficult to sustain an interest in a system of concepts whose terms have significance only in their reference to existence unless he took account of that reference. It is hard to see what difference there would be between a physics that held good of no matters of fact and a mere game. Physicists are serious students of nature; they are not playing games. If they wish to play games there are many much easier to play than physics, and any game is but child's play in comparison with a science.

Does this make a game of mathematics? For mathematics is pursued without reference to its truth or falsity concerning matters of fact. The answer is clearly in the negative. Mathematics is not a game; it is a most important body of knowledge. Although it abstracts from and neglects all reference to actual existence, mathematics is still the study of the nature of existence. What it has abstracted are aspects of real existence. The unique feature of mathematics is that its abstractions have content in themselves, as ideal entities, apart from their original reference to existence. So mathematics has its own world, a world formed by abstraction. But since the world of mathematics is formed by abstraction from actual existence it is not cut off arbitrarily or absolutely from the real world. For mathematics is the sole source of our knowledge of those aspects of actual and possible existence which have their own inherent intelligibility, and so can be investigated and explored only in abstraction from existence.

It may not be too much to say that our knowledge of those aspects of existence which we can obtain only at the level of mathematical abstraction is our one direct access to the inner rational and intelligible structure of physical existence. As Jacob Bronowski says, "The aim of science is to break the code of nature." [5]

> In whatever way we seek or exchange information about the world, we do not seize its underlying units themselves: what we learn is always about their organization. When in science, or in life, we analyze experience into parts, the meaning that we reach for lies not in the parts but in the structures which they form.[6]

As the skeletal structure of a living animal can be seen by us directly only when the skeleton is removed from the animal, reconstituted from its parts, and mounted; so the intelligible structure of physical being can be seen directly by human intelligence only as

[5] Ibid.
[6] Ibid, p. 426.

that intelligible structure is removed from existence by abstraction and reconstituted as the abstract entities which are the subject matter of mathematics. Only by means of such an instrument can the sciences give us genuine knowledge of the inner structure of real existence. Without this instrument, scientific knowledge would not be knowledge *of* nature; it would be knowledge only of how to use nature for our own purposes.

Why is not the intrinsic structure of physical existence directly apparent to our minds? Why do we have to abstract quantity and form it into mathematical objects before we can apprehend the intelligible structure of quantitative being? Perhaps we may find an answer to this question in the fact that all our contact with physical existence is by way of our senses. In sense perception we discover what things are; we are able in this way to grasp in awareness the nature of things that exist beyond ourselves. What we apprehend by way of our senses is truly intelligible, but the senses are incapable of revealing or exposing its intelligible structure. The senses can bring to our minds what is intelligible in itself, but in order to discover the intelligible structure inherent in what the senses communicate the intellect must perform upon that material its acts of analysis and abstraction. If the intellect could see directly into the nature of other things, as in the awareness which man sometimes attributes to God, then neither mathematics nor the sciences would be necessary as instruments of knowledge.

It is my conviction [said Albert Einstein] that pure mathematical construction enables us to discover the concepts and the laws connecting them which give us the key to the understanding of the phenomena of Nature. Experience can of course guide us in our choice of serviceable mathematical concepts; it cannot possibly be the source from which they are derived; experience of course remains the sole criterion of the serviceability of a mathematical construction for physics, but the truly creative principle resides in mathematics.[7]

SUMMARY

Although mathematics is concerned directly with abstract entities and their relations it has relevance to real existence be-

[7] *On the Method of Theoretical Physics*, The Herbert Spencer Lecture, Oxford, June 10, 1933 (New York, Oxford University Press, 1933), p. 7. By permission.

cause what is taken from the actual by thought in abstraction can be returned by thought to the actual. The problem here is no different from that involved in any kind of abstract thinking. Abstraction is grounded in the partial identities and uniformities which can be discerned among the differences and pluralities of actual existence.

The process by which we take note of uniformities and identities among the objects of experience is generalization. This, however, is merely the entrance to science; generalization poses rather than solves scientific problems. Generalizations of common sense and those formulated in ordinary language are not very useful, as they stand, in scientific investigation. If their meaning is to be made precise and if we are to avoid turning them into empty assertions, they must have content of their own which is independent of their reference to existence. Consequently they become useful for scientific inquiry and provide a basis for logically controlled inference only when reformulated in mathematical terms. An understanding of the facts of nature can never be obtained merely by observing those facts; to discover their intelligible relations with each other we must find some mathematical structure which those facts exemplify.

Scientific formulations, like mathematical, do not specify in themselves to what actual situations they are relevant. They differ from mathematical formulations, however, in that they have meaning only so far as they are relevant to some area of fact. Where they are relevant, scientific laws provide our only access to the inner, rational and intelligible structure of physical existence. Direct experience of physical existence is sensory; and although what sense experience apprehends is truly intelligible, its intelligibility is not revealed in sense experience itself. The intellect cannot intuit other things directly, so it must take the material provided by sense perception and uncover the intelligible structure of the objects perceived by its processes of analysis and abstraction.

QUESTIONS FOR STUDY AND DISCUSSION

1. *Terms:* confirmation, definition, generalization, law, stipulation. uniformity.

2. Why do not the conditions that make mathematics relevant to existence apply likewise to a game, such as bridge or chess?

3. Identify the use of existential dialectic in the section on "The Relevance of Mathematics to Existence."

4. If the entities of mathematics are conceptual constructs would such an entity exist if no one were thinking it? (Consider what "exist" means in this context.) Granted that a certain door continues to have the same rectangular shape whether anyone thinks that shape or not, what about rectangles? Were there rectangles, as distinguished from rectangular things, before anyone ever formed the concept of a rectangle? (If inclined to answer this question in the negative, consider carefully what is involved in any suggestion that a mathematical entity *begins* to exist.)

5. Illustrate Toulmin's distinction between natural history and science.

6. How does a "law of nature" exist? Is it a part of nature? A property of nature? A mathematical structure? A way of conceiving nature?

7. Restate the following as tautologies:
   (a) It is wrong to steal.
   (b) It is a violation to drive faster than the posted limit.
   (c) All physical bodies occupy space.
   (d) College students have gone beyond the secondary school level.

8. What is the difference between the use of stipulation in scientific inquiry and such cases as: "He is the better candidate because he is the Republican," or: "You want to know why this is so? I'll tell you why. It's so because I say it's so."

9. Examine: Any statement of causal relationship approaches a tautology as it becomes more complete.

10. If a law of nature at most delineates the structure of a uniformity, are we ever warranted in denying the possibility of an occurrence on the grounds that it would be in conflict with that law?

PART III

Philosophy
of
Nature and Man

CHAPTER 8

The Physical World

THE WORLD OF COMMON SENSE

The physical world as we consider it on the common sense level is generally understood to be composed of *things*, which we sometimes call substances; of the *properties* or *qualities* of those things; of *relations* among things; of *processes* or *events* which we recognize as *changes* that occur in things or in their qualities or relations; of *space*, in which physical things exist and in which events take place; and of *time*, in which changes occur and in terms of which we distinguish between *past*, *present*, and *future*. The physical world also contains living beings, and we generally think of these as rather sharply different from nonliving physical beings. Some living beings we recognize as having *minds;* and although we may think of mind as non-physical, yet minded living beings exist and act in the physical world. In this chapter we shall be concerned with the physical world in its basic physical nature alone, leaving our discussions of life and mind for later chapters.

The common-sense view of the world is very old. Its main features of thing, quality, relation, change, space, and time have been recognized in our own civilization, in one form or another, for as long as we have records. The earliest philosophies were inquiries into these features of the world; they were attempts to reconcile apparent conflicts which arose when men first began to try to understand these basic characteristics in relation with each other. How can the same thing change? If it changes then surely it is not the same. What things are basic in existence, and what things are derived by some process of change from those basic things? What is the nature of motion, which involves both time and space? How can the same thing move from one place to another? In spite of difficulties and paradoxes which early and later thinkers were able to uncover, the common sense way of thinking of the world has persisted.

It is true that scientific discoveries have made some changes in our common-sense views, but these changes concern almost entirely our ideas of the extent, complexity, and constituents of our world. We no longer think of the earth as the center of the universe, and of the sun and moon and planets and stars as belonging to earth's immediate spatial surroundings. We have at least heard of many of the hundred-odd chemical elements and no longer suppose that the whole of physical existence is composed of the four elements of earth, water, air, and fire. We are aware also that the "elements" are quite complex and are composed of many kinds of more basic particles. Only a few of the names of these particles have come into popular speech, the proton and electron and possibly the neutron, but people who read newspapers are aware that there are others. None of those differences in our common sense ideas, however, have touched the basic categories of the common sense view. It is quite likely, for example, that most people think of the electron as a thing in motion and as having qualities and existing in relation with other very small physical particles.

SOME COMMON-SENSE CATEGORIES

It will be helpful to review briefly a few of our basic common-sense concepts. This of course is not a common-sense inquiry, for it requires systematic reflection. Ordinarily we think *with* these categories, not *about* them.

A basic concept we constantly use is that of a physical substance or entity, and we distinguish substances or entities from events. A physical substance is spatial; it has qualities; it endures and changes; it has powers or capacities. An event, in contrast, happens to things. It is in some sense a part of the duration of things, or an interaction among things. An event has a beginning and an end and some unity or continuity. We say that substances change, that events happen to those substances; we do not say that substances happen to events. Nor do we say ordinarily that an event changes; the event is the change.

Aristotle defined change as "the actualization of that which is potential, in so far as it is potential." [1] Although this statement appears to be very abstract, it is faithfully descriptive of what we find in direct experience. We find a continuity in change, for example, not merely the replacement of one thing by another. So when iron rusts, the rusted piece of iron must in some sense be the same piece of iron as the one we had before rust was apparent. If someone merely removed a piece of iron that was free from rust and put a rusty piece in its place we should not say that the original piece of iron had become rusty. We can express this idea of continuity in change by saying that the iron before it rusts has the potentiality of rusting. Although it may have no rust on its surface, its surface is so constituted that on exposure to moisture it will combine with oxygen in such a way that rust is formed. The qualification, "in so far as it is potential," thus points to the fact that the change is from potentiality to actuality rather than merely the substitution of one actual state by another.

Substances have qualities, and a quality is a part of a substance's nature. The quality is not, strictly, a part of the substance but a part of its nature. We cannot divide a substance so that its qualities are over here by themselves and the rest of the substance is over there. We can only analyze a substance and *think* of its qualities alone. Where we distinguish between quality and quantity, we think of a quality, such as a color, as a part of a thing's nature which is not itself analyzable into parts. A quantity, on the other hand, is a part of a thing's nature which can be analyzed into parts.

To be spatial is to have distinguishable parts which coexist during the same time. A physical substance, we say, has extension. By this we mean that it has coexisting parts which are not parts of each other. To be temporal is to have distinguishable parts or properties which occupy the same place and so to be in process of

[1] *Physics*, Book III, Chapter 1, 201a 10-11.

change. A cause is an agent of change; a thing is called a cause when its action is such that changes occur in other things. An end is a state toward which a substance or a set of substances is tending. A purpose is a preview of a possible end with the intention of realizing that end. We no longer think of the physical world as purposeful in itself, but we do ordinarily think of it as including processes which contribute toward the realization of ends, such as the physical processes involved in the growth of living organisms.

These concepts involve a wide range of problems which have made up a considerable part of the subject matter of philosophy throughout its long history. The beginning student who wishes to consider some of the problems which have been encountered in the attempt to think these concepts coherently might examine Zeno's paradoxes concerning space and time and motion. He will find a more recent analysis in F. H. Bradley's *Appearance and Reality*, and still more recent ones in the works of Alfred North Whitehead, especially in *The Concept of Nature, Science and the Modern World*, and *Process and Reality*.

COMMON SENSE AND LANGUAGE

It has been suggested that the explanation of the stability of our traditional common-sense view of the world is to be found in the nature of our language. Other cultures with languages which have markedly different structures from our own language, it is suggested, also have quite different ideas about the world. We think in terms of substances and qualities and relations and changes, the argument goes, because we think in accordance with the structures of our own language. Our language is composed of substantives and verbs, and so we think of things or substances and events or acts; our language has adjectives and prepositions, and so we think in terms of qualities and relations. If we had been born into a culture with a language of very different structure we would think of the world in a quite different way. "All theoretical cognition takes its departure," says Ernst Cassirer, "from a world already preformed by language; the scientist, the historian, even the philosopher, lives with his objects only as language presents them to him." [2]

[2] *Language and Myth*, translated by Susanne K. Langer (New York, Harper and Brothers, 1946), p. 28. By permission.

Cassirer points out that our concepts are formed primarily not on the basis of similarities of appearance but "different items bear the same name, and are subsumed under the same concept, whenever their *functional* significance is the same." [3] For example, in the Kate language of New Guinea

> there is a word *bilin*, which denotes a certain kind of grass with tough stems and roots that are wedged firmly in the soil; the latter are said to hold the earth together during earthquakes, so that it does not break apart. When nails were first introduced by Europeans, and when their use became popularly known, the natives applied this word to them— as also to wire and to iron rods, in short, to everything that served the purpose of holding things together.[4]

According to Edward Sapir, language exerts a control over experience itself:

> Language is not merely a more or less systematic inventory of the various items of experience which seem relevant to the individual, as is so often naively assumed, but is also a self-contained, creative symbolic organization, which . . . actually defines experience for us by reason of its formal completeness and because of our unconscious projection of its implicit expectations into the field of experience.[5]

This concept of the relation of language and thought might suggest that where our thinking is inadequate the remedy is to reconstruct our language. A new language, however, would have to be constructed by means of the thinking we are already able to do, and if our thinking is controlled by the language which made that thinking possible in the first place, we are not likely to get far in constructing a new language. There is another side to this question, however, as Professor Irving M. Copi points out:

> As has been suggested by the comparative study of American Indian languages and those characterized as standard average European, sufficiently different natural languages embody different views of the world. . . . The construction of a particular formalized language, then, cannot decide a philosophical issue: it is rather the case that one's prior acceptance of this or that philosophical position will determine

[3] *Ibid*, p. 40.

[4] *Ibid*, p. 41, n. 17.

[5] "Conceptual Categories of Primitive Languages." Quoted in *Language, Thought, and Culture*, edited by Paul Henle (Ann Arbor, University of Michigan Press, 1958), p. 1.

what artificial symbolic language he will be led to construct and find congenial.[6]

No one would doubt that there is a close connection between the language of a particular culture and that culture's common sense ideas of the world. But to suppose that the question is one of whether the language is the source of the ideas or reflects the experience of those who have developed that language surely is to oversimplify the problem. It is not a case of all of one or all of the other. Certainly as individuals we have been greatly influenced by our language; our language has predisposed us to perceive and to think in certain ways. Furthermore, we think with language as our tool, a tool that is indispensable to human thought of any complexity; and so it is not easy to suppose that man first develops a definite way of thinking about his world and then fashions a language to express that way of thinking. It is just as difficult, however, to suppose that language develops independently of human thinking. The relation of thought to language is more intimate than either such one-sided view recognizes.

Language and thinking develop together. As identities are noted under the pressure of practical needs, ways of preserving that notice are found. Even at its lowest levels awareness is a matter of constantly shifting attention. Organic needs, with their rhythms, and their rhythms of rhythms, involve highly differentiated responses. Where symbol-forming equipment is present, with its physical basis in the highly developed central nervous system of man, patterns of response and of sensory experience are fixed in terms of symbols. This very situation leads to a tremendous complication of experience and response, for the symbol is the means by which experience becomes cumulative in the individual's consciousness and communicable to others. Increased range and complexity of the language of a society provides the individual who is born into that society with the means of more extensive synthesis and more refined discrimination of objects than he could ever achieve alone. In this sense, language directs experience. On the other hand, the pressures of living make it necessary to attend to new distinctions and relationships. The method of meeting that need is by the modification and extension of language, and this

6 "Artificial Languages," Chapter 4 of *Language, Thought, and Culture*, edited by Paul Henle (Ann Arbor, University of Michigan Press, 1958), p. 114. By permission.

sometimes leads to the creation of artificial languages or vocabularies.

There are reasons to believe that our common sense categories do fit quite well into the nature of actual existence. One such reason is the fact that although we have changed our ideas about the extent and complexity of our world we still retain our basic common sense categories. It may be objected that this is the case only because our scientific way of thinking has not yet penetrated popular thought. But to this objection we may reply that scientists themselves, who understand quite well the basic ideas of scientific thought, still use the common-sense categories when they are thinking about their world in their ordinary nonscientific dealings with it. The so-called language of the physical sciences, for example, differs from ordinary language not only in vocabulary but in its syntactical structure. The structure of the physicist's "language" is mathematical. Instead of using the subject-predicate sentence structure of ordinary speech, he thinks and writes and even at times speaks in equations and mathematical functions. But when a physicist identifies what it is he is talking about in the language of physics, he uses ordinary language structure to do so. When scientists lunch together, play bridge, go fishing, or fall in love, they use the language of the rest of us. This can scarcely be a matter merely of not having sufficient scientific understanding of these other affairs, for physicists show no evidence of even attempting to transfer their mathematical way of thinking to common sense situations.

Common sense ideas are very different from scientific ideas, but this does not mean that if one set of ideas is valid the other is not. The question is not the question of which is true. Yet there is a problem here, and we must consider this problem in order to avoid serious misunderstanding and to reach some kind of coherence in our ideas of existence.

COMMON SENSE AND SCIENCE

We are all familiar with the way in which we see and think the same thing from different perspectives and in different contexts. We can describe a painting, for example, in terms of its subject matter, in terms of the technique of the artist, in terms of its composition or arrangement of line and color, in terms of its place in the career of the artist or in the history of art, in terms of its religious or sociological or even political significance. All of these differ from one another, and what is relevant to one is seldom relevant to another. There can be no direct conflict between them, although there may be conflicts with respect to some of their implications. But we do not ask which of these descriptions is true, simply because they differ. All significant description and comment about things is relevant to some purpose or interest; since we have various interests and purposes, no single comment can be relevant to all of them. No one kind of account of anything can be all the truth about it.

For some human interests the common sense conception of the world is inadequate or irrelevant. In the areas of technology and science, for example, we cannot discover what we want to know if we remain at the common-sense level and use its categories alone. The special interests which we attempt to satisfy by the methods of science are mainly of two kinds. There is a practical interest in achieving some control of events and processes in our world, and there is the theoretical interest in knowledge for its own sake. Common-sense knowledge does give us a measure of control, but only so far as we are willing to take things as we find them and make little effort to break them down into their components and reconstruct them in terms of our own specifications. The primitive processing of clay and smelting of ores, the fabrication of buildings and furniture and vehicles from materials found in nature are all examples of practical uses of natural materials on the basis of common-sense knowledge. This may be expert knowledge in that only the initiated are in possession of the more effective techniques, but in the earlier stages such knowledge involves nothing more than what can be learned from direct experience and from trial and error methods. The achievements of modern technology, however, as in the plastics industry, in the new work in metals, and in electronics, require scientific knowledge.

Although modern technology is an important product of science, yet, as we have seen, the basic interest which leads to scientific inquiry is theoretical rather than practical. Pure science is a search for intelligibility; it is an attempt to reach a kind of understanding of nature which is not possible at the level of common sense. The trouble with common sense is not that it is false or that it is unintelligible. Common sense cannot be simply false, although of course it may be mistaken in this or that detail; its basic categories must be sound, else we could not start from common sense in order to go beyond it to science. Neither is common sense unintelligible, else we could not start from common sense and hope to reach any intelligible conceptions as a result of scientific inquiry. The defect of common sense for the theoretical interest in nature is that its intelligibility cannot be seen and grasped on its own level. Scientific inquiry is an attempt to uncover and make explicit the abstract intelligibility of that world of nature we encounter directly in ordinary experience.

Both philosophy and science are attempts to understand existence, but they are different kinds of approaches. Perhaps it is not too misleading to say that philosophy seeks a general framework of concepts in terms of which we can organize our more specific knowledge. Scientific inquiry is always concerned with specific and limited problems. Philosophy seeks for logical relations among our common-sense concepts and for ways of revising those concepts with the aim of reaching an inclusive and coherent view of existence in all its known aspects. Every problem in philosophy seems directly or indirectly to involve every other problem. The philosopher is constantly driven by the need for coherence. In contrast, a science can contain incompatible theories without any great embarrassment to those who are working in that field. Norbert Wiener has commented:

> Physics is at present a mass of partial theories which no man has yet been able to render truly and clearly consistent. It has been well said that the modern physicist is a quantum theorist on Monday, Wednesday, and Friday and a student of gravitational relativity theory on Tuesday, Thursday, and Saturday. On Sunday the physicist is neither but is praying to his God that someone, preferably himself, will find the reconciliation between these two views.[7]

Such a situation may be disturbing to those scientists who also have some philosophical interests, but they are not likely to be disturbed by it often in their scientific work. Scientific inquiry is essentially abstract inquiry which isolates in order to understand. Thus the intelligibility disclosed by scientific inquiry is an abstract intelligibility, it is the transparent intrinsic intelligibility of the mathematical schemes which are the instruments of scientific analysis.

As more and more of the results of scientific inquiry have been

[7] *I Am a Mathematician* (Garden City, N. Y., Doubleday and Company, Inc., 1956), p. 109. By permission.

assimilated into our common sense view of the world, new problems have arisen for philosophers. The apparent conflicts between our scientific knowledge and traditional religious beliefs, moral attitudes, economic and political practices and institutions, have posed the problem of working out a unified grasp of existence in which these conflicts can be reconciled. Scientific inquiry takes its departure from common sense, but it leaves common sense behind. One of the important tasks of philosophy today is to try to discover the underlying logical relationships among the basic concepts of all these varied fields of knowledge and thought and practice. The great modern intellectual revolution has been the scientific revolution. Our pressing philosophical problem is the reinterpretation of traditional modes of thought in the nonscientific areas. The aim is not to make the nonscientific areas into new branches of science; it is rather to discover the relevance of the results of scientific inquiry for common sense thought and for other specialized fields of interest.

In the remainder of this chapter we shall examine the philosophical aspects of three kinds of theories concerning the physical world: prescientific theories, the conception of nature which emerged in classical modern physics, and the changes in that conception which are the result of recent developments in physics.

PRESCIENTIFIC THEORIES OF NATURE

Early theories of nature in which attempts were made to understand natural processes in terms of nature itself, as distinguished from the mythologies, seem mostly to follow the same basic pattern. They are attempts to find those elemental entities in nature whose combinations and interrelationships will account for other things. The elements traditionally recognized in Greek thought were earth, water, air, and fire. Often there were sets of elements arranged in pairs of opposites, and the four Greek elements lend themselves easily to such arrangements, as in distinctions between the hot and cold, the wet and dry, the light and heavy.

If we ask what led men to attempt to discover elements, the question is hard to answer, for we cannot very well put ourselves back into the perspective of earlier civilizations. But one of the more plausible explanations, and one that receives some support from what we know of early Greek thought, is that man was baffled by the fact that the world he knew seemed to be a combination of orderly and disorderly change. It was likely late in the development of human life, during the past few tens of thousands of man's hundreds of thousands of years on the earth, that he recognized the presence of regularities in the processes of nature. The sequences of day and night and of the seasons were likely among the earliest of those to be noted. Much more recently the differences between the regularity of the apparent motion of the stars and irregularity of the apparent motion of the planets were noted.

Even today in many primitive cultures there is no idea of these regularities as in any way inherent in nature. Their occurrence is supposed to be contingent upon the proper measures being taken. It may be thought, for example, that if the appropriate ceremonies are not performed the sun will fail to appear. There are also people in the most highly civilized cultures who pray for rain in time of drouth and for the cessation of rain in time of floods.

The early conceptions of natural regularities considered them as somehow imposed upon an original disorder or chaos. Primitive creation stories emphasize the primordial chaos and always have some agency or divine power which brings order into the original disorder. The same approach is reflected in some of the early Greek philosophies of nature, particularly in the pre-Socratic physicists. Even in Plato's creation myth the Demiurge imposes order upon an original disorder:

> Desiring, then, that all things should be good and, so far as might be, nothing imperfect, the god took over all that is visible—not at rest, but in discordant and unordered motion—and brought it from disorder into order, since he judged that order was in every way the better.[8]

It is quite probable that early concepts of physical law were constructed on the model of civil law, for society achieved a considerable degree of order long before men were able to think of an order of nature. It would be a plausible conjecture that they were able to think of nature as orderly only because they had the experience of order in society. So the early ideas of physical law were likely projections of ideas of civil law. Anaximander is reported to have said, for example, that limits are placed upon the encroachment

---

[8] *The Timaeus*, 30A, translated by Francis M. Cornford in *Plato's Cosmology* (London, Routledge and Kegan Paul, Ltd., 1937), p. 33.

of opposites upon one another, because unlimited encroachment would be unjust.

The parallel between men's ideas of nature and the social order as constructed by custom and legislation is admirably developed by Professor Robert Scoon. The early law codes, he points out, were intended "to facilitate a readjustment *after* the normal order had been disturbed." So also the early philosophers began their thinking with "the apparent conflicts between natural elements, such as heat and cold, or winter and summer." Just as the concern of society is a restoration of order, so the working of nature was similarly conceived:

> The first philosophers had observed that in this ostensible confusion there were traces of regular activity, which they undertook to explain. But instead of developing the idea of a determined sequence of events or mechanical causation, they kept the apparent strife and introduced regularity in the form of an *ex post facto* readjustment. . . . Regularity . . . was a retroactive justice, a compensation for previous irregularity by subsequent irregularity in the opposite direction.[9]

The central problem of early Greek philosophy was the problem of reconciling change and permanence. How can the same thing undergo change? If it changes, it is not the same; if it is to remain the same, it cannot change. This, of course, is the basic version of the problem of the relation of order and disorder. The idea of order is the idea of an arrangement that does not change, or else a change which in a sense remains the same. In the latter case, change occurs but the same sequence is repeated. The sun is never in the same position in any two successive periods of the day or week or month, but its motion apparently is repeated over and over again always in the same sequence. Every year that series of motions takes place. So we have change with an unchanging pattern. But how can the same sun be in different places? How can the same plant go through different phases of growth? These are more fundamental questions, and these were the questions with which philosophy and science began.

There are two obvious directions in which an answer to this more fundamental question may be sought. We may take perma-

---

[9] Robert Scoon, *Greek Philosophy Before Plato* (Princeton, Princeton University Press, 1928), pp. 18-19. By permission.

nence as basic and try to explain the appearance of change, or we may take change as basic and try to explain the appearance of permanence. Anaximenes, for example, thought that the apparent change of one thing into another was only a matter of change of density. A more dense element such as water becomes air by rarefaction, while air becomes water by condensation. Such changes can be directly observed when water boils and turns into steam, and when steam condenses. Springs of water in the ground might also be understood as the transformation of earth into water, and the accumulation of silt in the mouth of a river as the change of water into earth. In contrast to this approach, we may take change as basic and regard the apparently permanent as only a special case of change. Heraclitus, for example, declared that all things change and that nothing ever remains the same. The apparently permanent is never a case of something unchanging; it is rather a more or less temporary balance of forces.

The main trend of early Greek thought was in favor of the permanent as basic and change as either illusory or as something to be explained in terms of the permanent. The final outcome of this line of speculation was reached by the Greek Atomists. They held that the world is composed of a plurality of minute, invisible, indivisible particles which are in constant motion. These particles, the atoms, differ in size and shape. They have no weight, and so they may be said to have nothing but quantitative characteristics. The things we perceive in our world are really intricate combinations of these atomic particles. The coming to be of familiar things is a process by which many atoms form temporary clusters, and the destruction of the things we perceive is only the separation of the atoms as the clusters break apart. The only actual change is a change of location, or motion in space. Since the atom is affected neither by its motion nor by its location, there is some question concerning the sense in which we can say that change of any kind can really occur in such a scheme. Nothing ever alters the atoms themselves or the space in which they move, and these are the only realities. On the other hand, there is motion; but if every part of space is identical with every other part, can we say that the motion of atoms is any kind of change?

As we shall now see, early modern physics accepted the main features of the Greek atomic theory's reconciliation of permanence and change. The revolution in modern physics of the past half-century occurred with the discovery that those traditional concepts provide an inadequate foundation for our understanding of the processes of nature.

EARLY MODERN PHYSICS

The physical theories developed by such scientists as Galileo and Newton were, in general, in the framework of Greek Atomism.[10]   Although Greek Atomism was entirely speculative, the physics of Galileo and Newton which developed within that speculative framework was genuinely scientific. Atomism itself, as the underlying theory, was not subjected to scientific investigation. Atomism continued to be generally taken for granted by physicists until they reached the point where the results of scientific inquiry came into clear conflict with the underlying assumptions of that theoretical scheme. A new conceptual structure then had to be developed, and in its basic features this was the work of Einstein, Planck, Fermi, Bohr, Heisenberg, Schrödinger, and others.

In spite of the radical revolution which has occurred in recent physics, the older scheme is still used in those cases where it is applicable. The scientist's willingness to make limited use of a general conceptual structure in spite of the fact that he recognizes it to be in conflict with other areas of knowledge is a trait which often puzzles the nonscientist. For some time, for example, two apparently conflicting theories have been used as conceptual schemes in understanding different sets of facts concerning light. Even today parts of the pre-Copernican astronomy are still useful in navigation.

Since change is what makes things unpredictable and interferes with our understanding of them, the obvious remedy is to eliminate change. We cannot simply deny change, but we may be able to put it where it will make the least trouble. So the strategy of early modern physics was (1) to reduce all the apparently different kinds of change to one kind, motion in space, and (2) to remove matter from the influence of change. The latter was done by postulating the homogeneity of space, by reducing all matter to mass and its qualities to quantity.

Out of this came what Professor Philip Wheelwright calls "the

[10] See E. A. Burtt, *The Metaphysical Foundations of Modern Science* (Garden City, N. Y., Doubleday and Company, Inc., 1955), pp. 86-87, 231.

classical kinetic theory of nature." This theory is based upon the following principles:

(1) *The kinetic postulate:* Every occurrence can be described in its essentials in terms of matter and motion. Matter means no more than that (whatever it is) which moves.

(2) *The postulate of telic neutrality:* An explanation of whatever occurs should be given without reference to telic categories—i. e., with reference neither to a tendency inherent in the process itself (an "entelechy"), nor to a cosmic mind or purpose, nor to effective values. . . .

(3) *The causal postulate:* Every occurrence takes place according to strict causal law—i. e., as strictly determined by some set of previous occurrences.

(4) *The postulate of conservation:* Something remains constant amidst change—whether it be conceived as matter, mass, energy, or certain physical relations.

(5) *The quantitative postulate:* All significant differences can eventually be described in quantitative, and therefore potentially measurable terms.

(6) *The postulate of logical economy* ("law of parsimony"): Of two explanations, both of which do justice to the observed facts, the logically simpler one is to be preferred.[11]

It is important to note that none of these is a statement of fact which can be checked by observation. To say that "every occurrence can be described in its essentials in terms of matter and motion" is not to make a generalization from observations. It means that if there are processes not explainable in terms of matter and motion those processes are excluded from the physicist's "nature." These principles are stipulations which defined the conditions and objects of inquiry for physics. The important question is not their "truth" or "falsity" but their usefulness as organizing principles. When phenomena which had been understood in terms of these principles showed themselves on further inquiry to be incompatible with these principles, new organizing principles had to be found.

The beginning of the end of the usefulness of the traditional scheme of thought as the basic conceptual scheme of physical science came with the study of electromagnetic phenomena. Efforts were made to adapt the mechanical concepts and modes of explanation which had been used so successfully in physics in the middle of

[11] *The Way of Philosophy*, Revised Edition (New York, The Odyssey Press, 1960), p. 102. By permission.

the nineteenth century. Even Clerk Maxwell, whose contributions to the field of electromagnetic phenomena were to be so significant, first attempted to understand electrical and magnetic forces in terms of mechanical models.

> Lines of force, Maxwell supposed, were tubes of ether rotating on their axes. The centrifugal force of such rotations caused the tubes to expand sideways and contract lengthways. . . . But two neighbouring tubes, rotating in the same sense, would move in opposite directions at the points where they touched, a conception which was not feasible mechanically. Maxwell supposed therefore that there were layers of particles between the tubes of ether, the particles rotating in a direction opposite to that of the tubes, like ball bearings or idling wheels. If all the tubes of ether rotated at the same speed, the particles would not change their positions, but if not, a given particle would move linearly with a speed which would be the mean of the circumferential velocities of the tubes on either side. . . . Maxwell considered that the particles were electrical in character, and he thought therefore that such a motion of the particles would constitute an electric current.[12]

Maxwell's own important contributions to the physics of electricity and magnetism came only as he abandoned the attempt to construct explanations in terms of mechanical models. He concentrated rather upon mathematical equations and their application to optical phenomena.[13] The experimental verification of such principles on a wider basis waited upon the perfection of instruments and techniques for the extension of observation far beyond the range of anything yet achieved at that time. With the development of instruments for the investigation of submicroscopic processes, the production of high velocities, precise measurements of very small intervals, and the exploration of vast regions of space, many traditional concepts were found to be no longer applicable. They are still useful for the study of phenomena within the range of ordinary observation upon the surface of the earth, but not in the study of the very small or the very large. Thus some of the principles of traditional physical science have been shown quite conclusively not to be typically characteristic of our cosmos. They are relevant only to a very limited range of the physical processes with which we are now acquainted.

[12] S. F. Mason, *Main Currents of Scientific Thought* (New York, Abelard-Schuman, 1953), pp. 390-91.
[13] *Ibid*, p. 371.

THE REVOLUTION IN PHYSICS

According to the principles of traditional physics all processes are theoretically reversible. If change is motion and if space is homogeneous, there is no sequence of motions more privileged than any other. In the study of heat exchange, however, it was found that this process had to be treated as irreversible. It seemed difficult even to imagine that if two bodies differing in temperature were placed close together the heat of the cooler body would pass from it to the warmer. As was noted in an earlier chapter, the problem of heat was a puzzling one for early modern physics. The field of thermodynamics developed certain postulates of its own, and not all of them could be brought into harmony with the basic assumptions of physics.

This was recognized by Fourier who contended, early in the nineteenth century, that the study of heat was a field distinct from mechanics:

> But whatever may be the range of mechanical theories, they do not apply to the effects of heat. These make up a special order of phenomena, which cannot be explained by the principles of motion and equilibrium.[14]

In his *Main Currents of Scientific Thought*, Mason comments:

> The second law of thermodynamics and its molecular interpretation gave a physical meaning and a direction to the passage of time which had been lacking hitherto in the Newtonian system of mechanics. In principle the mechanics of the Newtonian world were reversible. A cannonball theoretically could rebound on striking a target and retrace its path back to the cannon from which it came. According to the second law of thermodynamics, such an eventuality was quite impossible. The orderly, undirectional motion of the projectile would be continuously transformed by the frictional resistance of the air into heat, that is, into the random, disorderly motions of the molecules of the air and the projectile, and finally all vestiges of the orderly linear motion would be destroyed when the projectile reached its target, the orderly motion being transformed into the random thermal motions of the projectile and its target. Such changes were irreversible:

[14] Joseph Fourier, *The Analytical Theory of Heat*, translated by Alexander Freeman (Cambridge, Cambridge University Press, 1878), p. 2.

mechanical energy was permanently lost to the world when it was transformed into heat, and when the heat was dispersed.[15]

This is the concept of entropy, and with the study of atomic and subatomic processes in recent physics it has been found necessary to extend the concept of entropy. The result has been the formulation of two largely speculative theories concerning the cosmic process as a whole. There are those who hold to a "continuous creation" theory and those who defend an "evolutionary" concept of the cosmos. We can do no better than to quote Milton K. Munitz's description of these two views:

> In the arguments offered by Bondi, Sciama, and Hoyle, who are among the chief protagonists of the "continuous creation" theory, we find the universe assigned an infinite time-scale. In its gross features, the universe is thought of as being ever the same, no matter at what point in time it is considered or from whatever station in space it is viewed. Matter, it is claimed, is created continuously in elementary form. It is out of such randomly produced particles that eventually agglomerations of matter of the size of galaxies and clusters of galaxies come to be formed. While the continuing expansion of the universe removes some galaxies from our range of observability, other newly-formed systems come to take their place and thus help to keep the universe in a "steady-state."
>
> In opposition to this view are those who favor an "evolutionary" world picture, like Lemaître or Gamow. They would account for the variety of observational facts . . . in terms of a universe that "originated" at some finite epoch in the past. The event which marked such an origin is pictured as both cataclysmic in its proportions and unique in the thermonuclear and other physical conditions which it possessed. It is from such a beginning, conceived as a "Primeval Atom" by Lemaître and as an extremely compressed state of matter called "ylem" by Gamow, that the present constitution of the universe is taken as having evolved.[16]

In Newtonian physics the processes of the physical universe, the various motions of matter, were understood as having conti-

[15] Mason, *op. cit.*, p. 402.

[16] *Theories of the Universe*, edited by Milton K. Munitz (Glencoe, Illinois, The Free Press, and New York, The Falcon's Wing Press, 1957), p. 274. By permission. See the following essays in this volume: George Gamow, "Modern Cosmology," pp. 390-404; Hermann Bondi, "Theories of Cosmology," pp. 405-12; D. W. Sciama, "Evolutionary Processes in Cosmology," pp. 413-18; and Fred Hoyle, "Continuous Creation and the Expanding Universe," pp. 419-29.

nuity in their variations of direction and velocity and as taking place in the framework of an absolute space and an absolute time. If any object changed the rate of its motion, it would have to pass through all intermediate velocities from the lower to the higher, and if, remaining in motion, it changed direction it would have to pass through all directions from the earlier to the later. All actual measurements of motion were relative, for the rate and duration of one motion could be measured only against some other motion. The one conceivable exception to this would be the measurement of motion against absolute space and in terms of absolute time. But since we have no access to absolute space and time in our experience, this exception did not modify the relativity of motion so far as physics was concerned. Newtonian physics had no finite absolutes that were accessible to observation.

Maxwell's equations opened the way for what may be described as a new science of physics side by side with the traditional mechanical physics. "From X rays to radio waves, including the visible waves of light," comments Leopold Infeld, "all this rich and wide world of radiation is governed by field laws which seem to have little in common with the mechanical view." [17] Infeld points out that the earlier physics would have rejected the idea that radiation cannot be understood in mechanical terms.

> No orthodox physicist of the nineteenth century would have agreed with such an interpretation. The idea of two different physics, two alternative modes of thought, would have been unacceptable to him. He would have insisted that the field view is not essentially different from the mechanical view and that a consistent and completely satisfactory mechanical explanation could be found for electromagnetic phenomena.[18]

Such a hope, however, would fail for the reason that a mechanical explanation of electromagnetic phenomena would require a material medium through which electromagnetic waves are propagated. The absence of a material medium for the propagation of electromagnetic waves "is precisely the characteristic feature that distinguishes them from any other waves." [19]

New theories of light have introduced two finite absolutes into

[17] *Albert Einstein* (New York, Charles Scribner's Sons, 1950), p. 12. By permission.
[18] *Ibid.*
[19] *Ibid*, p. 13.

physics. It has been found that the energy of radiation varies in discontinuous amounts or *quanta*. This is contrary to the principles of the earlier physics which hold that all physical variations are continuous. Although quanta vary in size, depending on the wave length of the radiation emitted or absorbed, the quantum of energy which belongs to a specific wave length of radiation is a multiple of the speed of light divided by that wave length, and Planck's constant, *h*, which is 0. 000 000 000 000 000 000 000 000 006 55. This minute quantity may be considered the minimal absolute of the physical world.[20]

The other absolute, in contrast with the minimal absolute, is a maximal absolute. Light has been found to have an absolute velocity of approximately 186,284 miles per second. Unlike other velocities, which are relative to the motion of the observer, the velocity of light is the same no matter what is the state of motion of its source or of the observer. An automobile that travels sixty miles per hour over the highway is traveling only twenty miles per hour with reference to another automobile traveling forty miles per hour. The same automobile would be going at the rate of one hundred miles per hour relative to a third car moving in the opposite direction at forty miles per hour. The velocity of light, however, is the same no matter what is the velocity of its source.

The recognition that we depend on signals, such as light, in our observation of the motion of bodies led to the conclusion that space and time cannot be treated as separate. To locate a body, we need not only its space coordinates but a time coordinate as well. Further, the time intervals between events vary with the motion of the observer. Signal A may be earlier than signal B to one observer, and B earlier than A to another. No meaning can be given to the question of what the "real" or "true" interval is in itself, apart from its relation to some other physical event.

Two consequences of the new concepts of physics help to bring out the significant contrast between the newer and the earlier physics. These are: (1) that the mass of a body increases with increase in velocity so that the mass approaches infinity as the velocity approaches that of light, and (2) that kinetic energy itself has mass. Thus the separation of mass and energy in the traditional physics has been superseded by the discovery that mass and energy

[20] For a helpful elementary and non-technical exposition of some quantum theory concepts, see Infeld, *op. cit.*, pp. 100-01.

are convertible. Mass may be understood as a special case of energy, as a condition of internal stability or equilibrium of physical forces. In the fission of an atom this internal equilibrium is upset and a part of the energy which had been held in equilibrium is suddenly released.

One of the important implications of the new physics for philosophy is the inescapable conclusion that the physical world is a dynamic order. Nothing in it is static. The apparent permanence or endurance of a physical substance is a more or less temporary equilibrium of enormous physical forces. The whole cosmic scene may be understood as an almost incredibly complex event, a vast space-time panorama of interacting forces which, in their interaction, achieve many different states and orders of temporary equilibrium. In a sense the world of Heraclitus, where everything flows and where we cannot step into the same river twice, has replaced the world of the Atomists, where a plurality of absolute physical particles are in motion in empty space.

THE PROBLEM OF UNDERSTANDING THE PHYSICAL WORLD

The revolutionary concepts of the new physics bring us back again to a problem considered in an earlier chapter, the problem of the relation of the world as understood by physics to the world of ordinary experience. Which "picture" of the world is the true one? So long as we stay within the conceptual framework of classical physics we are able to construct imaginary models of physical structures and processes. Such models aid greatly our understanding of the processes they represent. To some extent the model reproduces the relationships being studied, and the accessibility of the model makes it possible to study those relations in detail. These models are constructed from the materials of ordinary experience, and it requires only a certain ingenuity to adapt those materials to the needs of the model. We also use diagrams and maps for the same purpose, to isolate and present for direct examination the structures and relationships of physical processes.

The new physics, however, has gone beyond the limits of the models we can construct from the materials of ordinary experience. The intelligibility of basic physical processes, as we understand those processes today, is not so much mechanical as mathematical. We can no longer treat a model as in any sense a picture or a representation, and physicists have had to learn to think their objects without the aid of pictures or models. Actually the models of the classical physics were no more pictures than were the mathematical equations which those models exemplified geometrically. The temptation to treat models as if they were pictures was one source of the idea that there is a conflict between the scientific and the common-sense views of the world. The new physics is too complex to use the familiar geometry of the space of ordinary experience, and this has the advantage of removing the tendency to take the model for the reality.

The question of which is the true view of the world, the common-sense view or the physicist's picture, now appears in a new light. For it is apparent that the physicist no longer has a picture to compete with the common-sense view. The two are not opposing alternatives but complementaries. The world as we find it in ordinary experience is that perspective of the real world which is relevant to our existence as living organisms in physical, psychological, and social interaction with our environment. In physics we discover this same world, but from a quite different perspective. The perspective here is intellectual and conceptual; we discover something of the intelligible order of the physical world. To dissolve the world of perception into scientific concepts and to try to interpret the physicist's concepts in terms of our direct experience are equally erroneous approaches. Certainly the physicist must take the world of ordinary experience seriously.

The modern physicist and anyone who would understand what he is up to [says Dr. Condon], must therefore learn to work in two worlds. One is a world of brass and glass and wax and mercury and coils and lenses and vacuum pumps—above all a world of electronic amplifiers and photo-multiplier tubes. The other is a world of visualization and creative imagination, dealing with concepts and constructs appropriate to atomic dimensions (or, in cosmology, to a domain too vast to be encompassed by direct human perception).[21]

It is also a mistake to try to interpret scientific concepts in terms of the objects of ordinary experience. For scientific concepts

[21] Edward U. Condon, "Physics," in *What Is Science?* edited by James R. Newman (Copyright 1955, by James R. Newman), p. 105. Reprinted by permission of Simon and Schuster, Inc., New York.

are not formed merely by ordinary abstraction; they involve the complex mathematical constructs which are necessary in order to expose to our understanding the underlying intelligible structure of physical existence. But this is a logical intelligibility, not perceptual.

As our mental eye penetrates into smaller and smaller distances and shorter and shorter times [comments Erwin Schrödinger], we find nature behaving so entirely differently from what we observe in visible and palpable bodies of our surroundings that *no* model shaped after our large-scale experiences can ever be "true." A completely satisfactory model *of this type* is not only practically inaccessible, but not even thinkable. Or, to be precise, we can, of course, think it, but however we think it, it is wrong; not perhaps quite as meaningless as a "triangular circle," but much more so than a "winged lion." [22]

It betrays misunderstanding to ask whether a table top is a smooth, level, hard, continuous surface or whether it is a dynamic structure of molecules, atoms, and subatomic particles. For it is in terms of these dynamic structures that we account for the smooth, hard, continuous table top of ordinary experience. This is not to say that things are simply what we perceive them to be. They *are* what we perceive them to be, but they are not *merely* what we perceive them to be. Things are also what we conceive them to be when we think in terms of the concepts of physical science. We cannot understand our physical world in terms solely of what appears to ordinary experience. We discover what these things "really" are, or at least a part of what they really are, only when we understand their appearances in terms of the mathematical relationships which account for those appearances, that is, which make those appearances intelligible.

When we go from ordinary experience to scientific explanation we neither deny nor abandon the first in favor of the second. As Whitehead has said,

science is rooted in . . . the whole apparatus of common-sense thought. That is the *datum* from which it starts, and to which it must recur. . . . You may polish up commonsense, you may contradict in detail, you may surprise it. But ultimately your whole task is to satisfy it.[23]

[22] *Science and Humanism* (Cambridge, Cambridge University Press, 1952), pp. 25-26.

[23] A. N. Whitehead, *Aims of Education* (New York, The Macmillan Company, 1929), pp. 159-60. By permission.

SUMMARY

The world of common sense is a world of substances, qualities, relations; of space and time and causality; of means and ends, purposes, and values. Much of the history of philosophy is an account of attempts to deal with the problems which arise from these categories. Common-sense concepts are deeply rooted in our language, and although our language predisposes us to think in terms of these categories we need not conclude that such a mode of thought has no other foundation. The persistence of these categories and their continued use wherever we are dealing with our world at the perceptual level, in spite of the radical changes which have occurred in scientific theory, suggest that common-sense categories express something which is profoundly true of the real world.

Progress in scientific understanding leads to apparent conflicts with common sense, and many of the details and assumptions of common sense are shown to be false. The theoretical study of nature, from prescientific speculation through the Newtonian scheme to the revolutionary theories of the present century, has required many readjustments of our common-sense ideas. This raises anew the problem of just in what terms we are to understand the physical world.

Common sense and science are not mutually exclusive alternatives between which we are forced to choose. They are rather two different perspectives which are not only complementary but also have a continuity. Scientific understanding begins with common sense, and in his work a scientist constantly assumes the soundness of the common-sense interpretation of the world and uses its categories in dealing with the world as it confronts him in perception. It is from the world of ordinary experience that the problems of science arise, and it is that same world which scientific inquiry seeks to understand. But scientific understanding is conceptual, not perceptual; and as it is a mistake to try to replace the perceptual with the conceptual, it is equally in error to try to grasp the conceptual schemes of scientific thought in terms of perceptual models.

Questions for Study and Discussion

1. *Terms:* energy, entropy, kinetic, mass, mind, physical, purpose, telic.

2. Compare "house" and "thing," with respect to their functions as words. We know the nature of what we refer to when we talk about a "house." Is this in any sense the case when we use "thing"? What is "thing" the name of? Or is "thing" a word which has only a language function, such as the word "of."

3. Illustrate the influence of language in the control of attention.

4. Is there any way you might express the differences between past, present, and future without using differences in tense?

5. (a) We encounter such expressions as "the language of science," and "the language of mathematics." Are these references to different languages or to special vocabularies?

   (b) Ordinary language uses the subject-predicate relation; mathematics uses equations and functions. Does this mean that mathematics has a different grammar or syntax?

6. If common sense and scientific knowledge are cases of knowledge of the same world from different perspectives, what kind of knowledge is the knowledge that this is the case?

7. Does "exist" have the same meaning in the following statements:

   (a) Houses exist.
   (b) Elections exist.
   (c) Space-time exists.
   (d) Triangles exist.

8. Are diagrams and models of molecular and atomic structures partial pictures or are they only ways of denoting certain mathematical relationships? What difference does it make?

CHAPTER 9

The
Nature
of
Life

BIOLOGY AS A CHALLENGE TO THEOLOGY

In contrast with the bitter disputes aroused by the new astronomy, early modern physics developed without much excitement or popular interest. Its achievements were expressed in mathematical formulas and in gradual improvements in technology. When significant progress began to appear in the study of living organisms, however, conflicts with traditional ways of thinking came into the open. Just as the Hebrew-Christian sacred writings and theology had been widely accepted in Western culture as authoritative concerning such scientific questions as the origin of the earth and of life and of man, so the new achievements in the sciences, especially in geology and biology, were looked upon as definitive refutations of the Biblical view.

Nearly a century ago, for example, Thomas Huxley was defending the theory of evolution in public lectures and debates against the attacks not only of prominent clergymen but of noted scientists as well. He saw the concept of evolution as a victory for the scientific spirit over traditional modes of thought:

> . . . the longer I live and the more I learn the more hopeless to my mind becomes the contradiction between the theory of the universe as understood and expounded by Jewish and Christian theologians, and the theory of the universe which is every day and every year growing out of the application of scientific methods to its phenomena.
>
> Whether astronomy and geology can or cannot be made to agree with the statements as to the matters of fact laid down in Genesis—whether the Gospels are historically true or not—are matters of comparatively small amount in the face of the impassable gulf between the anthropomorphism (however refined) of theology and the passionless impersonality of the unknown and unknowable which science shows everywhere underlying the thin veil of phenomena.[1]

As late as the 1920's an American state legislature passed a bill forbidding the teaching of evolution in the public schools of the state. In one of the public spectacles of that period William Jennings Bryan and Clarence Darrow clashed in debate at the trial of a young high school science instructor charged with teaching evolution. Perhaps it was a symptom of the confusion with which the relations of science and religion have so long been clouded that the supposed interests of religion were represented by a professional politician who knew nothing of theology or of the serious and responsible work which had been done in the critical study of the Bible by devout Jewish and Christian scholars. Nor was it a contribution to clarification that the supposed interests of science were represented by a lawyer whose reputation rested upon skills and intellectual processes completely foreign to the scientific mind, that is, upon the ability to identify himself emotionally with the cause he was defending and to induce such identification in judges and juries.

It is easy to look back with a smug feeling of superiority and amused condescension at the debates between Thomas Huxley and Bishop Wilberforce in England and between Clarence Darrow and William Jennings Bryan in America. Many of us pride ourselves on a more sophisticated understanding of both science and religion. But the kind of confusion which makes the evolution debates seem

[1] Leonard Huxley, *Life and Letters of Thomas Henry Huxley*, Second Edition (London, Macmillan and Company, Ltd., 1913), Volume I, pp. 344-45. By permission.

so silly to us today is a kind of confusion which still shows itself in other forms in contemporary thought. Over and over again, we see confusion concerning the kind of problems to which solutions are proposed, and we still find many attempts to deal with problems in one field by methods and evidence drawn from an entirely different field of study. If biological science and theology are distinct fields of study then the problems of one cannot be solved by the methods and data of the other. If a theologian appeals to evidence from biology in support of a theological thesis the soundness or unsoundness of his biological theory is subject entirely to biological tests of evidence. Likewise an attempt to use theology to support a biological hypothesis would require a theological test of truth. There can be no theological test of a biological theory or biological test of a theological theory. In so far as a supposed biological theory is subject to theological tests it is not biological but theological. In so far as a supposed theological theory is subject to biological tests it is not theology but biology.

This does not mean that one field of inquiry has no implications for another field of inquiry. What it does mean is that the question of the truth or falsity of the principles established in one field can be resolved only by work in that field itself. If a theologian finds his beliefs challenged by a biological theory, the conflict between biology and his theology is no evidence whatsoever that the biological theory is false. To discredit the biological theory he would have to do his work in biology. Nor can the biologist say that the truth of his theory shows the falsity of the theologian's position except to the extent that the theologian is confusing his theology with biology. To show the falsity of a theological position the biologist would have to do his work in theology.

What, then, is the significance of conflicts in the results of work done in different sciences and disciplines? There are, of course, different answers to this question in different circumstances. Often the apparent conflict comes from the kind of confusion we have already noted. But where the conflict is genuine it is a signal to be cautious about premature finalities, and it is an encouragement to workers in both areas to re-examine their evidence and reasoning. Conflicts cannot be resolved by fiat, nor by extending the authority of one discipline into the area of another. If they are not removed by work done in one or the other or both of the fields, in each case by the methods and with the evidence appropriate in that field, then those conflicts must be left standing as testimony that there is unfinished business.

As so often in the history of Western thought here, too, advances in one field led scholars in other fields to become more critical of their own assumptions, to re-examine their methods, and to consider more carefully just what questions properly belong to their own specialties. The impact of biological theories of evolution and of the physical basis of life came as a challenge to long accepted views in religion and theology. The progress of biology in the nineteenth century contributed nothing positive to the content of theology but it was one of the strongest influences in forcing the reconsideration of the methods and scope of theology which has taken place during the present century.

BIOLOGY AS A CHALLENGE TO POLITICAL THOUGHT

The impact of biology has been felt not only in religion but in politics and social theory as well. Social Darwinism, for example, has been a strong force in political thought and its effects have been felt widely in the world.[2] The ideology of Hitler's National Socialism rested on a theory of race which appealed to spurious and misinterpreted biological data. Any attempt to support political theories with biological evidence or to evaluate biological work on the basis of political tests is an example of the same kind of confusion which occurred in the conflicts between science and religion. It is obvious that no amount of scientific work or weight of scientific evidence could ever convince a Hitler that his political theory was wrong unless he were willing to evaluate that evidence in scientific terms and from the scientific perspective. The test of truth for Hitler's biology was an ideological test, and since he knew nothing of biology or of any other science he saw in this no incongruity.

Frequently a political or ideological position is defended by pseudoscientific arguments, and sometimes even competent scientists are so confused by these tactics that they prepare serious and

[2] For a study of the influence of the concept of social Darwinism in this country, see Richard Hofstadter, *Social Darwinism in American Thought* (Philadelphia, The University of Pennsylvania Press, 1945).

solemn scientific refutations. Not many years ago, for example, a great stir was made in Western scientific circles by "Lysenkoism" in Soviet Russia. Lysenko, a Soviet bureaucrat in charge of certain agricultural projects, had claimed success in experiments designed to oppose the generally accepted scientific theory of genetics. He published "evidence" supposed to demonstrate the inheritance of acquired characteristics. His views were endorsed by Stalin and were given official backing by the Soviet government, and Soviet biologists were forced into line with the Lysenko doctrine.

Some American biologists attempted to demonstrate the falsity of Lysenkoism by reviewing the scientific evidence and showing its conflicts with Lysenko's arguments. The point that some of these biologists missed was the fact that Lysenkoism was not a scientific theory at all. The evidence in its support was no more scientific than the "evidence" ordinarily presented by a candidate for Congress for or against foreign aid or high tariffs. Lysenkoism was a political doctrine, not a scientific one.[3] The issue was ideological, not a question of what the facts are. That the case for Lysenkoism was argued under the guise of a scientific hypothesis was simply a tactical movement in a far-reaching domestic political operation undertaken by Soviet rulers. Stalin and his associates had no interest in the question of the truth of Lysenko's doctrine; they were interested solely in what they wanted people to believe. They did not call for an independent investigation by competent geneticists under strict scientific controls but exercised their political authority to take the question completely out of the hands of the scientists.

Another influence of biological concepts on political thinking is found in the application of the idea of organism to the state. Seventeenth and eighteenth century political and economic theories tended to be mechanistic. Adam Smith, for example, conceived of society as composed of individuals as the primary units, related to each other externally in accordance with general laws which belong to the system as a whole and govern the action of each unit in the

[3] The political background of Lysenkoism was recognized in such articles as those by H. J. Muller, "The Destruction of Science in the USSR," and "Back to Barbarism—Scientifically," in *The Saturday Review of Literature* for December 4 and 11, 1948. See also C. D. Darlington, "A Revolution in Soviet Science," in *Discovery*, Volume 8, No. 2, February 1947, reprinted in *The Journal of Heredity*, Volume 38, No. 5, May 1947, pp. 143-48.

system. It is noteworthy that the concept of society as an organism was developed in the nineteenth century by those whose thinking in many instances had been influenced by the theory of organic evolution, while mechanistic theories of society were retained by those who, like Jeremy Bentham and James and John Stuart Mill, were little influenced by the concepts of biology.

Biological science does have political and social and educational implications. It would be very difficult, for example, for anyone acquainted with genetics to accept the idea of the inherent superiority of the descendants of some single remote ancestor. Educational or political discrimination against racial groups requires something other than a biological justification. But biology does not itself provide political principles any more than it provides religious and theological doctrines. A political theory is likely to be quite unsatisfactory in the long run if it rests its case on a false biology, but there is nothing in politics to provide any test of truth for biology.

BIOLOGY AS A CHALLENGE TO PHYSICS

The progress of the biological sciences has had its impact not only on religious and political ideas but also on the concept of science itself. The problem of the nature of life is more fundamental and more important than the issues debated by the evolutionists and their opponents or the political and ideological implications of a theory of genetics. The problem of the nature of life takes us into a basic question in the philosophy of science, for the advance of biological science presents a challenge to the very conception of scientific understanding and explanation which was developed under the influence of early modern physics.

Early modern physics had its foundation, and made most of its important advances, in the conceptual framework of mechanism. All physical action was understood in terms of the quantitative relations of material units in space, and this mechanistic scheme provided a fruitful approach to the scientific problems of that period. But living organisms seem, at least on superficial inspection, either to defy the laws of mechanics or to be beyond the reach of those laws. As a result, two extreme views appeared among those interested in the biological sciences. There were the mechanists who took the position that there is nothing in living organisms which cannot be understood in terms of the laws of physics and chemistry. Opposed to the mechanists were those who contended that living organisms do have certain characteristics which cannot be understood in physical and chemical terms but require us to recognize some non-physical principle of organization. Those who took this view were vitalists.

The challenge of vitalism was not only a challenge to mechanism in biology; it was also a challenge to the position of physics as the most adequate and successful expression of the idea of science. The vitalist contended that the methods and concepts of physics are not adequate for our understanding of nature, and in this he attacked the idea of the unity of science which had played so important a part in the development of modern thought. Mechanism upholds the ideal of a final explanation of all natural phenomena in physical-chemical terms; vitalism claims an exemption from the sovereignty of physical science in behalf of living organisms.

As we shall see more specifically in our study of mechanism and vitalism, these theories are not scientific hypotheses. The issues between them are not to be decided by scientific evidence. Mechanism and vitalism are rather conflicting positions which scientists take with respect to the import and significance of the scientific knowledge we have. The mechanist tends to accept as normative the information and conclusions obtained by the use of the methods of the physical sciences alone. The vitalist tends to take as normative the properties which seem to be distinctive of living organisms in contrast with physical systems. Mechanism and vitalism are also standpoints from which evidence is evaluated and which even, sometimes, influence the investigator in his selection of evidence. They are philosophical theories, and the issues between them turn not on what the observed facts *are* but on the question of what those facts *mean*.

From biology came a challenge to physics much more serious than that of vitalism. This was the theory of evolution, formulated by Darwin as a scientific hypothesis and supported by scientifically controlled observation and experiment. Although the implications of the concept of evolution for traditional mechanism were slow to be recognized, they gradually modified the scientific outlook. Eventually the challenge of biology to physics resulted in a victory for biology, in the sense that certain basic concepts of the new physics show the influence of the biological concept of organism.

We shall now examine the issue between mechanism and vitalism, the two sharply opposed theories of the nature of the life process which were formulated as interpretations of earlier scientific work in biology. This will lead us into consideration of some of the implications for this problem of the concept of evolution.

MECHANISM

The term "mechanism" suggests that structures and processes in nature can be understood best if we think of them on the model of a machine. The physics and astronomy of Galileo and Newton are prime examples of mechanistic thinking. We shall look first at some of the apparent differences between a machine and a living organism in order to see the distinctive features of a mechanism. We shall then see how the mechanist attempts to understand the apparently non-mechanical characteristics of a living organism.

Perhaps the first difference we think of in comparing an organism with a machine is that the organism seems to be self-starting and self-moving, while the machine has to be put into motion from the outside. The machine can be kept going only by supplying it with some kind of fuel or energy from the outside. In a sense this is true of the organism also, for it obtains energy from food, the atmosphere, and the sun. But there is a significant difference at this point between organism and machine. The energy the organism obtains from outside itself is not available to it and effective in its activity until that material has been, as we say, assimilated. The food and other energy upon which the organism subsists must be transformed so that it enters into the very chemical structure of the cells of the organism. The energy that makes a machine go, on the other hand, does not itself become a part of the machine. Gasoline is vaporized, drawn into the cylinders of a gasoline engine, and exploded by a spark. The force of these explosions moves the pistons. The product of the exploded fuel is expelled from the cylinders and new fuel takes its place. At no point does the fuel need to become a part of the motor in order to do its work.

Since a machine uses its energy source without incorporating that energy into its own structure, the parts of the machine are not changed in the course of their work except by such mechanical effects as wear and corrosion. *A machine is thus a complex structure whose parts are linked together externally and remain the same whether within the structure or removed from it.* The parts of two engines of the same design are interchangeable, and a piston or connecting-rod has the same shape and the same physical properties whether it is connected with other parts in a motor or lying by itself on the work-bench. A human arm, however, is no longer an arm after it is amputated from the body, for it can exist and function as an arm only as it is linked with the rest of the organism by way of skeleton, blood vessels, and nerve connections.

> Classical mechanism [says Karl W. Deutsch] implied the notion of a whole which was completely equal to the sum of its parts; which could be run in reverse; and which would behave in exactly identical fashion no matter how often those parts were disassembled and put together again, and irrespective of the sequence in which the disassembling or re-assembling would take place. It thus implied the notion that the parts were never significantly modified by each other, nor by their own past, and that each part once placed into its appropriate position, with its appropriate momentum, would stay exactly there and continue to fulfill its completely and uniquely determined function. . . . [The concept of mechanism excludes] the notions of irreversible change, of growth, of evolution, of novelty, and of purpose.[4]

The mechanist's answer to this difficulty is to point out that our account of the organism is too superficial. When we look at the organism as a whole it does seem to differ from a machine in the way in which it makes use of the energy available to it. But the scientific approach requires that we consider the organism analytically and look at the basic processes that constitute its life activity. If we study the chemical processes of nutrition at the level of molecular activity we may find that the machine model is quite adequate and that the difference is not between the mechanical and non-mechanical but between the mechanical at the macroscopic level and the mechanical at the microscopic or submicroscopic level.

If the molecular or atomic components of the organism are the same whether they are parts of the organism or not, then even if the organism does not resemble a machine on the macroscopic level

[4] "Mechanism, Teleology, and Mind," *Philosophy and Phenomenological Research*, Volume XII, No. 2, December 1951, p. 187. For a listing of the common characteristics of living beings and a discussion of the question of what is distinctive about them, see Warder Clyde Allee, "Biology," in *What Is Science?* edited by James R. Newman (New York, Simon and Schuster, 1955), pp. 235-36.

it is a mechanism on the microscopic or sub-microscopic level. All kinds of machines, macroscopic and microscopic and sub-microscopic, are rendered intelligible in structure and operation when we discover their unit parts and understand the relations which link these parts to each other in a single operating structure. The only significant differences between these different machines are differences of design and of complexity. The mechanist believes that eventually even the most mysterious functions of living organisms —assimilation, response to stimulation, integration of behavior, reproduction with genetic continuities—will be understood in terms of basic physical and chemical reactions. Nearly fifty years ago Jacques Loeb, the noted physiologist, wrote:

> In spite of the gulf which separates us today from such an aim I believe that it is attainable. As long as a life phenomenon has not yet found a physico-chemical explanation it usually appears inexplicable. If the veil is once lifted we are always surprised that we did not guess from the first what was behind it.[5]

The mechanistic concept is particularly useful and agreeable to the scientific enterprise on two counts. In the first place, it fits so well the analytic emphasis in scientific inquiry. As Deutsch points out:

> To this mechanical model corresponded a characteristic analytic method: to seek a set of simple, unchanging elements acting by simple unchanging laws. Such simple elements were discovered as atoms, corpuscles, or waves in physics; as molecules and elements in chemistry; as "economic men" in economics; and as "increments of pain or pleasure" in the ethics and philosophy of Jeremy Bentham.[6]

The mechanist has no qualms about studying even the most minute parts of a mechanism in isolation from other parts; for, on his view, to isolate a part is not to change it, provided analysis has been carried far enough. Furthermore it is an obvious advantage to be able to concentrate on a restricted area and to specialize in the study of different parts and functions without reference to their relations with the rest of the structure.

The second advantage of mechanism is that the concept of a complex structure as composed of units externally related to each

---

[5] *The Mechanistic Conception of Life* (Chicago, The University of Chicago Press, 1912), p. 26.

[6] Deutsch, *op. cit.*, p. 188.

other makes possible the most direct application of basic and elementary mathematical calculations to that structure. Arithmetic and algebra provide us with the relations of abstract units, and geometry provides the abstract space in terms of which we can understand external relations. A mechanical design is an exercise in applied geometry, and a machine is made by shaping matter in accordance with mathematical specifications.

MECHANISM AS A PHILOSOPHY

Mechanism is not a scientific hypothesis, open to verification or refutation by scientific investigation. Mechanism is rather for many both a point of view under the control of which scientific investigation is undertaken and that which gives meaning to the results of scientific investigation. This was expressed some thirty years ago by a great American scientist, C. Judson Herrick: "Natural science is mechanistic by definition. We naturalists are investigating natural mechanisms and what they do, how they run, and what they make." [7]

What if the facts do not seem to fit the theory of mechanism? Herrick answers this objection not with scientific evidence but by *stipulating* mechanism as the only point of view from which a scientific study of nature can be undertaken. This position, of course, cannot be the result of scientific investigation, for according to Herrick no investigation would be a scientific study of nature if it were not mechanistic. So, if the facts do not seem to fit the concept of mechanism, revise the concept. The only other alternative he saw is to relegate the facts to the realm of the supernatural, and this is to remove them from the field of scientific study:

Now, when our experience with nature—including human nature —is enlarged to include events that do not fit into our traditional mechanistic scheme of things, some of us are content with an appeal to a supernatural, that is, non-mechanistic, realm to help us out, but others of us feel that possibly there is something wrong with our ideas of mechanism in general.[8]

[7] "Mechanism and Organism," *The Journal of Philosophy*, Volume XXVI, No. 22, October 24, 1929, p. 592.
[8] *Ibid.*

In the latter case, says Herrick, we are not to abandon mechanism but to revise it. Mechanism is "by definition" the point of view of natural science.

Thus, for Herrick, mechanism is not something open to question except on the part of those who have an inadequate understanding either of the concept of mechanism or of natural science. No conceivable fact could possibly invalidate the theory of mechanism, for if any fact seems to do so then that fact either is not a natural fact at all or else it is mechanistic in a way that we do not yet understand. Whether this is a good philosophical argument or not, it is a philosophical argument. Its only defense is a rational defense; it is an appeal to what *must* be true, not to what we find to be the case when we examine the objects of nature. "Mechanistic by definition" means mechanistic by stipulation.

Once it is admitted that the concept of mechanism may be subject to revision, we must ask just what the concept of mechanism is. What is essential in it, that differentiates it *as mechanism* in all its various forms? For example, Herrick admits that the traditional concept is inadequate.

> The behavior of electrons and quanta of energy does not conform with the traditional concept of mechanism. . . . Yet this behavior is not capricious or lawless; if it were, it would not submit to the very elaborate mathematical treatment which is our best way of investigating it.[9]

Herrick says that he has a conception of mechanism "that embraces all that is recorded in classical mechanics and a great deal more."[10] What he means by a "mechanism" in the broader sense which he proposes for the term, seems to be a system of events in which each event is in causal relation with preceding and succeeding events. For example, in arguing that mental activities are mechanistic he says:

> The mental components are effective factors in the control of the course of events because they are real results of preceding natural events and real causes of the succeeding events. They are effective naturally because they are not disembodied epiphenomena or parallel phenomena, but vital functions of very substantial physical organs. They are, accordingly, as mechanistic as the muscular functions, and they

9 *Ibid,* p. 590.
10 *Ibid,* p. 595.

are as genuine vital processes as these last when viewed in their strictly biological relationships.[11]

Not only do we have here again an excellent illustration of the important point that mechanism is a philosophical position and not a scientific hypothesis, but we have also an illuminating illustration of the very confusion between the two that we have tried to show is so important to avoid. Herrick refers to the concept of an "Order of Nature," that is, of nature as a mechanistic scheme, as a "legitimate generalization of natural science," and as a "scientific induction." "This scientific induction," he says, "has no necessary metaphysical implications of any sort." Why does it have "no necessary metaphysical implications"? Because

> our experience is limited and will always be finite. It can never take us to ultimates, to absolutes, or to the essential nature of things-in-themselves; for it gives us only things-in-relation, and only partial views of the relationships at that.[12]

It is only too plain that an argument such as this is no generalization from the facts as we discover them. It appeals rather to what Herrick supposes we *have* to think. In other words, it is what the facts seem to him to mean for thought, and he arrives at this conclusion not by inspecting the facts but reflecting on them and constructing a conceptual scheme in terms of which their meaning may be understood. His argument that "the behavior of electrons and quanta of energy . . . is not capricious or lawless" is also an appeal to what we have to think rather than to anything that can be established by observation and scientific induction. This "behavior" *cannot* be lawless if scientific induction is to apply to it, for scientific induction pertains only to the orderly. We see this by reflective thought. Or, in Herrick's words, if this behavior were lawless, we could not apply to it "the very elaborate mathematical treatment which is our best way of investigating it." [13] His argument rests on a view of what reflection shows us *must* be true rather than what observation and generalization show us *happen* to be true.

If we look back at the early development of mechanism in scientific biology, its philosophical character will be even more obvious. Some of the most important foundations of scientific biology

11 *Ibid.*
12 *Ibid,* p. 590.
13 *Ibid.*

were established by the group known as "Helmholtz's School of Medicine," composed of Emil DuBois-Reymond, Ernst Brücke, Hermann Helmholtz, and Carl Ludwig. It is significant that these scientists adopted biological mechanism not as a conclusion reached on the basis of scientific evidence but as the principle upon which they proposed to operate as scientists. DuBois-Reymond wrote:

> Brücke and I pledged a solemn oath to put into effect this truth: "No other forces than the common physical-chemical ones are active within the organism. In those cases which cannot at the time be explained by these forces one has either to find the specific way or form of their action by means of the physical-mathematical method or to assume new forces equal in dignity to the chemical-physical forces inherent in matter, reducible to the force of attraction and repulsion." [14]

Ernest Jones comments that " 'unity of science,' 'science,' 'physical forces' were not merely directing ideas or hypotheses of scientific endeavor: they became almost objects of worship. They were more than methods of research—they became a *Weltanschauung*." [15] Certainly no scientific hypothesis can be established by taking an oath, nor are the results of scientific inquiry known before the inquiry is carried out. Mechanism in biology was, for the Helmholtz school, not a scientific hypothesis but a commitment based on a philosophical view of nature and the cosmos.

Such problems as the basic structure of the nerve cell and whether or not the nervous systems of higher and lower animals were composed of the same elements were significant to these men not merely as scientific problems. This latter problem, says Ernest Jones,

> was highly controversial at that time. The philosophical and religious implications seemed to be very disturbing. Are the differences in the mind of lower and higher animals only a matter of degree in complication? Does the human mind differ from that of some mollusc—not basically, but correlative to the number of nerve cells in both and the complication of their respective fibers? Scientists were searching for the answers to such questions in the hope of gaining definite decisions —in one way or another—on the nature of man, the existence of God, and the aim of life.[16]

[14] Quoted by Ernest Jones, *The Life and Work of Sigmund Freud* (New York, Basic Books, Inc., 1953), Volume 1, pp. 40-41. By permission.

[15] *Ibid*, Volume 1, p. 43.

[16] *Ibid*, Volume 1, p. 46.

VITALISM

As we have seen, the mechanist attempts to explain the apparently non-mechanical features of living organisms by breaking the organism down into its parts, and ultimately into physical-chemical structures. The difficulty with this approach is not in what it accomplishes but in what it omits. The fact remains that an organism seems to have a unity; and no matter how complete the physical-chemical explanation of its constituents may be, the organism as a whole appears to be non-mechanical in its makeup and operation. This has led some to the view that in order to account for the existence and functions of organisms as wholes we need something in addition to its physical constituents and mechanical laws. This is vitalism.

The vitalist does not attack mechanism as such; rather it is more his concern to recognize its limitations and to supplement it with a non-mechanical principle where mechanism seems inapplicable. Indeed, vitalists have been so much in agreement with the basic soundness of mechanism as applying to the physical world, that they have explicitly defined the vital principles as non-physical. The organism, for vitalism, is a physical-mechanical system plus a nonphysical vital principle which accounts for the existence of the living organism as a whole and for the nonmechanical functions of its operations as a whole.

As Karl W. Deutsch says, the *organism* as the vitalist conceived it, was

> a mechanism with restrictions: with restrictions on the possibility of analysis into separate parts, and of re-assembly from them; and restrictions on the extent of possible change in structure or function of either the parts or the whole. Perhaps the most severe restriction was the postulate that certain parts of it could never be known: the "imponderables," routed from physics and chemistry during the eighteenth century, reappeared as "vital force" or "vital spirit" in later "organismic" thinking. The implied sharp separation between these mysterious "miracle parts" and the ordinary knowable elements of the system, and usually, the presumed unchanging characteristics of both the knowable and the "imponderable" elements, then led to the classical picture of an "organism" with certain parts eternally mysterious, and with no chance of fundamental re-arrangement of its elements.[17]

[17] Deutsch, *op. cit.*, p. 189.

Vitalists have attempted to specify the nature of these "miracle parts" and to show how they can operate within the physical system of the organism without making that system an exception to the laws of physics. An outstanding example of this is found in the work of Hans Driesch, who was perhaps the chief spokesman for vitalism a half-century ago. According to Driesch, the organism possesses in addition to its mechanical activities and physical constituents a special nonmechanical *"individualising* causality" which he calls "entelechy." Entelechy

> is itself neither "an energy" nor "a material substance" of any special kind. . . . Entelechy is an agent *sui generis,* non-material and non-spatial, but acting "into" space, so to speak; an agent, however, that belongs to nature in the purely logical sense in which we use this word.[18]

Driesch attempted to show how such a causality can act in a physical system without violating the principle of the conservation of energy or physics' laws of action. He tried to meet this problem by confining the action of "individualising causality" to the realm of the possible; it acts on possibles before they become actual. The action of such an agency is consistent with physical laws, Driesch says,

> if only we suppose that the non-mechanical agent which is the bearer of individualising causality is able to *suspend* such happening as is *possible* on the basis of pre-existing differences of intensity and as *would* occur without the suspension. *Suspending possible changes* and *relaxing* suspension would then be the two modes orf "action" of the bearer of individualising causality.[19]

Driesch's distinction of actual and possible into two realms and his restriction of individualizing causality to the possible is stated even more explicitly:

> If we say that entelechy, whenever it ceases to suspend performed material becoming, allows a "possible" happening to become "real," we do not mean to imply that any obstacle to becoming, in the mechanical sense, is removed by entelechy; for such a removal in the mechanical sense, such an Auslösung, would require energy, and entelechy is *per definitionem* non-energetic. Entelechy only allows that

[18] *The History and Theory of Vitalism,* translated by C. K. Ogden (London, Macmillan and Company, Ltd., 1914), p. 204.

[19] *Ibid,* p. 203.

to become real which it has itself held in a state of mere possibility—not what has been in this state simply as a result of physico-chemical influences.[20]

EXAMINATION OF MECHANISM AND VITALISM

It is plain that vitalism, like mechanism, is no scientific hypothesis. The existence of the entelechy is a conclusion reached by thought as it reflects on the disparity between the make-up and action of an organism and the physical-chemical processes recognized by mechanism. The vitalist is convinced that the existence of an organism cannot be understood adequately on mechanical principles. But since he accepts the mechanist doctrine that all physical action is mechanical, he cannot interpret the distinctive organismic functions as physical. Because they are not mechanical, he concludes, they can be accounted for only by a nonphysical agent.

Here we have two theories concerning the nature of life which supposedly represent two mutually hostile points of view but which turn out to be making the very same basic assumption, the assumption that all physical existence and action is mechanical. The mechanist says that living beings are nothing but mechanisms; the vitalist says that living beings are mechanisms *plus* a nonmaterial ingredient. The difficulty with both views may be that the basic assumption which they both make is a false one. Each in its way has something of positive value to contribute to our understanding of life, but both views perhaps are fatally weakened by a common false assumption.

The application of our knowledge of physics and chemistry to the study of living organisms was the great step toward establishing biology as a science. But the fact that physics and chemistry are applicable to living organisms does not mean that in their physical make-up organisms exist only as mechanisms. The mechanistic approach to the study of life is a perspective which yields rich results, but the fact that it is relevant and significant as a way of studying certain aspects of life does not mean that it is the only perspective for the study of organisms. Mechanism as a philosophy

[20] *Ibid*, p. 205.

is the product of the "nothing-but" fallacy. Such thinking infers that since the mechanist perspective helps us to understand the nature and functions of organisms, it follows that organisms *exist* as mechanical systems.

As long as mechanism was the only perspective under which fruitful scientific study of nature could be undertaken it is understandable that those who pioneered in the scientific study of living organisms should have tried to understand the nature and functions of life solely in mechanistic terms. It is understandable also that those who were convinced that mechanism was inadequate should see no alternative except the postulation of non-physical entities in addition to the physical, as parts of organisms. What was needed was a new perspective from which to approach the study of nature.

This new perspective began to emerge with the theory of organic evolution, a theory which became a significant scientific hypothesis with Darwin's publication of the mass of factual evidence he had collected in its support. For the first time nature was studied scientifically as *history*. The organism was understood as a process in time and as the product of continuous changes reaching back as far into the past as life has existed. For the first time modern science saw change and process as constituting the very essence of natural entities and not as something imposed upon them externally.

In a strictly mechanical system basic internal change is impossible. Where all parts are analyzable into units and where each unit is acted upon externally by other units, the only change possible is a change in the external relations of those units. Nothing can, so to speak, "get inside" the unit and affect its make-up. External forces can only move it from one place to another. In such a system, of course, the only forces external to one unit are the motions of other units. But since what *actually exists* in such a system are the units themselves, their shifting space relationships constitute no change in their own constitution. It makes no difference to the nature of any unit *where* it is or what other units it collides with. It remains ever the same. The units do not change; the space in which they move does not change: so nothing real changes.

Once we admit real change into a physical entity, that entity can no longer be understood in mechanical terms except as we can regard its components as units. This is what has happened not only in biology but in physics as well. The atom is no longer a unit;

rather it is a complex structure which possesses only the stability which is maintained by the repetition of internal processes. But the constituents of the atom, such as electrons, protons, positons, etc., cannot serve as mechanical units. These are energy forms. The electron can be described as a particle for certain purposes; in other relations it is represented as a wavicle. The atom is a relatively stable dynamic equilibrium, and this means that it is a temporal process. Whether the subatomic particles are events would be difficult to say; if so, they would seem to be "events" in a different sense than that which we ordinarily attach to the term. It is plain, however, that they cannot be understood as ultimate material units somehow persisting unchanged through time. Erwin Schrödinger tells us that

> it is better to regard a particle not as a permanent entity but as an instantaneous event. Sometimes these events form chains that give the illusion of permanent beings—but only in particular circumstances and only for an extremely short period of time in every single case.[21]

EVOLUTION

The concept of organic evolution includes not only the idea of progressive change of form and organization but also the idea that later stages of development are the realization of *potentialities* inherent in earlier stages. Thus life is a dynamic process; it is no mere reshuffling of fixed and finished units by forces external to those units.

This does not mean necessarily that the potentialities actually realized in a particular phase of evolution are the only ones present in earlier stages. The environment plays a part in evolution, for the environment provides selective factors that help to determine which of perhaps many potentialities will actually be realized. We are familiar with this principle in the development of the individual person. A child may have the innate ability to become a scientist or a poet, but whether either of these potentialities is realized depends partly on the opportunities offered by his environment. No doubt there are hundreds of thousands of people in our land who have the intelligence to study higher mathematics successfully but who have

[21] *Science and Humanism* (Cambridge, Cambridge University Press, 1952), pp. 27-28.

never gone beyond the level of elementary high school algebra and geometry. Similarly the evolution of related but significantly different forms of living organisms corresponding to environmental differences indicates the presence of more potentialities in the earlier stages of life than ever actually develop.

Indeed we may go so far as to say that in some sense the whole sweep of development which has taken place in the evolution of life was potential in its earliest stages. If the earliest stages developed from inorganic structures then we may go still further and say that the most advanced products of organic evolution were potential in the earliest state of our solar system, even before the planets were formed. *The physical constituents of our world then were not only what they then would have appeared to be in their physical make-up alone, if they could have been observed, but were also the bearers of unimaginable ranges of potentiality.*

The process by which certain possibilities of change inherent in living organisms are realized while others remain unrealized is called "natural selection." In so far as there is in the life process a tendency on the part of the individual organism and on the part of the species to maintain themselves in existence it is plain that both the individual and the species must be able to adapt themselves to differences in the environment. In individuals of the higher forms of life this appears as learning; in the species it appears as evolution.

We are not concerned here with the nature of the process of selection, or with questions of just how genetic variation originates. Those are scientific questions. Our concern is rather to understand something of how a process of evolution *exists*, and to consider this especially in contrast with the way in which a mechanical system exists. Both mechanism and vitalism, it will be remembered, consider the physical world to be composed of static, fixed entities which do nothing of themselves and which undergo no change except change of position in space.

The inadequacy of mechanism, as a standpoint from which to understand the make-up and activities of living organisms, can be summed up in this way: a mechanism contains no possiblity of real change, and thus excludes the potential. Vitalism agrees with mechanism in its interpretation of the physical order. But since the vitalist cannot ignore the significance of the distinctive characteristics of the organism, characteristics which he considers nonmechanical in all their features, he adds something non-physical to the physical system. Mechanism excludes the potential from the actual altogether; everything exists in its final and absolute form. Vitalism does not exclude the potential, but in order to get the potential into the actual the vitalist has to bring it in from the outside. For the vitalist there is no more real potential *in the physical* than for the mechanist; in order to have any potentiality in the organism, the vitalist has to appeal to a non-physical principle.

The vitalist's separation of the potential and the actual is illustrated in Hans Driesch's attempt to explain how entelechy can have a causal effect upon the organism without violating the law of conservation of energy. Individualizing causality, he says, acts on possibles *before* they become actual. But he fails to see that the concept of a possible as something which can be acted upon turns the possible into something actual. Not only does the idea of the possible as something which can be acted upon treat the possible as something actual, it treats it as something *material*—in the classical sense of "material." Driesch thus attributes potentialities to a potentiality! Once the potential is separated from the actual, it either dissolves into nothing or becomes a new kind of actual. Mechanism illustrates the first alternative; vitalism illustrates the second.

The concept of evolution represents a radical break with the mechanistic conception. For if evolution is genuine, if real change occurs in nature, then there must be in nature, at any stage of development, more than is actual at that stage. Such a concept presents difficulties, and none of the attempts to make it intelligible in terms of traditional mechanism have been successful. The theory of emergent evolution, for example, is an explicit recognition that evolution is a process of genuine development in which new forms do appear, and it takes its stand as a theory in opposition to the traditional concept of mechanism.[22]

The philosophical problem we must face if we are to take evolution seriously is the question of how the potential exists. One thing seems plain: a world which contains potentialities is neither a static nor a finished world; only dynamic existence can have poten-

---

[22] See C. Lloyd Morgan, *Emergent Evolution* (New York, Henry Holt and Company, 1923). For some of the difficulties involved in the interpretation of the factual evidence for organic evolution, and for an excellent analysis of possible variations of mechanist-vitalist theories, see John G. Kemeny, *A Philosopher Looks at Science* (Princeton, D. Van Nostrand Company, Inc., 1959), Chapter 12.

tiality within itself. Mere abstract possibility, such as susceptibility to external changes, gives way to real potentiality when entities are understood in dynamic terms as events. It is no mere accident of verbal relationships that the concept of the potential is also the concept of potency; that is, of power. There can be no doubt but that the problem of how the potential exists can be dealt with only by reckoning with the significance of the temporal character of our world. Whatever else may be involved, we may be sure that a world of real change and genuine potentiality exists in some sense as an event. It is a world of directional, irreversible change. It is significant that some of the most striking event-characteristics of our world have been revealed in the new physics.[23]

Recent developments both in biology and in physics seem to show the inadequacy of mechanism not only as a philosophy but even as a basic working hypothesis to guide scientific investigation. To recognize this is not in any way to deny that a mechanistic hypothesis may be very useful as an operating procedure in limited investigations. It is hard to see on what other basis early modern science could have developed. Without the guiding concept of the cosmos as a machine, for example, the work of Newton might have been impossible. Mechanism has been a useful guide in biology as well; in spite of its weakness as a theory of how organisms exist, mechanism does have fruitful applications in bringing to light valuable information concerning life processes. But we must not confuse the usefulness of a conceptual framework provisionally adopted for certain investigations with the question of how the organism exists. Mechanism, says Joseph Needham, is "applicable everywhere, but final nowhere." [24] In its wide applicability lies the usefulness of mechanism as a method; in its lack of finality we find its inadequacy as a philosophy. Whatever kind of world this is, and whatever the final nature of living organisms may be, they are so constituted that limited areas and specific structures can often profitably be studied as mechanisms. But life processes can be understood in mechanistic terms only when they are taken in abstraction from the living organism in its unity and in its temporal

[23] For a significant statement of a philosophical position in which the concept of power is central, see Andrew Paul Ushenko, *Power and Events* (Princeton, Princeton University Press, 1946).

[24] *Time: the Refreshing River* (London, George Allen and Unwin, Ltd., 1943), p. 20.

dimension. The fact is that organisms *exist* as temporal unities; and the further we go in our scientific understanding of life, the more important it becomes to recognize this fact. As more adequate mathematical techniques for the study of temporal spans become widely available, we may expect far greater advances in the study of life than any so far achieved.

SUMMARY

The development of scientific biology appeared as a challenge to traditional ways of thinking not only in religion and theology but even in physics. The many conflicts and controversies which developed were largely occasioned by confusion concerning the subject matter appropriate to the various disciplines. In addition to such conflicts, some of the data and conclusions of biology have been given quite illegitimate political and social interpretations.

The impact of biology upon the basic concepts and assumptions of physical science has been great. In its earlier stages, biology tended to borrow its concepts from physics; but the new physics has begun to show some influence of biological patterns of thought, particularly in its recognition that physical processes are intrinsically temporal and dynamic and thus "organismic" in character.

The controversy between mechanism and vitalism reflected the assumption, common to both parties to the controversy, that physical processes are mechanistic in character. The mechanist contended that all apparently mechanistic properties of living organisms would eventually be shown to be physical in character, while the vitalist argued that these properties were nonmechanical and hence nonphysical. With the recognition that the assumption common to both points of view is open to serious challenge, a challenge which has come from physics itself, the controversy loses its significance and the issue must be stated in different terms.

The theory of evolution is in direct conflict with the assumptions of mechanism. For the first time objects in nature are studied scientifically as histories, with duration and change as of their very essence rather than as externally imposed upon them. As never before in modern scientific thought, the world of nature in even the most basic physical processes is conceived as dynamic existence. There is reason to think that the scientific study of living organisms helped to set the stage for this transformation of the basic concepts of physical science.

QUESTIONS FOR STUDY AND DISCUSSION

1. *Terms:* entelechy, evolution, material, mechanism, organism, vitalism.

2. Suppose chemical analysis were to show that the paper or ink of a supposed important historic document was of a kind first manufactured many years after the purported date of the document. Would this be a case of conflict between chemistry and history? Are there any similarities between this and supposed conflicts between science and religion?

3. Why has biology met so much greater resistance from popular thinking and common sense thinking than has, say, the theory of relativity or the quantum theory? Why has this opposition been so highly charged with emotion?

4. Examine: Both mechanism and vitalism exclude real change from physical existence.

5. Which is the more significant conflict, that between mechanism and vitalism or that between mechanism and evolution?

6. Contrast the organism as machine with the organism as history.

CHAPTER 10

Mind and Body

THE DISTINCTION OF BODY AND SOUL

The dualism of body and soul or mind is one of the basic facts of human experience. Only by the formation of a special theory can it be challenged. As Professor Howard D. Roelofs points out,

> opponents of Dualism and Interaction need on occasion to be reminded that it is *experience*, not theory, which initially presents dualism and interaction, that monisms, naturalistic and idealistic alike, initially appear as *theories* challenging experience.[1]

Dualism, says Professor Arthur O. Lovejoy,

> is the way of thinking natural to man as soon as he becomes even a little reflective about certain facts, of which most are matters of ordinary experience, and all have long been generally accepted.[2]

The distinction between body and soul is as basic as the distinction between night and day and between the seasons. Man ob-

[1] "A Case for Dualism and Interaction," *Philosophy and Phenomenological Research*, Volume XV, No. 4, June 1955, p. 470.

[2] *The Revolt Against Dualism* (Chicago, The Open Court Publishing Company, 1930), p. 11. By permission.

serves it as directly as he observes weather signs, as directly as he observes the difference between safety and danger, and between friend and foe. That the distinction is basic does not mean that man cannot be mistaken about it. To direct experience the earth seems to be at rest while the sun moves across the sky. That this happens to be an inadequate and misleading notion cannot be shown by any other direct experience or by any collection of direct experiences apart from theory. The truth of dualism is not guaranteed by the fact that we think quite naturally in such terms until we are convinced to the contrary by theoretical considerations. But the special position of dualism, in contrast with monistic theories, does mean that dualism is usually the starting point in man's attempt to understand himself. It suggests also that whatever theory we finally arrive at ought to do justice to the facts of experience expressed in terms of the dualism of ordinary thought.

The distinction of soul and body comes to us out of the dark past. The distinction is primitive, prehistoric, and no one can trace its origin. But we can easily imagine how plausible, even almost inevitable, the distinction might be to early man when he began to act according to conscious plan and purpose.

There is an obvious difference between what we see ourselves to be when we watch our own bodies in action, and what we are aware of when we turn our attention to such experiences as seeing itself, to fearing, hating, loving, deciding, and remembering. The difference is even more striking when we compare what we can observe in others with these acts of awareness we observe in ourselves. For although we cannot observe in others the acts of awareness we suppose them to have, yet we can see the movements of their bodies and hear the sounds of their voices. This alone might not be sufficient to lead to a distinction of soul and body, for there might be no difficulty in supposing that the movements of other bodies were accompanied by the experiences we find ourselves to have. There are certain special kinds of experience, however, which would be difficult for primitive thought even to recognize as taking place if the distinction between body and soul were not made.

One of the most important of these special experiences, no doubt, was the experience of dreaming. The dreamer, when he awakens, recalls a hunt or a combat in which he engaged after lying by the fire to sleep. Yet his companions assure him that his body was right there with them during all that time. What can he suppose, except that for a while he was away from his body? Of course while he was absent from his body he still had a body, for what he remembers doing is something that involved bodily activity. But plainly the body he had with him was not the one he ordinarily used, for his usual body was lying quiet and relaxed by the fire. The soul, ghost, or spirit was a kind of replica of his ordinary body; an "ethereal" body that could come and go unnoticed by other observers.

Another fact that made this distinction so important was the fact of death. Death and sleep have an obvious similarity. They seem to differ only in degree and in the fact that in death the soul which has left the body does not return to it again. It is likely that most of the deaths witnessed by early man were violent deaths. In such cases it was easy to suppose that injury to the body made it no longer habitable by the soul which had left it. Even in nonviolent death the rapid corruption of the body would lead to the same supposition. In any case, here seemed to be a most striking fact of experience, a matter of common knowledge, which showed unmistakably that there is a difference between a body animated by its soul and one which the soul has left.

Death may well have had a significance beyond the fact of separation of soul and body. A dead body differed from other physical things with which man had been familiar; a dead body was something which *had been* alive and then no longer was. We do not know what went on in the thought of early man but apparently something like this gave to a dead body a special meaning. In a sense, death itself, no matter how it might have come about, was an *unnatural* thing. It was unnatural because all natural things are besouled. Plants, clouds, streams and rivers, mountains, the moon and the stars, all of these man once thought to be animated by souls. The primitive outlook, in other words, was animistic. Man at that stage had no concept of dead, lifeless matter. But in the death of an animal, and especially of a man, there was a very special case in which the soul separates from body and leaves the body behind.

That a dead body was somehow thought of as unnatural is further supported by the fact that primitive man had no conception of natural death. Every case of death had a specific cause. Often the cause was obvious, as in the case of violent death. But even when not obvious, it was assumed that some agency, seen or unseen, was responsible. The existence, then, of a dead body was the existence of something artificial. In their natural state bodies were alive, not dead; for them to become dead, something had to *make* them dead.

As we have already seen, the soul that separated from the body was not what later thought would call an immaterial being. It still was composed of a *stuff*, although a very subtle stuff that was invisible under ordinary circumstances. But since the departure of the soul from the body was also the body's loss of all its animal functions, it was obvious that the real person was to be identified with the departed soul and not with the body that was left behind. In many primitive societies it was thought that even the permanently separated souls did not go far away. They remained in close proximity and were always available, to those who knew how to get in touch with them, for consultation and assistance.

With the emergence in Greek philosophy of the idea that man's experiences and conscious functions (such as perceiving, remembering, imagining, and reasoning) are immaterial activities, the concept of soul gradually gave way to the concept of mind. In the Greek language the distinction is not clearly drawn, but the Greek word, *psyche*, which may be translated either as *soul* or *mind*, came to be used by the Greek philosophers to refer to the immaterial part of man's nature. In modern English, "soul" is seldom used now outside of a religious context. The problem which has been of special concern to philosophy is that of the relationship to man's physical make-up of such apparently immaterial functions as perception, thought, and volition; this is the problem of the relation of mind and body.

DUALISM

Philosophical reflection upon the nature of man is of course very recent in comparison with the long period of human existence. But very early in the development of philosophical reflection the concept of mind underwent considerable change. In this instance reflection followed its usual course. The first step was to clarify the distinction between mind and body by making that distinction more definite. The more importance we place on our inner life of thought and feeling and will, the more concerned we are to avoid mistaking the outer for the inner; and the greater the difference between our notion of mind and our notion of body, the less danger there is of confusing them. One result was to emphasize in theoretical speculation the difference between mind and body and to think of this not only as signifying different ways of existing but also as a value difference. Mind and body were recognized as more than merely distinguishable; they were thought of as existing as separate entities which have come into a temporary combination. Not only are they separate entities, but they have different kinds of existence. Thus the soul or mind came to be thought of, as by Plato, as having its true home elsewhere, and as being a stranger in this world held here only by its imprisonment in the body. To be imprisoned is something evil, and so the body became in a sense the enemy of the soul, an agency of evil.

Philosophical dualism, the product of the attempt to form clearer ideas of the nature of mind and the nature of body, became the source of new problems. Primitive man did not ask how soul and body happened to get together; his question was always what, in this or that unusual circumstance, was the cause of their separation. But the more clearly defined in reflective thought became the distinction between mind and body, the more pressing became the problem of what makes possible their juncture in man. Plato himself made little effort to discuss this problem conceptually. It was one of the topics concerning which he felt he could communicate more effectively by the use of myth and allegory.

The more clearly we distinguish mind and body, the harder it is to see how they can have anything to do with each other. If we understand mind as immaterial substance, without parts, non-spatial, and capable of such functions as thinking and willing, then what relation can mind have to body? If we conceive body as extended, divisible into parts, and active only by change of place, then there seems to be nothing in body with which mind can make "contact," and nothing accessible to body which can be found in mind. Such considerations as these led Descartes to consider body and mind to be distinct substances, each of which exists in a way entirely different from that of the other. Descartes says:

there are *certain* activities, which we call *corporeal*, e.g. magnitude, figure, motion, and all those that cannot be thought of apart from extension in space; and the substance in which they exist is called *body*. . . . Further, there are other activities, which we call *thinking* activities, e.g. understanding, willing, imagining, feeling, etc., which agree in falling under the description of thought, perception, or consciousness. The substance in which they reside we call a *thinking thing* or *the mind*, or any other name we care, provided only we do not confound it with corporeal substance, since thinking activities have no affinity with corporeal activities, and thought, which is the common nature in which the former agree, is totally different from extension, the common term for describing the latter.[3]

The theories which result from attempts to solve the mind-body problem can be classified in four groups: (1) *dualism*, as in the case of Descartes, (2) *materialism*, (3) *subjectivism*, and (4) *integration theories*. Philosophical dualism is an attempt to retain both mind and body as independently real beings. Those who are not satisfied with the consequences of this attempt then either reject the reality of mind, and become materialists; or reject the reality of body, and become subjectivists; or reject the idea that the distinction of soul or mind and body involves different ways of existing. Each of these four basic views has two contrasting varieties.

Dualists have conceived the relationship of mind and body in two ways: in terms of *interactionism* and in terms of *parallelism*. The interactionist accepts the apparent mutual influence of body on mind and of mind on body as genuine. In spite of the difficulties in understanding *how* the motions of body can affect an immaterial and non-spatial mind and *how* the acts of mind can initiate motion in body, the interactionist is so impressed with what seems to be the *fact* of mutual influence that he refuses to abandon it in the face of the difficulties.

One of the few attempts to describe just how body and mind can act on each other was made by Descartes. After giving his reasons for supposing that the main seat of the soul is the pineal gland, he proceeds to describe how that gland might link together the activities of soul and body:

Let us then conceive here that the soul has its principal seat in the little gland which exists in the middle of the brain, from whence it radiates forth through all the remainder of the body by means of the animal spirits, nerves, and even the blood, which, participating in the impressions of the spirits, can carry them by the arteries into all

[3] *The Philosophical Works of Descartes*, translated by Elizabeth S. Haldane and G. R. T. Ross, reprinted by permission of the Cambridge University Press and Dover Publications, Inc., New York 14, New York, 1955, Volume II, p. 64 of the Dover edition.

the members. And . . . let us here add that the small gland which is the main seat of the soul is so suspended between the cavities which contain the spirits that it can be moved by them in as many different ways as there are sensible diversities in the object, but that it may also be moved in diverse ways by the soul, whose nature is such that it receives in itself as many diverse impressions, that is to say, that it possesses as many diverse perceptions as there are diverse movements in this gland. Reciprocally, likewise, the machine of the body is so formed that from the simple fact that this gland is diversely moved by the soul, or by such other cause, whatever it is, it thrusts the spirits which surround it towards the pores of the brain, which conduct them by the nerves into the muscles, by which means it causes them to move the limbs.[4]

This famous passage is an instructive example of what happens when a dualist tries to spell out in specific terms a way in which mind and body can be conceived to interact. Perhaps this amusing example has had a deterrent effect upon other dualists who might be inclined toward such speculations. Descartes tells us how the pineal gland might be supposed, in terms of the crude anatomical concepts of his day, to bring about motions in other parts of the body, and how motions in other parts of the body might be conveyed to the gland. But he tells us nothing whatever about how the soul moves the gland, or how the motions of the gland do anything to the soul. The only interaction Descartes describes is a supposed interaction between the pineal gland and the rest of the body; he tells us nothing at all about the interaction of the body or of any part of the body with the soul.

Parallelism is the theory that mind and body engage each in its own activity without having any influence on the other. Mental and physical activities are related, in the sense that what goes on in the mind at a certain time is relevant to what goes on in the body at that same time. The senses are stimulated by physical energies and the mind has the perception appropriate to that stimulation, but the physical stimulus does not *cause* the mental event nor does the mental event in any way depend on the physical event. A decision to perform a certain act is reached and the body performs the act. But the decision does not cause the physical action. The action is appropriate to the decision but its causes are all of them physical causes and the effects of the decision are all of them mental effects.

[4] *Ibid*, Volume I, p. 347.

There is thus complete independence of the mental and physical processes, but there is also a coincidence so that what happens in the one fits appropriately what happens in the other.

Leibniz, although not himself a dualist in the usual sense of the term, provides one of the clearest statements of parallelism:

> It must be confessed, moreover, that *perception* and that which depends on it *are inexplicable by mechanical causes*, that is, by figures and motions. . . . [The causes of perception] must be sought for, therefore, in the simple substance and not in the composite or in the machine.[5]
>
> These principles have given me the means of explaining naturally the union or rather the conformity of the soul and the organic body. The soul follows its own peculiar laws and the body also follows its own laws, and they agree in virtue of the *pre-established* harmony between all substances, since they are all representations of one and the same universe.
>
> Souls act according to the laws of final causes, by appetitions, ends, and means. Bodies act in accordance with the laws of efficient causes or of motion. And the two realms, that of efficient causes and that of final causes, are in harmony with each other.[6]

MATERIALISM

Parallelism plainly is not a view which we can support by appeal to positive evidence. It seems often to be a kind of last resort for dualists who are impressed with the difficulties of inter-actionism, particularly those who are convinced that the scientific outlook requires us to accept the physical order as self-contained, complete, and autonomous. If these dualists are to retain the mental along with the physical, they can do so only by denying to the mental any participation in or influence on physical activities. It is not surprising that many others who accept this attitude toward the physical would question the need for anything but the physical. From such considerations comes materialism: the view that only body is real, that mind is at most only appearance.

[5] *Leibniz Selections,* edited by Philip P. Wiener (New York, Charles Scribner's Sons, 1951), p. 536. By permission. By "simple substances" Leibniz means souls: "All simple substances may be called souls," while body is "composite substance." (*Ibid.*)

[6] *Ibid,* p. 549.

There are two varieties of materialism: *epiphenomenalism,* which accepts the mental only as a way in which the physical appears; and *behaviorism,* which rejects the concept of the mental entirely. For epiphenomenalism, mind has somewhat the same relation to body as a shadow has to the object which casts it. Our shadows follow us as we walk about, but they do nothing and have no effect on the bodies that cast them. So the mental is only a kind of accompaniment of certain bodily states, specifically of certain brain states and processes. The mental does nothing and its existence makes no difference to anything non-mental.

If the existence of the mental can be ignored, why admit it at all? According to materialism, what we call the mental is in reality physical. The only profitable concern we can have with the mental is to try to uncover the physical processes that constitute its real nature, and this is the contention of behaviorism. Thus John B. Watson, the psychologist who popularized behaviorism a generation ago, considered that thinking consists actually of subvocal excitations of the speech organs:

> The term thinking ought to be made to cover generally all implicit language activity and other activity substitutable for language activity. . . . Thinking then might become our general term to cover all sub-vocal behavior.[7]

Behavior is composed of stimulus and response, and the organs of response are muscles and glands.[8] Thinking is activity of the speech muscles, not strong enough to make a sound.

The following sweeping assertion by Leslie A. White is expressive of an extreme form of the materialist conception of mind and of its relation to nature:

> Everything in the cosmos can be interpreted in terms of matter and energy, whether it be a star, atom, cell, or man. All life is, of course, an organization of matter-and-energy. Mind, too, is but a form of motion of matter cellularly organized. Culture is merely the name we give to matter-and-energy in symbolic form. Chopping wood, singing a song, breathing a prayer, loathing snakes, hungering after righteousness, all are examples of matter in motion. We may thus distinguish various forms and, in a sense, strata of forms, of energy:

[7] *Psychology from the Standpoint of a Behaviorist,* Third Edition Revised (Philadelphia, J. B. Lippincott Company, 1929), p. 356.
[8] *Ibid,* Chapters I, V.

cosmic, galactic, organismic, physiological (intraorganismal), psychological (extraorganismal), and cultural (suprasomatic).[9]

SUBJECTIVISM

Just as some thinkers who are impressed by the difficulties of dualism avoid those difficulties by denying the reality of the mental, so others attempt a similar escape from the problem by denying the reality of body. Both materialism and subjectivism arise out of a preceding dualism. Which of these alternatives to dualism a thinker accepts, if he is to go one way or the other, often depends on his basic evaluations. If he has been impressed primarily by the importance of the physical sciences, his rejection of dualism may incline him toward materialism. If his primary concerns are with man's aesthetic, moral, or religious experience, he is more likely to be attracted by some form of subjectivism. There are two main varieties of subjectivism: *spiritualism*, the view that all existence is composed of minds and their contents; and *idealism*, the view that all existence is composed of ideas or mental states. Subjectivism often combines spiritualism and idealism in a theory that nothing exists except minds and their ideas.

There are a number of examples in the history of philosophy of such a transition from dualism to subjectivism. One such case is found in neo-Platonism as a reaction to Plato's dualism. Plato's material world tended to turn into mere illusion, the negation of truth and reality, and came to be thought of, in its true nature, as immaterial. Plotinus says that "what we know as Nature is a soul, offspring of a yet earlier Soul of more powerful life." [10]

A similar development, quite different in detail and motive, is found in early modern philosophy. Descartes' dualism may be said to have set the problems of much subsequent modern philosophy. In both of the two main streams of his influence his original dualism was abandoned, and in each case it was the mental that survived as real.

[9] "Ethnological Theory," in *Philosophy for the Future*, edited by Roy Wood Sellars, V. J. McGill and Marvin Farber (New York, The Macmillan Company, 1949), p. 375. By permission.

[10] *Enneads*, III, viii, 4, in *The Essence of Plotinus*, compiled by Grace H. Turnbull (New York, Oxford University Press, 1948), p. 110. By permission.

Cartesian rationalism, on the Continent, culminated in the philosophy of Leibniz, who saw the world as a system of levels of souls, or *monads*, in which the higher are distinguished from lower only by degrees of consciousness. Empiricism, in England, passed from the dualism of Locke through the spiritualism of Berkeley and reached its final stage of development in Hume, whose philosophy was completely separated from spiritualism. Hume repudiated all meaning for the idea of existence apart from awareness; he abandoned the soul, or mind or self, as the subject of awareness, leaving nothing to which existence may be ascribed except particular states of consciousness.

For Berkeley, all existence is comprised of minds, or spirits, and their ideas:

> Some truths there are so near and obvious to the mind, that a man need only open his eyes to see them. Such I take this important one to be, to wit, that all the choir of heaven and furniture of the earth, in a word all those bodies which compose the mighty frame of the world, have not any subsistence without a mind, that their *being* (*esse*) is to be perceived or known; that consequently so long as they are not actually perceived by me, or do not exist in my mind or that of any other *created spirit*, they must either have no existence at all, *or else subsist in the mind of some eternal spirit;* it being perfectly unintelligible and involving all the absurdity of abstraction, to attribute to any single part of them an existence independent of a spirit.[11]

Hume went further and refused to admit the existence of the mind as anything but a collection of ideas. What is a mind or self? It is "nothing but a bundle or collection of different perceptions, which succeed each other with an inconceivable rapidity, and are in a perpetual flux and movement."[12]

One of the more serious difficulties with subjectivism is that it lumps together as mental both the acts of mind and the content of experience. We may admit that the act of perceiving is a mental event and that only a mind can perceive. But this may not require

[11] *A Treatise Concerning the Principles of Human Knowledge*, Part I, Section VI, in *A New Theory of Vision and Other Select Philosophical Writings by George Berkeley*, with an Introduction by A. D. Lindsay. (Everyman's Library, New York, E. P. Dutton and Company, Inc., 1910), pp. 115-16.

[12] David Hume, *A Treatise of Human Nature*, edited by L. A. Selby-Bigge (Oxford at the Clarendon Press, 1928), p. 252. Other important parts of Hume's argument developed here will be quoted in Chapter 11.

us to admit that *what is perceived* is mental. The term "perception" is ambiguous: sometimes we use it to refer to the act of perceiving and sometimes we refer to what we perceive. It is possible that this ambiguity plays an important part in the development of Berkeley's subjectivism from Locke's theory of ideas. In contrast, we may consider Whitehead's view that "what is perceived is a part of nature and not merely content of mind."[13] When I see trees and grass and sky before me I see things that are extended and colored and which have shape. But my ideas of trees and grass and sky are not extended ideas, or colored ideas, or ideas which have shape.

INTEGRATION THEORIES

The difficulties with dualism do not always lead to the repudiation of either mind or body. Some thinkers accept dualism in spite of its difficulties, on the grounds that the difficulties of understanding the relation of mind and body are less than the difficulties created by repudiating either side of the dualism. In other cases the difficulties encountered in trying to understand the dualistic relation lead to an attempt to reconstruct the concepts of mind and body. Such an influence of Plato's dualism is seen in the work of his great pupil, Aristotle. So also in modern philosophy Spinoza attempted to deal with the difficulties of Cartesian dualism by considering mind and body to be not realities in their own right but, in their essences as thought and extension, to be attributes of one identical substance.

We may call such attempts to reconstruct the concepts of mind and body, "integration theories." They all deny any final and ultimate separation of mind and body; they deny, further, that either mind or body can be taken to be complete in itself. We may distinguish two main kinds of integration theory: *the double aspect theory*, and *hylomorphism*. Spinoza's philosophy illustrates the double aspect theory; and Aristotle's, the hylomorphic.

The double aspect theory is not so much an attempt to understand the relation of body and mind as it is an attempt to remove

[13] Quoted by permission from Victor Lowe, "The Development of Whitehead's Philosophy," in *The Philosophy of Alfred North Whitehead*, Second Edition, edited by Paul Arthur Schilpp (New York, Tudor Publishing Company, 1951), p. 80.

the problem. If we think of body and mind as two aspects of the nature of an underlying reality, a reality which we can know only in terms of those aspects, then we no longer are concerned with questions of how body influences mind and how mind influences body, or how the mental and physical can act in harmony when neither influence the other. For we no longer think of body and mind as two different kinds of things; they are different aspects of the same thing. The very thing we see as body we also experience as mind. Spinoza states his version of the double aspect conception as follows:

> Before we go any farther, we must here recall to our memory what we have already demonstrated, that everything which can be perceived by the infinite intellect as constituting the essence of substance pertains entirely to the one sole substance only, and consequently that substance thinking and substance extended are one and the same substance, which is now comprehended under this attribute and now under that. Thus, also, a mode of extension and the idea of that mode are one and the same thing expressed in two different ways. . . . For example, the circle existing in nature and the idea that is in God of an existing circle are one and the same thing, which is manifested through different attributes.[14]

At another place Spinoza states that "the mind and the body, are one and the same individual, which at one time is considered under the attribute of thought, and at another under that of extension."[15]

A recent example of the double aspect theory is found in Whitehead's philosophy. Whitehead rejects dualism as an incoherence and considers that all actual occasions are what he calls "prehensions," each of which is a grasping of aspects of other actual occasions into a unity. Each actual occasion has its private side and its public side:

> The *duality* of private subject and public object is a fundamental fact stamped on the face of experience. To achieve coherence [comments Victor Lowe in his account of the development of Whitehead's thought] Whitehead begins with the principle that, "The sole concrete facts, in terms of which actualities can be analysed, are prehensions [of objects by subjects]; and every prehension has its public side and its private side." But, further, his basic conceptions are intended

---

[14] *Ethic*, translated by W. H. White, in *Spinoza Selections*, edited by John Wild (New York, Charles Scribner's Sons, 1930), pp. 149-50. By permission.
[15] *Ibid*, p. 171.

to be so inclusive in scope, and so interlocked, as to overcome all the classical dualisms of metaphysics: mind and matter, God and the world, permanence and transcience, causality and teleology, atomism and continuity, sensation and emotion, internal and external relations, etc., as well as subject and object. Thus, e.g., "physical" inheritance from the environment, and novel "mental" reaction to it, are both, in principle, ascribed to *every* occasion, as respectively its "public" basis and its "private" culmination.[16]

Hylomorphism resembles the double aspect theory in that two aspects of a substance are recognized. It differs from the double aspect theory in two respects. First, the two aspects are not body and mind but matter and form. The concept of matter differs from that of body in that matter is taken to be anything that can receive a form. Matter is equivalent to potentiality. The concept of matter is also a relative concept. For example, atomic structures may be conceived to be in their own right combinations of matter and form, but in relation to the molecule the atom would be matter. Form is not equivalent to the mental, but is wider than the mental and includes shape and structure and all determinable pattern. The second way in which hylomorphism differs from the double aspect theory is in its understanding the relation of the two aspects. This theory cannot pass off the question of how the two aspects are related merely by referring them to an underlying reality which is known only in terms of its aspects. For hylomorphism, the reality *is* the synthesis of matter and form which constitutes the individual substance.

What we call the mental is included by Aristotle within the functions of *soul*, a more inclusive concept for him than mind. All things are composed of matter and form, and in living things the form is soul. All living things are besouled, and different levels of life differ in the level of soul realized.

> Of natural bodies some have life in them, others not; by life we mean self-nutrition and growth (with its correlative decay). It follows that every natural body which has life in it is a substance in the sense of a composite.[17]

[16] Lowe (*op. cit.*), pp. 106-107. The Whitehead quotation is from *Process and Reality* (New York, The Macmillan Company, 1929), p. 444.

[17] *De Anima*, 412a 14-16, *The Basic Works of Aristotle*, edited by Richard McKeon (New York, Random House, 1941), p. 555. by permission of Oxford University Press.

Plants have only the vegetative soul, by which are performed the functions of nutrition and growth. Animals have vegetable and animal souls, and the animal soul performs those functions peculiar to animal existence, such as movement and sensation. In man there is vegetable, animal, and rational soul. The rational performs the functions of thought, such as abstraction and reasoning.

In no case is body a separate entity, joined to another entity, soul; rather the living body is matter organized and functioning under the pattern of soul. Matter itself is something with only the potentialities of organization, incapable of realizing such organization by itself. Soul is the organizing principle. An individual living being capable of maintaining its own existence in interaction with its environment is a composite of form and matter constituting an organized whole. In order to be this, it must contain both a material capable of organization and an organizing principle.

> But since it is also a *body* of such and such a kind, viz. having life, the *body* cannot be soul; the body is the subject or matter, not what is attributed to it. Hence the soul must be a substance in the sense of the form of a natural body having life potentially within it.[18]

. . .

> If, then, we have to give a general formula applicable to all kinds of soul, we must describe it as the first grade of actuality of a natural organized body. This is why we can wholly dismiss as unnecessary the question whether the soul and the body are one: it is as meaningless as to ask whether the wax and the shape given to it by the stamp are one.[19]

The relations of matter and form in living organisms is understood in terms of a process of development. The organism has temporal existence, and it exists as a process of development from potentiality to actuality. As soul is the form of body, so the activity of soul is the realization of the potentialities of body. Sensation, for example, is the realization of potentialities of the matter which constitutes the sense organs, just as digestion is the realization of potentialities of the digestive system. In Aristotle's technical terms, the relationship is stated as follows:

> Since then the complex here is the living thing, the body cannot be the actuality of the soul; it is the soul which is the actuality of a

[18] *Ibid*, 412a 18-21; McKeon. *ibid.*
[19] *Ibid*, 412b 4-8; McKeon. *ibid.*

certain kind of body. Hence the rightness of the view that the soul cannot be without a body, while it cannot *be* a body; it is not a body but something relative to a body. This is why it is *in* a body, and a body of a definite kind. . . . Reflection confirms the observed fact; the actuality of any given thing can only be realized in what is already potentially that thing, i.e. in a matter of its own appropriate to it. From all this it follows that soul is an actuality or formulable essence of something that possesses a potentiality of being besouled.[20]

From such a standpoint as Aristotle's it is clear that dualism has been abandoned. The individual, it is true, is a kind of composite, but not a combination of two different kinds of existing substances. Soul and body are not separate beings, but are inextricably joined in the composite substance which is the living being.

If we consider the majority of them [the affections of the soul], there seems to be no case in which the soul can act or be acted upon without involving the body; e.g. anger, courage, appetite, and sensation generally. Thinking seems the most probable exception; but if this too proves to be a form of imagination or to be impossible without imagination, it too requires a body as a condition of its existence. If there is any way of acting or being acted upon proper to soul, soul will be capable of separate existence; if there is none, its separate existence is impossible. In the latter case, it will be like what is straight, which has many properties arising from the straightness in it.[21]

For Aristotle the individual reality is both *formed matter* and *embodied form*. Neither matter nor form by itself is actual. Matter by itself would be sheer potentiality, with nothing in it actual. Form by itself would be only a way in which material might be organized, but would not be the organization of anything. Form by itself would be equivalent to organized nothing. Form by itself, however, must not be confused with Aristotle's concept of form which is its own matter; that is, with God.

MIND-BODY THEORIES AS POSTULATES

When we compare these various theories of mind and body we see one striking difference. Some of them are attempts to understand the relation of the mental and the physical and attempt

20 *Ibid*, 414a 17-22, 25-28; McKeon, *op. cit.*, p. 559.
21 *Ibid*, 403a, 5-13; McKeon, *op cit.*, p. 537.

to give reasons to support the position taken. Others seem to be little more than standpoints which are adopted because of other considerations. Both kinds of view are philosophies; but the one is the outcome of philosophizing, while the other is often only a case of having and using a philosophy without actively engaging in philosophy. The first type of theory is an argument; the second type is a postulate.

Parallelism, epiphenomenalism, behaviorism, and the double aspect theories are postulational theories. If reasons are advanced to support them, those reasons are usually negative or extraneous ones. The argument ordinarily advanced in support of parallelism, for example, is the inability to reconcile the causal interaction of mind and body with the principle of the conservation of energy. This seems to be an extraneous consideration and to involve confusion of one field of inquiry with another. The principle of the conservation of energy is an important consideration where we are dealing with body in terms of physics, but the problem of the relation of mind and body is not a problem of physics. A theory of interaction which involved conflict with established principles of physics would indeed be suspect, but as we shall see this is not the kind of interaction which seems to occur in the mind-body relation.

Epiphenomenalism seems little more than a way of avoiding the mental in connection with the study of the physical. The view can hardly be stated without fatal inconsistency, for it seems to assert that the mental is something which really happens and yet does nothing and has no place in reality. An attempt to understand the relation of mind and body on the analogy of a shadow and the object which casts that shadow is not enlightening. For the shadow is not itself a positive physical thing, it is the absence of light. Yet not even the epiphenomenalist understands mind to be the absence of body; it is rather a nonbodily accompaniment of body. We know how shadows exist; but how, on this view, do minds exist? What is there in the nature of bodies which enables them to be thus accompanied by something which does nothing and makes no difference to the body it accompanies? The "shadows" they cast are *conscious* shadows; surely here a better analogy than the absence of light would be its presence. The difficulty with epiphenomenalism lies in the fact that on its own terms not only the theory of epiphenomenalism but the whole range of scientific knowledge is nothing but a series of inert and passive feeling-states. Judgment and truth-claims, however, are positive acts; their occurrence as positive acts cannot be denied except in truth-claiming judgment.

Behaviorism is epiphenomenalism with the epiphenomena abolished. For behaviorism there is nothing but body; the so-called mental is composed of nothing but physical responses of a low level. The problem of behaviorism is the problem of how anyone could have seriously advocated such a position. Behaviorism appeared first in the study of animal behavior, and it was a salutary reaction against the prevailing practice of interpreting animal behavior in terms of human experience. Behaviorism at this stage was a methodological principle, the principle that nothing should be attributed to animal action and response except the behavior which could be observed. There was to be no place in a scientific animal psychology for speculation about any supposed mental states or experiences the animals might have. This same principle was extended to the study of the human infant; and then, as a move to give to human psychology the scientific rigor of the physical and biological sciences, the principle was advocated for the whole field of psychology.

So long as behaviorism remained a methodological device no philosophical issue arose. It is true that there were questions about its adequacy and appropriateness as a method, particularly in its application to some phases of human psychology; but such questions concerned only the psychologist. Behaviorism acquired a philosophical significance when some of its advocates began to contend not merely that conscious experience should be ignored in any truly scientific study but that there is no conscious experience. We can understand such a contention only as a verbal move in a polemic of philosophical attitudes and assumptions. If it were true then, of course, no one could know what he was saying. To deny all conscious experience is to say something the meaning of which no one who has conscious experience can apprehend. To argue that consciousness does not exist as a substantive, as William James does in one of his essays,[22] is meaningful whether we accept the argument or not. But to deny that there is conscious experience is to go even further than to deny that anyone can ever know anything. The import of the denial is in conflict with the very existence of the denial itself.

[22] "Does Consciousness Exist?" in *Essays in Radical Empiricism* (New York, Longmans, Green, and Company, 1912), pp. 1-38.

The double aspect theory is not open to such charges as those which stand against the other postulational theories. The double aspect theory suffers from the fact that the case which supports what is distinctive about the theory is solely negative. Like parallelism, the double aspect theory denies interaction; but the double aspect theory carries its negation a step farther. Those who hold it are unwilling to accept what seems to be either the miracle or the chance coincidence of a parallel activity of two unrelated and mutually exclusive systems of existence. So they insist that underlying the apparent duality of mind and body is an actual identity. But this is merely assumed. What kind of identity it is they do not and, on their own principles, they cannot tell us. The underlying unity is unknown and unknowable except in terms of its diverse manifestations in body and mind; thus on this view it cannot be known *as* a unity. To call it neutral is to add nothing positive to its negative characterization.

THE CASE FOR SUBJECTIVISM EXAMINED

This leaves dualism with interaction, the two forms of subjectivism, and hylomorphism as the theories of the mind-body relation for which positive argument is developed. When we compare these theories we see immediately that the primary issue is the question of whether the mind-body relation concerns two distinct kinds of existence or whether only one kind of existence is involved. Dualism, of course, is the position that mind and body are two distinct realities. Subjectivism denies their separate natures, and asserts that the apparently physical realities are in truth either minds or ideas. Hylomorphism interprets the difference between mind and body as the difference between form and matter; they are distinguishable but not separate. The issue thus seems to turn on the question of what is real. If we are dualists, then a positive theory of the mind-body relation will require some conception of interaction. If we cannot understand the possibility of interaction then we will have to choose between subjectivism and hylomorphism. If we choose subjectivism it is at the price of denying the real existence of body. If we are reluctant to do this we may take the position that mind and body are both real, but only in union as form and matter and not in separation from each other.

Spiritualism and idealism are philosophies which have their foundation in a theory of knowledge, and their adequacy as theories of the mind-body relation is primarily the question of their adequacy as theories of reality. In other words, the arguments for the subjectivist types of mind-body theories are arguments of a wider and more fundamental reach. Leibniz, for example, was led to the conclusion that all real entities are minds (monads) not because that position provides a solution of the mind-body problem but because he thought that only if the real is mental can we make intelligible the fact that physical motion is dynamic and not merely passive. Actually, when he came to the problem of the relation of the lower level monads which compose the body to the conscious monad which is the mind, Leibniz was forced into a theory of parallelism.

Berkeley's philosophy was a combination of spiritualism and idealism. Minds exist, and these minds possess ideas, the ultimate source of which is God. The world of nature, of mountains and trees and clouds and stars, is a world composed of ideas. But Berkeley did not arrive at this position as a consequence of the difficulties involved in understanding the relation of mind and body as distinct kinds of substance. He reached it from an analysis of perception. Once he did reach it, of course, the special problems of interaction in a theory of dualism had disappeared. The situation in the case of subjectivism consequently seems to be this: if on other grounds you reach a position of spiritualism or idealism, the problems of the relation of mind and body will disappear. But subjectivism has seldom if ever been arrived at as a result of a direct consideration of the mind-body problem. Apparently there is nothing to be found in a direct attack on the mind-body problem to suggest the non-existence of either mind or body. Such a suggestion would seem to come from other sources.

THE ISSUE BETWEEN DUALISM AND HYLOMORPHISM

Interactionist dualism and hylomorphism have much in common. Both theories make a clear distinction between mind and body and both theories recognize a two-way influence of mind upon body and of body upon mind. The chief difference seems to be that for dualism mind and body are two substances of two different orders of being, while for hylomorphism mind and body are the formal and material aspects of one substance—the individual human being. The difficulties with dualism turn on the question of how these two substances of different orders of being can interact.

The typical criticism of interaction, a criticism we have already mentioned as leading some to accept parallelism or to reject dualism altogether, is that the causal action of body on something not physical and the introduction of physical changes resulting from a nonphysical cause would both be violations of the law of conservation of energy. An additional argument against interactionism is the difficulty of conceiving how a physical object, which acts by motion and the release of energy, could bring about a change in a mental substance which is not in space at all and thus not within the reach of any physical process. How a mental substance can produce motion is equally difficult to understand, for since a mind is not in space it cannot move and so cannot make physical contact with anything in space.

One answer to this difficulty, developed with great effectiveness by Professor Howard D. Roelofs, is to point out that interaction of mind and body is not a causal affair at all, for

> we know what it takes for one body to do something to another body, and we know that the mind does not have that. Energy is required and the mind lacks it. Again, we know what happens when one body does affect another, the first loses energy. But the body loses no energy in its relations with the mind. Therefore, there can be no interaction. I accept the whole argument, but only and precisely in its own terms. Note what they are. Here Interaction is taken to be energy exchange, what one body does to another body. But the mind is not another body, nor the body another mind. Neither one pushes the other around, as if both were bodies; neither one communicates *ideas* to the other, as if both were minds.[23]

The interaction of body and mind, Professor Roelofs argues, is one of response rather than causation:

> What happens when mind and body interact is this: to a specific state of the body, probably a specific state of a specific part of the body, the brain, and a state proper to that part, the mind responds with a change *proper to it*, an idea, a feeling, a perception, as the case may be. This response is determinate: the mind feels what the body determines. On other occasions, to a specific state of mind, a state proper

[23] Roelofs, *op. cit.*, pp. 467-68.

to the mind, let it be a specific intent of will, the body responds in a manner proper to it, the body moves. This response is also determinate: the body does what the mind wills. This is control, in both directions, without exchange. That is why I use the term response.[24]

If we ask how mind can respond to body we are not left entirely in the dark. For we have instances of such response in those innumerable awarenesses of body in ordinary perception. It is not difficult to suppose that these explicitly conscious awarenesses are mediated by more elementary and unconscious cognitive responses of mind to specific brain states. A noncausal response to the presence and action of something else is quite intelligible if that response is cognitive. But what concept can we form of a response which is both noncausal and noncognitive? If this body is to respond to an act of will what relation does it have to mind to make that response possible? It is not aware, as body, of the mind's purpose. If somehow the body does respond to the act of will the bodily action will be other than what it would have been if the act of will had not occurred. This means there will be changes in body processes, changes of energy discharges and of movement, and these are physical changes. Are they uncaused?

Professor Roelofs' answer is to say that the fact of interaction requires us to accept in both mind and body a capacity beyond those ordinarily attributed to them. "Further this capacity functions, so far as the evidence goes, only in a specific situation, the union of body and mind in one being."[25] It is not body as body which has a capacity to respond to body, but mind united with body in one being. Nor is it mind, simply as pure intelligence, that has the capacity to respond to body, but mind united with body in one being. We are neither pure intelligences nor mere bodies:

> We are minds and bodies united in single beings. It is clear, at least to me, that what we can learn of minds and bodies in that union, should be conclusive as to what each can do *in that union*. It is true that we have considerable knowledge of what just bodies can do. But it is simply fatuous to take the activity of body in isolation from mind as exhaustive of what body can do in union with mind.[26]

The question thus comes to be the question of the nature of the union of body and mind. Body can do in that union what body

24 *Ibid*, p. 468.
25 *Ibid*.
26 *Ibid*, pp. 468-69.

cannot do out of that union. This immediately suggests that such a union is a transformation of body, of its mode of existence. Such is close to the contention of hylomorphism that body, as the material of the individual person, is united with mind as the form. As such, body is no longer mere body. It is body informed with mind. Mind is no bodiless intelligence, but mind embodied.

Professor Roelofs recognizes that the weakness of dualism is its inability to give an account of the unity of body and mind:

> When I attend as persistently and comprehensively as I can to what I myself am, I then find Dualism defective in its account of my unity. . . . *Functional* unity is provided. What is lacking is an adequate account of man's *essential* unity. How is man both two natures and yet one person? [27]

He points out further that in emotion we have a peculiar fusion of body and mind.

> Could either a pure intelligence or a pure body *shudder?*—"tremble convulsively with fear, horror, or aversion?" Could either a body or a mind by itself *laugh?* These are not interactions of two components, not a constant conjunction of two components. The shuddering, the convulsive trembling with fear, is one in its own essence, and that which alone can shudder, the embodied soul, is one . . .[In this union we have] both the interaction of a dualism and a unity which transcends interaction.[28]

What kind of unity transcends the interaction of body and mind and yet includes that interaction? Perhaps our best way to identify this is to say that it is the unity of a self, or personal unity. What exists is the person, and the person simply cannot be adequately understood as a combination of mind and body. It is a new level of existence, just as a living organism is a level of existence in which the physical constituents acquire a new way of existing.

How do we account for the fact that there are different levels of existence? If we account for this in terms of evolution, then, of course, we may be asked how we account for the fact that evolution has occurred. At some point we are forced to recognize that we are dealing with ultimate facts. That there are different levels (including levels of inorganic existence, living organisms, and persons) may not be something to be accounted for at all; it may well rather

[27] *Ibid*, p. 474.
[28] *Ibid*, p. 476.

be that these are ultimate facts in terms of which we account for other things. On the other hand, we may find the existence of the world itself to be a fact which is not intelligible in itself, and this may lead us to existence which transcends the world itself. But if we accept the assumption that all existence is intelligible, and if we take evolution seriously, we may find it difficult to deny that even in its most elementary state this world was something more than physical in its potentialities.

The problem of mind and body thus gives way to a different problem, the problem of the nature of a self and of its mode of existence. Perhaps the best we may say concerning the mind-body problem is that it is insoluble on its own grounds because the nature of the self cannot be understood in terms of any kind of relation of distinguishable aspects of the self. Professor Roelofs finds dualism defective, he says, "in its account of my unity." But why should the unity of a self be understood in terms of the relation of body and mind unless that unity is the consequence of the union of these two kinds of beings? Perhaps the distinction of body and mind, as aspects of my own existence, is the consequence of reflective abstraction. The dualism of body and soul or mind, which was stated at the beginning of this chapter to be one of the basic facts of human experience, may need to be reinterpreted, just as we need to reinterpret the apparent fact of direct experience that the sun moves across the sky of an earth which is at rest. Even if dualism is true, in the sense that both mind and body are genuine aspects of our existence, it is inadequate in its supposition that our existence is the result of a union of mind and body. The double aspect theory explains nothing; it merely asserts the existence of both aspects, and the abstract structure presented in the hylomorphic theory needs to be supplemented by a more adequate account of a self's mode of existence. In our next chapter we shall consider directly the question of the nature of a self and its mode of existence.

SUMMARY

The distinction of body and soul or mind is a distinction which arises out of basic human experience, and its genuineness is seldom doubted except under the influence of theory. Reflection upon this distinction and the problems involved in the attempt to understand the relationship of mind and body have given rise to may different theories. These may be classified as follows:

I. Dualism
    A. Interactionism
    B. Parallelism
II. Materialism
    A. Epiphenomenalism
    B. Behaviorism
III. Subjectivism
    A. Spiritualism
    B. Idealism
IV. Integration theories
    A. The double aspect theory
    B. Hylomorphism

Of these, parallelism, epiphenomenalism, behaviorism, and the double aspect theories are not so much conclusions reached by reflection upon our experience of minds and bodies as they are positions taken because of other considerations. Interactionist dualism, spiritualism, idealism, and hylomorphism are the views for which positive arguments are presented. Of these, the two forms of subjectivism are implications of a theory of reality which in turn is based on the theory of knowledge. In so far as the mind-body problem can be considered in its own right and apart from wider considerations, the issue thus seems to be between interactionism and hylomorphism.

The attempt to understand interaction without attributing physical properties to mind or mental properties to body leads to a recognition that body in union with mind is not the same as body apart from mind, and that mind in union with body is not the same as what mind would be apart from body. This brings the theory of interactionist dualism very close to hylomorphism. The weakness of interactionism is in its inadequate account of the unity of the self, and the weakness of hylomorphism is in its abstractness. The body-mind problem can be dealt with adequately perhaps only if we take a different approach and consider directly the question of the nature of a self and how it exists.

1. *Terms:* behaviorism, double aspect theory, dualism, epiphenomenalism, final cause, hylomorphism, idealism, integration theories, interaction, monad, parallelism, pre-established harmony, prehension, rationalism, soul, spiritualism.

2. Does the primitive distinction between body and soul constitute a genuine dualism, or is it a distinction between parts of a composite being which are essentially of the same order of existence?

3. Is parallelism compatible with freedom of the will?

4. Examine the aphorism of a nineteenth century materialist: The brain secretes thought as the liver secretes bile.

5. How far is it possible to differentiate the physical and the mental in the following activities: speaking, walking, digesting, dreaming, thinking, deciding?

6. Is Whitehead's version of the double aspect theory closer to dualism or to hylomorphism?

7. Examine the implications of the theory of evolution for the problem of mind and body. Are any of the body-mind theories discussed in this chapter incompatible with evolution?

CHAPTER 11

The
Self
and
Freedom

WHAT IS A SELF?

No theory does justice to our experience which takes the self to be solely physical or solely mental or to be only a conjunction of a body and a mind. As in the case of the relation of an organism to its physical constituents, the self is a higher organization which has properties and powers not to be found in its constituents at lower levels of integration. The unity characteristic of a self is a unity of awareness and of action, the unity expressed in our ordinary use of the personal pronouns in their primary meanings. To say "I," "we," "you," or "he" is to refer to a self. The self is that which we designate by the use of these pronouns. What we refer to when we use these words includes the physical, for we find nothing strange in such statements as: "He is not here," or "I am overweight." On the other hand, we do not ordinarily use these pronouns to refer to the body in such a way as to exclude the mental, for we speak of "*my* body," "*your* body," and so on. We say:

"Jones's arm was broken," but we do not say: "A part of Jones was broken."

The unity characteristic of selves is most plainly seen on the side of experience. Experience of course is not confined to selves. Presumably it is coextensive with animal life at least. We cannot get inside the experience of lower animals but we can make fairly plausible inferences from their behavior and from our knowledge of the kind of learning they are capable of. Animals do not use language, in the strict sense of responding to symbols. Words and phrases may be used as signals to release activities in animals that they are prepared to perform by instinct or learning. But there is no indication that animals can have a truly symbolic response to words, that on hearing the words the animal can become aware of what the words refer to. If someone refers, in my hearing, to "the Court House on the town square" I am aware of the building to which he refers. A dog might be taught to trot down the street to the building when the phrase is spoken as a signal, but the words would not have symbolic meaning for him in the sense that on hearing them he would think of the building itself. That this difference between man and lower animals is physical as well as mental is a plausible inference from the differences found in the higher brain centers, particularly in the development in man of the language centers and the forebrain, and from the fact that although animals can be trained to react to words as signals they seem not to learn to *use* artificial signs to communicate.

The conscious functions linked with language are functions of the unity of awareness. Among these are memory, the present awareness of the past; imagination, abstract ideas which have a certain independence of control by present objects of experience; and anticipation and purpose in which future possibilities are envisaged in idea and accepted by the self as directive of its action. In all these acts, self-awareness is at the center of the experience. A recurrence in idea of a past experience, for example, would not be a memory if the self which had the past experience were not the same self which has the memory. In fact we could not distinguish between past and present without identity in self-awareness. The gradual emergence of self-awareness in children is seen in the gradual development of a recognition of time intervals and of the relation of the present to other parts of the day and week and year. Evidence of self-awareness appears also in the child's ability to distinguish between himself as subject and himself as object, between the "I" and the "me."

If we try to identify more specifically the nature of this unity of awareness which is characteristic of a self we find ourselves at a loss as to where to look for it.

> There are some philosophers [said David Hume], who imagine we are every moment intimately conscious of what we call our SELF; that we feel its existence and its continuance in existence. . . . For my part, when I enter intimately into what I call *myself*, I always stumble on some particular perception or other, of heat or cold, light or shade, love or hatred, pain or pleasure. I never can catch *myself* at any time without a perception, and never can observe anything but the perception. When my perceptions are remov'd for any time, as by sound sleep; so long am I insensible of *myself*, and may truly be said not to exist. . . . I may venture to affirm of . . . mankind, that they are nothing but a bundle or collection of different perceptions, which succeed each other with an inconceivable rapidity, and are in a perpetual flux or movement. . . . The mind is a kind of theatre, where several perceptions successively make their appearance; pass, re-pass, glide away, and mingle in an infinite variety of postures and situations. . . . The comparison of the theatre must not mislead us. They are the successive perceptions only, that constitute the mind; nor have we the most distant notion of the place, where these scenes are represented, or of the materials, of which it is compos'd.[1]

Hume is clearly right about one thing. We do not find the self as one among the many other objects of experience. If it is the self which has the experience then the self, by itself, can hardly be what is found in the experience. But here Hume leaves something out. Because of his oversimplified theory of what experience is, he overlooks our experience of the acts of the self such as the acts of perceiving and remembering and imagining.

Hume himself recognizes that his own position makes it impossible for him to admit that we have any awareness of *acts* of the mind, for since the mind is nothing but a succession of impressions and ideas there is nothing there to act. In his discussion of how we distinguish between imagination and memory, for example, Hume does not even consider the possibility of a direct awareness of these acts. He considers only two possible explanations. The first one is

[1] *A Treatise of Human Nature*, edited by A. L. Selby-Bigge (Oxford at the Clarendon Press, 1928), pp. 251-253.

that the difference lies in the *kind* of ideas we have in each instance. He rejects this on the ground that in both imagination and memory our ideas are derived from impressions "and can never go beyond these original perceptions." The other possibility is that the difference lies in peculiarities of the *arrangement* of ideas of memory and imagination. He rejects this because we cannot recall past impressions to compare them with present ideas in order to find out whether these present ideas preserve the original arrangement of certain past impressions. He concludes that the only difference between the memory of a past event and something we merely imagine or fancy

> lies in its superior force and vivacity. A man may indulge his fancy in feigning any past scene of adventures; nor wou'd there be any possibility of distinguishing this from a remembrance of a like kind, were not the ideas of the imagination fainter and more obscure.[2]

Hume's analysis thus raises an issue concerning the facts of experience. Are we aware only of sensory content, feelings, and inclinations; or are we aware also of the *acts* of perceiving, imagining, remembering, willing, and desiring? Many of us would insist that we are aware not only of what we perceive but, on reflection, we become aware also of the acts of perceiving. Unless, however, when our attention is directed toward other objects we also have at least a dim awareness of the act of awareness as well, there would be nothing for reflection to attend to and bring into clear awareness. So, too, in thinking, imagining, remembering, desiring, willing, and in every act of awareness we are aware of the act as well as of the object toward which that act is directed.

Ordinarily our attention is on the object of awareness. When we reflect, in another act of awareness, we can attend to the act while the object recedes from the center. It may now be asked, in what act of awareness we become aware of the self alone, and this seems to be the question Hume was asking. In these terms, the question is unanswerable. For Hume asks us to find an awareness of the self apart from our awareness of other things and apart from our awareness of the acts of self. What would the awareness of the self, as thus isolated, be? It would not be a perception, nor a memory, nor an image, nor a concept. For the "bare" self has never been exposed to us in its bareness, and we have no reason to suppose that it exists

[2] *Ibid*, p. 85.

as a *bare* self at all. The self exists as acting, as perceiving, remembering, imagining, thinking, willing, deciding, wishing, loving, hating, fearing, regretting, and so on. If reflection is looking for a bare self that is somehow detached, as it were, from its acts, then there is nothing for reflection to find and to place in the center of awareness.

Hume fails to recognize the bipolar structure of experience. He seems to suppose that the awareness of something is simply a case in which something, as it were, "shows up." This is not what happens in awareness. At the distinctively human level, at least, awareness is complex; and awareness of self is given along with awareness of object. The content of awareness is no simple fact, such as "green, oblong patch," "strident noise," and such. Our awareness is rather, "I am seeing that oblong green patch of grass," or "I am hearing that noise of a power saw," or "I am remembering that delightful visit." Harmon M. Chapman calls attention to the fact that such expressions as "The children are home," "The milk has arrived," and so on

> are all elliptical expressions and carry with them even in the natural attitude an implied "I think that . . . ," "I see . . . ," and so on. As Kant correctly put it, the "I think" must be able to attend every act of consciousness.[3]

Along with this content is also the penumbra of awareness of specific space and time relationships to other things and other experiences. Professor John Wild points out that it is in this complex bipolar structure of experience that we find the self in its existence. When we attend to the act of awareness of a previous awareness, we take that act out of its existential context and make an object of it. When we get it as an object we do not get it in the act.

> I do not believe that traditional thought has been correct [says Professor Wild] in supposing that I gain a clear awareness of my own act only by a second reflexive act, or in idealistic language, that I can know one consciousness only by another consciousness intending it from the outside. My existing awareness, in its first act, opens into a world horizon which is ever present as encompassing any specific object that I intend. But this horizon belongs to my existence, and can never be objectified. Hence when I look at an original awareness as an object, from the standpoint of a second act, it is torn from its

[3] "Realism and Phenomenology," in *The Return to Reason*, edited by John Wild (Chicago, Henry Regnery Company, 1953), p. 32. By permission.

world context, and is reduced to the level of a peculiar subjective object, or subject, within a world that is not its own.[4]

Where awareness of the acts of the self is lacking, and just to the extent that it is lacking, other knowledge as well is impossible. I do not *know* that a conclusion I reach by reasoning is valid unless I am aware that I am reasoning. I do not *know* that the tree I perceive is really there unless I am aware that I am perceiving. If I plan to spend $7.00 of the $20.00 I have in my pocket, I cannot *know* that there will be $13.00 left unless I am aware that I am performing the act of subtracting. I do not first subtract, and then, on reflection, make the happy discovery that this is in fact what I was doing. We often find ourselves uncertain about our memories. This is not merely, or perhaps ever, because the image lacks vividness; for I may be quite sure I saw a certain person at a certain place yesterday even though my present image is dim. When we are uncertain about a memory the uncertainty is usually, if not always, about whether we are remembering or imagining the specific detail concerning which we are uncertain. So also the deceptive nature of illusion and hallucination is confusion within the moment of awareness, but a confusion of one *mode* of awareness with another.[5]

If we ask now, "What is the self?" we may answer first that it is the coming together and sustaining of experience in a dynamic unity in which different experiences manifest their relevance to each other. Secondly, the self is a unity of action in which motive, goal, and means are held together in conscious relevance and action is guided by that awareness.

If we ask, "How are we aware of the self?" we may answer that we are aware of the self by catching it in act. Awareness is bipolar: perception, for example, is not mere awareness of an object present to the senses but is awareness of the self perceiving the object; memory of a past event is awareness of the self remembering the event. The self, as distinguished from the objects of awareness, is the "I." And what is the "I"? It is what shows itself in the act of perceiving, remembering, imagining, reasoning, desiring, deciding, regretting, and so forth.

[4] "Contemporary Phenomenology and the Problem of Existence," *Philosophy and Phenomenological Research*, Volume XX, No. 2, December 1959, p. 168.

[5] See Chapman, *op. cit.*, pp. 23-24.

AWARENESS OF THE PAST

An equally serious oversight in Hume's analysis is his failure to see the significance of the fact that we are aware not only of "some particular impression or other," but also are aware, as he says, that perceptions "succeed each other" and "are in a perpetual flux or movement"; perceptions "pass, re-pass, glide away, and mingle"; the mind is constituted of "successive perceptions." Hume fails to see that the awareness of a succession of perceptions cannot itself be merely one of those successive perceptions. Only an awareness with an identity of its own in distinction from its objects could be an awareness of those perceptions *as* a succession.

The unity of awareness characteristic of a self is one which in some way includes more than the present moment. Unless my present memory of a sound I heard a moment ago is an awareness that somehow reaches into the past I cannot properly be said to remember. Suppose it is said that I have an image which I refer to the past, but that what I am aware of now is itself wholly in the present. The difficulty is that if my awareness does not in some sense actually reach into the past then there is no past in my awareness to which to *refer* the present image.

At this point we are confronted with a serious problem. In some sense, what I am aware of now in memory is something that existed in the past. But my awareness takes place *now*. How, then, can it be said to "reach into" the past? Clearly we need to make some distinctions, otherwise we shall find ourselves supposing either that we can actually reverse the order of time and bring back the past in its real existence, or else that we are not aware of the past at all but are aware of a deceptive present, of a present which masquerades as a past. That the first of these cannot be the case is plain from the fact that the supposed return to the past would take place after the past event itself and thus would not be a genuine reconstitution of the past in its actual existence. On the other hand, if we are not aware of the past at all, but merely of a present which is disguised as the past, then we destroy the basis upon which we understand the time relation itself. How could we have the illusion of experiencing the past unless we had had a genuine experience of the past?

The first step in avoiding the worst of these difficulties and paradoxes is to examine the relation between past and present. As Professor Wild points out in another place,

> in reality the past exists only so far as it is actualized in a present *now*, and the future exists only in so far as this present *now* is beginning it in potency. All that actually exists is a *present*. So there are no *real* relations between things existing at different times. There are only *mental* relations, which have a real foundation, so far as the mind accurately remembers what actually happened in a preceding *now*, no longer existent, or accurately anticipates what actually will be in a non-existent future.[6]

This distinction may be somewhat differently stated as one between the *nature* or *essence* of something in the past and the *existence* of that past event. Certainly we cannot bring the past in its existence into the present, for this would be to change its real relations with the present and thus make it something other than what actually happened. But a present existence can carry in it something of the nature or essence of a past existent. I look at a picture taken years ago. The picture which I see exists now, but there is a partial identity of what this picture shows with the nature of that something in the past. In this present picture there is an arrangement of line and color partially identical with the arrangement of line and color which was shown by the object that was photographed in the past. I see a distant star. What comes to me is a light pattern which exists in my field of vision now, light which left the star many years ago. I do not now see the star in its existence of perhaps hundreds of years ago. The conditions under which the light from the star has traversed the intervening space to my eyes are such that the light has preserved something of the same pattern it had when it left the star. Here is a partial identity of a present light pattern with the physical nature of a past existent, an identity which enables me to know something of *what* the past was in spite of the fact that I cannot confront the past situation in its actual existence.[7]

On the other hand, no awareness of the past is possible, and thus no reconstruction in the present of a past to which we could refer, unless present awareness in some sense contains a past. Here we need to try to answer the question of *how* the past, in Professor

[6] *Introduction to Realistic Philosophy* (New York, Harper and Brothers, 1948), p. 346. By permission.

[7] For an interesting discussion of this problem, see Paul Weiss, *Modes of Being* (Carbondale, Southern Illinois University Press, 1958), pp. 207-09.

Wild's words, "is actualized in a present now." Certainly the present moment of experience is not a mathematical instant, a mere one-dimensional mathematical line, as it were, separating past from future and with no "breadth" of its own. Nor is the present moment a static given amount of time that is simply there. On the contrary, the present moment of experience is a dynamic forward moving awareness, pushing ever beyond itself (into the future) and moving ever beyond itself (from the past). It is the *movement* that is distinctive, not any given amount of presentness. I am immediately aware of the past in this sense: that I am constantly aware of the present *in process of becoming past*. Of course I cannot go back and pick up a piece of the past and move it into the present in order now to inspect it. But right now I am aware of the passage itself, and from the structure of the dynamic present I am able to construct the whole vast framework of time in which I locate events whose nature or essence I capture again in the present.

HOW DOES THE SELF EXIST?

If we ask how the self achieves its unity, and establishes the continuity of experience that we find in the awareness of self-identity, we find two ways in which this question is approached. This is not surprising, for awareness seems to be a dual structure, with *acts* of awareness and the *objects* of awareness. We may try to understand the unity of the self as a relationship among the objects of experience, or we may try to understand the unity of the self as a unity in the acts of awareness.

The attempt to understand the unity and continuity of awareness in terms of relations among the objects of experience seeks for certain features or relations among these objects which will account for the connections we find between present and past experience. Some of the features which have been proposed as significant are *resemblance, contrast*, and *contiguity* in space and time, and *causal connection*. The experience of an object which resembles a previously experienced object tends to *revive* the earlier experience. Thus the unity of awareness is explained as the presence in the same experience of two or more objects having certain relations among themselves. There are laws of association in accordance with which these relations are established in experience. *White* suggests *snow* and *snow* suggests *cold*. We go so far even to say that white "makes us think" of snow, and snow "makes us think" of cold. *White* also suggests its contrast, *black*. The sight of a building may lead to the recall of a past experience in that building, such as a painful session with a dentist. In these and other ways the relations of the objects of experience are supposed to account for the unity of awareness which is at the basis of our self-awareness. We may go again to Hume for an illustration of this conception:

> As all simple ideas may be separated by the imagination, and may be united again in what form it pleases, nothing wou'd be more unaccountable than the operations of that faculty, were it not guided by some universal principles, which render it, in some measure, uniform with itself in all times and places. Were ideas entirely loose and unconnected, chance alone wou'd join them; and 'tis impossible the same simple ideas should fall regularly into complex ones (as they commonly do) without some bond of union among them, some associating quality, by which one idea naturally introduces another. This uniting principle among ideas is not to be consider'd as an inseparable connexion; for that has been already excluded from the imagination: nor yet are we to conclude, that without it the mind cannot join two ideas; for nothing is more free than that faculty: but we are only to regard it as a gentle force, which commonly prevails, and is the cause why, among other things, languages so nearly correspond to each other; nature in a manner pointing out to every one those simple ideas, which are most proper to be united into a complex one. The qualities, from which this association arises, and by which the mind is after this manner convey'd from one idea to another, are three, *viz.* RESEMBLANCE, CONTIGUITY in time or place, and CAUSE and EFFECT.[8]

By virtue of such associations the "bundle or collection of different perceptions" which make up the self, according to Hume, is constituted and maintained. "Here is a kind of ATTRACTION," Hume comments, apparently with Newton's theory of universal gravitation in mind, "which in the mental world will be found to have as extraordinary effects as in the natural, and to shew itself in as many and as various forms." [9]

The difficulty with this theory of the self is that the very experiences out of which the unity of the self is to be constructed are experiences which themselves already involve that unity. How

[8] Hume, *op. cit.*, pp. 10-11.
[9] *Ibid*, pp. 12-13.

could I recognize a resemblance, or a contiguity, or a causal connection unless I already had a unified awareness? It is true that we often associate, say, by resemblance without an explicit awareness that this is what we are doing. But if the past experience were the experience of one consciousness and the present experience that of another, what connection between the objects could there be for either awareness? On Hume's view, every single experience is a separate consciousness. Only if there is already a unity of the self which has the two objects in its experience, can resemblance or any other link between them lead from the awareness of one object to awareness of the other.

The fact that self-awareness comes gradually is no evidence against the view that the unity of the self is to be found in the acts of the self rather than as derivative solely from the objects of experience. For self-awareness in the act of perceiving an object or remembering the past or deciding a course of action, or in other acts of the self, is not clear and sharp. Attention here is on the object; awareness of the self attending and performing its own functions is a part of the total awareness which is now in the background. Not until we turn attention, in reflection, toward the act of the self can we discern more clearly something of its structure. This of course is another act, and in it we examine the former act now out of its own existential context; for the only act now actually going on is the act of reflecting on our previous act. Such reflective experience, however, contributes toward a more explicit awareness of the self as we find it in act.

We have here something of the same relation between direct experience of an object and reflective analysis that we find in listening to music. As we hear a musical composition being played we are aware, dimly and vaguely, of the formal structure of that music. To center our attention on the formal structure itself we have to turn attention away from the moving sound which is the music. But after attending to the structure and returning to the music, we find our listening enhanced by a more explicit awareness of relations of themes and of dynamic patterns even when we are attending as directly as we can to the sound itself.

It is when we ask how the self exists that we see where its unity is to be found. The self exists, so far as we can tell in our direct and reflective experience, in those acts of perception, memory, thought, imagination, desire, purpose and will. These are what we find the self to be doing, and so we may say that the self exists in the performance of these acts.

The traditional doctrine that the self exists as substance is based on the principle that an act requires something that acts. In other words, to be in act is first of all to *be*, and to be something with a nature of its own. Of course substantiality is not something we sense or perceive; we *think* it. To deny that the self is substance would be, on this interpretation of substance, to deny that there is anything that acts in perception and thinking and in the other acts we attribute to the self. In one sense the self is its acts; it exists *in act*. But the specific acts are acts of one self and are expressions of definite powers which that self has. The important point of the substance conception of the self is in its denial that the self is simply a collection or even an integration of experiences. The self exists first of all as an active *being*—as the power of desiring, intending, deciding, doubting, believing, knowing, etc.

The self exists as act, and there are two important and distinctive characteristics of the action of a self. First, the self exists as *an act which goes beyond the present*. This is especially plain in memory and anticipation. As has been mentioned before, in memory a *present* experience somehow reaches into the *past*. We have an awareness *of* the past *in* the present. A picture may be of something past, but the picture is not an awareness of the past. It is *our* awareness which uses the picture to recall the past.

Only a self can make judgments about the past and about the future, and only a self can consider the present in terms of the relation to the past and to future possibilities. As one consequence of this ability to be aware of what has come to it in past experience, the self is able also to consider the present in terms of its relation to what is absent in space as well as in time. Having learned the permanent spatial relationship of places, we are able from that time on to orient ourselves no matter in which of those places we may be. Not only spatial orientation but innumerable patterns of relationship become available to us as parts of the framework and setting of present experience. Thus in conscious awareness the fragment of existence which is directly present now is supplemented and filled out in idea in more or less approximation, depending on the extent of our knowledge, to the reality to which it belongs in fact. At the basis of all this is the time-transcending character of the self's awareness.

The time-transcending character of the self enables it also to reach beyond the present into the future. In our knowledge of things we form definite concepts of *what* those things are, of their basic and relatively permanent natures. In so far as we know *what* a thing is and how it acts, and in so far as we are justified in assuming that the things we know will exist in the future and will have the same nature they now have, to that extent we know something of what will be happening in the future. I have every reason to believe that the tree I see now in full leaf will drop its leaves in the coming months, stand bare and leafless through the winter, and leaf out again in the spring. For it is the nature of this kind of tree to go through such a cycle so long as it lives. I know also that there are other possibilities. There are diseases that may kill the tree; a windstorm can uproot it; lightning may strike; or I may decide to cut it down in order to make the space available for something else. I may not be sure which of these alternatives will be realized, but from my knowledge of the nature of the tree and of plant diseases and weather conditions and from my knowledge of my own interest and preferences for the use of my property I do know something very definite about future possibilities.

This second distinctive characteristic of the action of a self is its power to know what some of the future possibilities are, and its power to choose, within limitations, which of those possibilities shall be actual. The self exists most completely and at its fullest in the act of decision. At any moment a self is a focus of existence. The unity of my experience includes the natures of things which have never been united in fact. Something I see now, reminds me of a scene from my childhood. This present event and that earlier event were never present together and never can be present together in actual occurrence, but they do come together in my experience. I can deal with one thing in the light of its relations with other things with which it has had no contact and between which the only connection runs through my awareness of both. As the unity of the self is a focus of relationships from the past, so also it is a center from which radiate future possibilities. The decision I make is the determining factor in the selection of the actual from among these many possibilities. A moment before the decision is made and acted upon, many possibilities remain available; the moment the decision is made and carried out, the instant the word is spoken or the fingers release the letter in the mail-drop or the telegram is put on the wires, at that moment one of the earlier possibilities begins its existence as an actuality and all those which are in conflict with it are left behind as mere ghosts of what might have been.

In decision we do, in a sense, make fact. We serve as agents in the never-ceasing process of change which is the actual world. Thus decision has a creative aspect. Our ideas of the future have a part in making the future. But there is another sense in which decision is creative. For we not only influence the course of other existence in the decisions we make, we also create ourselves. We ourselves are, at any moment in life, truly unfinished in our nature. There are possibilities open to us and in our choices and decisions we contribute to the realization of some of these possibilities and to the elimination of others. We create ourselves just to the extent that we adopt our own purposes and do not simply take to ourselves the purposes and goals which other people urge upon us. So far as we form our own standards of judgment and evaluation, instead of passively accepting the norms which happen to be generally accepted in our society, we make ourselves to be the kind of persons we become.

> As a self [says Richard Kroner], man is under obligation to determine himself; he is not like all other things in the world determined by his "nature." In a way he has no nature at all, because he has a will. By nature, man is neither good nor bad; he is good or bad by his will. The will is the center of man's moral self. Through his will he makes himself the man he is. He determines his "nature," his individual character.[10]

THE PROBLEM OF FREEDOM

The ability to choose, to exert some control over the course of events by our own decisions, suggests that a self is in some sense and to some degree a free agent. For if my acts as a self are controlled by other things then I am only a channel through which other things act. If this is true then I only seem to decide; in fact my decision is only a reflection in my awareness of relationships of forces over which I have no control. We seem to be free. We feel like free agents in our action. Yet we are influenced by

[10] *The Primacy of Faith* (New York, The Macmillan Company, 1943), p. 112. By permission.

other things and by forces we do not understand. This presents a problem, a problem which is both theoretical and practical: How far do influences and forces outside of ourselves control our choice and our decisions? Are we to any significant extent capable of acting without such control? If we are not capable of acting in freedom then our impressions concerning what the self is and how it exists are lamentably in error.

The problem of freedom is not a problem which can be solved by searching for new factual evidence. It is a problem of interpreting and understanding the significance of facts we already know. Our sense of our freedom is a part of life as we live it from day to day, from hour to hour and from moment to moment. Not often do we reply to a suggestion: "I am not free to act," or "My hands are tied." Sometimes we do, but these times are rare in comparison with such responses as, "I'll see," or "I'll think it over," or "I haven't made up my mind yet." At the same time we are aware of strong forces pulling us this direction and that. Sometimes a decision seems to come of itself without any specific act of choice we are aware of making. So often our decisions seem to oppose rather than carry out our preferences. We discover later that an earlier decision was influenced by attitudes we were not aware of when we made it, and we wonder how far such unconscious influences extend and whether perhaps our sense of autonomy is not entirely an illusion.

Thus we face the issue of freedom or determinism. Our initial assumption is that of freedom, and common sense supports us in this assumption. As infants and in early childhood we no doubt felt ourselves at times to be omnipotent. Only gradually and painfully did we become aware of our limitations and discover how powerful are the forces that influence our actions. Then as we learn something of the nature of our world in the physical and biological sciences, and as we discover some of the laws and courses of human behavior in our study of psychology and of the social sciences, we are led to consider the possibility that our sense of freedom is just an illusion. We feel the force of Spinoza's statement:

> Thus an infant thinks that it freely desires milk, an angry child thinks that it freely desires vengeance, or a timid child thinks it freely chooses flight. Again, a drunken man thinks that he speaks from the free will of the mind those things which, were he sober, he would keep to himself. Thus a madman, a talkative woman, or child, and people of such kind, think they speak by the free decision of the

mind, when, in truth, they cannot put a stop to the desire to talk, just as experience teaches as clearly as reason that *men think themselves free on account of this alone, that they are conscious of their actions and ignorant of the causes of them.*[11]

THE CASE FOR DETERMINISM

Determinism should be distinguished from fatalism, with which it is often confused. People who are fatalists believe in a kind of partial determinism, that certain important events in a person's life are predetermined by forces beyond his control in such a way that some specific outcome is ordained in each case no matter what the circumstances may be. For example, a person may be a fatalist about the day of his death. He may believe that the day on which he will die is already fixed and that nothing whatever could change that date. Even if he knew when it was to be, it would be useless for him to try to protect his life. A car would hit him, a stray bullet strike, or he might slip and fall and break his neck. Even if he should stay in bed on the fated day, something would happen; a heart attack, or an earthquake, or something else will destroy him. The soldier in combat who shows no fear because he believes that there is just one bullet "with his name on it," and that no other bullet can be fatal, is another example. So long as that bullet does not come his way, his life is safe; if it does come, it will seek him out inexorably and there is no point in trying to avoid it. Such beliefs are often linked with superstitions such as astrology and numerology, or with certain theological concepts.

Fatalism differs from universal determinism in two ways. The fatalist usually thinks that these crucial events are governed by forces or powers that are in some sense purposive in their activity. Something looks ahead, as it were, and when the appointed time comes intervenes to control events so that the preordained one will occur. Universal determinism is usually thought of as a control exercised not by some power that anticipates the future but entirely by preceding causes. The second difference is that where fatalism may admit freedom in every aspect of life except for the few fated occurrences, determinism is conceived as universal and all-inclusive.

---

[11] *Ethics*, translated by A. Boyle (Everyman's Library, New York, E. P. Dutton and Company, 1910), pp. 88-89. Italics not in the original.

Nothing escapes its net. For fatalism, in short, nothing makes any difference to the outcome once it is preordained; for determinism, everything makes a difference.

Determinism goes with mechanism, and the case for mechanism is a case for determinism. The essential point of mechanism is the conception of mutual externality of the parts and the existence of each part in independence of the others, together with the idea that the action of any one part is brought about by the action of something else. Thus no mechanism is self-moving and no mechanism can operate in isolation. Since each part depends on something outside itself for its action it follows that the nature of the action is partly under the control of something outside the moving part. What happens depends also, of course, on the make-up of the part itself. But this also is the result of the action of something else. No machine and no part of a machine makes itself. The conclusion is plain: every mechanical action is completely controlled by external causes.

Let us look at two variations of a simple mechanism—the mechanism of a strip of wood or metal attached vertically, at one place only, to a nonmoving base in such a way that the strip swings freely. If the strip is attached at its center to the base, its movement will be different when force is applied than when it is attached at the end of the strip. For one thing, when the strip is whirled about its center of gravity, its motion will be smooth and deceleration will be uniform; when the strip is attached by one end, the motion will not be smooth, for the strip will move faster on its downward path than on its upward and there will be a pendulum action before it comes to rest. These differences are in all respects differences *given* to the parts of the device by the arrangement in which they are placed; they are not differences brought into being by the way in which those parts exist in and of themselves.

Determinism as applied to human activity is usually an aspect of some more fundamental mechanistic conception of human existence. This need not be materialistic, for the mental also can be understood in terms of mechanism. The association theories in nineteenth century psychology, for example, were or tended to be mechanistic. Ideas were conceived as psychic units which entered into and passed out of relationship without themselves being changed. In association psychology the possibility of an idea undergoing change required that it be complex; its change consisted only of the addition or removal of constituent parts from the complex. Thus the final units were simple ideas, and everything else was to be explained by the linking and separating of simple ideas. Ideas were passive entities; all mental activity was something that happened *to* ideas. In some theories the mind was differentiated from ideas and had certain powers of combining and separating; in other theories the mind itself was nothing but the play of ideas. Their source was usually thought to be in sensation.[12]

A quite different type of psychological determinism is found in the work of Sigmund Freud. Freud's primary concern was with the affective side of human life, and especially with emotional disorders. But he was convinced that not only our temperaments and dispositions but even our so-called intellectual processes are governed by original instincts and by traumatic experiences of infancy and early childhood. Thus the mental make-up and the activities of the adult mind are controlled by structures and experiences over which no direct control is possible. Personality and emotional patterns can be changed, and a person's emotional disturbances can often be cured, by his becoming conscious of the early experiences of which they are the consequences; but this does not mitigate the complete determinism in which the mind is caught. For such changes are brought about as a result of what we may call a reshuffling of basic drives, and this is always under the control of and for the satisfaction of some aspect of the original instinctual nature. The belief in freedom, Freud argues, arises from the fact that some of our ideas are determined by unconscious factors and thus we are not aware of their causes. In our more important decisions we have a feeling of psychic compulsion, of being unable to have decided otherwise than we did. This feeling of compulsion he accepts as a true reflection of what actually is the case in such decisions.

On the other hand, it is in trivial and indifferent decisions that one feels sure that he could just as easily have acted differently, that he acted of his own free will, and without any motives. From our analysis we therefore need not contest the right of the feeling of conviction that there is a free will. If we distinguish conscious from unconscious motivation, we are then informed by the feeling of con-

[12] The classic expression of the association theory is found in James Mill, *Analysis of the Phenomena of the Human Mind* (1829). The chapter on "The Association of Ideas" is included in *Readings in the History of Psychology*, edited by Wayne Dennis (New York, Appleton-Century-Crofts, Inc., 1948), pp. 140-54.

viction that the conscious motivation does not extend over all our motor resolutions. . . . What is thus left free from the one side receives its motive from the other side, from the unconscious, and the determinism in the psychic realm is thus carried out uninterruptedly.[13]

When we consider the question of whether determinism is true or false, we find a special difficulty facing us. To demonstrate directly the truth of determinism would require us to show that nothing can ever act freely. The case for freedom does not face such a problem. For we can defend freedom as actual within a quite limited range of activity and still admit determinism in everything else. One act of freedom is enough to demonstrate the possibility of freedom. But the determinist must show that freedom is impossible, that *nothing* acts spontaneously; for him to show that one act is determined contributes nothing at all to his case. The point is that determinism is essentially a negative position while belief in freedom is essentially a positive position. Because of this a demonstration of the truth of determinism is seldom if ever attempted.

Instead of argument in support of its truth, the case for determinism is usually in the form of an argument in support of its adoption as a working hypothesis or as a point of view. In the context of the passage from Freud quoted above, he refers to absolute determinism as an "assumption." Although Freud himself believed firmly in the truth of determinism, he presents it here as a working hypothesis. These alternatives have quite different philosophical consequences. To accept determinism as a working hypothesis applicable to any area in which the concepts of mechanism provide guidance for scientific investigation, is a necessary procedure. For the reservation of any area from the reach of determinism is also its exclusion from the range of certain kinds of scientific investigations. Indeed, the willingness to accept determinism as a working hypothesis in specific areas in biology and in psychology, for example, has made possible much of the important progress which has occurred in those sciences. To the extent that scientific inquiry is thought to require the principles of mechanism as its prerequisite, determinism will be accepted as a working hypothesis in application to every field in which it is hoped to apply the methods of science. To recognize this does not mean to agree that the only possible scientific inquiry

[13] *Psychopathology of Everyday Life*, from p. 162 of *The Basic Writings of Sigmund Freud*, translated and edited by Dr. A. A. Brill. (Copyright 1938 by Random House, Inc.) Reprinted by permission of the Brill Trust.

is an application of the principles of mechanism, for if non-mecha-nistic concepts are applicable, as they seem to be even in certain areas of physics, determinism is not a necessary assumption.

The case for the *acceptance* of universal determinism is the case for advocating the universal application of the methods of science, *plus* the case for considering the concepts of mechanism to be essen-tial to any truly scientific inquiry. Quite rightly the determinist objects to an arbitrary restriction of scientific inquiry, to the reser-vation of any area of existence and the prohibition of the scientific study of that area. In so far as one is convinced that all existence is knowable scientifically and is convinced also that the methods of science which operate under the guidance of mechanistic concepts are final, one will hold to universal determinism. The apparent excep-tions to determinism will be considered, with Spinoza and Freud and others, as nothing but evidence of our ignorance, as challenges to further extension of scientific inquiry. The case for determinism is thus the case for a certain policy in our thinking. It may be a tactical policy, where determinism is accepted as a working hypothesis for certain limited areas of inquiry; or it may be a strategic policy, where determinism is a part of a general philosophy or world view. There are some today who feel that determinism as a strategic policy was easier to accept in the background of nineteenth century scien-tific thought than in the context of twentieth century science.

THE CASE FOR FREEDOM

Perhaps most of those who believe in the fact of free-dom simply take it for granted. Those who have considered the problem as a problem and who retain their belief in freedom, are convinced of the reality of freedom either because the arguments against it have not been convincing or because the arguments in sup-port of freedom have been convincing. Arguments in support of freedom are of two kinds: those which support the claim that the assertion of freedom is true and those intended to justify the accept-ance of freedom as a working hypothesis or basis of action.

The support of belief in freedom by an appeal to direct expe-rience may be quite convincing to some, but obviously it does not convince those who reject the reality of freedom. Determinists may remind us that people who believe that the sun moves across the face of the earth from east to west are accepting the authority of direct experience. Only by interpreting certain observations made under careful controls, and interpreting these under the guidance of hypotheses not based on direct experience but on mathematical calculations, do we discover that our direct experience of the motion of the sun is misleading. So it is with freedom, determinists argue. We seem to be able to choose between alternatives independently of various influences pushing us in one direction or the other, but according to the determinist the truth is that we are misled by appearances. As Spinoza said, we have the impression that we are free to act because we are ignorant of the causes of our action. So although a belief in freedom based on appeal to direct experience may be convincing enough to one who holds it, yet as it stands it does not establish the case for freedom. If we are to make a case for freedom, either we must help the determinist discover something about his own experience he has missed so far, or else we must bring reasons in support of the contention that in this instance direct experience is trustworthy. It is apparent that the case for freedom must be established by argument if it is to be established at all. We shall consider first some attempts to justify the assumption of freedom as a working hypothesis, and then consider some arguments in direct support of the truth of the belief that man is free.

Those who accept the reality of freedom as a working hypothesis must come to terms with determinism if they are to justify their policy. Until recently in modern thought, opposition to determinism was quite properly interpreted as opposition to the unlimited extension of scientific explanation. Some libertarians believe that there are certain areas of existence, particularly the human personality, which are not appropriate areas of scientific study. Our knowledge of these existences must come exclusively, they thought, from literature and philosophy and religion. But attempts to build a wall around certain objects to protect them from scientific study have never succeeded for long. When scientists find techniques to study these objects and develop an interest in doing so, the walls crumble. Only in a successful authoritarian society can any areas be protected even for a short time from scientific study if there are those who are determined to carry on such a study. The best way to stimulate inquiry is to try to prevent it.

Other libertarians make no attempt to exempt any areas of existence from scientific study; rather they contend that no matter how important is the knowledge we get from the use of the methods of science, those methods are limited and the knowledge they provide is incomplete. However much we may discover in scientific inquiry about an object there is always something more to be learned in other ways. Scientific inquiry is not to be barred from any area, on this view, but no matter where it is undertaken or how far it is carried the results obtained will be incomplete. We have already seen examples of this position in our study of scientific knowledge and its methods. All scientific inquiry, for example, makes certain assumptions about real existence, and if we are to examine these assumptions we shall have to use some other method than the method of science. All inquiry makes assumptions concerning what is of value, and the truth of such assumptions can be examined only by the methods of philosophy. The validity of scientific methods cannot be investigated by use of the methods under examination. So, too, the defense of freedom lies outside the reach of scientific investigation. No matter how far it is carried, according to this argument, the scientific study of man will neither justify nor refute the claim that man is free; for in his freedom we have an aspect of man's nature which is beyond the reach of the methods of the sciences. This view questions not the truth but the relevance of science.

One of the fundamental issues in contemporary thought between determinism and freedom is precisely this issue: Are the sciences the sole sources of informative knowledge concerning existence? Those who believe that they are the sole sources of genuine factual knowledge are also quite properly convinced that what appears to be the ability by man to choose between alternatives, without the choice being compelled by factors ultimately beyond his control, is a misleading appearance. Further advances in scientific technique and knowledge, they will insist, will show us the causes we are not now able to see. Those who believe that man is really free must appeal to something other than scientific knowledge. As we compare these points of view we see again that the argument for determinism is basically a negative argument. On its positive side it is the hope that science will advance its boundaries; its factual basis is the fact of our ignorance.

The argument for freedom as a working hypothesis, that we are justified in assuming that we are free and in acting on that assumption, is sometimes pragmatic. To act *as if* we are free is a way of action which *works*. To act as if we had no real choices inhibits effort, and leads us to avoid facing issues. Sometimes this is combined with the appeal to direct experience, and we are told that if we act as if we are free we shall discover that in truth we are free.

Such an argument begs the question. It assumes that we are free to choose whether we shall act as if we are free. The determinist's reply is that the belief that we are choosing to act as if we are free is itself determined, and that the action we carry out in the context of this belief is done under compulsion. Belief in freedom may itself be one of the compelling factors in our behavior.

The positive argument for the reality of freedom has two sides. The first side is an argument in existential dialectic, that significant denial of freedom is impossible unless freedom is a fact. In other words, there is a contradiction between what I mean when I deny that I am free and the fact that a claim of truth is asserted. The other side is based on an examination of the nature of thought and its relation to action, particularly the place of values in action. We shall look at each of these arguments briefly.

If I deny that I am free, if I assert that everything I do and say is something I am compelled to do or say by forces beyond my control, then I impeach any claim of truth for what I say. Once we begin to suspect that someone we are dealing with is making statements he has been coerced into making, we cease to treat his statements as communications of what he means or intends. We take them rather as indications of the nature of the influences which are operating upon him, just as the verbal expressions and statements of a person who is mentally ill are significant as symptoms of the underlying disorder. The determinist, according to the implications of his own avowed position, cannot help claiming to be a determinist. Does he mean what he says? If he cannot help saying what he says there is no more reason for a non-determinist to think he says it because he means it than to think he says it because of some other influence. It all depends upon which influences are the stronger. By his own admission he is powerless to speak independently of the influences upon him and to say what he says simply because it is the truth.

Father M. C. D'Arcy uses this argument against the Freudian variety of determinism:

> The power of the mind to judge and to judge the nature of its own act makes it independent of the conscious or unconscious forces. The new psychologists themselves admit this in fact; they are bent on

discovering the true working of the human psyche, and in their researches they are relying on the intellect and in their conclusions they are, as they think, judging truly. Were their own theory entirely true their judgment would have itself to be a rationalisation, and so they would have cut off the branch on which they are sitting.[14]

Sometimes I say something the way I do because I am irritated or uncomfortable and sometimes I say something the way I do because it is the truth. There is a great difference in what *because* refers to in the two instances. In the first instance, *because* means *cause:* in the second instance, *because* means *reason*. If I apologize later for an impatient remark, I may say, "I didn't mean that," and my explanation will be understood to indicate that something other than my intent to conform my speech to fact caused me to speak as I did. But suppose that I make the same comment about a statement made under circumstances in which there was no reason to suspect that I had any other intent than to tell the truth. A stranger asks me how to get to the Post Office. I say, "Go down this street a block and turn to your right." As he starts away, I call to him: "I didn't mean that." What could the stranger think except that I had a momentary lapse of attention when I first spoke, or else that I need therapy?

Unless we are free to choose what we shall say, and to choose it solely in accordance with what the facts are, the claim that we are speaking truly is meaningless. It, too, is only a symptom of something else. Where the claim of truth for what we say is significant, however, *what the facts are* is not itself a cause or influence which makes us speak. Our speech and communication is motivated, but if the motive is a desire to communicate truth then that motive cannot be successfully fulfilled unless there is freedom to choose and to reject the various verbal formulations which come to mind. The determinist states the case for determinism and once we understand what

[14] *The Nature of Belief* (New York, Longmans, Green and Company, 1931), p. 79. The argument that thinking must be free in order to be either true or false, and that thus we cannot even discuss the problem of freedom meaningfully unless we are free, made a profound impression upon William James. He was introduced to this argument, after he had published his own "Dilemma of Determinism," by reading Renouvier's *Deuxième Essai*, Pt. XVII. Renouvier, in turn, had been influenced here by Jules Lequier's *La Recherche d'une première vérité*. On this see Ralph Barton Perry, *The Thought and Character of William James* (Boston, Little, Brown and Company, 1936), Volume I, pp. 658, 661.

he says we realize that if he is right he cannot help saying what he is about to say and that if what he is about to say is false he is not free to alter it to conform with the truth. Only if some other influence makes him change his words, and only if this change *happens* to fit the facts, is what he says true. If the determinist were right truth-telling would always be an accident.

A being who is not free cannot even recognize truth. This is why we are so insistent that those on whom we depend for true judgments and decisions—judges and juries and scientists and scholars—shall keep themselves free from influences that would have causal effects on their judgments. If we understand the dangers that lurk in prejudice and in personal interests and preferences then the desire for truth will lead us to seek always to avoid confusing our personal desires and interests with the evidence that gives logical support to the conclusions we reach. In other words we seek the maximum freedom to accept or to reject various suggestions and conclusions solely on the evidence itself.

As we have already seen, argument in philosophy is argument in support of a thesis. There is a difference, however, between having a conviction that a thesis is sound by virtue of the strength of the evidence which supports it and believing that a thesis is true because of a personal stake in its truth. If we are searching primarily for satisfying beliefs we follow the latter course. If we are philosophers, however, we desire above all to find the truth no matter what bearing it may have on our personal interests. This does not mean we are to be indifferent; it means that our primary concern is our desire to find the truth. We have to learn to want to see all other hopes destroyed and all other desires frustrated if that is the way the evidence is.

Freedom in speaking and freedom in acting are not arbitrary freedoms. We do conform our speech to truth and we do conform our action to our purposes. The point is that truth and purpose are *guides* of action, not *compulsions*. The way in which they influence us is through the values they rest upon. When I come to appreciate the value of knowing the truth, and when I come to appreciate the personal and moral and aesthetic values of realizing certain other goals in life, I desire these goals. They do not force me to act, for, as goals, they are not real beings. At present they are only possibilities. Of course the *idea* of a goal is something actual, and my possession of the idea may compel me to act in a certain way. But if so it is not the goal that I conform to *as a goal;* I only react to the idea as a prod or as something that pushes me in one direction or another. In such case the idea operates as a cause, not as a reason.[15]

THE FREE SELF AND NATURE

The position we take concerning the problem of freedom may be a position we take because it is implicated in a general point of view. On the other hand, our position on the problem of freedom may be one of the principal considerations which lead us to take the general view of ourselves and our world which we do take. As we have already seen, the first alternative is characteristic of determinism; the second is characteristic of philosophies of freedom. As might be expected these represent very different interpretations of existence.

Determinism tends toward the idea of existence as a universal, all-inclusive, interconnected system. Every distinguishable item is completely interconnected with others. Thus determinism tends to be monistic, to accept what William James called the "block-universe" idea. Whether a materialism or an idealism, the determinist's philosophy sees the individual part as completely dependent on other parts. The only absolutely complete explanation is the whole itself. Thus he looks outside of human behavior for its explanation; he looks outside human personality, to understand its nature and make-up; he looks to causes outside of institutions and societies in his attempt to explain why they are what they are.

The libertarian tends toward a pluralism in his philosophy. The unit of existence is the individual, not the system. The system of existence is a system of different levels, each having its own characteristic nature; and it is a system of autonomous individuals, each of whom contains within himself a considerable part of what explains his action.

At this level the issue is between the attempt to understand man as a function of the world, to explain him in terms of non-human

[15] One of the few attempts to meet this argument will be found in Lucius Garven, *A Modern Introduction to Ethics* (Boston, Houghton Mifflin Company, 1953), p. 96. For a discussion of Professor Garvin's criticism, see Samuel M. Thompson, *A Modern Philosophy of Religion* (Chicago, Henry Regnery Company, 1955), pp. 181-85.

antecedents and causes, and the contention that our most significant datum is man's existence as a self which has some degree of autonomy. We cannot explain the power to explain, consequently man as man does not have a nature in terms of which we can explain his actions. In some profoundly significant respect, man makes himself; in his decisions and in the actions by which he carries them out, he brings himself to be.

To take the concept of human freedom seriously would affect profoundly our attitude toward man and his relation to nature. The implications of such a view of man's existence are well expressed by Professor John Wild: Man

> is not a thing at all, for a thing is just what it is. But a man is never just what he is. He is free and able to determine himself by his chosen projects. . . .
>
> This freedom to make himself separates man radically from all subhuman entities of nature. They simply are *what* they are, and do what their natures determine them to do. Man *makes himself.* He is not merely something different. He is something different existing in a different way. . . .
>
> . . . There is a terrible chasm between us and all sub-human things. These entities, as science dispassionately reveals them to us, are quite unlike ourselves. We have been thrown into a universe where we are surrounded by vast ranges of speechless and unfeeling being. We stand alone in a world which is foreign to our existence; where, without comforting delusions, we cannot feel at home.[16]

This sharp contrast between man and nature may suggest a perspective from which we may understand and appreciate the difference without having to look upon it as a conflict. Men become determinists when their search for understanding proceeds upon the assumption that to account for something is to explain it in terms of other things. The concept of cause enters at the point where we find that our understanding of *what a thing is* fails to make intelligible *what that thing does.* Here we have to look outside the thing itself for something to account for what it does. In our discussion of scientific explanation we found, however, that the identification of a cause is not sufficient. The causal relation by itself shows only *that* there is a connection, not *what* the connection is.

Scientific explanation is the discovery of the intelligibility of

[16] *The Challenge of Existentialism* (Bloomington, Indiana University Press, 1955), p. 77. By permission.

these connections. It accomplishes its end by integrating cause and effect into a single event and explaining the action in terms of the internal, mathematically intelligible structure of the event. The problem of freedom versus determinism may be resolved if we see that when this point in scientific explanation is reached the idea of determinism loses its usefulness. What a thing does is here understood partly in terms of its own structure, not solely in terms of other things which are outside of it and acting upon it. Perhaps it is significant that modern physics tends to attribute a kind of spontaneity to its ultimate units.

The answer to determinism in human action might be found by discovering what it is in the agent himself which makes his action intelligible. Here, however, the scientific approach loses its relevance. The method by which intelligibility is achieved in science, by way of mathematical relationship, is the method we have to use when we are dealing with things from the outside and when we have no direct awareness of their internal constitution. Ourselves, however, we see from within. The intelligible explanation of human action is thus in terms of purpose, means and end, and the concept of the self and of its possibilities which guides choice.

SUMMARY

The self has a unity of its own; it is no synthesis of parts or conjunction of body and mind. The unity shows itself in experience as a unity of awareness in the form of a consciousness of self which is involved in our awareness of other things. Experience has a bipolar structure of subject and object in which awareness of self is given along with awareness of object. Thus our basic awareness of the self does not come by making the self an object.

The kind of unity which constitutes the self must be a unity which somehow transcends the present moment in time. Present awareness must somehow reach into the past and the future without itself being or containing something past or something future. How this can be is seen when we discover that the present moment of experience is not something static but is a dynamic forward moving awareness. Awareness of the present is also an awareness of the past in the sense that it is awareness of a present in process of becoming past, and it is an awareness of the future in the sense that it is an awareness of a present which is transforming what were future possibilities into present actuality.

The self exists in its acts of perception, memory, thought, imagination, desire, purpose, and will. The self exists in a space-transcending and time-transcending act in which past, future, and the existentially remote are brought into a present unity of knowledge. The unity of the self is also a unity of action manifested in decision. This action includes also the acts by which the self makes itself to be the kind of self it becomes.

Such a conception of the self involves us in the problem of freedom. Determinism is usually the outcome of a mechanistic interpretation of existence. It derives its strength in our own culture from the association of physical science with the mechanistic interpretation of nature. The case for determinism is the case for the view that ultimately everything can be understood scientifically together with the view that every truly scientific inquiry must employ the concepts of mechanism.

The case for freedom has two sides: the case for the acceptance of freedom as the basis for action, and the positive argument that the fact of freedom is established directly by the evidence. The positive argument for freedom, in turn, has two sides: the dialectical argument that meaningful denial of freedom is impossible unless freedom is itself a fact; and the argument that distinctively human action is guided rather than caused by motives and goals.

Whereas determinism is usually a conclusion implicated in a philosophy which is arrived at mainly from consideration of other issues, freedom is often one of the chief foundations upon which a more general point of view is built. This may lead the libertarian to a sharp opposition in his thought between man and nature. Such a distinction may be appreciated without being regarded as a conflict if we differentiate between the conditions of intelligibility in scientific inquiry and in our awareness of ourselves.

QUESTIONS FOR STUDY AND DISCUSSION

1. *Terms:* decision, determinism, fatalism, freedom, pluralism, pragmatism, spontaneity.

2. What is involved in language communication besides reaction to words as signals?

3. When I perceive a tree I am aware of the tree. I can turn attention then to the awareness of the tree, and so be aware of being aware of the tree; and then I can attend to my awareness of being aware of being aware of the tree. What is to prevent an infinite regress here?

4. Are the distinctions of past, present, and future, distinctions inherent in duration itself or are they distinctions introduced by us in our experience of duration?

5. What meaning can you find in the statement: "For all we know time might reverse itself"?

6. When an astronomer "looks at" a distant star what does he actually see? Compare this question with the question of what we hear when we listen to a phonograph record.

7. Distinguish between awareness of the succession of ideas and an idea of succession. Does Hume confuse these?

8. Examine: The self is what it does.

9. All mechanism is deterministic, but is all determinism mechanistic?

10. No matter what I can do about it I am going to die; no matter what I do, summer will pass and winter will come. Are these examples of fatalism?

11. Can the question of freedom vs. determinism be settled in general terms, or does it arise significantly only in specific circumstances and have to be considered in the light of that specific situation? Examine the latter alternative as itself an argument for freedom.

The World
of Values

CHAPTER 12

The
Nature
of
Value

VALUE JUDGMENTS

At first sight our statements of evaluations look like any other statements. They have subjects and predicates; they purport to be statements about something, and they ascribe some attribute to the object or situation the statement is about. If we say: "Stealing is wrong," we are talking about a kind of action, *stealing*, and we are saying something about this action that characterizes it, namely, that it is *wrong*. Our statement seems in all respects to be parallel with such a statement as: "Stealing is difficult."

If we look more closely at these two statements, however, we find one important difference. To say that stealing is wrong is to express disapproval of stealing, but no such meaning is involved in the statement that stealing is difficult. The latter statement might be made in a context of approval or disapproval, or it might be made quite independently of any such attitude. One person may mean that the thing that makes stealing attractive to him is that its difficulties and risks are exhilarating; another may mean that the difficulty of stealing without getting caught leads him to avoid stealing. In still another case the statement may express only an observation of a fact with, say, the wonder that so many people are willing to go to so much trouble for so little gain. To say, however, that stealing is wrong is to pass judgment upon the act of stealing. A judgment of approval or disapproval, whether the approval or disapproval is moral or aesthetic or whatever it may be, is a value judgment.

To be a value judgment, a judgment must *express* approval or disapproval. To say, for example, "I disapprove of stealing," is not a value judgment. This is a descriptive judgment. It describes my attitude toward stealing but is not itself expressive of that attitude. It may be descriptive of my value judgments or it may be the kind of thing I would say if I were not sure whether or not stealing is wrong and yet had a personal attitude of disapproval toward it. If someone says, however, "He is right in disapproving of stealing," then that person is expressing a value judgment concerning another's practice in making value judgments. To say that things are *good* or *bad, better* or *worse;* that things are *beautiful* or *ugly;* to say that something *ought to be done* or *not done*, or *ought to be admired* or *not admired* is in each case to express a value judgment. In value judgments we do more than merely attribute some quality or characteristic to something. What is this *more* which value judgments express?

A value judgment seems to express some sense of coercion or necessity that is lacking in descriptive judgments. If I believe that it is wrong to steal I am not merely characterizing stealing but expressing what we might call provisionally a sense of need not to steal. Whether or not to steal is not like the question of whether or not to eat or read a certain book or play golf. Whether I do these other things or not is simply a matter of preference or of taste. But if I believe it is wrong for me to steal I consider that to yield to the desire for immediate gain would be to act contrary to another and a more basic demand. But what is the nature of this more basic demand, and what makes it more basic than my desire for the advantages of a successful theft?

One thing that is obvious about our experience and action is that we do not act solely in terms of the immediate situation. Not only do we have established habits of action; we also have established policies of action. We have rules, or regularities, in our choice-making procedures, and we accept some of these rules or regularities as having a controlling position with respect to others. It appears to be a basic condition of the possibility of making value judgments that we have definite policies of choice and action and that when those policies are in conflict we recognize that some of them take precedence over others. Thus if I mean, when I say it is wrong to steal, that my policy of not stealing is the one in control whenever that policy comes in conflict with, say, my policy of doing whatever is to my financial advantage when the opportunity arises, then there is a very definite, specific, and recognizable difference between my value judgments and my descriptive judgments.

We can see this difference more easily in moral than in aesthetic judgments, but careful attention will show its presence in the latter as well. When I say that this picture is good art, or that one performance of a symphony is artistically better than another, I may mean that what I call the better work or performance satisfies or is in conformity with certain aesthetic rules which take precedence over other rules which might have been satisfied. Likewise, to say that this is a poor picture may be to say that the regularities (style, or pattern) it embodies are in conflict with certain others which have a position of priority.

Judgments of logical value may be similarly interpreted. To say that a proposition is false is to say that its truth claim is in conflict with another truth claim which has priority or takes precedence. For most of us the truth claim of a perception takes precedence over whatever inclination we may have to believe something to be true because that is the way we like to imagine it. Not only when what we see and what we dream are in conflict do we reject the dream, but most informed people in our culture reject dreams on principle as sources of information concerning what happens outside ourselves. We accept basic beliefs about the relation of experience to fact which are in conflict with the acceptance of a dream as such a report. The demand for logical consistency and the rejection of contradiction are basic policies of our thinking. Perhaps it can be shown that they are necessary policies, but not all who accept them as basic are aware of the case which may be presented in support of their necessity. To say that a certain statement is the one that *ought* to be made, that it is the *true* statement, can be understood to mean that a denial of this statement would be in conflict with a more basic assertion to which it is our policy to subordinate statements of this order.

We may say, to sum up our account at this stage, that the distinctive feature of value judgments is that they involve certain *commitments* which we have already made and to which we give priority. Of course these commitments may change, and if they do then our value judgments also will change; whether any of these commitments are final is another question. So also is the question of whether these commitments are true or false, or even whether they are the kind of assertions which can be either true or false. If they are policies only, then they may not be truth claims at all.

A value judgment may carry with it also the idea that anything in conflict with the commitment which the judgment expresses is destructive of the value order itself and must be rejected if that order is to stand. This also shows itself in the sense of compulsion or necessity so often apparent in truth claims. We cannot permit an inconsistency to stand without challenge because acquiescence in it would destroy the very meaning of the truth claim itself. Or I may reject a possible course of action not only because it is undesirable and contrary to my commitments, and so is something on which I turn my back; I may feel compelled to do all I can to prevent its realization because such an outcome would be destructive of the values which give meaning to my choices. We oppose some political policies because we think them unwise or unnecessary; we oppose others because they would be destructive of the political order itself or of the values which the political order is intended to realize. A member of a college or university faculty may oppose a policy and use every means he can to defeat it because in his opinion that policy would make the whole educational enterprise, or some important part of it, meaningless or absurd. A state of affairs which would destroy my freedom to choose or to exercise other of my functions as a person would be a possibility against which I should have to contend not merely to avoid this or that undesirable state of affairs but to avoid the loss of everything that makes life as a person significant. In cases such as these the element of necessity in value judgments is very strong and may in fact dominate for a time at least all that one does and thinks.

It should be noted that this interpretation of value judgments is presented as one possible interpretation. It would be somewhat arrogant to say that this or that is what people mean when they express approval or disapproval. The only way to find out what a person means by a statement is to discover what he intends to communicate. So people may express quite different meanings in their value judgments than that indicated in our present discussion. The important point of this interpretation is that it does make a value judgment distinctive. The difficulty with some other meanings is that they leave nothing in the value judgment but description, so that there is nothing at all distinctive about it; or else the difference between value judgments and descriptive judgments is so wide that the so-called value judgment loses its character of being a judgment. Some of the problems involved in these other interpretations will be considered later.

THE BASIC ISSUE OF VALUE THEORY

The way in which we ordinarily formulate our value judgments suggests that value properly belongs to the things and situations to which we attribute them. When we say that a person was courageous in his rescue of another from drowning we seem to be saying something about that person. We may admire his courage, but when we say that he was courageous we ordinarily think of courage as a value and thus as a kind of *good*. We are saying that he is, in this respect, good. Such an interpretation is expressed by G. E. Moore, for example, in his characterization of ethics:

The peculiarity of Ethics is not that it investigates assertions about human conduct, but that it investigates assertions about that property of things which is denoted by the term "good," and the converse property denoted by the term "bad." [1]

The character of things as good is known as directly and immediately as is, for example, a thing's color:

My point is that "good" is a simple notion, just as "yellow" is a simple notion; that, just as you cannot, by any manner of means, explain to any one who does not already know it, what yellow is, so you cannot explain what good is.[2]

This conception of values, however, may seem inadequate on the ground that it fails to do justice to the element of necessity involved in value judgments. Referring to our moral judgments of right and wrong, in which the element of necessity or compulsion is usually explicit, Moore says:

[1] *Principia Ethica* (Cambridge, Cambridge University Press, 1922), p. 36.
[2] *Ibid*, p. 7.

I am, in fact, unable to distinguish, in its main features, the moral sentiment excited by the idea of rightness and wrongness, wherever it is intense, from the total state constituted by a cognition of something intrinsically evil together with the emotion of hatred directed towards it.[3]

Thus what for many is a central feature of value experience is identified by Moore as an emotion and thus as something subjective. But if we go this far toward subjectivism, why not go all the way?

If, when I say that someone was courageous, I mean that I accept a certain kind of behavior, such as taking a risk in order to save another person from death, or having priority over a contrasting kind of behavior, am I not expressing a kind of demand I make of human action in such a circumstance? I approve the act of saving a life, I would disapprove the act of one who allowed another to drown. Why not simply recognize, then, that value judgments are judgments of approval and disapproval solely in the sense of expressing our attitudes toward things? Because of some peculiarities of our language, we happen to express these approvals and disapprovals in a way that disguises their true character and leads us to confuse them with statements about the nature of objects. The value judgment in such a case would be more properly expressed as a statement not about the object but about *me*. As subjective rather than objective, a more accurate statement than "He is courageous" would be "I have an attitude of approval toward his act," or "Hurrah for him!"

Here seems to be a basic issue of value theory: Are values subjective or objective? Are values objective facts, characterizing the situations about which we think and toward which our action is directed, or are they characteristics of our own ways of thinking and feeling? When I say that something is good, am I talking about the thing itself, as Moore contends, or about my attitude toward the thing?

According to Edward Westermarck,

Men pronounced certain acts to be good or bad on account of the emotions those acts aroused in their minds, just as they called sunshine warm and ice cold on account of certain sensations which they

[3] *Ibid*, p. 218.

experienced, and as they named a thing pleasant or painful because they felt pleasure or pain.[4]

A classic expression of this view is found in Hobbes' *Leviathan:*

> But whatsoever is the object of any man's Appetite or Desire; that is it, which he for his part called *Good:* And the object of his Hate, and Aversion, *Evill;* And of his Contempt, *Vile* and *Inconsiderable.* For these words of Good, Evill, and Contemptible, are ever used with relation to the person that useth them: There being nothing simply and absolutely so; nor any common Rule of Good and Evill, to be taken from the nature of the objects themselves.[5]

If value judgments are merely expressions of emotion or attitude, and so are subjective, then there are important consequences for our interpretation of human behavior and human affairs. To say that stealing is wrong is to say only that I do not like to have stealing take place. To say that people *ought not* to steal is to say only that my preference is that they refrain from stealing. It means strictly, on this view: Would that people did not steal![6] Thus its strict meaning is expressed not in a statement about something but in an optative sentence. If I do express this in the form of an assertion about something then the assertion will be about me that I wish or desire that people would not steal. Thus to change the value of an action from wrong to right we have only to change our preferences. If I no longer prefer that people refrain from stealing then I shall no longer refer to stealing as "wrong." The remedy for evil then is to change our attitudes; and in many cases this is much easier than to change things.

When we look at the history of a civilization we do find that the value judgments commonly made in one period give way to quite different judgments in later periods. We find also that different societies differ widely in what they approve and disapprove. We in our own society disapprove strongly of cannibalism, but in some societies, including those of our own remote ancestors, to eat human flesh has been considered a duty and has brought moral satisfaction.

---

[4] *The Origin and Development of the Moral Ideas,* Second Edition (London, Macmillan and Company, Ltd., 1924), Volume I, p. 4.

[5] Thomas Hobbes, *Leviathan* (Everyman's Library, New York, E. P. Dutton and Company, n.d.), p. 24.

[6] For such an interpretation of the language of value judgments, see Charles L. Stevenson, *Ethics and Language* (New Haven, Yale University Press, 1944), especially Chapter II.

The nature of flesh has not changed, nor have the processes of eating and digestion. It is our attitude toward the act that has changed. In one or two generations the attitude toward marriage and divorce has greatly changed in our society, as have the attitudes toward many of the actions toward which there were widespread religious and moral taboos a half century ago.

On this view of the nature of value, morality is understood simply as the *mores* of a society. An act is immoral if it is contrary to what is generally practiced in the society. The whole matter is one of custom and social acceptance. The sanctions of morality, the various punishments inflicted for violation of the mores, range from expressions of disapproval through social ostracism and the various forms of punishment provided for those convicted of violating the laws.[7]

The subjectivity of values seems even more obvious in aesthetic judgment. What is aesthetic approval or disapproval except a matter of taste? And what is the difference between good taste and bad taste except the difference between what is generally liked, or what is liked by the elite, and what is disliked? Whether we like or dislike a work of art seems to depend largely on familiarity or its lack. New styles and forms are nearly always attacked. If they are taken up by groups which have prestige, or if their specimens are plentiful enough so that people are sufficiently exposed to them to become familiar with them, these novelties are accepted. Distortion in painting, dissonance in music, functionalism in architecture all have run such a course.

Logical values, true and false, likewise are interpreted as relative to belief and disbelief. Here again the whole question becomes one of accepting or rejecting certain basic assumptions. Change our assumptions and we change the true into the false and the false into the true. To accept or reject is to express an attitude, a commitment. Even the demand for logical consistency, and thus the very existence of such cultural constructs as science and mathematics, is the expression of an attitude. The only difference between the true and the false is again a difference between what is generally accepted and what is not. Knowledge consists of the basic beliefs of a society together with the subordinate beliefs considered in harmony with those basic ones. The harmony may be logical consistency, but so far as

[7] The two volume work by Edward Westermarck, cited above, is an elaborate and important study of morality as custom.

popular belief is concerned it is more likely to be a harmony of atti-tude, especially the agreement with the attitudes of other people.

Whatever may be the final significance of subjective theories of value, they have contributed much to our understanding of the is-sues and our recognition of factors in value judgments which are all too easy to overlook. These theories have made us see that there is a subjective element in such judgments, the element of commitment or demand or espousal. Without this we should be indifferent in our thought and awareness; and if indifferent we should not even attempt to control and guide our actions. These theories have also forced us to face the fact of relativity in value judgments, the fact that differ-ent historical periods, different cultures within the same historical period, and different social groups within the same culture have dif-ferent value attitudes. Any adequate theory of value will have to ac-count for this marked variation. Granted that subjectivism has been of great service to value theory, the question of its own adequacy still remains.

EXAMINATION OF SUBJECTIVISM

The issue between subjectivism and objectivism in the theory of values turns out to be the question of whether our state-ments of value principles or norms may be said properly to be true or false of objects. If statements of value principles are optative state-ments then either they are in such form, e.g.: "Would that men did not steal," that *true* and *false* do not apply; or they are in such form: "I wish that men did not steal," that the statement is *about* the person who expresses the judgment. The latter statement is true or false, but the question of whether it is true or false is only the question of whether the speaker correctly represents his attitude or is lying. If we try to formulate our statement so that it is about the object and yet exposes only an attitude, for example, "Stealing is something of which people generally disapprove," then it loses its status as a value statement and becomes a statement of alleged fact about popular at-titudes.

We have here the source of the difficulty that many find with subjectivist theories of value. As soon as value standards are looked upon as neither true nor false they seem to lose their authority. If the question of whether stealing is wrong is merely a matter of how we feel about it, then how can we say that we *ought not* to steal? If the difference between Beethoven and the latest fad in popular music is only in our likes and dislikes then it surely seems absurd to take the time and trouble and study necessary to reach some understanding of Beethoven's music. If only we keep our likes simple we shall find life much less complicated. What this issue amounts to is the question of whether values *ought* to be realized, and the "ought" is stronger with some values than with others, or whether there is no point in saying that values ought to be realized. Our whole civilization, particularly in its religious, educational, and political aspects, rests on the assumptions that there are values that ought to be realized and that some of these are so important that the choice cannot be left to the individual. Of course it is possible that our civilization stands on a false foundation.

The theory that value judgments and norms are only expressions of emotions or imperatives is exposed to one serious challenge. The challenge is appropriate as soon as the subjectivist suggests or implies that this theory *ought* to be held. If a subjectivist so much as hints that this is the truth of the matter and consequently the objectivist ought to accept it as his own view, then we are surely entitled to ask him which way he wants it to be. Westermarck, for example, refers to "the error we commit by attributing objectivity to moral estimates." [8] Is he suggesting that it is *better*, in the usual sense of the word, not to attribute objectivity to moral estimates? At another place he seems to be reassuring us concerning subjectivism:

> Far from being a danger, ethical subjectivism seems to me more likely to be an acquisition for moral practice. Could it be brought home to people that there is no absolute standard in morality, they would perhaps be somewhere more tolerant in their judgments, and more apt to listen to the voice of reason. . . . Far above the vulgar idea that the right is a settled something to which everybody has to adjust his opinions, rises the conviction that it has its existence in each individual mind, capable of any expansion, proclaiming its own right to exist, and, if need be, venturing to make a stand against the whole world. Such a conviction makes for progress.[9]

Does Westermarck mean that it is *better* to be tolerant and to be "more apt to listen to the voice of reason"? What does he mean, in

[8] Westermarck, *op. cit.*, p. 13.
[9] *Ibid*, pp. 19-20.

the context of his own theory, by his statement that subjectivism is far *above* the vulgar idea, and what does he mean by *progress?* Does the subjectivist mean that this is the truth about the matter, or does he mean only that this is how he feels about the matter? Does he mean that other right-thinking and carefully observant people will agree with him if they examine the question carefully; or does he mean to say only, "I wish that others would see this as I do, and am here announcing that their doing so would induce a pleasant feeling in me"? If his subjectivism is to be consistent then it appears that he can mean only that this is how he feels about the matter. But if so, why is this statement of how he feels any more significant than, say, an announcement that he likes his eggs scrambled?

The subjectivist may reply that his contention that this is the truth of the matter is not a value statement at all; it is a descriptive statement setting forth the facts. But is there any point to his stating what he takes to be the truth, or even to looking for the truth, except on the assumption that the truth is what we *ought* to believe? If he says, "This is the truth," and we reply: "Well, what of it?" what then can he say without abandoning subjectivism? He may say: "The truth is what I prefer to believe; I wish to avoid holding beliefs that are false." We may reply: "Why tell anyone else what you prefer? Why should anyone else care about your preferences? Furthermore, why should anyone else think that you are telling the truth about what you prefer. You certainly cannot think that you ought to tell the truth, and so anyone you talk to is well advised to suspect that you are lying in order to pave the way for some deception which will be in your own interest."

To hold a theory which involves a denial that we ought to believe the truth and that we ought to tell the truth about what we believe is to hold a theory which renders meaningless any claim of truth in its own behalf. If I say, "I do not admit that I ought to believe the truth," then what meaning do I intend that statement itself to convey? Might I not as well say, "No statement I utter, including this statement, is true"? The fact that I utter the words may be understandable if, for example, I am rehearsing a line or listening to the sounds of the words or exercising my voice. But to utter these words as a truth claim is to make a statement the truth of which is in conflict with the act of claiming truth for the statement.

We are no better off with the argument that the question of the truth or falsity of value principles need not be raised at all, that the only pertinent question is whether they are relevant or applicable. Their true function, it may be argued, is to bring order and coherence into human action. But why bring order and coherence into human action? Suppose I say I prefer disorder and incoherence? The reply may be either simply to reiterate a preference for order, or to use force to make me conform in my action; or to insist that in some sense I *ought* to prefer order and coherence. Reiteration gets nowhere; to use force is to abandon argument; to contend that I *ought* to have a different attitude is to introduce objectivity into the value theory.

VALUE JUDGMENTS AND TRUTH

Subjectivism denies that value statements are statements of fact and concludes that they are neither true nor false of objects. A simple objectivism contends that value statements are true or false of objects and fails to recognize the difference between a statement about *what is* and a statement about *what ought to be.* If we happen to be satisfied with neither view and are looking for a more adequate standpoint, our best approach, as we have seen before in dealing with opposing theories, is to look for a false assumption which the two views have in common. There are two ways in which theories can conflict logically. They may be mutually contradictory, in which case one must be false and the other must be true; the problem is to discover which is the true one and which the false. Or they may be contraries, in which case they cannot both be true but may both be false. If they are both false, then we look for an alternative which differs from both. What follows is the presentation of such an alternative.

Subjectivism and objectivism agree on one point: they both assume that only statements of fact, of what is the case, are true or false. We can see how easy it is to make this assumption; for if a statement is true or false it presumably agrees or disagrees with something. It must refer to something beyond itself as a report of what that something is or a report that it is, else there is nothing for the statement to be true or false of. Thus it is supposed that a statement must refer to an actual state of affairs or else not express a truth claim at all. We may agree that a statement must refer to *something* if it is to have anything to be true or false *of,* but need we assume that what it refers to is in every case an actual state of affairs? Statements can refer also to what is possible, to what is imaginary, to what is constructed by thought. Actual fact is only one mode of being; both subjectivism and objectivism assume that actual fact is the only mode of being.

We do claim truth for statements which refer to other than actual existence. It is true, we say, that Hamlet hated his stepfather, and yet Hamlet and his stepfather are fictional beings. It is true that the square root of nine is three, and yet if mathematical objects are conceptual constructs there are no such actual existences as a nine and a three. In view of this distinction between actual existence and other kinds of being we might say that value judgments refer to a world of being other than the actual world. Plato argued that values cannot ultimately be mere matters of fact but belong to a changeless and immaterial world of Forms. So impressed was he with the prior and basic position of values in knowledge that he insisted that the world of Forms is the real world and that what we call the actual world is a world of appearance which is only partly real.[10]

If we take descriptive judgments and value judgments to refer to two entirely different realms of being then we find ourselves in a different kind of difficulty. If I say that Jones pays his debts, I am describing his behavior. If I say that Jones is good, what kind of reference am I making? "Jones" refers to an actually existing man whom we both know, but "good" would refer to something in another realm of being. How can "good" then pertain to or be asserted meaningfully of Jones? We do not say that Jones is a square root, or that he is a descendant of Hamlet. Square roots belong to the realm of mathematical objects, and Hamlet's descendants, if any there were, would belong to a fictional world. If value judgments are to claim truth when they are to be asserted significantly of actually existing things, then they must refer to something and what they refer to must have some connection with actual things. But if value judgments are to be distinguished from descriptive judgments then they cannot refer simply to what things actually are.

How can we make a statement about an object, a statement that is true or false, and yet not make that statement solely about the object's actual nature? Once we put the question in this form we can see immediately one possible answer. A statement may be about an object and yet not be a report of what that object actually is, pro-

[10] See Plato, *Republic*, VI, 505, 508, 509; VII, 518.

vided the statement is about what the object *may* be or *can* be. Existing things not only have the properties and qualities they show in their actual nature; they have potentialities as well. When we say that a thing is good or bad we may be referring not alone to what it actually is nor alone to what it is potentially, but to *the relation between its actual and potential nature*. Whenever we say that this or that object is a good specimen, we are referring to its actual nature in comparison with certain potentialities which it once had.

Although we need to distinguish between what a thing is actually and what it is potentially, we must be careful not to separate the two. As Wilbur Marshall Urban has pointed out, the potential along with the actual, and value along with existence, belong to the essential nature of the real:

> The perceptual object, the aesthetic object, the historical happening, the moral act—what are these objects when the value element is abstracted? . . . Value has meaning only in connection with things. . . . But it makes a great difference whether we think of objects existing in their own right and incidentally possessing value, or think of their value as the very essence of their reality. If the latter view is adopted . . . we shall cease to contrast judgments of reality with value judgments in any absolute sense.[11]

It may be that psychologically our value judgments go back to our earliest awareness of the relation of what we actually find to what we expected to find. If the expectation was pleasurable and if it is fulfilled in fact then we regard the object that fulfills it as good. If we are disappointed with what we find then we call the object a poor specimen. It is literally *unsatisfactory* in failing to *satisfy* our expectations. In some such way we may have learned to make value judgments. But for many of us this is not what we come to mean by our value judgments. As we mature and as we come to have more adequate conceptions of our world and learn to conform our judgments to its nature, we come also to form our value standards in accordance with the real potentialities of things rather than in accordance merely with our own wishes and preferences. Our wishes and preferences are never eliminated from the picture, but many of us

[11] *The Intelligible World* (New York, The Macmillan Company, 1929), p. 157. By permission. For a distinction between values as essences and actual existence, but with values given a role of participating "in determining reality," see Nicolai Hartmann, *Ethics*, translated by Stanton Coit (New York, The Macmillan Company, 1932), Volume I, p. 220. See also pp. 221, 222-23, and 251 of the same volume.

do attempt to govern our preferences in accordance with the real potentialities of actual existence rather than evaluating the potentialities in accordance with our wishes. Many psychologists consider this the basic quality that distinguishes the mature person from the immature.

An actually existing changing thing has, at any stage of its development, alternative possibilities. Some of these possibilities are mutually exclusive. A rosebush may grow strong and healthy if regularly fertilized and protected from insects, blackspot, and mildew. Another rosebush of the same variety and from the same stock may be weak and sickly if unattended. The same bush cannot realize both of these potentialities together. It may be healthy for part of its life and sickly for the rest. But at any particular time it is in one or another state of health. At one extreme we consider it a good specimen; at the other, a poor specimen.

Another aspect of the problem of value judgments and truth is the problem that presses upon us in our day to day decisions. If value judgments are in some significant sense true or false, how do we go about finding out which are which? It must be recognized at the outset that there are no simple formulas we can use to answer such questions. Values come to be appreciated only through experience. We have to be open to values; and we have to be receptive and patient, not yielding to the snap judgment of the first look. The discovery of values requires also exposure to varied and competing values in the same area. The maturely sensitive and responsive person must be able to appreciate the appeal and the positive worth of the alternatives he rejects. We do not respect the moral judgment either of the wanton, who knows no values except the cheaper ones of immediate sensual gratification, or of the prig who knows no values except negative ones. The person who resents modern art or modern music, who refuses to place himself at its disposal in a willing effort to find what values it offers, is no competent guide to esthetic value. Nor is the person who simply rejects as outmoded and old-fashioned every work of art which is not a challenge to tradition.

Although there are no easy formulas by which we can determine the truth or falsity of a value judgment, still there is a device which helps us in the first stages of such a problem by making explicit the issues to be faced. A helpful first step in the examination of a value judgment is to ask ourselves why we have decided as we have. I look at a painting and something about it disturbs me. In some way it seems just not "right." I may simply dismiss it, as of no interest, or I may follow up my initial impression by asking myself what is wrong. My specific value judgment here is that this painting is not effective, that it fails somehow to hold attention as a successful painting does. A brief study may reveal that the composition presents so neat and symmetrical a balance as to seem static and inert. There is no successful resolution of tension because all tension has been excluded; the painting needs a more dynamic balance. At the other extreme I may find that a composition lacks unity; it breaks too easily into two different pictures. In either of these cases, I bring out into the open the standard that was implicit in my original judgment: that in compositions such as this a dynamic balance is better than a static one; or, that a composition should have a unity which prevents its parts from falling away from each other and becoming, as it were, separate compositions externally linked together.

Those who have had some exposure to elementary logic will recognize that this can be formulated as a syllogism. The specific value judgment is the conclusion. The reason given for the conclusion is a descriptive statement, a judgment of fact, concerning the object: the composition is static in its balance, or it lacks unity. From this descriptive statement as the minor premise and the value judgments as the conclusion of a syllogism, we can in each instance construct the only major premise which will complete a valid syllogism: that static compositions of this order are esthetically inferior, or that compositions which lack unity are inferior. The next step, of course, is to subject the standard, which now has become explicit, to examination.

The illustrations we have considered here concern esthetics. How does our theory of value, the theory that value concerns the relation of the potential to the actual, apply to such a problem? A painting is not a natural object in process of development, such as an animal or a plant, with inherent tendencies which are realized or frustrated by external causes. On the other hand, what do we mean by such esthetic judgments as those we have been considering if they do not in some sense reflect a comparison of possibilities? If I am convinced that a composition fails esthetically because of its too static character, am I not contrasting this composition with other possible ways of handling the same subject? Many value judgments fail to be explored; they are little more than reflections of immediate likes and dislikes and, as such, hardly deserve the name of value judgments. But it would seem that an examination of a value judgment would require some awareness of other possibilities and a comparison of this actuality with what would have been actual if another possibility had been realized.

Our problem now is the problem of standards. How do we tell the difference between the kind of relation of actual to possible which we call good and the kind we call bad? If we say that excellence, in character and behavior and in art and in understanding, is the realization of certain possibilities and the exclusion of others, how do we tell which possibilities constitute excellence in their realization and which possibilities are destructive of excellence when realized?

VALUE STANDARDS

As already suggested, we may find a clue for the discovery of value standards by considering the basis upon which we distinguish good and poor specimens in nature. A good specimen of a natural species of animal life is one in which the qualities and features we take to be characteristic of that species are found fully developed. Sometimes the standard is one imposed upon the species, as when we deliberately breed animals for certain characteristics. This is the case with dogs bred to show, with race horses and show horses, beef cattle, swine, and other domestic animals. It is the case also with plants which are developed for certain characteristics, such as the development of flowers and shrubs for aesthetic and decorative properties as well as for resistance to disease, hybrid varieties of corn and special varieties of other useful plants.

A little reflection makes it quite plain that value standards such as these are varied and in many respects arbitrary. The qualities desirable in a dog which is to be shown in competition may have some remote relation to the effectiveness of a dog in his natural state, but often that connection is almost impossible to see. Beef cattle are in fact little more than meat-producing organisms, and the qualities which make them the more desirable as sources of beef are qualities which would make their survival very difficult in a natural state. The lean, scrawny, tough, long-legged scrub would make short work of a grand champion steer if they were competing for food on the range. The variation and arbitrariness of the standards we use make it necessary, if the import of a value judgment is to be understood, to specify the standards by which we are judging. A good hunter may be a very poor specimen in the show ring; no animal is simply good in general, except in the sense that any existence is good.

Considerations such as these strengthen the case for the view that all our value judgments are relative. In a limited sense, they are relative. No specific value judgment means anything except by reference to some standard. But *relativity of values,* as ordinarily understood in philosophy, is a position which goes further than this. The relativist considers also that our standards are entirely subjective and arbitrary. We can say what is valuable and what is not with reference to a specified standard, but we cannot say what standards we ought to use. Or, if we do evaluate our standards, we evaluate them with reference to other standards and thus at any stage the standards we use are arbitrary. If we try to push this back we find no stopping place; we find an endless regression.

The difficulty which some find with relativism is its inability to justify any standards in preference to any others. The whole matter is one of arbitrary choice, or of historical accident; there is no question of right or wrong standards. So if a person wants to be a highly developed specimen of a skid-row bum there is no reason why he should hesitate to work toward that end. It is among his potentialities; and which of those potentialities is to serve as his standard of evaluation is a matter of arbitrary choice. Such an outcome seems to render meaningless all striving for excellence and all satisfaction in achievement. It destroys the significance even of its own claim to be true. To contend that truth is not itself a value is not a sufficient reply, even if such a contention can be shown to be sound. The effort to establish the truth of a complete relativism supposes at least that knowledge of truth is a value; otherwise the expenditure of the effort is absurd. Our task now is to examine the possibility that there are some principles of value which are absolute.

A SEARCH FOR ABSOLUTE VALUE STANDARDS

Men have looked in many directions for absolute value standards, and consequently there has been much conflict in the results of that search. What appears to one to be obvious and compelling is challenged by another. Others have abandoned all attempts at a rational search for absolutes and have accepted the deliverances of some authority. The attempts to establish rational standards by philosophical reflection and argument are nearly always attempts to find those standards as involved in or implicated by the nature of being; it is the theory that the difference between what ought to be in actual existence and what ought not to be can be found in the nature of the world order itself. The following argument is a statement of one version of this position. The argument will first be stated with respect to the difference between good and bad, considered somewhat more broadly than in the moral sense of the terms alone. We shall look, first, for some objective and nonarbitrary basis upon which to distinguish between good and bad specimens.

At any stage in the development of an individual we may suppose there are alternative possibilities, and that some of the various possibilities are inconsistent with each other. A man may not be able, for example, to prepare for and have a satisfying career both in law and in engineering even if he has outstanding aptitudes for both. The long period of professional study which each demands and the very different activities involved in the two professions would make their simultaneous practice very difficult. Of course he may choose a career of law practice in which he specializes in engineering cases. This is an additional possibility, but obviously he would not be practising as an engineer. On the other hand, a man can be a lawyer or an engineer and still be successful as husband and father; within limits he can achieve some distinction as an amateur in golf or tennis or some other sport, and there are innumerable hobbies he can pursue; he can be a poet or a painter, or an amateur historian.

The same principle operates in areas where the problem is not one of deliberate choice. The young child may develop, in character and personality, in one of different directions. He may learn to face reality and to deal with his problems on their merits, with an attitude toward life in which he makes reasonable demands and accepts reasonable satisfactions. Or he may live his entire life under the control of infantile emotional demands which lead him to interpret the problems of adult life in terms of a child's conception of their significance. Even after he becomes an adult he may make his decisions, demand his satisfactions, and approve or condemn on the basis of a world he has constructed in fantasy. Most of us would say that the first alternative is the better one. Is there any foundation in the nature of man, and of existence itself, for this judgment?

Let us look at one feature of these alternatives. From what we know of the actual process by which human beings mature we may say that the first alternative involves the effective exercise of an ability to think objectively and to control one's actions in accordance with the results of that thinking. Such an ability is not exercised by the person who develops in the other direction. Now let us assume that both persons, when young children, were fully equipped as human beings, of normal intelligence and with normal human potentials. In childhood neither one was capable of controlling his actions by rational judgment operating in the light of adequate knowledge and understanding. In both, however, this was a genuine potentiality. Not only was it a genuine potentiality but it also represented a level of activity toward which earlier stages seem to be tending as their proper fruition. Many psychologists today believe that the emotional storms and stresses of early childhood and adolescence provide the means by which the individual is able to fashion a self of his own; a self capable of dealing with the real world in terms of what that world is and for the sake of ends appropriate to his own nature. Those whose development fails to get beyond the earlier stages are, then, in this sense incomplete products of the process by which mature human beings are produced. As in this way incomplete, they are also defective.

Why is such an incomplete development defective? Surely not merely because something possible is at one stage left unrealized, for the actualization of any one potentiality is bound to leave others unrealized. It is rather because there are structures and activities in earlier stages which seem to exist only for the sake of something that will come later. To use the words of Professor Eliseo Vivas, such development involves

a notion of structural preformations inherent in the incomplete thing, such that the thing is endowed at an earlier stage of its development with the power of completion along certain lines which are determinate within limits.[12]

[12] *The Moral Life and the Ethical Life* (Chicago, The University of Chicago Press, 1950), p. 209. By permission.

The cerebral development of the new-born child is incomplete. There are brain structures, for example, in process of physical maturation which will serve later as speech centers. So far as we know, the immature speech centers in early infancy do nothing except grow and develop; they contribute nothing to the actual life of the infant at that time. This is even more obvious if we look at still earlier stages. The whole breathing apparatus of the human infant is complete and ready to function before birth. But it does not function until after birth. Here are structures and relationships of incredible complexity which contribute nothing to the life of the organism during the period of their formation. Their existence during that period is for the sake of later functions. These later functions are what make the earlier existence of these structures significant. So far as this process is left incomplete, to that extent the specimen is not merely limited but defective. To put it in plain language, the failure of existing structures to function in accordance with their nature means that there is no point to their existence.

This approach to value rests upon one basic assumption: *the principle that it is good to exist.* Only where there is a contrast between the existent and the nonexistent do we think in value terms. For us human beings, who exist in time and whose awareness transcends the present, the form of the contrast between the existent and the nonexistent which comes home to us most directly is the distinction between the actual and the possible. Although only those possibles which we adopt as ends are the ones which we consciously recognize to be valuable in their realization, still there are values we ought to recognize if the failure to realize certain possibilities renders some actual existence meaningless. For such failure means that there is an existence incomplete *in its existence;* that is, prevented from carrying out the act for which it exists. Such a situation is found particularly in the case of a thing which exists as a temporal duration in which development takes place. "The innermost meaning of time," says Urban, "is the inalienable difference between what is and what ought to be." [13]

We do not attribute value to entities which have some other mode of being than actual existence. No number, for example, is

[13] Urban, *op. cit.,* p. 159. See Nicolai Hartmann's argument that the relativity of values does not make them subjective, and that they are relative not "to the subject's opinion of them or to his appraisement of them, but to the subject's existence. . . ." Volume I, pp. 206-08.

valuable, or more excellent than another; nor is a word, simply as a word. Not even a possibility is valuable as such, although the fact that an actual existent possesses certain possibilities may contribute to its value as an existent. The value of an actual existent lies in the fact that it *is* the realization of possibilities.

The distinction between our awareness of something as being *actual* and as being *valuable* is thus the distinction between our recognition that it actually *is* and our awareness of it as the fruition of earlier potentialities. An existence which had in it nothing potential, such as the existence which theism attributes to God, would be not only nontemporal but also a being in whom there could be no distinction between existence and value.

The same principle, that it is good to exist, applies in a somewhat different way to esthetic values also. Esthetic values, which we attribute to the productions of human art, may be understood first of all in terms of the relation of the complete to the incomplete. The esthetic object, of course, is complete in itself. We do not ordinarily find fault with a painting or a musical composition because it is unfinished. Yet when we compare the actual work with what might have been done with such subject matter, we may find the actual work an inadequate fulfillment of the possibilities of the subject.

No theory of the nature of value can specify what values are supreme or what potentialities in human existence are highest. Our conceptual analysis can be only *about* values; what values are in themselves, we can discover only in direct experience or by means of some kind of communication which is not conceptual but enables us to feel directly the meaning of individual structures and relationships.

VALUE RELATIONS

Although the philosophy of value cannot get beyond abstract relationships and structures, there are important problems in this restricted area; and this is a field in which much work remains to be done. Considerable attention has been given to the analysis of moral values, particularly by Aristotle in ancient philosophy, by Kant and Nietzsche in modern philosophy, and more recently by Nicolai Hartmann. Most of what we know about value structure has come from conflicts of theories in ethics and esthetics. Since these have come to our attention through controversy we tend to think of them in terms of pairs of opposites. The following are some examples of ways in which various values may be related to each other. These relations are not necessarily constant; for example, different values may be opposed in some situations and mutually compatible in other situations, or a value may be instrumental in one relationship and intrinsic in another.

(1) *Opposition and supplementation.* Some values are mutually exclusive, so that a choice must be made between them; while others are mutually supplementary. Many values of the life of a scholar are incompatible with some of those of the life of a politician, such as freedom from immediate pressures in the first and the zest of living under pressures which cannot be controlled in the other. On the other hand, the values of one's occupation may be supplemented by the values of a recreation or a sport.

(2) *Instrumental and intrinsic.* Some values are for the sake of others, while some are for their own sake. There are certain kinds of information we acquire because we need to use it. Such information has instrumental value. There are some things we desire to understand for their own sake. Related to this distinction are also the distinction between *relative* and *absolute,* and between *proximate* and *ultimate* values.

(3) *Experiential and ontological.* Some values are values of experience itself, others are values of existence. Some things are good, for example, because of the pleasure they bring; other things are good in the sense that it is good that they exist.[14]

(4) *High and low, strong and weak values.* These distinctions, which we owe to the work of Nicolai Hartmann, express the distinction of high and low values in terms of our readiness to praise. A high value is one for which a person is praised and admired. Highly developed skills, for example, in which one takes advantage of unusual gifts are praised. A low value is one which is not worthy of praise. A strong value is one the absence of which leads to condemnation, such as ordinary honesty. A weak value is one for the absence of which we do not feel condemnation. As Hartmann points out, high values are weak values and strong values are low

[14] See Philip Wheelwright, *The Way of Philosophy* (New York, The Odyssey Press, 1954), p. 402, for a classification of value relations from which this one is partially derived.

values.[15] Some values are both low and weak, but it seems difficult to find values both high and strong. The main thrust of some religious teachings, however, might be understood as attempts to establish the strength of high values by advocating the rejection of strong low values in favor of high values. The arguments of pacifists also often point in this direction.

SUMMARY

Value statements may be distinguished from ordinary statements of fact as those which express an approval or disapproval which is based upon priority of commitment. The latter feature is the source of the necessity or compulsion we recognize in the concept of oughtness or obligation. The problem which such a distinction poses is whether the value which we attribute to things is truly a feature of things themselves or is only an expression of our attitudes toward things. To consider values simply as qualities of things seems to many to fail to do justice to the element of necessity in value judgments. To consider values as merely expressive of our emotions and attitudes, or of our likes and dislikes, destroys the basis upon which one person makes claims upon another.

One possible way out of this apparent dilemma is in the view that although values are objective they do not refer, as do descriptive predicates, to what the object actually is. Value statements are about objects but they concern the relation of what an object is actually to what it was potentially.

This raises the question of how we distinguish between true and false value statements and whether or not there are absolute value principles. Complete relativism is self-defeating, for it destroys its own significance as a theory. It is possible to have a basis for absolute value standards if we assume that it is good to exist. Value is the fulfillment of possibilities; disvalue is the destruction of possibilities in such a way that some actual existent is rendered meaningless.

[15] See Hartmann, *op. cit.*, Volume II, Chapter III. "The Gradation of Value."

1. *Terms:* appearance, commitment, descriptive judgment, mores, objectivism, ought, relativism, syllogism, value judgment.

2. Is decision concerning an act to be done or not done possible without making some assumptions or accepting some position concerning values? (This requires some consideration of what is involved in decision.)

3. Suppose you are over-charged in a store, or you receive a low grade in a course which the instructor explains by saying that he simply does not like you. You protest that such treatment is not fair. The other replies, "Why should I be fair?" How would you answer?

4. Consider an evaluation you are accustomed to make as nothing more than an emotional response. What factors would you have to take into consideration and what changes in your attitude would be necessary in order to replace this response with a reasoned judgment?

5. What is the difference between being impartial and being indifferent? Between being disinterested and being uninterested? Is there any distinction between impartiality and disinterest?

6. Distinguish subjectivity and relativity of values.

7. A robber demands your money at gun-point, you raise your hands, and he takes your money. Has he forced you to accede to his demand or was it your choice? Is it possible ever to compel action by physical force?

8. What do you understand by *moral force?* Is "force" used here literally or as a figure of speech?

9. Analyze some of your own value judgments in an effort to discover the standards which you take for granted in making those judgments.

10. What are some significant examples of values that are low and weak, low and strong, high and weak? Are there any values which are both high and strong?

CHAPTER 13

Ethics

THE PROBLEM OF ETHICS

Ethics is concerned with the two basic practical problems of human life: (1) What is worth seeking—that is, what ends or goals of life are good, and (2) what is a person responsible for—that is, what duties should he recognize and attempt to fulfill? Although these problems are not always in the forefront of our attention they are always at least behind the scenes ready to appear. Whenever we are faced with a choice and try to make that choice reasonably, we are forced to think of something more basic or more important than the immediate issue before us. For to have a *reason* for a choice, a reason that governs the choice, is to submit the issue to something more important to us than the rejected alternative. If I turn my back on a chance to enjoy a present pleasure for reasons of health or because I have promised to do something else at that time then I count my health or the keeping of my promise more important than the lost pleasure. If now I ask why I should care for my health or why I should keep my promises I must appeal to some interest still more important or more basic. The problems of ethics are the questions of just what these questions lead us to finally.

Our discussion of this problem here cannot possibly be an adequate consideration. We shall have to oversimplify, and we can consider only some of the alternatives. But our purpose here is to provide an introduction, not a solution, to the problems of ethics. An introduction can hardly avoid some reference to the history of ethical thought, but our purpose here is not to survey that history. The purpose of this chapter is to lead into a process of reflection upon these two problems, the problem of what is good and what is right. We shall begin with a way of thinking that is obvious and plausible. We shall then see some of the difficulties that emerge, and look at the plausible way of attempting to deal with those difficulties. This will lead us into an ethical theory which is in opposition to the first, and will be the occasion for an attempt to bring the two together in a synthesis.

THE ETHICAL SITUATION

Not all problems are ethical problems. Some problems are not practical problems at all; they are theoretical. They are questions we try to answer not because our action depends on the answers we find but because we want to understand. Some practical problems are not ethical, but are questions of technique. Our goals are already chosen; we know what we want. The problem is only the question of *how* to reach our goals. An ethical problem, then, is a practical problem, and it is the kind of practical problem in which we have to decide which goals to seek.

The ethical situation is one in which we have to make a choice.

The object of choice being one of the things in our own power which is desired after deliberation [Aristotle points out], choice will be deliberate desire of things in our own power.[1]

Although ethical problems are practical problems, the study of ethics is a theoretical activity; it is a reflective examination of the goals open to us and of the various ways by which men try to reach those goals.

In an ethical situation there are alternatives before us, and they are alternatives about which we are uncertain. Each is a real possibility, or at least it seems to us to be so, and yet no one of them is certain to be realized. The possibility that I shall die sometime, for example, cannot be an alternative in an ethical situation, for I have

[1] *Ethica Nicomachea*, 1113a 10-12, translated by W. D. Ross, in *The Basic Works of Aristotle*, edited by Richard McKeon (New York, Random House, 1941), p. 971. By permission of Oxford University Press.

no choice about whether I shall die sometime. But whether I shall risk my life in a venture I am contemplating may well be a matter of ethical choice. The ethical situation is one in which I am free to choose, at least free enough from other influences and pressures so that my choice really makes the difference between the realization of one possibility rather than another.

The thing that is distinctive about an ethical choice is that it is made in accordance with the results of one's own reflection and decision. It is neither forced upon one by outside pressures nor is it a mere acquiescence in the approvals and disapprovals which are characteristic of the social group in which we live. As we shall see later, the ethical situation can be distinguished from what we ordinarily call the moral, for morality in its wider sense includes the idea of conformity to the modes of action acceptable to and within the social community. In the narrower sense of ethical, a choice which is governed by social codes or by an authority or by another's prescription is not an ethical choice. However, the decision to allow one's course to be governed by such factors may very well be an ethical choice, provided *that* decision is made by us without coercion and on the basis of our own reflection and in accordance with principles we take to be fundamental.

There is no necessary conflict between ethical choice and conformity to the behavior expected of one by his social group. We tend, perhaps, to suspect that there is such a conflict because conformity is so often merely a matter of giving in to pressures. But conformity may also be the result of a deliberate decision made as a matter of kindness or consideration for the feelings of others; or it may express a recognition of the practical importance of respecting rules which are generally accepted. In such cases conformity is not an abdication of one's own will in favor of social pressures, but a deliberate choice made under the guidance of values to which one is committed. The rebelliousness of the young against authority is often the result of a failure to examine the reasonableness of what is required. Sometimes, of course, what is required is not reasonable, and resistance and rebellion may be in order.

People often confuse questions of technique and problems of exerting self-control with ethical problems. So far as I know what I want to accomplish and am bothered only by the question of how to go about it, I am not in an ethical situation. My problem is a technical one only, the problem of devising or discovering the means to an end already accepted. Some people also have little question in their minds about what they should do, but have considerable difficulty in doing it. Whatever the source of the trouble may be—psychological conflicts or immaturity or lack of character—the problem is not always an ethical one. It may be a psychiatric or an emotional problem; but whatever may be its cause, the difficulty is a personal weakness or defect. The victim of such difficulty may not so much need enlightenment, as training or treatment.

Many emotional problems, however, are character problems; they arise from the refusal to face life realistically, to come to terms with oneself and to appreciate fully the values available to man. A chronically dissatisfied person who is frustrated because he cannot get the things he thinks he wants, would be every bit as dissatisfied if he did get the things he thinks he wants. For he is wishing for things which do not satisfy, or else he does not have a personality structure stable enough to be capable of satisfaction. Such people are ineffective and weak, and in a sense, morally weak. For in its traditional sense, the word "virtue," which we associate so closely with morality, meant literally a kind of strength and effectiveness in making choices and carrying these choices out in action. In Aristotle's definition of *virtue,* this sense of the word is combined with concern for the ends toward which choice is directed and the application of a rational standard in the control of choice:

> Virtue, then, is a state of character concerned with choice, lying in a mean, i.e. the mean relative to us, this being determined by a rational principle, and by that principle by which the man of practical wisdom would determine it.[2]

Although character problems usually arise from faulty training and poor habits, their moral significance is recognized in all societies; and we usually hold people responsible for their actions even where they are plainly of weak character and chronically unsuccessful in governing their actions. The recognition that such weakness often has its roots in early childhood has encouraged a relaxation of responsibility on the principle that a person should not be "blamed" for what he cannot help. This attitude is perhaps justifiable in so far as the matter of blame is concerned, but the impulse to blame and the tendency to look upon moral guilt as some kind of stain are perhaps hold-overs from a pre-ethical stage of morality.

2 *Ibid,* 1106b 36-1107a 2, p. 959.

It is quite a different thing to hold a person responsible not only for what he can do but also for what he can learn to do, if we mean by this that he must take the consequences of his failures. This itself may be a necessary condition for the effective growth and maturation of responsible persons. Thus the question of what policy to take toward character weaknesses is itself an important ethical question. It is one of the ethical problems which is becoming more and more critical in our society, especially in the fields of economics, education, and criminology.

The question that confronts us in an ethical situation is the question of the basis of our choice. How are we to choose? What are the overriding considerations that we are going to recognize in this situation? We saw earlier that this question has two aspects: (1) What is the good? and (2) What is my duty? Among the many ethical theories which have arisen in man's long reflection on these questions, three stand out as basic alternatives:

(1) The goal of life is satisfaction, and our duty is to seek satisfaction.

(2) The goal of life is the fulfilment of our obligations, and in such fulfilment is the only genuine satisfaction.

(3) The goal of life is the most complete possible realization of our highest potentialities as selves.

As we shall see, the difficulties involved in the first view lead many thinkers into the second, which is in certain basic respects the opposite of the first. The difficulties with the second view lead some to the third, in the attempt to do justice to both the first and the second while avoiding their difficulties.

TRANSITION TO ETHICAL THEORY

Significant reflection on the problems of ethics does not take place in a vacuum but in the context of moral experience and of concepts which are complex enough to involve serious conflicts. These conflicts concerning morality may arise between social classes, between those of different economic interest, between those who have had contacts with other societies and those who have not, between different generations in a society undergoing rapid changes of custom, or between individuals who differ in temperament and experience. In most societies familiar to us and in most of those which have influenced our own culture the emphasis, in the education of the youth and in the institutional life of the society, is on duty and conformity. The nonconformist is feared as a danger to the group, and this fear is communicated to the young. Religious sanctions are of great importance in producing group solidarity, and the moral duties which are laid upon the individual are often interpreted to him in religious terms.

Since here as elsewhere reflection is likely to arise as a result of dissatisfaction with the conventional or of skepticism concerning popularly accepted ideas, the first tendency of reflection is likely to be in opposition to accepted beliefs. A person is led to question what he has been taught is his duty when there is something else he wants which is in conflict with what he is supposed to do. If the conflict is strong enough and if he is able to overcome his resistance to anything which would alienate him from an attitude of conformity (a resistance instilled by his early training), then he may conclude that what he *wants* is more important to him than what he is expected to do. We may say that to rebel against custom and authority is to act on the principle that the good for me is to get what I want rather than to do what is expected of me.

Now the difficulty for thought begins. Formerly I was told what to do, first by parents and relatives, then by the laws and customs and expectations of the wider group. Now that I propose to cut myself free of these demands and controls, I shall have to decide for myself. But should that not be easy? I am aware of what I want. Yet when I act on present desire I find that the result is often disappointing. I thought I wanted something, but when I got it I found that I do not care for it. Then, too, I have conflicting desires, and this is most frustrating. I am unable to choose between them, for at this stage I have no basis of choice except the presence of desire itself; so either I satisfy none of them or else the ones rejected in action remain to tantalize me in imagination. From such difficulties as these the impulse to reflection must often come.

Reflection in such a situation may be nothing more than a mulling over of various alternatives, a kind of imaginative foretasting of the different possible satisfactions, which then ends with a yielding to the attraction that comes out the stronger. This kind of reflection does not provide an ethics or a moral theory. We do not have ethics until reflection is rational reflection, and until conclusions are accepted solely on the ground that they are logically implied by what we have consciously and deliberately accepted as the basic assumptions on which we propose to live our lives. But rational reflection means thinking in terms of concepts. Here it means a search among the various possible satisfactions in the effort to discover what about them makes them desirable. Thought first looks for what is common to the different cases so that, once found, this knowledge may be used in comparing, accepting, and rejecting possible courses of action in the future.

The obvious feature common to all satisfying experiences is of course simply the fact that they do satisfy. If we want to go further, and find out the difference between those that satisfy more and those that satisfy the less, then we examine the experience of being satisfied. The one feature common to all such experiences, and a feature capable of considerable variation in strength, is the feeling of pleasure. The one feature common to all disliked situations is their unpleasantness. Thus the common feature of all the desirable objects is not in the object itself but is a property of our experience of the object. If we are to try to control our action so that as often as possible we shall get what we want, then we should aim at the greatest possible amount of pleasure with the least possible pain and unpleasantness. This theory of the good is *hedonism*.

PSYCHOLOGICAL AND ETHICAL HEDONISM

There have been two varieties of hedonism. One has been called *psychological* hedonism, since it is the position that we do as a matter of fact always seek pleasure. No matter how altruistic our intentions may seem to ourselves to be, the actual motive is our desire for pleasure or our desire to avoid unpleasantness. A man may give money to a beggar because to refuse would make him feel ashamed of himself, and this would be unpleasant. Or he may enjoy the gratitude expressed by the recipient, or he may get a thrill of pleasure from his own pride in his generosity. Sometimes a conscious recognition of the true motive of an act would be unpleasant, and so we repress that awareness and rationalize the act in terms of motives of which we are proud.

Such observations as these, and the recognition that in all emotion the feeling-tone is an important and prominent ingredient, have led to the generalization that all activity is for the sake of obtaining pleasure and avoiding unpleasantness. The feeling-tone of an emotion is plainly a factor which makes the difference between the desire to repeat some emotional experiences and the desire to avoid others. The discovery that much of our motivation depends on unconscious memories of emotional experience in infancy and early childhood makes even more plausible the hypothesis that all our motives are pleasure motives. In the words of Jeremy Bentham, the noted founder of utilitarianism, "A motive is substantially nothing more than pleasure or pain, operating in a certain manner." [3]

In apparent contrast with psychological hedonism is *ethical* hedonism. This is the view that we *ought* to seek pleasure. The principle upon which human life should be lived and the standard by which choices should be made is the principle of maximum pleasure and minimum unpleasantness. It is often argued that psychological and ethical hedonism are mutually inconsistent, for if we do always seek pleasure then what is the point of the contention that we *ought* to seek pleasure? And if it does make sense to contend that we ought to seek pleasure then surely sometimes we fail to do so. One does not commend to a person an act one knows he is going to perform anyway.

This objection fails to consider that even if all motivation is the desire for pleasure yet the fact that pleasures differ greatly in intensity and in duration makes it possible for us to miss much pleasure that is available to us. Knowledge and experience improve the effectiveness of our search for pleasure. We learn that some pleasures deceive, that in their immediate appeal they hide from us the pain and suffering which will follow when they are gone. The overweight person, the diabetic, or the person with an ulcer avoids forbidden foods not because his appetite is deadened by his physical condition but because he knows the unpleasant consequences of present indulgence. Ethical hedonism is the doctrine that the best life is one of careful control of our activities, in the light of our own experience and of the experience of others, to the end that we shall have the maximum of pleasure with the minimum of pain and unpleasantness.

When, therefore, we maintain that pleasure is the end [said Epicurus], we do not mean the pleasures of profligates and those that

[3] *An Introduction to the Principles of Morals and Legislation*, (New York, Hafner Publishing Company, 1948), p. 102. By permission.

consist in sensuality . . . but freedom from pain in the body and from trouble in the mind. For it is not continuous drinkings and revellings, nor the satisfaction of lusts, nor the enjoyment of fish and other luxuries of the wealthy table, which produce a pleasant life, but sober reasoning, searching out the motives for all choice and avoidance, and banishing mere opinions, to which are due the greatest disturbance of the spirit.[4]

This policy is quite consistent with the recognition that all action is for the sake of pleasure, as psychological hedonism contends. Bentham's initial statement in the Introduction to his great work, *The Principles of Morals and Legislation*, bring psychological and ethical hedonism together in a single principle:

Nature has placed mankind under the governance of two sovereign masters, *pain* and *pleasure*. It is for them alone to point out what we ought to do, as well as to determine what we shall do. On the one hand the standard of right and wrong, on the other the chain of causes and effects, are fastened to their throne. They govern us in all we do, in all we say, in all we think: every effort we can make to throw off our subjection, will serve but to demonstrate and confirm it. In words a man may pretend to abjure their empire: but in reality he will remain subject to it all the while.[5]

Ethical hedonism may be regarded as the kind of supplementation of the natural law expressed in terms of psychological hedonism, a supplementation which is possible when intelligence intervenes in nature. Ethical hedonism is the injunction to learn the lesson of what our nature is, and to enhance the effectiveness of our action by use of what we learn from experience about the conditions of pleasure and unpleasantness. The harmony of such an ethics with the economy of nature itself is expressed in Epicurus' maxim: "Nature is weak towards evil, not towards good: because it is saved by pleasures, but destroyed by pains." [6] Hedonism identifies all value with pleasure, all disvalue with pain or unpleasantness. Although hedonists do not always make this identification with the frankness of Epicurus' reduction of aesthetic value to pleasure, the principle ex-

[4] *The Extant Writings of Epicurus*, translated by C. Bailey, in *The Stoic and Epicurean Philosophers*, edited by Whitney J. Oates (New York, Random House, 1940), p. 32. By permission of Oxford University Press.

[5] Bentham, *op. cit.*, p. 1.

[6] Epicurus, *op. cit.*, p. 42.

pressed is the same: "I spit upon the beautiful and those who vainly admire it, when it does not produce any pleasure." [7]

PLEASURE AND THE OBJECT OF DESIRE

Critics of hedonism have often objected that this ethical doctrine involves a serious confusion concerning the basic facts of human action, especially purposive action, the kind of action with which ethics is chiefly concerned. The confusion to which these critics refer is that between the object of desire and the feeling-tone of the experience of failing or succeeding in the attempt to obtain the object desired. I get pleasure from eating, for example, because I desire the food. I desire food because I am hungry. If I am sated with food the prospect of more food is revolting, not pleasant. I enjoy a book or a play only if it interests me. The interest is primary; pleasure is a consequence of satisfying an interest, and to have satisfaction interfered with is unpleasant. There are no such things as pleasures in general, at least in normal experience; all pleasure is linked with interest in objects. [8]

Critics of hedonism admit that sometimes we do seek objects for the sake of the pleasure those objects bring, but unless there remains some interest in the object for its own sake it ceases to bring pleasure. This is illustrated by the rapid changes of interest we see in the growing child. As he matures the child's interests change, and what gave him intense pleasure a short time before no longer appeals to him.

To such critics the hedonist may reply by raising a question: "What is this interest in the object except a desire for the pleasure it will bring?" He points out that although we do have certain organic and psychological and social needs, yet if the actions which tend to satisfy those needs were unpleasant and the actions which tend to thwart them were pleasant our very survival would be threatened. He might well point out that we have here the source of the ethical problem. Because some things which are harmful are also pleasant we have to learn to control our actions and to govern ourselves in ac-

[7] *Ibid*, p. 51.
[8] A full and clear statement of this criticism may be found in Thomas Hill Green, *Prolegomena to Ethics*, Fifth Edition (Oxford at the Clarendon Press, 1906), pp. 177-85.

cordance with the maximum pleasure principle. For to call these acts harmful is to say that they bring eventually more unpleasantness than pleasure. The desire for pleasure is what "makes us go." Without it we would be merely passive, completely apathetic, incapable of action.

The difficulty with this line of attack on hedonism is its failure to reach the true issue in ethical theory which hedonism raises. So far as the positive facts to which he appeals are concerned, the hedonist's position is a strong one. Many who find hedonism unsatisfactory recognize the positive contributions of hedonism to our ethical understanding; their objection concerns what hedonism denies and what it ignores. But the non-hedonist who is capable of appreciating the contributions of hedonism is not the kind of thinker who is likely to be effective in pointing out the shortcomings of hedonism. Such understanding is made possible by the examination and criticism brought against hedonism by hostile criticism, by thinkers who place the whole ethical emphasis on an entirely different aspect of moral experiences. To such criticism we now shall turn.

PLEASURE AND OBLIGATION

Hedonism is least satisfactory to those for whom the primary and distinctive aspect of moral experience is duty or obligation. Where the hedonist is concerned above all else with the *good*, there are others who are concerned above all else with the *right*. They object to hedonism because of its failure to do justice to moral obligation. To say that I enjoy something and to say that the thing I enjoy is good are statements which the hedonist must consider identical, except in so far as he means by the good the maximum possible enjoyment. Even so, it is the enjoyment itself that marks the object as good; more enjoyment would mean only more good. In Epicurus' words:

I summon you to continuous pleasures and not to vain and empty virtues which have but disturbing hopes of results.[9]

Beauty and virtue and the like are to be honoured, if they give pleasure; but if they do not give pleasure, we must bid them farewell.[10]

[9] Epicurus, *op. cit.*, p. 47.
[10] *Ibid*, p. 46.

Hedonism's difficulty in accounting successfully for the factor of obligation appears when we ask of the hedonist the grounds on which he asserts that we ought to seek the maximum pleasure with the least unpleasantness. True, once we discover that the results of our action are to some extent within our control, we may *desire* to seek to maximize our pleasures and minimize the disagreeable. But on what ground can the hedonist consistently say we *ought* to do so? If he means we ought to because pleasure is good, can he mean anything more by "ought" than that it is good to seek the good? What does this mean except that it is a pleasure to seek pleasure? Thus the hedonist, in saying that we *ought* to seek pleasure, is only pointing out that in addition to the pleasure we seek there is another pleasure, namely, the pleasure of seeking pleasure.

The hedonist might very well accept this as an accurate account of his meaning of "ought," and be content with it. "Here," he might say, "is the true significance of what has been misunderstood as some kind of moral force or compulsion independent of, or even in opposition to, the desire for pleasure." But there is another difficulty involved in the hedonist position which he may be reluctant to accept. This is in what it implies concerning the demands we make upon others. Perhaps it would be very difficult to answer a hedonist who was consistent enough never to claim a right or assert that another person owed him any service or consideration. But perhaps also it would be difficult to find such a hedonist in a society such as ours, where the very fabric of that society is woven of rights and duties.

When the words of a popular song voice a plea to "be my love, for no one else can end this yearning," they express the attitude of hedonism. It is not the other who is the object of love for his or her own sake; the other is merely a means to an end, an instrument for the elimination of my own unpleasant state. A nonhedonist might well reply: "Who cares about your yearning?" But even another hedonist, to whom such a plea is addressed, might reply: "Don't talk to me; I just don't yearn to end your yearning!"

What can a hedonist say about what we commonly call an injustice except that it is unpleasant? If he says to a man who is robbing him, "You ought not do this," what can he mean consistently with his own position except: "I dislike having you do this," or, "You will not enjoy the consequences of this act"? Suppose the hold-up man replies, "Well, my friend, the consequences in your wallet I'll enjoy all right; as for the rest, I am happy to take my chances." What can the hedonist say to this? "You ought not do this" means either: "It is unpleasant to me for you to do this," or, "Your act will bring you something unpleasant." As Epicurus said:

> Injustice is not an evil in itself, but only in consequence of the fear which attaches to the apprehension of being unable to escape those appointed to punish such actions.[11]

The difficulty becomes acute when a person obtains his pleasure from inflicting suffering on others. Many participants in a lynch mob apparently get a rapturous thrill from their act. What, on the hedonists's grounds, can they be said to owe the victim? His pain belongs to him alone, not to them.

The hedonist can exhort another to consider more carefully the prospective pleasures and pains involved. From his own experience he may assure another that an act will have pleasurable or painful consequences which the other person knows nothing about. But he cannot say, with the meaning we ordinarily give to the statement: "You ought not." The hedonist may reply that we are too prone as it is to say "You ought not," and that it would be refreshing to our society to have more people whose only advice to others is to seek pleasure; and there are times when many of us would sympathize with this observation. But will the hedonist feel the same way about the matter when the search by others for their pleasure interferes with his and they laugh at his protests? There seems something incongruous about a hedonist protesting against injustice or claiming a right.

A recognition of this difficulty and a concern for the social or public applications of hedonism in nineteenth century English thought led to *utilitarianism*, a theory developed by Jeremy Bentham, James Mill, and his son, John Stuart Mill in the attempt to give a social reference to hedonism. The principle is not to seek merely my own pleasure, for since the good is pleasure the greatest good will be the greatest amount of pleasure. So I should seek the "greatest happiness of the greatest number." This provides a criterion of good and of right. The answer to a question of what should be done, either by an individual or by a legislative body, will be found by calculating the net total happiness of the alternative proposals.[12]

Is utilitarianism the abandonment of hedonism? Utilitarianism

---

[11] *Ibid*, p. 38.
[12] See Bentham, *op. cit.*, Chapter I.

appears to set up pleasure, the existence of pleasure whether yours or mine, as an objective value; while for hedonism the value is the pleasure as experienced. A consistent hedonist values another's pleasure only in so far as his awareness of another's pleasure is pleasant to him. The value for him, then, is not the other's pleasure itself, but the hedonist's pleasure in seeing the other enjoy himself. A hedonist may well reply to the utilitarian that the only grounds on which he can seek the happiness of others is that it gives him pleasure to watch or contemplate their enjoyment. But if he is so constituted that he gets more pleasure from the misery of others, then it is their misery that he would promote. Nothing counts for him but the quality of his own experience.

When Bentham faces this issue directly, he seems to accept the hedonist interpretation of the principle of utility:

> What motives . . . can one man have to consult the happiness of another? by what motives, or, which comes to the same thing, by what obligations, can he be bound to obey the dictates of *probity* and *beneficence?* In answer to this, it cannot but be admitted, that the only interests which a man at all times and upon all occasions is sure to find *adequate* motives for consulting, are his own. Notwithstanding this, there are no occasions in which a man has not some motives for consulting the happiness of other men. In the first place, he has, on all occasions, the purely social motive of sympathy or benevolence: in the next place, he has, on most occasions, the semi-social motives of love of amity and love of reputation.[13]

But about whose pleasures is a man concerned when he acts from "the purely social motive" of benevolence? Of course he is concerned about the pleasures of those who are the objects of his benevolence, but only because of his own pleasure in their pleasure. "The pleasures of benevolence are the pleasures resulting from the view of any pleasures supposed to be possessed by the beings who may be the objects of benevolence." [14]

THE ETHICS OF DUTY

The difficulties which are found in hedonism by those who see duty or obligation as the significant content of morality

---

13 *Ibid*, pp. 312-13.
14 *Ibid*, p. 36.

lead to the formulation of a view directly contrary to hedonism. For such thinkers hedonism can have ethical significance only as it is based on duty, the duty to seek pleasure. Without this hedonism is not an ethics at all; it is only a theory that it is pleasant to seek pleasure. From the view that the duty to seek pleasure is the only content that could make hedonism a moral theory the distance is short to the conclusion that conformity to duty is the whole of morality. Immanuel Kant said:

> The value of life for us, if it is estimated by that *which we enjoy* (by the natural purpose of the sum of all inclinations, *i.e.* happiness), is easy to decide. It sinks below zero; for who would be willing to enter upon life anew under the same conditions? who would do so even according to a new, self-chosen plan (yet in conformity with the course of nature), if it were merely directed to enjoyment? [15]

For hedonism all the value of an act is in the consequences, in the pleasurable or unpleasant character of those consequences. But if the moral quality of an act is wholly in its conformity to obligation, then the consequences make no difference. If I ought to tell the truth then it is wrong for me to lie no matter how much misery I cause by my refusal to lie. I can take the consequences of an act into account only as they are involved in my duty. If I have a duty to avoid injuring others then I must act accordingly, not because injury to another is in itself an evil but because for me to injure another would violate my own obligation.

Of course there are many good things in life, and we seek these things for ourselves and for those for whom we care. But such goods have nothing to do directly with morality.

> To be kind where one can is duty, and there are, moreover, many persons so sympathetically constituted that without any motive or vanity or selfishness they find an inner satisfaction in spreading joy and rejoice in the contentment of others which they have made possible. But I say that, however dutiful and amiable it may be, that kind of action has no true moral worth. It is on a level with other inclinations, such as the inclination to honor, which, if fortunately directed to what in fact accords with duty and is generally useful and thus honorable, deserve praise and encouragement but no esteem. For the

---

[15] *Kant's Critique of Judgment,* translated by J. H. Bernard, Second Edition, Revised (Hafner Library of Classics), p. 358, n. 1. Reprinted by permission of Hafner Publishing Company.

maxim lacks the moral import of an action done not from inclination but from duty.[16]

Thus Kant distinguishes sharply between acts done in accordance with duty and acts done *from* duty. Only the latter have moral significance. Sympathy and warmth toward others may even be a hindrance to morality.

> Even the feeling of sympathy and of warmhearted fellow-feeling, when preceding the consideration of what is duty and serving as a determining ground, is burdensome even to right-thinking persons, confusing their considered maxims and creating the wish to be free from them and subject only to law-giving reason.[17]

There are all sorts of good and desirable objects which fall outside the realm of the moral, but these are all good because they are good *for* something or because they happen to be desired. The only moral good is a good *character;* that is, righteousness, uprightness, conformity of action to duty. In Kant's words, the only thing good in itself is a good will. A person who governs his action by what is right, who does what he does not because he desires the result but solely because it is his duty to do so, is the person who has attained the moral good. Here is moral value, and here is the highest achievement of man as man.

> Thus morality and humanity, so far as it is capable of morality, alone have dignity. Skill and diligence in work have a market value; wit, lively imagination, and humor have an affective price; but fidelity in promises and benevolence on principle (not from instinct) have intrinsic worth. Nature and likewise art contain nothing which could replace their lack, for their worth consists not in effects which flow from them, nor in advantage and utility which they procure; it consists only in intentions, i.e., maxims of the will, which are ready to reveal themselves in this manner through actions even though success does not favor them. These actions need no recommendation from any subjective disposition or taste in order that they may be looked upon with immediate favor and satisfaction, nor do they have need of any immediate propensity or feeling directed to them. They exhibit the

[16] *Foundations of the Metaphysics of Morals,* in *Critique of Practical Reason and Other Writings in Moral Philosophy,* translated by Lewis White Beck, New York, 1956. Reprinted by permission of the publisher, The Liberal Arts Press, Inc.

[17] *The Critique of Practical Reason,* Beck, *op. cit.,* p. 222.

will which performs them as the object of an immediate respect, since nothing but reason is required in order to impose them on the will.[18]

The emphasis in the ethics of duty is on human freedom and autonomy. For one thing the very idea of obligation seems to presuppose freedom. To say that a person is obligated to do something which is not within his power to do seems obviously inconsistent. For another thing, to say that moral action is action which is taken because of the obligation to take it, puts within the agent's own awareness and decision the difference between taking one action rather than another.

The ethics of duty separates the moral quality of an act from the particular consequences and from the desires and preferences of the agent, and rests the issue of right or wrong on reason alone. Only if I have some concept of what my duty is can I decide whether I should do this or that. But my concept of what my duty is must be in the form of a general principle, else it could not be applied to this or that specific occasion. Thus when I arrive at a conception of what my duty is I am setting up a rule of action for myself. I do for myself here what a legislature does for those who live under its laws: I legislate for my own future conduct.

This legislation is not only under rational control in its applications, but it is itself the expression of a rational will. The distinctive feature of duty or obligation is the element of necessity it contains. A so-called "duty" not recognized as binding would be a contradiction in terms; so far as it is not binding it is not a duty. If we ask now what kind of compulsion is involved here we see immediately that the compulsion cannot be an external one, for in so far as any action is done under outside pressure it is not being done as a duty. Of course I may recognize a duty to submit to outside pressure, and for this reason I may submit; but in such case I am not acting under the control of the outside pressure. The compulsion we find in obligation must be an inner compulsion; obligation compels only when it is recognized.

Inner compulsions are of two kinds. One of these is emotional compulsion. Anger, hate, love, adoration all have their modes of expression. In hate we feel *impelled* to say things for which we have no evidence; we say them because of the emotional tension we feel and because their expression brings a relief from that tension. Our

[18] *Foundations of the Metaphysics of Morals*, Beck, *op. cit.*, p. 92.

emotional disturbances are notoriously independent of our deliberate control. We can learn to control them, but the exertion of such control modifies the emotion itself. Even deliberately to get angry is to give our attention over to control by images and memories and associations which arouse the feeling. Any other deliberate "anger" would be only an act. The other kind of inner compulsion is that which we find in our rational thinking, the compulsion of logical necessity. I cannot believe two mutually contradictory statements if I am aware of their mutual contradiction. Nor, if I accept one proposition, can I refuse to accept another the denial of which would be inconsistent with the former proposition. Here the complusion is internal to my own thinking. My own intellectual insight into the logical relations is the sole condition of my awareness of the necessity. It is not a necessity imposed upon me from outside. Nor is it a necessity which operates by our abandoning control of our own thought; rather it becomes apparent only as we do control our thought in accordance with its own inner nature and exclude from the determination of our conclusions everything that is not logically relevant.

The moral agent, on this view, is thus a law to himself. Anything that is a law to itself is, in its proper activity, an end in itself. Moral agents then are ends, not means; and to treat a person as a moral agent is to treat him solely as an end and never as a means. Not only is he an end, but he is a self-legislating end.

EXAMINATION OF FORMALISM

The difficulty which many find with the ethics of duty is in its formalism. We are told that the good consists in the fulfillment of obligation, but what is our obligation? We are to act in terms of rational principles, legislating for ourselves as autonomous rational agents. But what legislation are we to adopt? Surely there is something involved here in addition to mere conscientiousness; it must make a difference what we are conscientious about. The trouble with the fanatic seems to be that he is conscientious about the wrong thing. We all have seen people so preoccupied with what they take to be their duties that they fail to ask whether they have rightly identified their duties. "I feel it is my duty to tell her what I think of her behavior," may be spoken quite sincerely so far as the speaker's conscious intentions are concerned and yet may be a disguise for an act of cruelty which brings considerable emotional satisfaction to its perpetrator. Few human acts have been done more sincerely from a sense of duty than those in which men have slaughtered their neighbors and even their kin for the sake of a religious or political principle. The most hideous wrongs suffered by weaker groups in society at the hands of stronger ones have had their sincere and gifted moral defenders.

Kant's formula of duty illustrates the difficulty we face when we try to make any formula do the whole task of solving our ethical problems. So act, Kant advises, that you can will that the principle of your action should be a universal law.[19] Are you tempted to lie? Then consider whether you can will that all others shall lie. Reflection will show you that the advantage you hope to gain from lying is possible only in a situation where people generally tell the truth and assume that others do likewise. If you could, by an act of will, bring it about that everyone would lie then your own lie would be worthless to you. Thus, if you act on Kant's principle, to lie is irrational. The real problem, however, is not often whether I shall lie but rather the problem of what is and what is not a lie. Is a lie any statement known to be false? Of course not, if the false statement is not intended to deceive. Is a lie, then, any statement known to be false and intended to deceive? Then in much of our business and sport and even most games we engage in systematic lying. But this is accepted as a part of the activity, and interpreted accordingly. Is a lie any statement known to be false and intended to deceive, and used where the intended victim is not warned by the accepted conventions to be on his guard? This is so vague it could not possibly work in practice. Every deception that was successful would be interpreted by its victim as a lie and by him who used it as a recognized practice. It would seem that we can say only that a statement known to be false and used for *wrongful* deception is a lie.

The difficulty of defending such a rule is shown in Kant's own attempt to apply it to a specific case. A French critic, Henri Benjamin Constant de Rebecque, attacked Kant as defending the position that it would be wrong "to lie to a murderer who asked whether our friend who is pursued by him had taken refuge in our house." Constant's thesis, which Kant is here concerned to answer, is:

[19] *Ibid*, p. 80.

To tell the truth is . . . a duty, but it is a duty only in respect to one who has a right to the truth. But no one has a right to a truth which injures others.[20]

This assumes, Kant argues in effect, that a lie is wrong only under circumstances in which it harms others, and that there are circumstances in which a lie does not harm others. The latter assumption is false, and consequently even if we accepted Constant's first assumption there would be no circumstance to which it could be applied. A lie necessarily harms others, for even if in my lie

> I do not wrong him who unjustly compels me to make a statement, nevertheless by this falsification . . . I commit a wrong against duty generally in a most essential point. That is, so far as in me lies I cause that declarations should in general find no credence, and hence that all rights based on contracts should be void and lose their force, and this is a wrong done to mankind generally. . . . For a lie always harms another; if not some other particular man, it still harms mankind generally, for it vitiates the source of law itself.[21]

Kant's argument here assumes that the statement to the murderer cannot be avoided, that one must either lie or reveal the presence of the intended victim. It is perhaps at this point that most of us would differ from Kant. In another place in this essay he has said: "Each man has not only a right but even the strict duty to be truthful in statements he cannot avoid making, whether they harm himself or others." [22] But is there ever a situation in which we cannot avoid making statements? To make a statement is, on Kant's own principles, a voluntary act. Confronted by a murderer seeking your friend who has found refuge in your house, would you be restricted to a choice between a "Yes" or a "No"? Few of us would have trouble in thinking of many other things to say and questions to ask, but even more appropriate might be the attempt to restrain or detain the would-be murderer. Most of us would like to think that there is more moral grandeur in an attempt to protect a friend even at the risk of one's own life than calmly to reveal his hiding place in order to preserve one's own moral integrity or to avoid the risk of vitiating the source of law.

[20] Quoted from Constant's essay, "On Political Reactions," by Kant, in "On a Supposed Right to Lie from Altrustic Motives," Beck, *op. cit.*, p. 346.

[21] *Ibid*, p. 347.

[22] *Ibid*, p. 349.

We say it is wrong to steal. But what is stealing? To steal is to take *wrongful* possession of another's property. Is it wrong to kill? As long as people have uttered the command, "Thou shalt not kill," they have been killing with good conscience. We kill in war; officers of the state kill in the execution of sentences of death; the law recognizes homicide to be justifiable in some cases where it is committed in defense of life or property. The rule we accept is that it is wrong to kill *wrongfully*. Rules such as these turn out to be either not binding or to be tautologies. Of course it is wrong to do something that is wrong. This is an important principle, just as is the principle that a thing is what it is and not what it is not. But the one principle tells us nothing about the differences between right and wrong just as the other tells us nothing about what a thing is. These are limiting principles; their violation is a mark of irrationality or meaninglessness.

A second difficulty with formalism is found in the fact that its practice is inconsistent, at least in spirit, with the principle of freedom and autonomy on which it is based. If the only morally significant act is one in accordance with what the self legislates for itself, then how can the self-legislation be considered binding? A legislature, so far as it is acting in a sovereign capacity, cannot bind itself. A law is passed; nothing except something outside the control of the legislature can prevent it from repealing that law the next day. So far as I am an autonomous agent acting in freedom, I cannot now bind myself in a future situation. To do so would be to abdicate my autonomy. If another person relies on my promise it is because he is convinced that when the time for performance arrives I shall decide to keep that promise. This is of the essence of a promise. If when I agree to a future performance I allow the power of action in the future to be taken away from me and entrusted to another, then it is not on my promise that anyone relies but on the arrangements that have been made for the action to be taken independently of me.

To live by rules is not to live as an autonomous and free agent; each rule chips away some part of future freedom. To live by rules is to assume that we have adequate knowledge of what the future will require of us. To live by rules is inconsistent with the fact that every situation is unique. Of course we learn from experience, and what we learn we formulate in terms of generalizations. But the application of a generalization can never be automatic in any situation of importance; for we always have before us the question of whether this situation is in fact one to which the generalization applies. If it does apply then we have the additional question of just how it applies. As we shall see later, this does not mean that there is no place for rules in life. Many things we do are routine, and do not require specific decisions each time they are done. But if we are acting in freedom we are always ready to set aside any routine if the occasion seems to call for that. There is a place for rules in moral discipline; they may be indispensable instruments in the preparation of a person for the exercise of freedom. But such rules do not fulfill their purpose until they are transcended.

TOWARD A SYNTHESIS

Perhaps the difficulty with hedonism and formalism both is oversimplification. It would be hazardous and presumptuous to say that they are simply wrong. The thinkers who have worked out these points of view were not fools. The errors of a great thinker are errors which can be seen only in the light of his own contributions to the problems on which he has worked. We have said elsewhere that often the more adequate point of view is to be found in a synthesis of opposing views. But unless the opposing views have been worked out there is nothing to synthesize, and unless their mutual opposition has been made explicit there will be no awareness of the need to synthesize. A view which is different from commonly accepted assumptions is not likely to be formulated except by someone who is dissatisfied with the commonly accepted position, and the inadequacies of this new view are not likely to emerge except at the hands of someone who considers it to be false. After two conflicting positions have been developed it becomes possible to consider whether they can be brought together in a more comprehensive position which does justice to both.

As we have seen before, one way of approaching a synthesis of opposing views is to examine the points of agreement and disagreement. Two views sometimes may be seen to be complementary except for their negations. For example, moral experience is concerned with problems of what is good and what is right. If in saying that it is concerned with the problem of what is good we rule out the problem of what is right, and if in saying it is concerned with what is right we rule out consideration of the good, then the two positions stand in stark opposition to each other. But in order to be thus opposed to each other, these two views have to agree on something more fundamental: that good and right are not both basic characteristics of the moral situation but that one is reducible to the other. The only basic disagreement concerns the question of which is which.

The two positions may perhaps be reconciled if we can show that good and right are mutually complementary, that neither is reducible to the other but that each involves the other. Our examination of these two points of view may have suggested a way of bringing the good and the right together. We saw that the significance of moral rules is not in what they prescribe positively but in their demand for consistency and in their function as limits. Duty and obligation may serve as the negative and formal aspect of an ethics which also has a positive content.

When something that has an initial appeal to us as desirable is discovered in actuality to be undesirable, we usually make that discovery by finding it to be inconsistent with some other end which is even more important. The idea of obligation may very well be the way in which a person understands this relation as he views it in terms of his own basic policies. The conviction that I have a duty to perform may rest on a recognition that my failure to perform that act will negate or destroy an end which has positive value. Otherwise how can the duty have positive content? From what other source can any positive content come? We have seen that the difficulty with formalism is that obligation is empty when it stands by itself. But it need not stand by itself, and if we have positive goals to achieve then the formal aspect of ethics may lie in the need to act consistently with those goals. Although these goals at their best may involve something more than mere pleasure, yet hedonistic theories have done us the great service of showing that ethics requires a content desirable in and for itself.

Once we recognize positive value and the demands of duty to be complementary rather than opposed, the way is opened for a conception of value much broader than hedonism admits. Hedonism is restricted to the immediate in its value theory; if we recognize the validity of the claims of duty, immediacy is transcended. A step toward this may be seen even in some forms of hedonism itself, where a present pleasure is sacrificed for a future pleasure. However, once we admit that this *ought* to be the case, then we abandon the conception of good as a subjective quality of experience; for now we are saying that it is good for man to have pleasure, in the sense that this is the way he *ought* to exist. Thus we take moral value out of the merely subjective and attribute to it an objective status. It is a short step from this to see that man has many potentialities and many kinds of satisfaction that are available to him besides merely the experience of pleasure.

THE UNION OF DUTY AND GOOD

Our exploration of two divergent paths of ethical theory has brought us to a position where we can see them approaching one another. What is man's duty? It is to seek the good, to work toward the attainment on the widest scale of the highest values he can reach. His own nature with all its potentialities and the world in which he exists with its potentialities provide him with the material out of which he is to shape his life. His life is lived in time; he pushes into and helps to make a future he cannot foresee. At every step he is faced with the need to compare possibilities, to evaluate, and to decide which shall be actual. It is in these acts of knowing, appreciating, comparing, and deciding that he exists to the fullest as a person. Failure to know what is accessible to his awareness and relevant to his interest; failure to appreciate values—both those he will espouse and those he will relinquish; failure to compare these values in the light of his own goals; failure to decide for himself under the guidance of his own knowledge and appreciation of values—and this includes the willingness to re-examine his goals in the light of new values: to fail in any of these is to fail as a person.

Anything in which anyone has ever found satisfaction is a possible good. Nothing that exists, nothing that happens, is evil in itself. The only evil is the frustration by something good of something better. The only goods we are justified in neglecting are those which can be secured only at the cost of giving up something better. The saddest negation of life is nihilism in action, the denial or ignoring of positive values. Our guide in this, in the earlier stages, is the experience of others. It is plausible to assume that what the most cultivated and most widely experienced have found to be of absorbing interest is something which any person whatever will find absorbing, provided he makes adequate contact with it, and provided he is not defective. The more demands an interest makes upon our powers of knowledge and of imagination and the more involved we are in situations where the course of events hangs upon our own decisions, the greater our satisfactions and our sense of the worth of life. The more we occupy ourselves with trivialities, with merely "putting in the time" in drifting here and there under the push and pull of outside influences and accepting the immediately attractive at face value because we have nothing else to work toward, the more bored and dissatisfied and worthless we feel ourselves to be.

Satisfaction in one's work, for example, is likely to have a direct relation, first, to the degree of independence one has in making decisions, and secondly, to the importance of what does depend upon one's choices. To work only under the control of others in a fixed routine, a condition which has existed so widely in our modern system of industrial production, can be a dehumanizing influence. The effect is worse where the worker has no awareness of what his own work contributes to the final result. Satisfaction is limited also even where one has a considerable freedom in deciding how to do his job if he cannot recognize much of importance in what he does. Perhaps one of the quickest ways to destroy a man's humanity would be to compel him to work under rigid rules at such a job as carrying heavy stones from one location to another and then taking them back again.

On such a view as this, there is a place for discipline as well as for satisfaction; in fact, the greater satisfactions all depend upon successful discipline. A person who achieves genuine freedom and autonomy in the choices and decisions he makes concerning the most important issues which confront him will likely find that he has achieved such autonomy as the result of having gone through a number of levels of discipline. The lowest level of discipline is to submit under duress to a rule established by others. The next level is to submit voluntarily to an external rule, under the influence of an appreciation of the values at stake. The next level is to submit to a self-devised and self-imposed rule; and the final achievement is to be free from all rules, and to be able to act in accordance with a trustworthy and true appreciation of the competing values as they are encountered in a specific situation.

But a last question remains: Why should a person choose the way of the fullest possible exercise of his powers in preference to a life of passive acquiescence? Societies under the influence of some of the Eastern religions do teach their people to seek the goal of release from struggle and effort, of Nirvana. In this question we are brought to the limits of ethics. The answer to this question is not an answer which ethics itself can provide; it can be found only in our theory of existence. The issue between the Western and the Eastern traditions, in their conception of the good life, is a metaphysical difference. The difference is in their conception of the relation of our existence to the good. The basic assumption of much Eastern thought is that existence as we know it, finite and temporal existence, is evil. The goal of life should be to remove desire, to inhibit striving, to lose ourselves in the all-encompassing ocean of being in which differences are overcome and all is one.

The basic assumption of the Western tradition is that existence is good. The criterion by which the better is distinguished from the poorer is one of fullness and inclusiveness of existence. What man's good is depends on his potentialities. His working standard is the standard of completeness. He chooses best when he chooses those ends which contribute the most to the realization of other ends and exclude the fewest of the higher values. Value is fullness of existence. The ultimate is an absolute union of value and existence; and this would be creative existence. The highest goal for each man is the closest approach he can make to that ideal.

Although in direct conflict with each other, the Western and Eastern traditions have a common assumption. They differ, in that for the West finite existence is good and for the East it is evil. They differ also in that for the West the actual existence of finite beings in time is reality, and not mere appearance or illusion. In the tradition of the East, finite temporal existence is illusion; the real is behind the veil of appearance, and is to be reached only by giving up finite existence in time. So, not in spite of but by virtue of their differences, the Eastern and Western traditions unite upon a common assumption which underlies both of these conflicting views: the identity of value and reality. Whatever is real, the highest goal for man is found in his closest approach to reality. Man's obligation is to be real, and this is to realize in himself the highest potentialities accessible to him. Whether the highest potentiality for him is to deny his finite and temporal existence, or whether it is to exist in the process of active experience, thought, appreciation, and decision, it is in any case to find the good in the real.

SUMMARY

Ethics is concerned with two basic questions: What is good? and What is right? The ethical situation is one which involves alternative courses of action as genuine possibilities open to our choice and decision. A choice is ethical, in the strict sense of the term in which it is distinguished from the more general category of the moral, when it is made reflectively in accordance with one's own basic concept of what is good or right rather than in response to emotional pressure or group influence.

Three kinds of ethical theories may be distinguished: (1) Those for which the good is primary while right or duty is relative to the good. (2) Those for which the right or duty is primary and comprises the whole content of the good. (3) Those which attempt a synthesis of good and right.

Hedonism illustrates the first of these types of ethical theory. Pleasure is the only good; pain or unpleasantness, the only evil. Our only duty is to seek the maximum of pleasure with a minimum of unpleasantness. A difficulty arises, however, if the hedonist attempts to justify a claim upon another. To assert a claim upon another is to say that the other ought or ought not to do something. The hedonist can say, consistently, that it would please him for another to act in a certain way, or he can warn the other of unpleasant consequences which will follow his intended act. The attempt to broaden hedonism into a social ethics in utilitarianism did not succeed in getting beyond subjective pleasure, for on hedonist principles I can desire that another person shall have pleasure only if it is a pleasure for me to contemplate that eventuality.

Those who are impressed by the importance of obligation interpret the moral good in terms of duty alone. In Kant's version of this theory other goods have no moral or ethical significance. Reason alone discovers and applies the basic moral imperative. This turns ethics into a strictly formal affair and compromises even the principle of autonomy upon which this theory is based. It is an ethics of rules which are binding by virtue of their rational nature and universality, but which, the closer they approach universality, the emptier they become. Duty has no content, and the ethical principle becomes: It is right to do what is right and wrong to do what is wrong.

Hedonism and formalism agree in assuming that the good or

the right must be primary and that in either case the other must be a function of the one. A third possibility appears when we see that the good and the right may be complementing aspects of the basic value situation. Duty and the demands of formal rational consistency constitute the negative or limiting side of our search for value, while the good is the positive content of any realization of possibilities. Whether realization is in positive action or by way of negation, value and reality are ultimately one.

QUESTIONS FOR STUDY AND DISCUSSION

1. *Terms:* authority, character, choice, conscience, duty, formalism, happiness, hedonism, moral, natural law, Nirvana, obligation, right, sanctions, self-realization, utilitarianism, virtue.

2. Consider a decision you made recently and which required some deliberation before you were able to make up your mind what to do. Can you define the issue in such a way as to identify the advantages and disadvantages of each alternative? What does the decision reveal concerning your own judgment as to what is most important? How far did this process of reflection actually go when you made your decision?

3. Examine the advantages and disadvantages of conformity (a) in campus life, (b) in study and course work, (c) in family life, (d) in business, (e) in the practice of a profession. In each case identify the areas in which conformity is ordinarily found or expected.

4. Can commitment to any values be final and absolute, or is it always conditional? In discussing this question consider the extent to which our conception of what a value is depends upon the circumstances of the situation. For example, are there any changes in circumstances which would alter drastically the meaning of a commitment (a) in carrying out the terms of a contract, (b) in marriage, (c) in loyalty to the State?

5. Contrast the Aristotelian concept of *virtue* with popular uses of the term.

6. Which of the chief ethical theories discussed here (hedonism, utilitarianism, formalism, and self-realization) are primarily egoistic and which are primarily altruistic?

7. (a) Illustrate the difference between seeking an object for the sake of the pleasure it will bring and obtaining pleasure from the satisfaction of a need.

(b) Suppose a hedonist argues that man's basic need is for pleasure, and therefore man should seek pleasure before all other things. Is this argument itself in support of hedonism or in conflict with it?

8. Children generally accept correction or reprimand from their parents in quite a different spirit than when it comes from an outsider. Does the child's relation with his parents throw any light upon the psychological foundations of morality? Consider in this connection the Freudian doctrine of the id, superego, and ego, and the parts they play in character development.

9. Distinguish between good and evil character, and between strong and weak character. Can a weak character ever be either good or evil? Are all evil characters strong characters? In considering these questions consider carefully the ambiguities in our ordinary uses of "good" and "evil."

10. Examine the following argument: Those who believe that it is sometimes justifiable to lie should always be careful, if the question of their attitude upon this matter should arise, to lie about their own belief. Consequently, we can believe a person's statement about this question only if he says he believes it is right to lie. It follows from this that the only people we can believe are either liars or fools.

11. Examine: All ethical theories agree that the aim of life is to get what you want; they disagree only on what it is you really want when you become fully aware of your potentialities and of the available alternatives. Does it make any difference to your position here whether you take "want" to mean primarily *desire,* or take it to mean primarily *need* or *lack?*

CHAPTER 14

Art

THE PROBLEM OF THE SIGNIFICANCE OF ART

Preoccupied as we are with our daily duties and personal ambitions, indoctrinated with the primary importance of the practical, few of us in twentieth-century America pay much attention to art. We hear music, but seldom listen to it; we see pictures and reproductions of serious painting in magazines and on walls, but seldom look at them; we go to the theater, watch television dramas, read novels, run through a few verses we may find on a special page or tucked away in the extra spaces of a magazine, but we take these things as entertainment and a means of relaxation. Yet if we consider whom our civilization has honored and revered above all others we find a curious discrepancy with the ones among our contemporaries whom we consider important. This has likely been true of other generations and of other countries, although in our own time the contrast seems to be even greater. Those who are remembered as the great men of the past seldom had fame and honor while they lived. Even when they did receive recognition, the true quality of their greatness was not recognized.

This paradox may well be the consequence of the fact that our immediate value judgments are not as reliable as later judgments. The reason for this should be obvious. Only later, after the event and after its consequences are seen, after the relations of the event to other events become more apparent, are we in a position to evaluate. We cannot see the object immediately before us in its true proportions. We have to stand back and see it in perspective and in its setting. So also with events and with people. Those who lived and worked with Shakespeare no doubt were aware primarily of some of his personal problems, the difficulties and minor satisfactions of his day to day routine. Perhaps his frustration and discouragement with the way a rehearsal was going, or his need to pay a loan, was what loomed large at the moment to his intimates. The urges of the immediate can hide from us the true measure of a man's greatness. This may be why, when we look back at the past centuries of our civilization, the great men include so few of the wealthy, or merchants, or inventors, and not even many of the politicians or soldiers.

The political and military great are often honored more for nobility of person and of character than for skill in their professions. We do not honor Abraham Lincoln particularly for his unusual and sometimes devious skills in political manipulations; we honor him for a vision that rose above politics and for a devotion not to immediate needs only but to the destiny of his country. Washington was not a military genius; he was a man for whom no defeat could be final in the light of a goal that concerned a future not yet even dimly seen. He did not have the skills of a party politician, but he had the insight and devotion of a statesman. In the long sweep of Western history, however, even Washington and Lincoln, Wellington, Marlborough, Caesar, and Alexander are not the ones who have given our civilization its stamp and character. They have preserved certain features of it, altered it in some ways, and opened and closed channels of influence; but our civilization is the gift of philosophers, scientists, artists, and prophets. When we call the roll of the great, these are they whose names make up the larger part of the list. Any society in which this is not the case is a society with a borrowed civilization; it has none of its own.

Such reflections force upon us the question, among others, of why art is important. What is there about a painting, a poem, a symphony, or a novel that can make it more important to society in the eyes of posterity than an invention or a business organization or a battle or an election? In our attempt to explore this problem we shall try first to come to some understanding of the nature of esthetic experience, and then we shall consider the significance of art.

ESTHETIC EXPERIENCE

Esthetic experience, as the term would suggest, is usually perceptual, although it seems that some people find esthetic properties in objects of thought. It is possible that much of the intrinsic appeal of mathematics is esthetic, and thinkers who value system and organization may often be influenced by the esthetic appeal of logical completeness. But we think primarily of perception, and especially of sight and hearing, when we refer to esthetic experience. Our problem at this point is to differentiate the esthetic from the nonesthetic.

The distinction can be seen plainly in ordinary everyday experience. Each of us, for example, sees and approaches and opens certain doors day after day, sometimes many times a day. How many of us could sit down and draw from memory an outline of one of those doors, showing the design of its panel and the shape and ornamentation of the knob and plate? Most of the time we merely see the door and the door-knob as something-to-be-reached-for-grasped-turned-and-pulled-open. Compare with this the kind of seeing that goes on as we watch a cloud move across the sky and note its changing shapes. Ordinarily a chalk board is simply something-to-write-on; but if we *look* at it, "take in" its appearance, we see its mottled color where chalk remains in different amounts, and we trace patterns of smaller and larger cracks on its surface. The difference between these two kinds of perception is the difference between perceiving something in terms of what it means for action or for some practical purpose and perceiving what the thing *is* itself. Esthetic experience is first of all the kind of experience in which attention is absorbed in what a thing is in itself.

Our earliest perceptions are almost certainly esthetic rather than practical, in the sense in which we have drawn the distinction thus far. We see children literally tasting the objects they handle. They are absorbed in the look and sound and feel of things. Only gradually do they learn what these things are for, and begin to attend not to the thing but to its use. An earlier age would call their absorption in the object of perception instinctive, but such a term is not very meaningful by itself. The impression is inescapable, however, that such absorption in the qualities of things is pleasurable. Even in our practical activities we sometimes find ourselves forgetting the goal we are seeking and directing our attention to objects we had not noticed for themselves. Something calls attention to the thing itself, and this often involves an especially pleasant or unpleasant feeling-tone. For example, I may be momentarily oblivious to what someone is saying if my attention is caught by an unusual quality of his voice.

What we are aware of when we attend to what is directly presented in sense perception has been called "esthetic surface." [1] In the case of sight, this is color quality and visual shape seen for what they are in themselves and not for what they may signify concerning something else. I may see the color of an apple only in the sense that by means of the color I become aware that the apple is ripe. This is not an experience of esthetic surface. The esthetic surface is the color itself—the way the red deepens at certain spots and fades out at others, here gradually and there abruptly; the contrast of the green skin at the stem and blossom ends of the apple with the brown of the stem and the grayer darkness of the dry remains of the blossom. By their attention to esthetic surface, painters discovered that shadows are not gray or black but blue and purple. Snow is not a blank whiteness but has in it every color of the spectrum. Our ordinary use of the names of colors shows how little attention we pay to color itself in ordinary experience. We call the European human stocks "white," but it is likely that the only human beings we have ever seen with white on their faces were clowns. We feel no unfitness in referring to the so-called races as "white" and 'black" and "yellow" and "red" because we use these names to refer not to what we *see* when we encounter members of those groups but to refer to what we *think* conceptually about them. We see only enough to recognize a classification. All this can be summed up in Professor Eliseo Vivas' compact and precise definition of esthetic experience as "an experience of rapt attention which involves the intransitive apprehension of an object's immanent meanings and values in their full presentational immediacy." [2]

[1] See D. W. Prall, *Aesthetic Analysis* (New York, Thomas Y. Crowell Company, 1936), p. 11.

[2] *Creation and Discovery* (New York, The Noonday Press, 1955), p. 95. By permission.

ESTHETIC FORM

We may attend to what a thing is or we may attend to what it means with reference to something else. Ordinarily our attention is of the latter kind, particularly as we pass from childhood into adolescence and maturity. For then we begin to be preoccupied with interests and needs that carry attention away from the present into future times and remote places. Even when, for the moment, we do forget our practical concerns and are absorbed in something directly present, the object of our attention often has only a weak hold on us. We look at a picture and before we realize it we are not attending to how the picture looks but are absorbed in thinking of something of which the picture reminds us. When we hear music and are carried away into dreams and memories we are no longer aware of the sound itself and of its own properties and inner relationships. The sound has become a means for recalling something else. Such seeing and hearing is not esthetic experience, or at best whatever esthetic aspect the experience may have is quite subordinate and unimportant.

One reason why ordinary objects do not hold our attention upon what they are in themselves is that we find so little there to attend to. What we do see or hear is already familiar to us and if, by a deliberate effort, we attempt to hold attention on the esthetic surface we soon become bored. However it is instructive to note just what happens when we do make such an attempt to hold our attention. In order to do this we have to note differences—differences of color and shade, of shape and size, changes in sounds and contrasts of pitch and timbre and duration of the sound. We note how these differences are related to each other; for example, here may be spots of different sizes with no initially discernible order. We discover near the center a series of spots which run to the right in order of size, each smaller than the one to its left. As long as we continue to make such distinctions we can, with some effort, hold attention on the characteristics of the object as presented. When we can no longer attend to such distinctions and discover relationships among the aspects we have noticed, either our attention wanders to something else or we go to sleep. This, by the way, is the basis of all techniques of inducing hypnosis, and it is also the way in which many people are able to put themselves to sleep at will. The trick is to hold attention by an effort of will on something so simple and undifferentiated, or so trite and familiar, that it has no attention-holding power of its own.

The differences and relationships we find in esthetic surface constitute esthetic form. One difference between a successful work of art and ordinary objects is that a work of art has an incomparably greater richness of esthetic surface. Compare, for example, a simple melody with the sounds and noises we hear as we walk down the street. The complexity of relations we can be aware of in hearing the melody, and the plain and obvious pattern of the changes in pitch, quantity, and loudness of the tones, belong almost to a different world of sound than the screech of automobile brakes or the sound of the wind or of the patter of rain. A sunset may be rich in color but usually there is little there to compare with the complexity of shapes and their interrelations in a painting which the artist has composed deliberately to bring to our awareness a certain complex pattern of colors and shapes. The very word "compose" carries the suggestion of what the artist, or composer of music, does. He places things together in patterns (forms) which have an intrinsic interest for the observer or hearer.

Even the simplest jingle will illustrate the attention holding power of form. Suppose someone remarks that he had heard of a chap who was having trouble with his wife. It happened that this man had a special liking for pumpkins, so he quite effectively took care of the matter by shutting up his wife in an empty pumpkin. On hearing this fantastic tale where would our attention be? Quite likely it would be darting from wondering what the speaker was driving at, through doubts concerning his sanity or sobriety, to questions of what wife would be small enough or pumpkin large enough for the former to go into the latter. A speculative mind might then perceive that here is a possible murder mystery. In all of this, attention departs from what is presented, and explores all sorts of related matters. But when we hear the familiar jingle:

> Peter, Peter, pumpkin eater,
> Had a wife and couldn't keep her;
> He put her in a pumpkin shell
> And there he kept her very well.

such questions do not arise, and incongruities do not distract attention. The form itself absorbs attention in such a way that the presence of something that conflicts with what we know, of something that is literally absurd, does not destroy our awareness of the content itself. To take note of the absurdities we have to change our perspective entirely and shake attention free from the magnetism of the form. Form gives to art an independence of the factual, and this freedom from the factual is essential to art. "Art bound down to facts, still more to thoughts, is lost," says Jacob Burckhardt.[3]

Form is the means of communication in art. In his work of art the artist communicates to the observer what he finds that seems to him to be significant in its own right. A painter sees certain intrinsically interesting relations of mass and color hidden within all the welter and chaos of the shapes and colors of a landscape. That they are intrinsically interesting is shown by the fact that once he notes them they do hold his attention. The landscape painter differs from the casual observer of a landscape mainly in this respect, that he is able to see these interesting patterns in spite of the shapes and forms that overlap them or in other ways distract attention from them. Perhaps it is an oversimplification to say that the true function of the painter is nothing more or less than to bring those patterns of shape and color into the view of the observer, but this is certainly an important part of what the painter does. In abstract art this may be the major or even the sole object of his work. Whatever else the work of art may be, it is always an attempt by the artist to communicate by means of the delineation of significant forms.

Here we have the suggestion of a partial answer to the question with which this chapter began, the question of why art is important. If there are patterns or arrangements, either found in nature or constructed from imagination without any specific model, which have instrinsic significance then art is important as the means by which these are discovered and communicated. If there are important characteristics of things which can be communicated in no other way then art is not only important, it is indispensable to our discovery of the resources of existence.

[3] *Force and Freedom,* edited by James Hastings Nichols, (Meridian Books, New York, The Noonday Press, 1955), p. 129. By permission of Pantheon Books, Inc., New York, publishers of the American Edition.

ART AS COMMUNICATION

We are all familiar with the fact that statements often convey much more than they say in the literal meanings of their words. The context or situation makes a difference in the interpretation we give to those statements. Some one hears a friend say casually: "I'll see you on Tuesday," and thinks nothing more about it; but this very same sentence would have quite a different import if spoken by someone who is to interview him for a promotion he is eager to receive. Variation in stress is a familiar way of conveying differences in meaning which the same words appearing in the same order in print could not show by themselves. In response to a statement, for example, I may say, "O, you did," in a way to express surprise, or doubt, or to show that I understand which person did the deed, or merely to confirm that I have heard what was said. Here we have communication not merely by the meanings of the words but also by the *way* in which the words are said. This is one kind of communication by means of form. The forms in these instances are the arrangements of stresses, pauses, and differences in pitch. Other familiar forms are those of rhyme and meter.

A familiar kind of form relation used in communication is metaphor. The very indirectness of the metaphor provides an emphasis on some aspect of the meaning conveyed, or makes explicit what could be brought out as effectively in no other way. Not only are otherwise hidden meanings made apparent, but the metaphor may be the means by which an attitude or evaluation is conveyed. Consider, for example, the impact of Lord Acton's aphorism: "The strong man with the dagger is followed by the weak man with the sponge." No literal statement of his meaning could say so much in so little and convey so forcefully a certain interpretation of political life.

Poetry provides our best examples of communicating by *how* something is said. Change the language of a poem and the meaning is lost; no paraphrase can be substituted for the original. Of course some meaning will be communicated by a paraphrase or a prose interpretation, but there are meanings in poetry for the expression of which the poetic form itself is indispensable. In serious poetry these meanings are so rich and subtle that some are bound to escape the reader. T. S. Eliot has observed:

A poem may appear to mean very different things to different readers, and all these meanings may be different from what the author thought he meant. . . . The reader's interpretation may differ from the author's and be equally valid—it may even be better. There may be much more in a poem than the author was aware of. The different interpretations may all be partial formulations of one thing; the ambiguities may be due to the fact that the poem means more, not less, than ordinary speech can communicate.[4]

This is the reason criticism and interpretation of literature is so important; it is why literature has to be studied as well as enjoyed. Different readers with different perspectives and approaches discover different ranges and levels of meaning. Their interpretations can alert a reader to meanings he otherwise would miss completely. The reward of such study turns out to be not only an incomparably more intense enjoyment but a deeper and broader comprehension of life and existence as attention is centered upon the dramatic relationships in which the meaning of life is to be found.

In their profounder aspects the devices of poetry are a mystery even to those who are most successful in using them. However it may be accomplished, we know that the coincidence of stress and quantity of sound with shifts of emphasis in meaning, together with variations in the relationships of changes of sound with changes of meaning, exert a uniquely effective hold on attention and on feeling. The cry, the chant, the sob, and the laugh are all direct expressions of emotion. Under some conditions to hear them is to respond with them oneself, and to respond with them is to feel the emotion they express. Poetry is a more subtle affair, of course, but its secret may be in the emotional roots of language. At any rate, we know that language did not originate as a means of impersonal and emotionally neutral communication; such a function is a late development, and is a function so far from the roots of language that it can be performed successfully only by means of artificial languages. The language of mathematics and the technical terminologies of the sciences are examples of languages developed expressly to avoid the emotional associations and value meanings of words.

A poet uses the sound properties of words to create a structure which communicates what the conventional meanings of words cannot possibly convey. Consider the following lines from Shakespeare's *Troilus and Cressida*:

> And scants us with a single famisht kiss,
> Distasted with the salt of broken tears.

Here every word in the first line except "and" and "a" and all of the second line except "of broken" has a "t" or "s" sound. Three times in the first line and twice in the first word of the second, the "s" and "t" sounds join. Not only is the theme of tasting made to stand out by means of the metaphor, but the distinctive consonantal sounds of the word "taste" itself bind the words of the lines together in a unity. At the end, a new metaphor is introduced unexpectedly, the metaphor of *broken* tears. The contrast of the phrase, "of broken," with what has come before is heightened by the absence from it of "t" and "s" sounds. Perhaps, however, the stroke of genius here is seen not in the sound structure so much as in the way that Shakespeare brings together the contrasting metaphors and unites them in the double suggestion carried here by the word "broken." In this one word two ideas come together: the idea of tears as the expression of a broken heart, and the idea of tears releasing their salt as they are broken by the kiss.

The effectiveness of poetry as communication becomes evident when we consider the length and awkwardness of the attempt in the above paragraph to describe what is done here by these two short lines and compare that with the impact of the poetry itself. The poetic effect is direct. It needs no explaining. Shakespeare did not write these lines to provide a sample of esthetic analysis. In fact we have to give up the poetic experience in order to construct or even to follow an analysis. The lines achieve a union of patterns of sound and meaning which communicates much more than what is said literally, even more than what could be said literally by any combination of words. When we reflect that "literal meaning" concerns strictly what a word carries our attention to beyond the word itself, we see even more plainly the contrast between the esthetic surface and the literal meaning. Poetry communicates by use of esthetic surface rather than by reliance upon literal meaning. The effectiveness of the communication lies partly in the fact that the meaning is conveyed by means of an expression which enables that meaning to be felt rather than conceptually cognized.

Another example of the use of word sounds will be seen in lines from one of Wordsworth's Lucy poems:

> The stars of midnight shall be dear
> To her; and she shall lean her ear
> In many a secret place
> Where rivulets dance their wayward round
> And beauty born of murmuring sound
> Shall pass into her face.

Here the "ear," "are," "er," "or," and "ur" sounds are prominent. They occur thirteen times in five lines, and contrast is effected by omitting them entirely from the third line. These sounds accord with the emotional content of the verses, and their use evokes the feeling desired by the poet. The metaphor of "rivulets dancing their wayward round" is freshened by the contrast introduced by means of the word "wayward." The alliterations of "beauty born of murmuring sound" are saved from banality by the impact of the metaphor in the last line.

A striking illustration of the importance of the mode of expression in poetry can be found by comparing two translations of the same passage. The following are translations of a passage in Aeschylus' *Agememnon*, where Cassandra tells of the vengeful murder Clytemnestra plans:

> Lord of the ships who laid waste Ilium—
> and yet not know that she-wolf's tongue.
> She licks her lord's hand—fawns with pricking ears,
> and bites at last, like secret death.[5]

Compare:

> Little does he know what that foul bitch,
> with ears laid back and panting tongue,
> will bring to pass with vicious snap
> of treacherous destruction.[6]

[5] Reprinted from *Three Greek Plays,* translated with an Introduction by Edith Hamilton, p. 217, by permission of W. W. Norton and Company, Inc.

[6] Philip Wheelwright, *The Burning Fountain* (Bloomington, Indiana University Press, 1954), p. 239. By permission.

ABSTRACT ART

The problem of the relation of form and content in art is one of the central problems of esthetics. We can see how in poetry, or in the forms of drama and fiction, communication is enhanced and made more effective by the mode of expression. But what about the more abstract arts? How does pure music communicate? Or abstract painting? Their content does not represent anything. An abstract painting is not a picture *of* anything. A string quartet or a piano sonata need not be *about* anything. What, then, is their significance? This question is a center of considerable controversy in esthetics, and it is one of the issues on which different esthetic theories divide.

Susanne K. Langer's definition of art as "the creation of forms symbolic of human feeling" [7] seems especially illuminating with respect to pure music and abstract art. We all recognize different ways of feeling, and we have names we use to refer to them, such as happy, sad, expectant, disappointed, angry, arrogant, etc. Certain sequences and combinations of sounds evoke these various ways of feeling. The importance of music may lie partly in the fact that it has such complex resources of tone and rhythm and pitch, all of which we use to express emotion, that it can bring us into contact with complexities of feeling-structure we could discover in no other way.

The appeal of music, however, does not depend on the arousal of actual feelings in us as we listen. We do not often become sad or tender or loving when we hear one kind of music, and angry or full of hate when we hear another kind. If music does have such effects it is because our attention is distracted from the music itself and we are reminded of past experiences in which such emotions were present. Songs often have intimate associations with certain emotional experiences, and the religious use of music is an example of this. But when we hear music simply as music our pleasure is in the listening itself.

We often obtain a kind of satisfaction in contemplating emotional patterns which we cannot secure by living through those emotional experiences. It can be pleasurable to contemplate a ter-

[7] *Feeling and Form* (New York, Charles Scribner's Sons, 1953), p. 40. By permission.

rifying event, and not in any way be terrifying. Children sometimes are so absorbed in the movement of a story that they actually feel fear. When combined with an awareness that the story is not real, this has its own kind of pleasure in the relief from fright which comes as the situation is recognized as play or fancy. A child enjoys being frightened if the fear is suddenly resolved. "Scare me again, Daddy," he pleads as he recovers from the startle of a playful lunge or a sudden drop in his father's arms. It is true that for many people such unreal emotional experiences are the whole appeal of the fiction they read and the dramatic performances they enjoy, hence our standard television and cinema fare. But this means only that many people are still children in their emotional development. With emotional maturity comes the pleasure of contemplating emotional experiences. This pleasure, while often not as immediately intense, is incomparably more satisfying than actually feeling the emotion itself, and the presence of emotion may in fact interfere with the esthetic experience. Professor Eliseo Vivas points out that esthetic experience actually excludes emotion:

> For rapt attention on an object excludes self-consciousness, and emotion cannot be present without the latter. . . . [He goes on to say, however:] Although sometimes almost totally devoid of emotion, the aesthetic experience need never be a cold experience. For if we distinguish, as we should, between emotion and feeling, it will be readily seen that it is the feeling that gives the glow to the experience and not the emotion.[8]

Put into intimate contact with forms of feeling by art, however, our emotional experience itself is greatly enriched. To know the nature of love opens to us complexities of the experience without which the emotion would be close to an animal level. How can we discover and recognize the dramatic subtleties of all kinds of human relationships if we have never contemplated the forms of human relationships as they are exposed to us in poetry and fiction? Unless we find these patterns of feeling apart from their involvement in our own emotions, we cannot look at them and consider them and discover *what* they are, for in the actuality of emotion our attention is held in the grip of the urgencies of the situation. The more we discover about the forms of feeling the more there is in experience itself that is accessible to our awareness and ap-

[8] Vivas, *op. cit.,* p. 96.

preciation. Only thus does emotional experience have any lasting meaning for us. Without such appreciation, the experience is simply here and gone; once gone, it is gone forever except for vague memories that never reveal its essence.

In pure music we find the elemental forms of feeling untangled from life and exhibited to us as sound in motion. These are basic forms of dynamic change which underly all conscious experience and exhibit the patterns of all human drama. Their expression in music, because of the qualitative richness of the sense of hearing and because music moves in time, makes possible the revelation of complexities and intricacies of patterns of sound we could not possibly recognize or follow in ordinary experience. Music shows us not only the forms of feeling, but it uncovers and exhibits potential complexities of those forms which could be discovered in no other way.

If we consider the nature of these patterns of sound we recognize that they have a dramatic structure. A musical composition exhibits a unity composed of contrasts, tensions and their resolution, the progressive unfolding of thematic material, and innumerable ways of exhibiting differences in unity and unity in difference. Each part is seen in its place in the composition as a whole. As we shall see later in more detail, the question of what a thing means is the question of what place it occupies in some structured unity. Such unities are communicated solely in terms of dramatic relationships. This is the case with all art. The artist, says Professor Vivas, "tells us what is the dramatic pattern of human life and thus defines for us its sense." [9]

Abstract painting and sculpture do in color and space what pure music does in sound. Dramatic structure, of course, is temporal; in painting and in other arts of spatial composition, the temporal factor is in the viewing rather than in the composition itself. Abstract painting and sculpture are the discovery and exhibition of complexities of space and color forms that are potential in the elemental relations. These modes of art likely have severe restrictions, but they accomplish something impossible to representative art: they separate completely the visual forms from other meanings. In representative art the viewer must make that separation in his own imagination if it is to be made at all. Abstract art does this for the viewer. The significance of abstract art is simply the signifi-

[9] *Ibid*, p. 122.

cance of such separation. If we must have the separation done for us in order that we may discover some kinds of formal relationships in space then abstract art is indispensable for that kind of discovery. The weakness of abstract visual art seems to lie in the comparative poverty of its forms when taken by themselves.

ART AND TRUTH

In what sense is a work of art true or false? If it is significant as art not in what it refers to but only in itself, then how can we say it is true or false? What more can we say of it than that it is and that it is interesting or moving? If we define truth narrowly as the correspondence of symbol with what it refers to then it would seem that the very thing we found to be distinctive of art precludes any distinction of true and false. But we do not need to conceive truth in such narrow terms, nor do we understand it in so limited a sense in our ordinary use of the word.

We make such statements as: "He is a true man," or "This is true courage." We mean that this instance is a specimen of the real thing. Some kind of standard is supposed, and to say that something is true in this sense is to assert conformity with the standard. When we say, "He is a true man," we probably mean that this is what a man ought to be, or that this man's actions are what a man's actions ought to be in this situation. But truth in this sense may mean much more than correspondence of the specimen with an ideal. The specimen may in fact be the very thing that reveals the ideal to us. We see man after man in trying situations, and in every instance we feel something is lacking in their handling of the situation. Then we encounter a person whose tact and understanding and moral courage and unselfish devotion lead us to exclaim, "There truly is a man!" *What he is* shows us something of what man ought to be when he realizes his potentialities most fully.

Truth in art may be understood as art's revelation of being, of resources and aspects of being which can be discovered in no other way. A work of art is false when it portrays its object in such a way as to falsify its nature. This does not mean that truth in art is confined to naturalism. Distortion and caricature are important esthetic instruments, and art can be completely abstract so that no question of "true" representation arises. But a novel that presents a man as experiencing genuine satisfaction in a life of superficial gratification might be false in the sense that real man does not have that capacity. Or, we may say, a "true" man cannot thus be satisfied. If, however, the intent is to show us a truly shallow version of human life then the portrayal may have esthetic truth.

Art can show us what it is like to be this or that kind of person not by describing or generalizing or constructing concepts, but by presenting a constructed specimen. The specimen is constructed under the control of the artist, we may say, to express an idea. The truth of the art lies, then, in the success with which the specimen expresses that idea. So far as the art work shows how this or that human character can *be*, it has truth. So far as an abstract painting gives us the "feel" of relationships among lines and colored spaces which can be found only in that specific arrangement of line and color, it has esthetic truth. What the painting shows are relationships which can be made explicit only in *this* unique composition. An abstraction without composition, a novel without plot or theme, a musical composition without unity and development, would lack esthetic truth.

Quite possibly, however, art is not only a source of esthetic truth but is also the instrument by which some of the most profound and significant truth about existence which is accessible to the human mind is discovered and communicated. If so, the significance of art goes far beyond the limits of the esthetic. Our failure to recognize the importance of art as a discovery of existence may well be regarded by later generations as a shameful and scandalous barbarism. In our tendency to interpret knowledge in exclusively conceptual terms, we have forgotten the roots in experience and existence even of that conceptualizing process itself:

> Symmetry, balance, all the laws of geometric composition [Herbert Read reminds us], were first made evident in art; the first science was a notation of the discoveries of the artist; mathematics arose as a meditation on artifacts.[10]

Art, as much as science, exposes what nature hides, and no more than scientific truth can be expressed by art can the truth that art communicates be expressed by science or philosophy. In Charles Morgan's phrase: "Art is news of reality not to be expressed in

[10] *Icon and Idea* (Cambridge, Harvard University Press, 1955), p. 50.

other terms." [11] This "news of reality" cannot be grasped in conceptual terms; it brings us into contact with existence in its individuality, with what cannot be caught and communicated in concepts. Again quoting Herbert Read: "It has always been the function of arts to stretch the mind some distance beyond the limits of the understanding;" [12] and it is the function of the arts, in the words of Jacob Burckhardt, "to body forth a higher life which would not exist without them." [13]

As we shall see in the next chapter art is of special importance as the instrument by which religious insights are communicated. It is necessary, however, at this point to look more carefully at the way in which art provides this most important contact with existence.

THE PARALLEL OF ART AND MATHEMATICS

An instructive parallel may be drawn between the cognitive functions of art and of mathematics. As we saw earlier, in our study of mathematics and science, mathematics is the instrument by means of which the conceptual intelligibility of factual existence is discovered and exhibited in scientific knowledge. In this mathematics is closely related to logic itself, which elucidates the basic rational structures of all conceptual thinking. But concepts are not the only instruments by means of which existence can be shown to make sense. In concepts we abstract common natures of things, and think these common natures apart from the things themselves. Conceptual thinking deals with universals, and in conceptual thinking the individual existent with its own distinctive individual character falls out of view. A laboratory specimen is thrown away once its chemical analysis is complete. It has no significance in itself; its importance lies wholly in its being a representative of a *kind* of material. A work of art, however, is not a specimen for anyone who is interested in it for its own sake. It is treasured and

[11] *Reflections in a Mirror*, Second Series (New York, The Macmillan Company, 1947), p. 91. By permission.

[12] Reprinted by permission of *Dodd, Mead and Company* from *The Anatomy of Art* by Herbert Read (copyright 1932 by Herbert Read), p. 68.

[13] Burckhardt, *op. cit.*, p. 127.

studied not for what it shows concerning other objects of its kind but for what it is itself.

A work of art, moreover, does not exist merely as something in itself. Art is an expression of what some aspect of existence means for an artist. The material which enters into an artist's work is what he has found to be significant. A serious novel or play expresses something of the meaning of life as the artist sees it. Here are familiar human situations presented in such a structure of idea and action in human conflict and emotion that hitherto unrecognized meanings of those situations are disclosed. There are different ways, for example, of coming to understand human jealousy. We can study its general characteristics, as a psychologist might, trying to discover the universal or typical causes and the common characteristics it manifests in different instances. Or we may engage in a clinical study, examining a number of cases and drawing conclusions from what we find. A third way of coming to understand jealousy seeks not so much to discover its causes and characteristics or to become acquainted with a large number of actual instances, but to grasp its meaning for human life. For this we would have to turn to literature and drama, and the instrument of disclosure and appreciation would be imagination rather than reason.

Knowledge about meaning is conceptual; *encounter with* meaning is by perception and imagination. Just as scientific inquiry can reach beyond the range of direct perception only by means of the conceptual constructs of mathematics, so the search for meaning and value can reach beyond the range of direct experience only by means of the imaginative constructs of art. Mathematics by itself is not concerned with the nature of actual existence but with such aspects of existence as quantity and order considered only in and for themselves. In like manner, art by itself is not concerned with the nature of actual existence as such but with certain aspects of existence which are taken apart by imagination and treated in and for themselves. As mathematics is used to disclose the intelligible structure of factual existence, so art is used to disclose the intelligible structure of value. When we use art in this way we go beyond the strictly esthetic level to what may be called the "revelatory level."

Universal essences and rational structures are grasped in concept; dramatic structures are grasped in feeling. In feeling we have our direct encounter with value. As a concept holds in a single act of thought some general character of things, a character encountered in many different instances; so in feeling we discover the unity of a process which extends through a period of time and contains different and contrasting phases. We *feel* dramatic tension, for example; we do not see it or hear it or touch it. We may think *about* it but tension is never presented to our awareness as the content of a concept. Conflicts and contrasts are felt before they are thought; and the unity within which differences stand over against each other and within which they are resolved, is a felt unity. Even the discovery of conflicts among concepts themselves is often by feeling, not by thinking.

The unities we feel in our response to value are either unities of temporal change or unities of spatial differences experienced in a temporal sequence. Since such unities are either themselves temporal or else apprehended in a temporal experience in which differences emerge as contrasts and are reconciled in some kind of harmony, it is appropriate to call them "dramatic unities." As we found in our earlier discussion of the nature of value and its relation to actual existence, value involves completion or closure; it is the realization of potentialities and as such is the completion of what before was incomplete. This is precisely what a dramatic unity shows. Tension and conflict are resolved, and that resolution is a completion of what before was incomplete. We cannot rest with conflict and have any feeling of satisfaction; imagination provides its own closure if existence fails. But the meaning of the closure cannot be grasped in awareness unless we encounter it *as* the resolution of a conflict. We have to go through the dramatic process either in actual experience or in imagination.

In this broad sense value pertains to conceptual systems as well as to existential ones, and we quite properly speak of logical values. But the experience of even a logical value involves feeling. Such experience is quite different from merely noting a logical function. It is one thing to note that a logical conflict has been resolved; it is quite another thing to be, as we say, struck by the resolution of a logical contradiction. Only in the latter do we *experience* value even in a conceptual system.

In so far as we experience a plurality of events as nothing more than a sequence we are unable to think of some of those events as more important than others. Facts by themselves, considered apart from their place in a structured unity, are all on the same level.

Value is discovered and experienced, in distinction from being merely thought about, in direct encounter with a dramatic pattern. Either the events experienced have a dramatic structure which is felt in the experience, or else there is a progressive unfolding in experience of interrelations among the components of a non-temporal pattern. Where direct encounter is lacking, communication of value can be by means only of something else which can be directly encountered. Art and art alone is the means by which value is communicated.

In philosophy and science the instruments of knowledge are logical forms, concepts and mathematical entities and relationships; and these are obtained by reflective abstraction and conceptual construction. The instruments of value experience and communication are esthetic forms, and these are obtained by imaginative abstraction. Philosophy and science, so far as they are true, show us the logical structure of existence; art, as far as it is true, shows us the dramatic structure of existence. Conceptual knowledge shows us the meaning of existence for thought; art shows us the meaning of existence for feeling.

ABSTRACTION IN SCIENCE AND ART

Although we detect dramatic form by means of feeling, we cannot depend on feeling alone to bring us into full awareness of the dynamic patterns of existence. Feeling, by itself, is inarticulate. Otto Baensch points out that since feelings

> are non-sensory qualities, our apperception of them is also of a non-sensuous sort. . . . There is no apperception so blind as the nonsensuous apperception of feelings.
>
> . . . How can we capture, hold and handle feelings so that their content may be made conceivable and presented to consciousness in universal form, without being understood in the strict sense, i.e. by means of concepts? The answer is: We can do it by creating objects wherein the feelings we seek to hold are so definitely embodied that any subject confronted with these objects and empathetically disposed toward them, cannot but experience a non-sensuous apperception of the feelings in question. Such objects are called "words of art," and by "art" we designate the activity that produces them.[14]

[14] "Kunst und Gefühl," *Logos*, II, p. 14 (1923), quoted by Susanne K. Langer, *op. cit.*, pp. 21-22.

As thought must isolate rational structure for theoretical knowledge, so imagination must lift out of our experience of actual existence the dramatic structures found therein if we are to give them our full attention. First, in the recounting of experience, dramatic relations are exposed by selection, emphasis, conflict, climax, and resolution. Then the mind deliberately looks to experience for material to work over and fashion into dramatic form independently of the circumstances of the original experiences themselves. By this means, and by this means alone, can the rich and varied relationships of dramatic forms be discovered. In the discovery of these forms, in religion and literature and art, the dramatic intelligibility of existence is found.

There are parallel processes of abstraction in science and in art. Although scientific inquiry takes its departure from our experience of objects and events in nature, yet, as we have already seen, scientific explanation makes those objects and events intelligible to us by the use of conceptual constructs which are never found in direct observation. What holds true here of conceptual abstraction also holds true of imaginative abstraction. Suppose I wish to know not something universal but something individual. Let us say that my attention is absorbed in this individual tree, and I am trying to see the precise outline of the edge of the tree against the sky. Here too, abstraction is necessary, but it is not conceptual abstraction; I am trying to grasp this object itself as an individual and to discover how the details I observe enter into that individual unity of form which has caught and held my attention. So I make a pencil mark which reproduces on paper the specific shape of the "edge" of the tree as I see it against the sky.

I may now carry this process of abstraction a step further. I note a contrast between the soft curves of the outline of the tree and the straight lines and angular shapes of other objects in the scene. Instead of drawing only the shapes I see, I may bring out this contrast in a composition deliberately designed to express the feeling aroused by the softness of the outline against the rigidity of the other shapes. So, too, we may set in relief by imaginative abstraction and construction some phase of the complex drama of human relationship, as shown in a play or a novel.

The tonal structures we call "music" [Susanne K. Langer points out] bear a close logical similarity to the forms of human feeling—forms of growth and attenuation, flowing and slowing, conflict and resolution, speed, arrest, terrific excitement, calm, or subtle activation and dreamy lapses—not joy and sorrow perhaps, but the poignancy of either and both—the greatness and brevity and eternal passing of everything vitally felt. Such is the pattern, or logical form, of sentience; and the pattern of music is that same form worked out in pure, measured sound and silence. Music is a tonal analogue of emotive life.[15]

As conceptual abstraction is the foundation of philosophy, science, and mathematics; so perceptual and imaginative abstraction is the foundation of art and religion. In both cases creation is the means of discovery.

> What the artist does [says Professor Vivas] . . . is to wrench from his subject matter something that is not fully realized in it. . . . The artist *creates* then, in the sense that he makes a dramatic structure out of subject matter in which the ordinary ungifted mind would not think of looking for it. But the structure is no more invented by him than it is by the physicist when the latter discovers the laws of the physical world and expresses them in the tools he has at hand. The writer *discovers* this structure, in the sense that the forms and the substance of his work are found by him in the data of experience which is the subject matter of his art.[16]

By creating a dramatic structure in which these forms may be exhibited the artist makes them accessible to the rest of us who would never discover them without his aid.

THREE LEVELS OF ART

Logical intelligibility is revealed with the resolution of logical conflicts; dramatic intelligibility appears with the resolution of dramatic conflicts and the discovery of the unity they express. As logical intelligibility can operate on a purely abstract or hypothetical level without committing us to any judgments concerning real existence, so we find dramatic intelligibility on the purely esthetic level. In so far as a work of art has an exclusively esthetic significance the artist is concerned with his forms and subject matter only as they enter into the composition of the work itself. In experience at the esthetic level as well, the esthetic object completely

[15] Langer, *op. cit.*, p. 27.
[16] Vivas, *op. cit.*, pp. 123-24.

absorbs attention just as the mathematical object absorbs the attention of a mathematician. The esthetic level of art, however, is not the only one, and if we are to have some understanding of the broader significance of art we need to consider other contexts of experience in which art has an important function.

We can see the development of art as involving three stages or levels which are not necessarily separate but are distinguishable. Art has its roots in the need to express or communicate a felt meaning found in some object or event. The artist creates his own pattern by such devices as selection, emphasis, contrast, distortion, and suggestion. His composition, with its own distinctive unity and thematic developments, shows something of the nature of the object it represents. At the most elementary level, pictorial art calls attention to some feature of an object by isolating its outline on a separate surface. Significance is shown at this level merely by calling attention to the existence of the feature itself. As in drawing and painting, so also in narration some aspect of an event is separated out from the welter of detail in which it was embedded in reality, and attention is called to its existence by putting it off by itself.

At the first level art is representational. The object or event portrayed is presented in accordance with what that object or event is already recognized to be. The work may be an idealization, as in some of the greatest of Greek sculpture, but if so it is the idealization of something actual. Portrait painting does not cease to be representational even when its flattery is so extreme as to be artificial, any more than the Hollywood version of feminine beauty becomes the less representational as it becomes the more stereotyped in its vulgarity. That a representation is poor does not make it any the less representational.

The distinctive character of representative art is found in the fact that the art work is intended to show something of what the artist sees or imagines the object to be. The art work is done in submission to what the work represents. The work does not have to copy its object literally, for distortion may be an effective way of exposing to attention something that is significant in the object. In such a sense even Duchamps's "Nude Descending a Staircase" and a Picasso profile with displaced facial planes are representational in so far as they are intended to reveal something in the nature of the object portrayed.

At the representational stage composition is instrumental. It is the means by which the artist shows the significance of something beyond the work of art itself. As the artist becomes absorbed in his composition, however, the role of the object portrayed may change so that the portrayal of the object turns out to be only a starting point for a work that is composed solely for itself. Here the representational function gives way to a strictly esthetic function, and the painting or poem no longer has its significance in what it reveals of the object. The work is important not for what it represents or for its effectiveness as a representation but for what it is. Both the representative and the esthetic levels may be present together, and certainly representation with no inherent esthetic values would deserve little attention as a work of art. But where both are present, one or the other is usually dominant. We are not particularly interested in the people who were the subjects of Rembrandt's portraits; our interest is in the works themselves, in what is *presented* and not in what is *represented*. Without the interest we have in the subjects of Gilbert Stuart's portraits, however, we should likely pay little attention to his paintings. The intrinsic musical values of Beethoven's Pastoral Symphony far overshadow its program content, while much religious music is seldom listened to for its esthetic values alone.

At the esthetic level, where forms found by the artist in actually existing things are varied and developed for their own sake, the artist no longer controls his composition in terms of the relations of his forms to the objects represented. *The control he exerts over his composition at the esthetic level is in terms of the relations of forms to each other.* The landscape painter who changes the position of a tree in his painting in order to meet the requirements of his composition has taken a step away from representation. To change the arrangement of what is found in order to satisfy the requirements of the composition is quite different from a rearrangement intended to focus attention upon some feature of the object or to express thereby its special significance. Art becomes exclusively esthetic, as in abstract art, when the forms used in a composition are so handled that they have no reference to anything beyond the composition itself. Art becomes completely esthetic also when the significance of the object portrayed consists entirely of its contribution to the composition.

At this level the self-contained character of the esthetic object is reflected in the esthetic experience, where attention is completely absorbed in the object. The feeling quality of the experience has no relation to any actual or supposed representational meanings of the work of art. According to Clive Bell, the one word which best expresses the distinctive quality of an esthetic experience in its more intense moments is "ecstasy." [17] This word is especially apt in the suggestion of its literal sense that we somehow "stand outside" ourselves in such an experience. Time and place and all personal concerns are gone. We are not so much moved as entranced. It is not an emotion we have but pure, intense, all-absorbing feeling.

In so far as it remains on the esthetic level pure art tends to develop in the direction of a preoccupation with form itself. Thus we have abstract painting as the result of experimentation with relationships of line, shape, and color—relationships first discovered in attempts to convey an impression of something objective. Similarly, as sound patterns overshadow the sense of the words in song the development is in the direction of pure music.

Art which has reached the esthetic level, however, does not always remain pure. In its preoccupation with forms of feeling, to use Susanne Langer's phrase, artistic genius probes deep into the esthetic possibilities of these forms and sometimes finds itself carried into the depths of the dramatic pulse of existence itself.

> Beauty has never been deposed as the mode in which man expresses those intuitions of form that lift his being out of our environing chaos and casualness [says Herbert Read]. But the serenity thus achieved was not enough—there always remained a nagging sense of the numinous, of a world beyond the world of immediate sensation, some transcendental realm.[18]

This is no mere return to representation. On the contrary, it may be the disclosure of levels of existence to which we have no other way of access. These may be modes of existence incapable of being revealed by anything imitative. It is as if the artist's preoccupation with art forms themselves, apart from any representative function they may have had originally, perfects those forms as instruments to catch and reveal deeper levels of existence. Of course the forms themselves often undergo modification in this develop-

[17] See *Art*, Fifth Edition (New York, Frederick A. Stokes Company, n. d.), Chapter I, especially pp. 29-30.
[18] *Icon and Idea*, pp. 51-52.

ment; art breaks through earlier limitations. Such art does not mimic or copy reality, and thus reveal the real by means of the unreal. Rather it conducts us into dramatic structures which are basic to existence itself. *What* we feel is *how* existence is. In feeling we enter the basic pulse of existence itself at levels deeper than we can reach in any other way. Instead of a return to representation this is an advance from the esthetic level to the revelatory. Poetry, painting, drama sometimes reveal, for example, the intimate dramatic structure of a human relationship in a way to show us something fundamental to the drama of the human situation itself, something not to be described in any literal way but to be grasped only as we are led by the artist to feel it.

The significance of pure music is almost exclusively esthetic, and yet the possibility of reaching a revelatory level must not be ruled out. J. W. N. Sullivan saw in Beethoven's late quartets a unique and incomparable revelation:

> In these five quartets we have the greatest of Beethoven's music, and much of it is different in kind from any other music he or anybody else ever wrote. In the last quartets, and particularly in the great three, those in A minor, B flat major, and C sharp minor, Beethoven is exploring new regions of consciousness. . . . But this inner world to which Beethoven had now retreated, although it no longer owed anything to fresh contacts with the outer world, was nevertheless a living and developing world. It not only contained elements which he had never before explored, but also elements that had never before existed. The last quartets testify to a veritable growth of consciousness, to a higher degree of consciousness, probably, than is manifested anywhere else in art.[19]

Art reaches the esthetic level by withdrawing from its object; at the level of revelation art returns to reality but no longer as representational. As revelatory, art *reconstitutes existence* in such a way as to bring out values otherwise undiscoverable. When art is revelatory of ultimate meanings it becomes an instrument of the religious consciousness. In its religious function, mainly in the forms of poetry and narrative, art seems to disclose ultimate meanings we can reach in no other way. It does this not by describing something we could know better by viewing the original, but by

[19] *Beethoven: His Spiritual Development* (Mentor Edition), pp. 123-124. Published by Alfred A. Knopf, Inc., and by Vintage Books, Inc. under license from Alfred A. Knopf, Inc. Reprinted by permission.

working such a transformation in our awareness that we are attuned to reality in its numinous dimension. By means of his religion man *feels* his place in the scheme of existence. Instead of the self-contained ecstasy of esthetic experience, he has in religious experience the feeling of participation in the cosmic drama.

SUMMARY

In esthetic experience attention is absorbed by the object perceived, its intrinsic qualities and forms, without reference to its use or function or anything extraneous to what the object is directly perceived to be. Qualitative richness and discernible arrangements of qualitative differences are what hold attention in esthetic experience. Esthetic form gives to art an independence of the factual, and it is by means of esthetic form that the artist makes available to others the intrinsic meanings he finds in his subject matter. Esthetic form provides a means of communicating meanings which can be disclosed in no other way. What is communicated in art is apprehended not conceptually but in feeling, and art has been defined as "the creation of forms symbolic of human feeling." Abstract art separates the basic visual and auditory forms from content which has extraneous significance and exhibits the complex relationships of these basic forms.

Art may be said to have truth in so far as it does present patterns and relationships inherent in its subject matter. Esthetic truth may be understood as integrity of composition and intrinsic significance of content. Works of art, however, may be true or false in a more important sense, as the discovery and communication of basic patterns of existence itself.

When we consider the cognitive function of art we find an important parallel between art and mathematics. As mathematics is the instrument by which the conceptual intelligibility of factual existence is discovered and disclosed in scientific knowledge, so art is the instrument by which the dramatic intelligibility of existence is shown. The one makes existence intelligible in terms of general or universal forms, the other in terms of individual forms. Just as universal essences and rational structures are grasped in concept, so dramatic structures are grasped in feeling. We apprehend essences in concept; we encounter values in feeling, and values encountered in our experience of objects can be communicated only by means of art.

Parallel with conceptual abstraction and construction in mathematics are the processes of imaginative abstraction and construction in art. The artist exhibits in his medium, such as line and color or moving sound or word arrangements, the perceptual forms he has found amid the sensory complexities of real existence. By creating a dramatic structure in which these abstracted forms may be exhibited the artist enables others to experience them in meaningful interrelationships.

In considering the relation of the art work to real existence we can distinguish three levels of art. The first level is that of representation in which some significant aspect of real existence is made accessible to awareness by presenting it apart from the object itself in a composition which is intended to show something of the intrinsic pattern of the object.

The second level is the esthetic level, in which the composition is significant solely for what it is in itself rather than as an instrument for revealing some feature of a really existing object. At this level artistic composition is governed entirely by the relation of forms to each other rather than by the relation of forms to the objects represented.

The third level is one at which the work of art not only reconstitutes existence in such a way as to bring out values otherwise undiscoverable but so transforms our awareness that we reach levels of experience which are otherwise unattainable. When art reveals ultimate meanings for human life and existence it becomes the instrument of the religious consciousness.

QUESTIONS FOR STUDY AND DISCUSSION

1. *Terms:* abstract art, esthetic experience, esthetic form, esthetic surface, dramatic pattern, immanent meanings and values, intransitive apprehension, naturalism (in art), presentational immediacy, representational art.

2. Can you think of any achievement of civilized society which does not rest finally on art?

3. Art is the root both of science and religion. How do you explain such different growths from the same root?

4. Do you see any connection between a child's propensity to handle and taste things and his delight in verse and rhyme? Does poetry always have a sensuous appeal?

5. Is the esthetic experience we have in fine art predominantly a passive experience, or does it involve an active participation by the viewer or listener?

6. (a) Compare overhearing music, hearing music, and listening to music.
   (b) Formulate a parallel set of distinctions to apply to painting.

7. Why are the fine arts exclusively visual and auditory but not olfactory, gustatory, or tactual?

8. Compare the following with respect to the experience of esthetic surface. To what extent is it a factor in each?
   (a) You look at the sky and notice that the clouds threaten rain.
   (b) You notice a cloud so shaped that its outline reminds you of a human face.
   (c) You note a contrast of color and shape as faster moving clouds cross in front of larger masses.

9. Give examples from reading, conversation, or watching an athletic event or writing a paper, of situations in which attention is seized and held momentarily by the esthetic surface.

10. (a) How does a landscape painting differ from the original landscape in esthetic form?
    (b) Can photography be a fine art?

11. Does it make any sense to ask what a poem means?

12. How do you account for the quite common emotional antagonism to abstract art?

13. Explain, illustrate, and examine the statement that the pleasure of contemplating emotional experience is incomparably more satisfying than actually feeling the emotion itself.

14. Compare: (a) This story is not true to the facts. (b) This painting is not true impressionism. (c) This story does not ring true. (d) This portrait does not show the face in its true proportions.

15. Is censorship of art or literature ever justified? (In discussing this question it will be necessary to consider carefully just what *art* and *literature* are.)

16. Describe a football game or some exciting event in two different ways: (1) to show its dramatic structure, and (2) to show its conceptual structure.

17. If art sometimes has a revelatory function, do you think it would be possible to confirm the truth of a claim of revelation? For example, how might Sullivan's statement about Beethoven's late quartets be subjected to examination?

CHAPTER 15

Religion

THE NATURE OF RELIGION

Religion is a basic human activity in which almost all other important human activities have their origins. Morality, art, science and mathematics, the various technologies by which man controls nature for his own purposes, originated in activities which were religious in nature. Only in the past few hundred years have these other interests been pursued independently of religion, for in earlier times every aspect of a human society reflected its religion. Irreligion not only did not exist, it could not exist; the very idea of irreligion was unthinkable. Impiety, yes; but impiety itself is a religious category.

There is a sense, however, in which we can say that where everything is religion nothing is. This is true in the sense that in such a society nothing is religious in distinction from the nonreligious. As the late Professor Archibald Allan Bowman has shown, the concept of the secular is itself a religious concept, for only in contrast with the religious do we have any notion of anything secular.[1] So the men of primitive societies probably did not think of themselves as religious; it is we who, looking back upon them from our own point of reference in a secular society, see their lives as suffused with religion. So, too, only from such a point of view as

[1] *Studies in the Philosophy of Religion* (London, Macmillan and Company, Ltd., 1938). See especially Volume II.

our own can any attempt be made to form a concept of religion and to try to delineate its distinctive character.

There have been many definitions of religion, and not all are in agreement, but the disagreements are mostly in matters of emphasis. Religion is belief and practice. In its broadest sense a religion is the set of beliefs and practices in which and by which a group expresses its idea of what is of final significance in life and existence and by which that group maintains itself in effective relationship with those ultimates. To be religious in this broad sense is to be concerned with ultimates in belief and practice. To be irreligious in this same broad sense is to be unconcerned with ultimates; it is to be absorbed entirely in the immediate.

Religions differ from each other primarily in what they recognize to be ultimate. Different ultimates require different practices. A god which is a projection of impulses of aggression and violence may require human sacrifice for its appeasement, while the conception of the ultimate as a rational unity may be expressed in disciplines of inquiry and meditation. In the simpler cultures at least, idea and practice are usually in close agreement, whether the idea of what is ultimate prescribes the practice or whether the persistence of traditional ritual induces the formation of religious ideas to explain the practice.

RELIGIOUS AND SECULAR PERSPECTIVES

The concept of religion as concern for ultimates in belief and practice may help us to understand why earlier societies were throughout religious while modern Western society has so marked a secular aspect. The possibility of a secular society seems to depend on the development of rational knowledge in philosophy and the sciences. Without philosophy and science we have no concept of immediate causes or explanations of events in distinction from ultimate causes and explanations. For the religious mind of earlier times everything that happened was, directly or indirectly, the action of the gods. Only for one who thinks of realities that exist and act in their own nature can any event be explained or understood apart from a reference to ultimates.

When men believe that things have their own nature and act in accordance with the nature they have, then men try to understand the events which occur by seeking to know the character of those things involved in the events. The growth of vegetation, storms and seasonal changes, the movements of the planets, birth and death, illness and recovery, are no longer explained as the actions of humanlike supernatural agencies who merely use these things in nature to carry out their own designs. We today understand the germination and growth of a plant in terms of the nature of the seed, of the chemicals in the soil, and of the light from the sun. The germination and growth of the plant is a joint action of these and other natural existences, each acting in accordance with its own constitution. Instead of using prayers and incantations and fertility rites, we prepare the soil with physical tools, keep it clear of unwanted plants, and enrich it with fertilizers. A storm is not for us an expression of the anger of the gods who are to be placated with offerings; a storm is a confluence of moving bodies of air with certain ranges of temperature differences.

The scientific understanding of nature came only gradually to be accepted even by the educated classes of our culture. In the early stages its application was pretty much restricted to astronomy and physics. Life and human existence, history and society, were still understood as direct expressions of divine activity. The tendency thus was to divide the world into two parts, the part to be understood scientifically and the part to be understood religiously. It was not long, however, before imaginative men, echoing a similar development in early Greek thought, suggested that all of nature is to be understood in terms of physical science. The principles of physical science needed only to be extended in order to explain life and mind and society in all their aspects. Either God was to have no place at all in this or, as with the deists, God was used only to explain the origin of nature. It is in this spirit that the development of science during the past few centuries has appeared to many as a persistent widening of scientific understanding at the expense of a corresponding narrowing of the area of existence to which religious ideas are relevant. Religion resisted the Copernican theory and was defeated. Religion then retreated, but made a stand against the theory of evolution. Again religion met defeat. If no other major battles have been fought there have been many skirmishes, but these seem to be on the decrease and the way seems open for the scientific exploration of all areas of existence.

In recent years, however, a new development has appeared.

The idea of the religious and the secular as conflicting and competing ways of interpreting existence has been challenged. Much religious thought today considers these approaches to be complementary instead of opposed. The religious and the scientific are different perspectives, and the understanding obtained in one is an understanding in different terms from that of the other. Since religious and scientific questions are different kinds of questions nothing but confusion comes from the attempt to answer one kind of question in terms of the methods and concepts of the other. On this view, the question is not how to divide the territory between religion and science; the problem is rather to bring each party to a better understanding of itself so that each will recognize its own limitations and will refrain from using its own distinctive methods in the attempt to deal with problems to which those methods are not applicable.

This double-aspect conception of the relation of the religious and the secular has its dangers. Something like it was tried in early modern times, when the scientific view was beginning to be seen as a serious threat to the religious interpretation of existence. At that time the doctrine of the twofold truth was proposed. Christian theology of the time asserted, for example, that the world had a beginning in time while Aristotelian science held that the existence of the world is eternal. In the face of such conflicts, and in order to retain both theology and science, some thinkers, such as Pompanazzi, proposed that there are two kinds of truth, theological and scientific or philosophical. The proposition that the world had a beginning in time is true theologically, but false philosophically. This, of course, is self-defeating, for it raises immediately the question of whether the doctrine of the two-fold truth is itself true theologically or philosophically. A double-aspect conception of the relation of the religious and the secular can succeed only if it is impossible for kinds of truth accessible in one order of knowledge to be in conflict with the truth accessible in a different order.

The distinction of perspectives makes it possible to view nature as a vast impersonal order without committing ourselves to the view that this is all that nature is or that this is the one true way to think of nature. Thus where it is convenient and useful to do, we can think of nature as a mechanical system without feeling compelled to deny to nature any non-mechanistic features it may have. In so far as we are applying mechanistic concepts to nature its nonmechanical features fall outside the scope of our thought. They are either irrelevant to our limited subject matter or, if they are relevant, then our mechanistic concepts are inadequate and should be modified. We need no longer be bound by the restrictions of an older view of the relation of thought to its objects, a view which assumed that if a scheme of explanation is true of anything it is true of everything. We recognize now a degree of freedom in choosing between different schemes of conceptual interpretation on the basis of relevance; and we recognize that to reject one mode of interpretation as irrelevant to our purpose in one inquiry is not to deny its relevance to other problems. Thus there is no conflict between the conception of nature as an impersonal order in connection with one kind of inquiry and a conception of nature as pregnant with purpose and value in connection with a different problem, provided neither of these is taken to be all-inclusive or as excluding all other ways of thinking.

From such an approach as this the traditional distinction between the natural and the supernatural may be seen in a different light. Instead of considering the natural and the supernatural as different realms of existence we might try the experiment of distinguishing them as expressing different perspectives of existence. Our concept of nature then would be our understanding of things in their own existence and in terms of their relationships with each other. The idea of a supernatural order might be understood as the dramatic expression of the scheme of interpretation in terms of which we get some glimpse of the ultimate meaning of existence. As such it would provide guidance toward the basic policies and attitudes which are appropriate for us to take toward ourselves, toward other persons, and toward the whole scheme of existence.

With such an approach in mind our first question will be: What kind of truth might we recognize as available in religion at its best without compromising the truth claims of philosophy, science, history and other human disciplines? Certainly we cannot here pretend to exhibit or communicate religious truth, for if there is such truth it can be discovered and communicated only in religion. Our concern is rather with the question of whether or not it is reasonable to suppose that there is any significant truth accessible to us in religion and, if so, what *kind* of truth it is and how it is communicated. These are not religious or theological problems; they are problems of the philosophy of religion. The aim of such inquiry is not edification but understanding, and we shall approach the problem of religious truth by considering the basis upon which religions can be compared and some problems involved in communication between those who have a religious commitment and those who reject all such commitments.

THE COMPARISON OF RELIGIONS

We speak of the higher religions, and this must mean that there are lower religions. The adherents of one religion consider their own to be true, and so they must look upon those in conflict with their own as false. Thus the comparison of religions usually involves two factors, and the range would be from the higher and truer to the lower and more false.

Reflection suggests that the difference between higher and lower religions is a difference between the values they embody and express. A high value is one the possession or realization of which properly inspires our esteem. It is a value toward which we do not have strong and immediate urges, but one which brings a satisfaction greater and more complete than the satisfaction obtained in lower values. Lower values press themselves upon us, as does the value of food when we are hungry or of rest when we are tired. The value of feeling ourselves to be more important than others, of vengeance, of mere physical sexual relief, and of gain at the expense of another's interest are all examples of low values. These are the goals we aim at so long as we follow impulse and are guided by immediate feeling. But the satisfaction we have in their attainment is thin and disappointing. Higher values do not have this immediate attraction for us. We have to learn to appreciate them. A sensitive and cultivated imagination is required in order to be aware of their attraction. Their attainment represents genuine achievement, and the satisfactions they bring are deep and lasting.

Benevolence or brotherly love and wisdom are examples of high values. They can be realized only in discipline of the emotions and of the intellect. Their cultivation requires the rejection of many ends which are inherently desirable and which have strong immediate appeal. The joys of bitter rivalries, the passions of possession and jealousy, and the stuporous veil of sensual indulgence which dulls the edge of perception and judgment have to be given up. A religion of love is a higher religion than a religion of conquest. A religion of wisdom is a higher religion than a religion of physical gratification. A religion of righteousness and justice is a higher religion than a religion of escape.

A religion may be considered true to the extent that its values are genuine values and not disvalues. A false religion is one which requires devotion to disvalues. That there are disvalues does not mean that there are evils in human life which are nothing but evils. No actual thing can be merely evil if evil is the absence and negation of good, and if everything that is, is good; but some things are better than others, and some things good in themselves are evil in relation to other things. A positive good becomes a relative evil at the point where it destroys or interferes with other and more important goods. The pleasures of the table are certainly positive goods, but when their indulgence endangers health they become harmful—provided the maintenance of health is more important than the immediate pleasures of the palate.

In two respects our discussion of the bases for the comparison of religions may be misleading. We have spoken as if one religion as such is higher or truer than another. In a sense this may be the case, if we refer to the insights and value interpretations which a religion can make available in its traditions and rituals. But it is plain that individuals who are adherents of the same religious doctrines, in name at least, and engage in the same outward ceremonies may have very different ways of understanding these things and find quite different meanings in them. Within the same religious community there may be those whose religion is low and false and others who have made that religion's highest and truest insights their own. There are differences between different subgroups such as the various Christian communions or Muslim sects or between the Sephardic Jews and those of eastern Europe. But within any one of these groups there are perhaps even greater differences. Although the resources of his religious community usually set the limits of religious attainment for the individual adherent, yet within these limits the level of religious development he attains depends on the use he makes of those resources.

In another and more basic respect the analysis presented above raises a serious problem. We have suggested a comparison of religions in terms of the values they embody and express, but such a comparison assumes that we ourselves have a valid scale against which we can compare the values of various religions. If our standard of value is itself based on religious commitment then we seem to be begging the question. If our standard is not itself an expression of religious commitment, then we are assuming that standard to be an ultimate against which religious commitments are to be judged. In the latter case, then, we are either criticizing religions because they are not something other than religion or else we are holding covertly to a religion we do not recognize to be a religion, and so are the victims of self-deception.

Much criticism of religion and advocacy of "humanistic" or "scientific" attitudes toward the problems of basic loyalties and commitments are actually arguments against religion in the traditional sense of the word. Such doctrines as those of "Humanism" or "Ethical Culture" may first be advocated by those within a religious community who disagree with the traditional beliefs of that community. Occasionally such dissenting groups retain sufficient agreement and identity to survive a complete break with the parent community, and even refuse any longer to consider themselves to constitute a religious community at all. Whether or not these groups are religious may be a merely verbal issue, or it may be a more substantial one. To the extent that absolute values are denied, it may seem that no commitment to ultimates can be admitted unless it be to the principle of relativity itself. In the latter case, whatever such commitment may involve we should likely find difficulty in recognizing it as a religious commitment. It would be only an intellectual stance, or a working assumption.

We appear thus to be left with two alternatives: Either we compare religions from within a religious framework, and consequently beg the question; or else we reject all religion as such (and thus reject all ultimate commitments) in favor of postulates or working assumptions. If we follow the latter course, can we consistently profess commitment to the sovereignty of truth itself? Moreover, can the sovereignty of truth be anything more than a working hypothesis, the hypothesis that the attainment of truth is desirable? Any conversation between adherents of this point of view and those holding a view that involves a religious commitment would be extremely difficult to sustain. Intelligent and informed people whose religious convictions have survived critical examination are inclined to doubt the seriousness of their opponents' arguments, for they cannot see how the search for truth itself can be much more than a game for those who have no ultimate commitments. On the other hand, those who reject religion on principle are on their guard lest their opponents, having deceived themselves, should now deceive them also.

Difficult as it may be, however, such conversation is not impossible. It is taking place constantly, whenever those of the different basic persuasions are willing to listen to and try to understand the view of the other side. This has been one of the great dialogues of Western civilization. The great religions have benefited from the criticisms of their enemies, and their doctrines are constantly undergoing re-interpretation. It is also the case that many who place themselves outside all religious commitments frequently discover that they do have commitments deeper than they had realized. It would be presumptuous to suggest any easy solution to this basic problem, but if more light is to be found the way to find it is for those of each side to attempt to appreciate the insights and persuasions of the other, and to do this so far as possible from the inside. One does not need to change sides to reach a significant appreciation of the other side; he needs only a willingness to open his sympathies and to dedicate his imaginative awareness to an appreciation of attitudes he rejects for himself.

Many of those whose own positive religious commitments have survived critical examination, and who have read widely among the more articulate and thoughtful critics of religion in a sincere search for greater enlightenment, have been disappointed repeatedly in what they have found. Just as many of those who dismiss art as unimportant make it very plain in what they say about art that they have never really listened to music or looked at a painting or attended to the language of a poem, so also many of those who dismiss religion as trivial or as simply false show very plainly in what they say that they have no awareness of what the religious person is talking about. If art is the instrument of communication in religion then those who cannot use the language can hardly be expected to discover the meanings conveyed by that language. C. S. Lewis comments:

> One who contended that a poem was nothing but black marks on white paper would be unanswerable if he addressed an audience who couldn't read. Look at it through microscopes, analyse the printer's ink and the paper, study it (in that way) as long as you like; you will never find something over and above all the products of

analysis whereof you can say "This is the poem." Those who can read, however, will continue to say the poem exists.[2]

Of course those who reject religion as meaningless may reply that the meaning which religion purports to find in existence is not found there but actually read into existence. The problem here is that of the nature of religious truth and its communication. The following two sections are a presentation of one way in which religion may be understood as a means by which truth can be discovered.

RELIGIOUS TRUTH

When we say it is true that Caesar crossed the Rubicon and that Charles I of England was beheaded we mean that the events referred to by these statements actually happened in the past. When we say that water is H_2O we mean that water is composed of the two elements, hydrogen and oxygen, in the proportion of two hydrogen atoms to one of oxygen. We are stating what the chemical structure of water actually is, what we should find if we separated the components of water and isolated them from each other. In all three cases our statements are descriptions of fact. Their truth lies in their conformity to the facts to which they refer. To understand the statements is to grasp in our minds something in the nature of the facts themselves. If we had been present we should have seen Caesar cross the river, or seen the axe fall on Charles' neck. If we properly perform the laboratory analysis of water then our tests will show that the gases into which the water is analyzed are hydrogen and oxygen.

But descriptive truth is not the only kind of truth we find in statements. Descriptive truth enables us to grasp in our minds something of the nature of the thing or situation to which the statement refers. Other statements have the kind of truth which, instead of giving us an awareness of the nature of something, put us in touch some way with its existence. For example, if someone says truly of a person that he is angry, the statement has descriptive truth. Anger is a kind of emotion, and we know what it means. The statement enables us to recognize that such an emotion is present in the person

[2] *Reflections on the Psalms* (New York, Harcourt, Brace and Company, 1958), pp. 116-17. By permission.

to whom the statement refers. But let us suppose that instead of simply being informed that so and so is angry we are told something like this: "Do you want to know how John feels this morning? Then let me tell you a story." The speaker then tells his story and we listen. As the story unfolds we may find ourselves absorbed in it; the story stimulates our imaginations and we see how a person feels in the circumstances related in the narrative. The speaker then remarks: "That is just the way John feels this morning, the very way you would feel if you had been through such an experience." We may reflect that in a sense we have been through such an experience. Hearing the story has enabled us to discover John's state of mind *by putting us in contact with* just such a state of mind. We discover *what it means to be* in such a state. If this is John's state of mind then we may say that the account has *existential* truth. We discover not something *about* John's feelings, nor do we share those feelings in the sense of having John's experience as our own. Upon hearing the story we do not become angry; or, if we do, it is our anger and not John's that we know. In so far as the story accomplishes its purpose it does so not by making us angry but by making it possible for us to appreciate the nature of John's anger. We discover what it is like for such a state of mind to *be* in the circumstances related.

Existential truth and its communication have much in common with esthetic truth. We have already seen that the communication of religious truth makes extensive use of art, and it may not be too much to say that art has its origin in such a function. Myth, poetry, music, painting, sculpture, and architecture originally were all ways of expressing and communicating religious meaning. For religion, supposing it has important truth to give us, is not a matter merely of informing us concerning fact by indicating which concepts pertain to which situations and events. Religion, like art, is a kind of experience in which we discover meanings we could come in contact with in no other way. Colors and shapes we discover by perception, and mathematical relations by thought. But the ultimate values of existence we can find only as our imaginations are stirred. We can discuss those values and compare them intellectually; but we can discover them for ourselves only by reliving in imagination the stories which communicate them, and by having our attitudes and emotions re-formed in song and poetry and visual art.

So far as a religion is true, its practice puts us in contact with what is ultimate in existence and value. The higher religions claim to do this by transforming us so that what is within us, in feeling and emotion and attitude, is truly the expression of the final principle of being itself. Those religions for which God is the source of all other existence, and is the ultimate union of existence and value, hold out the promise that those who follow their precepts will be transformed into God's likeness and find in themselves the reflection of his nature. So far as that promise is fulfilled by following their directions, by hearing and contemplating their stories, by submission to their disciplines, by allowing feelings and emotions to be formed by their music and art, then to that extent those religions are true.

THE COMMUNICATION OF RELIGIOUS TRUTH

Religious truth is almost entirely existential truth, and so we must not confuse it with the kind of truth we seek in history or science or philosophy. This does not mean that the narratives and poetry in which religious truth is expressed and communicated do not also contain ideas about what happened in the past and about the constitution of nature. A narrative that comes to us from a past age will be expressed in terms of the ideas of the world which were held by the people of that time. But if the significance of the narrative is in what it reveals to us concerning the ultimate values of life and existence then its historical errors and its pre-scientific ideas about nature are matters of little religious consequence. A factually confused and unhistorical narrative may express profound religious truth which so moves the hearer that his whole approach to life is radically changed. That this can and does happen can be understood without difficulty once we distinguish between the truth communicated and the mode of communication.

If the sacred story of a religion is true, it is true not because it gives us the facts of human history as a competent historian might give them, but because it gives us the meaning of history.

> It is the genius of true myth [says Reinhold Niebuhr] to suggest the dimension of depth in reality and to point to a realm of essence which transcends the surface of history, on which the cause-effect sequences, discovered and analyzed by science, occur. . . . But since

myth cannot speak of the trans-historical without using symbols and events in history as its forms of expression, it invariably falsifies the facts of history, as seen by science, to state its truth.[3]

A historian quite properly evaluates the historical accuracy of the story in terms of the facts as he knows them independently of the story. He accepts as historical fact only what tested historical evidence permits him to accept. But a historian, as a man, may also accept a narrative as an expression of religious truth, and in doing this he may find the ultimate meaning of the facts of history to be disclosed in a story of dubious historicity. Much religious obscurantism results from failure to distinguish between the truth the story communicates and the truth we may know or not know *about* the story.

The religious question is not whether the events of the story actually happened as history but whether or not the story reveals the meaning of existence. From the religious perspective we interpret facts in terms of the story, not the story in terms of the facts. This, however, is an interpretation not of the supposed "facts" which compose the story but of the facts of our own experience, the facts of life and of actual history. The story provides a framework of meaning in terms of which we glimpse the ultimate significance of life and existence. If we do have here such an encounter then the story is the instrument by which truth is given to us; the story offers truth in a form adapted to our condition. If we ask, "What here is the test of truth? What guides faith in its acceptance or rejection?" perhaps we can answer only that those who have thus discovered a meaning in existence have found something with which there is nothing they can compare.

Religious truth has much in common with esthetic truth; the relation of the two is much closer than the relation of religious truth with historical or scientific truth. Religion and art illumine existence so that we may see through them something of the value structure of the reality beyond them. They do not so much refer to that value structure directly as they reconstitute existence in such a way as to reveal its true values. Religion differs from art mainly in two respects: (1) the values it puts us in contact with purport to be ultimate values, and (2) religion leads not merely to the appre-

[3] *An Interpretation of Christian Ethics* (New York, Harper and Brothers, 1935), pp. 12-13. By permission.

ciation of the values it reveals but brings our lives into conformity with them.

History, art, and religion differ in the ways in which their dramatic structures are related to actual existence. History, of course, is no mere catalogue of facts. We never understand a historical event until we discover its dramatic pattern, the pattern by which it gathers variety into a unity, of conflict within conflict, of partial resolution and the eruption of new conflict. The historian must present his facts in a story, but he obtains the plot and the dramatic form from the events themselves. In art at the esthetic level, dramatic form may be suggested by existence but it is constructed and delineated for its own sake. In religion the forms of art are used to illuminate events by showing them in terms of a dramatic pattern which cannot be found merely by inspecting the events themselves.

Jacob Burckhardt made the comment that to the masses "the heart of any religion is a sealed book." [4] In religion there can be communication without the recipient of the communication understanding how it is done, just as a mother can communicate her love to her child without the child's awareness of what is taking place. But such communication is partial and relatively ineffective. If there is religious truth to be communicated, surely its communication will be more effective if those who receive it have some understanding of what it is not. To confuse religious truth with historical and scientific truth is to cloud the depths of religious truth itself. Such truth is received, as it were, in disguise. "I hazard the prophecy," said Alfred North Whitehead, "that that religion will conquer which can render clear to popular understanding some eternal greatness incarnate in the passage of temporal fact." [5] Only education will remove the disguise. When popular understanding includes knowledge of history and science the insights of religion perhaps may be seen more adequately for what they are.

[4] *Force and Freedom*, edited by James Hastings Nichols (Meridian Books, New York, The Noonday Press, 1955), p. 110. By permission of Pantheon Books, Inc., New York, publisher of the American Edition.

[5] *Adventures of Ideas* (New York, The Macmillan Company, 1933), p. 41. By permission.

THE IDEA OF GOD

The essence of religion is the conviction that existence has a meaning for man that he can find only as he places himself in proper relation to reality. This meaning is found not only or even primarily by theoretical inquiry but in active moral and spiritual relationships. The higher religions seem to teach that man becomes aware of his proper relation to reality by acts of worship, including prayer and contemplation and the guidance of attention by ritual symbols, and by means of oral and written narrative and poetry in which visions of man's true destiny and the factors which influence it are expressed. Some of these activities obviously cannot go very far without leading to an attempt to characterize the reality which man attempts to discover and toward which he desires to place himself in proper relationship. At primitive religious levels this reality is thought of in animistic terms, and at a somewhat higher level the animistic forces become personified and we have polytheism.

To refer to the ultimate in existence as "God" usually means that the ultimate is thought of as a being with which man can have moral and spiritual relationship. For a polytheism, of course, there is a plurality of such beings. But the line of distinction between an animism which thinks of the forces of nature primarily as powers and a polytheism which thinks of them as personal is at the point where man's relations to those forces involve personal response. At the animistic level he is a merely passive beneficiary or victim of their activities, except in so far as he himself knows how to exert power to counter or supplement their own. The only device available to him is magic. The powers of nature become personal when their relation to man is on a level of personal response and is influenced by man's attitude toward them. Violation of a taboo becomes disobedience of a command; fear of contamination and of bad luck becomes remorse for sin and fear of a deserved punishment; preventative magic is replaced by sacrifice and petition for favors. As the gods of a polytheism become more personal their relations with each other become personal. It is a short step from this to the conception that one of the gods is supreme, and then the supreme deity may come to be recognized as the only one. He then is no longer a god, but God.

Monotheism has three main forms: pantheism, deism, and

theism; and these differ primarily in their accounts of the relation of God to the world. For pantheism, God and the world are one. The world in its ultimate unity is God. The difference between God and the world is the difference between the world in its ultimate unity and some limited part of the world experienced or understood apart from the whole to which it belongs. Such separation or abstraction of the part from the whole is considered a distortion of the nature of that which is taken apart; to grasp its true nature we must see it in its place in the all-inclusive unity of reality. The destiny of the individual human person then is to lose his separateness and individuality, and to be absorbed finally into the One. In contemplation he can think his identity with the One; in mystical states he may experience it partially; finally he hopes to achieve it completely.

At the risk of oversimplification we may say that in pantheism the relation of God to the world is one of *immanence*. In deism we have a relation of God to the world which is the opposite of immanence: God entirely *transcends* the world. For pantheism either God is completely contained in the world or the world is completely contained in God, so that God and the world are identical; in deism, on the contrary, God and the world are completely separated and mutually exclusive. For deism God is the being who made the world, established its laws, and set it in operation. God may, on occasion, interfere with its operations and suspend its laws for some purpose of his own. He makes certain demands on the beings he has created, especially upon man to whom he has given the power to disobey him and his laws. God provides rewards and punishments to induce man to keep the laws God has established, and a future life to compensate for the inequalities of the rewards and punishments of this life. Thus the relation of man to God, as deism conceives it, is external and mechanical.

For theism God is both immanent and transcendent. He is the creator of the world and thus is not himself a part of the world; but he does not create the world as something that exists separately from himself. Although in no sense a part of the world, God is in some sense in the world and every aspect of the world is present to him. In creation God gives to the world its own existence, but this giving of existence is not an act done once and for all. Creation is continuous with the world's existence; the world's existence is continually a *given* existence. In most versions of theism, the relation of God to his world is providential. The world and all creatures are objects of his love and compassion, and the highest destiny for man is to find not the pantheist's identity of existence with God but the union of love.

It is significant that the higher theistic religions do not define their God, although their theologians may attempt to. The religious consciousness of God is always in symbols and figures. If a theist is asked: "What is God?" he might well answer this question by a series of questions and answers:

Does the world have an origin beyond itself? That origin is God.

Does the world have a meaning beyond itself? That meaning is God.

Does the world have value beyond itself, for the sake of which the world exists? That value is God.

Does the world have a unity which holds together its distinctions of time and space, a unity not itself exhausted in any passing moment or series of passing moments? That unity is God.

POLYTHEISM

We must now try to get beyond these abstract distinctions to see what some of the more important of them have meant to man in his struggle to maintain life physically and socially and in his hungry search for the meaning of his existence. The search for the meaning of life in religion is not concerned with its meaning for thought, but for attitude and action. The basic framework of a religious interpretation is in the form of stories by means of which a people find their own identity and are able to feel their place in existence. Since the Hebrew-Christian religious tradition is one of the primary sources of Western civilization and culture, in this and in the following two sections we shall consider an interpretation of the development of the ideas of God which have been held in that tradition. We shall trace these from their polytheistic background through the historical theism of early Hebrew thought to the universal theism of later Judaism and Christianity. Pantheism has had a minor part in this tradition and deism has appeared mainly as a modification or perversion of theism, and so no attempt will be made here to go further into these ideas of God.[6] Our examination of the Hebrew-Christian tradition will also illustrate the theory of religion and its relation to art which has been suggested in this and the preceding chapters.

The dramas of existence which have impressed themselves most firmly upon man's mind are those of the seasons, the chase, the cycle of vegetation, the cycle of procreation, physical combat, and such spiritual conflicts as those of desire against duty, of the immediate against the remote, of self-seeking against loyalty to others. The basic dramas of life which provide the subject matter of all primitive religions are those of the cycles of nature. To die and be buried and then to come to life again is the dramatic pattern of the course of the sun through day and night and of the growth of a plant from its seed. To pursue a quarry, sometimes to fail and sometimes to succeed, is the pattern of the chase and of battle. Marriage and procreation combine these two dramatic patterns into one.

When man first tried to find some ultimate meaning in his existence he saw himself and his society as part of a universal drama. He attributed to the world itself the dramatic patterns of combat, procreation, birth, death, and resurrection. The ancient polytheisms, Professor G. Ernest Wright points out,

> could not reach beyond the primordial, static chaos which was conceived as the dark and primeval ocean or "deeps" from which the salt and fresh waters on earth came. In Mesopotamia the "deeps" were personified as Apsu and Tiamat. Creation began by a sexual procreation on the part of this male and female pair, who produced a series of gods, the various elements of the universe as then understood. Order was achieved after a cosmic battle among the gods in which the younger and active forces won the victory over the static chaos, and proceeded to establish world order.[7]

Polytheism, however, can seldom rest content with a plurality of gods as the final explanation of existence. There is need to go behind the plurality to find some unity underlying the whole scheme of nature. The cycle of the seasons, for example, gives meaning to the acts of planting and harvesting, but what gives meaning to the

[6] For a fuller discussion of pantheism and deism, see Samuel M. Thompson, *A Modern Philosophy of Religion* (Chicago, Henry Regnery Company, 1955), Chapters 14, 15.

[7] From *Biblical Archaeology* (The Westminster Press, 1957), p. 101. Used by permission.

cycle of the seasons? What makes intelligible the fact that existence contains so varied a collection of powers and agencies? If polytheism understands creation as a struggle among the powers of nature then, in the words of Professor Wright,

> what was it in the world that kept nature orderly and with which the divine wills were themselves in harmony? It was believed that some principle of order had been established at creation, to which even the gods were subject. The Greeks spoke of this principle as *moira,* "fate," "destiny," what is fitting and proper. The Egyptians spoke of it as *maat,* usually translated as "truth" or "justice" . . . In Mesopotamia the words *parṣu* and *shimtu* seem to possess a similar significance. *Parṣu* is something mightier than the gods, a world order without which the gods would be nothing. Mankind has its *shimtu* or fate, a destination given it before existence.[8]

The idea of a principle of order inherent in the world of nature involves the concept of nature as a fixed and finished order of existence. What appears to be change is only repetition, and everything that happens to which any meaning can be given is predestined to happen just as it does. Man finds the meaning of his life and of the events of nature as pulses within the ever-recurring cycles which make up the order of existence. But what about the meaning of nature itself? Its principle of order has no source; we can say only that it is. Neither its existence nor the existence of the world it informs have any meaning. We can say of them only that they are. Their existence is senseless. To some reflective minds such problems become acute. What can be the point of winning or losing in the struggles of life? The struggle is never real, for the everlasting recurrence will go on relentlessly, each phase in the cycle giving way to the next as foreordained. Ultimately nothing makes any sense. We find eloquent expression of this in the words of the Preacher in the *Book of Ecclesiastes:*

> What does a man gain by all the toil
>   At which he toils under the sun?
> A generation goes, and a generation comes,
>   but the earth remains forever.
> The sun rises and the sun goes down,
>   and hastens to the place where it rises.
> The wind blows to the south,
>   and goes round to the north;

[8] *Ibid,* p. 102.

round and round goes the wind,
    and on its circuits the wind returns.
All streams run to the sea,
    but the sea is not full;
to the place where the streams flow,
    there they flow again.
All things are full of weariness;
    a man cannot utter it;
the eye is not satisfied with seeing,
    nor the ear filled with hearing.
What has been is what will be,
    and what has been done is what will be done;
    and there is nothing new under the sun.[9]

THEISM

We know little of the circumstances of the origin of monotheism. It seems to have emerged briefly in Egypt but was soon overwhelmed by a resurgence of traditional polytheism. The greatest achievements of monotheism are without question in the theistic religions of Judaism, Christianity, and Islam. These all have their origin in what we may call the historical theism of the Hebrews.

Historical theism differs from polytheism in two important respects. In the first place, it conceives the principle of cosmic order as neither a part of nor contained in the cosmos itself, but as transcendent. In the second place, this principle of cosmic order is in some sense a personal being. The significance of such a conception lies in its implications that the cosmic order is incomplete and thus still in the making, and that the cosmos is governed by a power with which man can have a personal relationship.

The Hebrews were nomads who wandered into a land already settled and found a culture far advanced over that of their own. For generations the Hebrews lived in the still more advanced civilization of Egypt. After leaving Egypt they wandered for years without finding a permanent abode. Finally they returned to Canaan, seized

[9] Chapter 1, verses 3-9, Revised Standard Version (New York, Thomas Nelson and Sons, 1952). All quotations from the Bible are from the *Revised Standard Version of the Bible*, copyrighted 1946 and 1952 by the Division of Christian Education, National Council of Churches, and used by permission.

its cities, and established themselves there. Out of such experiences this collection of obscure tribes somehow developed a profound conviction that the events of life are contingent, that man's future is not fixed beforehand but depends on the choices and decisions he makes in the course of his life. The universe is governed not by a universal deterministic principle but by a Creator who transcends the world and controls its operations in accordance with a moral law. The Hebrews, so far as we know, were the first to see the events of nature and of human society as historical, as having a reason for existing and a goal to achieve. Since the pattern of events is not one of immanent necessity but is in process of being fashioned by its Creator, that Creator can open the way for man to participate in its formation. Thus man's choices and actions may have a profound significance in the cosmic drama, something impossible in the world of polytheism.

In a theistic setting the forces of nature can no longer be personified as gods, for the God of theism is one. Not only is God one, but although he acts in nature and in history his existence is distinct from nature. For polytheism the events of life and of nature are all events in the lives of the gods. Although Hebrew theism drew a sharp distinction between the natural and the human on one side and the divine on the other, yet the distinction was not a separation. Man's life was given to him as something valuable, and if he lives his life in accordance with God's plan for him his life will be one of joy and achievement. The Hebrew people also had a destiny to achieve as a people chosen by God as his instrument; but to achieve this destiny it was necessary for that people to obey the law of God and to preserve itself from idolatry.

The law given by God opens the way to man's high destiny. Individual and nation need only to obey, on this condition the promises of God will be fulfilled. By thus making the future depend on present choices and decisions, what happens now is given a cosmic significance. Only an open future can give meaning to history. The future is the work of God in the sense that God has established his law, and his law binds man to the consequences of his own choices. If man sins he will surely die. But the future depends also on man, for man does not have to sin; and it is just as much God's law that if man is righteous he will live and prosper. Whether or not a man shall sin is not decreed by God; it is up to man himself. The righteous prosper, the unrighteous suffer; man makes the choice and God guarantees the outcome. Wrongdoers "will soon fade like grass and wither like the green herb."

> I have been young, and now am old;
> Yet I have not seen the righteous forsaken
> or his children begging bread.
>
> . . .
>
> Depart from evil, and do good;
> so shall you abide forever.
> For the LORD loves justice;
> he will not forsake his saints.
> The righteous shall be preserved for ever,
> but the children of the wicked shall be cut off.[10]

However simple and obvious in principle this solution of the problem of life seemed, things did not work out according to plan. There were many who did see the righteous forsaken and his children begging bread. Another Psalmist, after recounting the miseries and disasters which had come upon those people whom God had chosen and to whom he had made his promises, had this to say:

> All this has come upon us,
> though we have not forgotten thee,
> or been false to thy covenant.[11]

Polytheism had identified the natural with the divine and had found the meaning of nature and of human life in the lives and activities of the gods. Early Hebrew theism distinguished nature from God as God's creation, and found the meaning of life and existence in the acts which God performed in nature and especially in his care for his people in accordance with his promises to them. History was seen as the implementation of a solemn covenant between God and his chosen people, and every happening was interpreted in terms of the relationship established by God between obedience and reward and between disobedience and punishment. But the covenant failed. Its terms were not carried out by God in any recognizable way. History, like the forces of nature, had failed to disclose the meaning of existence and of human life. The Hebrews had seen history as transcending nature; it was necessary now to transcend history.

[10] Psalm 37, verses 25, 27-28, Revised Standard Version.
[11] Psalm 44, verse 17, Revised Standard Version.

When nature fails and history fails, where is man to turn? The obvious answer is to turn to the future. But even the future has failed, for the present misery of the righteous is not the future which was promised. To some there came now a glimpse of the mystery of God. The covenant still stands but, in spite of appearances, man actually had failed to fulfil its terms. The true law of God is beyond his grasp and its requirements are beyond his own unaided performance. The holiness of God came to be understood as the holiness of absolute righteousness rather than a separation enforced by taboo. Only by the suffering of the righteous can the terms of the covenant be fulfilled. Whether the Suffering Servant was to be Israel herself, or whether the Isaiah figure refers to an individual Messiah, or whether the two are seen in a mystical unity, the fulfilment of the covenant is in an act of free acceptance of suffering and a free assumption of guilt by one who ought not to suffer and who has no stain of guilt. The guiltless one suffers, and so takes upon himself the retribution God has established for sin. Since only God himself is righteous then only the suffering of God himself can save man from the consequences of guilt. Thus was resolved the basic dramatic conflict of the Hebrew religion.

The resolution of the dramatic conflict of historical theism may appear at first sight to be itself a part of the course of history. For the Messiah was to appear at a future time to usher in a new order of life and restore his people to their promised place. Even the early Christians, who believed that the Messiah had already come, looked forward to his return and to a period when his rule on earth would be established. Both the hope for a Messiah who has not yet appeared and the expectation of his return are interpretations which seem still to find the meaning of life and of existence in history. Yet these "future" events may be included in history only in an equivocal sense for they belong to a future that does not have historical continuity with the present. Thus a deeper insight may see them as not a part of our time dimension at all. Even in their most literally conceived form, however, the Messianic expectations point to a society and a world so changed as to have lost all continuity with present existence; for that transformation is recognized, by those who anticipate it, as in no sense growing out of what has come before but as the act of God from outside history and nature.

Thus the drama in which the meaning of existence is to be found is one which intrudes into history but is not itself a part of history.

Nor is it now conceived as a human drama. It is not the drama of a people struggling to obey God's commands, failing and undergoing punishment, brought back to obedience by leaders raised up by God, and failing even more disastrously but looking forward to final victory. The drama now belongs, like that of polytheism, to the realm of divinity itself. But this new conception differs from polytheism in an all-important respect: it is not the dramatic conflict of the powers of nature but the drama of the Creator himself, who created the world through love, who so loves the world that he maintains its existence in spite of the inevitable imperfections of finitude, and who takes upon himself the stain of evil and by that act transforms evil into good. Thus is resolved the dramatic conflict between the creative act and its inevitable consequence of evil. It was the transfer of the cosmic drama into the divine nature, together with the need to avoid a dualism of ultimates such as that of Zoroastrianism or of Manichaeism which led to the Christian dogma of the Trinity.

The gift to man of freedom and moral responsibility cannot erase the imperfections of finitude; on the contrary it transforms those imperfections into moral evil and sin. Failure and disaster are inevitable; but without them man could not exist as truly free, and thus as one made in the image of God. So God must permit evil to exist if man is to be free and morally responsible; but God can permit evil to exist without himself being evil only if he takes that evil into himself in such a way as to transform it into good.

Here we have a story which purports to show us the meaning of life and existence. By what criterion can its truth be tested?

THE TEST OF RELIGIOUS TRUTH

Does this great tradition in any significant way show us what the truth about existence and life is? To consider this question fruitfully we shall have to see what kind of a question it is in this context and take account of certain relevant considerations in the light of which it will have to be discussed.

First of all, it is important to try to grasp the underlying theme of Western religion. Perhaps the distinctive feature of our culture is its conception of man's freedom and creativity. A religion that places ultimates in a transcendent existence leaves the world open to change and manipulation. A religion that sees the source and goals and final values of human life in a transcendent existence frees man's imagination to entertain for himself any plausible possibility that occurs to him. The binding forces of custom and institution are loosened and the way is open for individual and social experimentation.

If man is to find meaning in his existence there must be some pattern or structure of values which can be expressed in human attitudes and choices. If man is free and if there are significant possibilities within his reach, now or later, which are not yet recognized, the meaning of human life cannot be found either in nature or in history. For if man is free then his own nature and the future course of history are both open and what is to be the actual pattern of human life rests to some degree upon man's own decision. The possibilities that confront us are limited, it is true, but they include both salvation and destruction. The consequences of our choices are largely beyond our control, but we can control our choices. History has much to teach us; but if we are free we cannot discover from history the meaning of life for ourselves, for we face a future not determined by the past and as different from the past as we choose to make it. If we act in freedom we shall make our choices under the guidance of the possible, not under the control either of the present or of the past.

If man is free he cannot do justice to the possible if he insists upon living by rule. No rules or codes of conduct can be final, for their acceptance as final would suppose that the way of the future has already been found. To think that the problems of life can be solved by a set of rules was the error of the early Hebrews. When Micah declared that the Lord requires only that we do justice, love kindness, and walk in humility, and when Jesus of Nazareth summed up the law in the injunction to love God with all our heart and mind and our neighbor as ourselves, principles of value were substituted for systems of rules. Man can discover the way to his highest destiny not by being shown what it is to consist of in fact but only by discovering the values life must embody no matter what the content of life may be.

Communication of values is possible, however, only in a work of art. We discover values directly by participation, but if we are to recognize and appreciate values beyond the range of our present and past experiences those values must be communicated to us in imaginative constructs. If we have a story that reveals the meaning of life we discover that meaning for ourselves as we live our lives and make our choices in accordance with the values which that story exemplifies.

Is the story true? The question of its existential truth is partly the question of the completeness of fulfilment its values provide. It must stand comparison with every rival story that moves our hearts. If there is an ultimate dramatic intelligibility to be discovered in existence it must be one in which all things that exist and all events that happen work together for good, and this must include human failure and evil as well as success and good. We can be satisfied with nothing less.

If we are to live both as free and so that our decisions and actions fit some meaningful pattern, we have to live according to some story. It can be a cheap and tawdry one, or it can be a rich and noble one. This question we can answer only by making our own comparisons. Classical atomism, for example, is a story with a dramatic pattern which deals with the problem of the meaning of evil, as do so many such dramas, by excluding it. Atomism is the drama of the motion, collision, cohesion, and separation of irreducible particles of matter in an otherwise empty space. The world it pictures is one that has no place in actual existence, and its appeal is entirely from its austere simplicity. In contrast, the story of the redemption of evil in divine suffering reveals a pattern of values which gives meaning to evil and turns failure into ultimate success.

Since we grasp values in feeling we may say that, in a sense, we find in feeling a test of the truth of religious commitment. But under what conditions can we trust our feelings? Is our feeling response appropriate to the values to which it is a response? Is our feeling a fit instrument for the discovery of value? To be able to respond to serious music or poetry in a way that is appropriate to the values expressed we have to give some analysis and study to the work. The feelings which the work happens to arouse in the lazy, the ignorant, and the tone-deaf are not significant. So, too, if we are to discern any truly significant dramatic pattern of existence we need a heightened sensitiveness. If there is a story that can reveal to us the ultimate meanings of existence surely one way in which it does so is by transforming the self, by making the self sensitive to values in their true proportion and relationships.

Although we cannot find the meaning of existence in history, still it is quite possible that history provides a significant test of religious truth. To compare conflicting religions is like the comparison of any conflicting stories. What makes us believe one man's story and disbelieve another's? Is it not the integrity of the one story and the way in which the other falls apart under cross-examination? History is the cross-examination of the stories by which man has tried to live.

Survival is thus a kind of evidence of truth in religion. But not all kinds of survival are on the same level. Just as it is one thing for a story to stand up when no one is able or willing to challenge it, so the survival of a religion not exposed to the challenge of other attitudes and of changing events may not be significant. Two kinds of survival may be of special importance as tests of truth in religion. There is the kind of survival in which a religion is able to take the insights of its rivals into itself and to transform them into its own image. This has been done by every great theistic religion. Then there is the kind of survival in which the same story shows itself capable of great growth in the depth of meaning it discloses and in its capacity to adapt to radically changing ways of life.

A few thousand years may seem too small a part of the span of human existence to serve as a test of history. But more has happened to man in this short time, almost inconceivably more, than in the hundreds of thousands of years he had existed before. What counts for man is not time as measured by the sun or the fixed stars but human time. A story which survives the repeated overturning of economic, political, educational, and even ecclesiastical systems, the clashing and mingling of alien cultures, and the complete transformation of man's understanding of nature and the cosmos and himself, would seem to have great resources of meaning. The theistic religions appear to have met this test with some success. Whether they can survive tests to come we do not know.

TRADITIONAL PROOFS OF THE EXISTENCE OF GOD

For those who accept a theistic religion and have never been bothered by any basic doubts concerning its truth the problem of the existence of God does not arise. In fact if it does arise for such ones, its very existence as a problem stands as a threat to their religion. From the theistic perspective the problem of the existence of God is not a religious problem at all, for without God a theism is impossible. The existence of God becomes a problem for a theist only as his religion is attacked at its roots, but when this happens he is faced with a philosophical problem. There is little point in telling him to have faith, for the ground of faith has disappeared. You do not strengthen a weakened foundation by piling upon it more and more of the structure it is supposed to support. The problem of the existence of God, however, is a philosophical problem to which men are usually driven by religious doubts. Although, as with Plato and Aristotle, arguments for the existence of God are sometimes developed primarily from philosophical considerations, such arguments usually arise in defense of a religious position. This does not alter their strictly philosophical character, and it is only on their rational soundness that their degree of success or failure is to be estimated. Whether they are convincing or not may or may not be significant; whether such fact has any bearing on their soundness depends on why they convince or fail to convince and on the competence of the judgment of the person concerned.

These arguments are sometimes referred to as "proofs," and in evaluating them we should remember what a proof is. A proof purports to show that a conclusion is so related to the evidence given in its support that if the statement of the evidence is true the conclusion is either probably or certainly true. A proof, that is, shows that the assurance of truth possessed by the evidence carries over to the conclusion. In inductive proofs, as these are generally understood today, the assurance of the truth of the statement of the evidence passes to the conclusion with some degree of probability. In deductive proofs the assurance of the truth of the premises is shown to attach with full force to the conclusion. Proofs of the existence of God are usually of a deductive kind.

Traditional proofs of the existence of God are of four main types: ontological, cosmological, teleological, and moral. This classification is not entirely satisfactory, for the latter three are closely related and might be considered as one group of proofs standing over against the first. The ontological proof argues from the idea of God to the existence of God, while the other three proofs argue from the existence of something finite to the existence of God. The cosmological proof, as its name suggests, goes from the existence of the world to the existence of God; the teleological goes from the supposed existence or fact of a relation of means to ends in nature to the existence of God; the moral argument contends that moral experience can be taken as significant only if God exists, that is, the moral proof may be said to go from the existence of moral fact to the existence of God. Thus while the ontological proof goes from the idea of God to the existence of God, the other arguments go from finite existence to God's existence—from the existence of the world, the existence of relations of means and ends, and the existence of moral relationships.

THE ONTOLOGICAL ARGUMENT

The classic statement of the ontological argument is by Anselm. After pointing out that we understand "God" to mean "a being than which nothing greater can be conceived," Anselm argues that such a being must exist, that the conception of such a being requires that being's existence. Although

> the fool hath said in his heart, there is no God . . . this very fool, when he hears of this being of which I speak—a being than which nothing greater can be conceived—understands what he hears, and what he understands is in his understanding; although he does not understand it to exist. . . . [But since the fool understands this then even he must see that] that, than which nothing greater can be conceived, cannot exist in the understanding alone. For, suppose it exists in the understanding alone: then it can be conceived to exist in reality; which is greater.[12]

In summary: We have an idea of God as a being than which nothing greater can be conceived. Either this being exists or does not exist; if this being does not exist we can form an idea of a being which is greater, namely, one that does exist; therefore, this being exists.

The usual criticism of Anselm's argument attacks his inclusion of existence among the attributes of God. We think of God, Anselm seems to be arguing, as infinite, eternal, omniscient, omnipotent, holy, just, compassionate, and existent. If we do not include *exist-*

[12] *Proslogium*, Chapter II, in *St. Anselm: Proslogium; Monologium; An Appendix in Behalf of the Fool by Gaunilon; and Cur Deus Homo*, translated by Sidney Norton Deane, Second Edition (Chicago, Open Court Publishing Company, 1910), pp. 7-8.

ence among the attributes, then we can think of a being greater than one that omits existence, that is, a being that has all the other attributes plus existence as well. The difficulty is that existence is not an attribute at all. To have existence or not to have existence does not indicate a difference in the *nature* of anything. As Kant pointed out in his criticism of the ontological argument, a hundred dollars in my pocket and a hundred dollars in idea are the same in nature; the only difference is that in the one case the hundred dollars exist and in the other they do not. It would seem that those who assert and those who deny the existence of God must have the same idea of God, else one would not be denying what the other asserts. One would be asserting the existence of one kind of God and the other would be denying the existence of another kind of God. Or, we may say, one would be asserting the existence of an existing God; the other would be denying the existence of a nonexisting God.

This criticism is cogent, but it does not do full justice to Anselm's argument. Anselm's point is that we have to think of God as necessary being, as that being which cannot not exist. There is no contingency in God as there is in the case of any finite being. Thus Anselm might have avoided the direct thrust of the criticism we have formulated if, instead of including existence among the attributes of God, he had pointed out that necessary existence is implied by them. This still, however, falls short of a proof of existence. We may admit that a most perfect being would have to exist and yet deny that Anselm has shown that there is such a being. We can see, intellectually, the necessity of God's existence from God's perfection only if we can grasp that perfection in idea. The trouble is that when we think of God as perfect our thought can reach only to the idea *that* God is perfect. Our thought cannot grasp that perfection as it is in God if God exists. If we could experience God's perfection as it is supposed to be in God, then God's existence would be evident to us. But since we cannot, the idea merely *that* God is perfect is not sufficient to *show* us his necessary existence. If we already believe in the existence of such a God as Anselm refers to, we believe in a being whose necessary existence would be evident to anyone who could understand what it is like to be God; but if we do not already believe in the existence of God, we are brought no closer to assurance by the fact that *if* such a being exists that being exists by necessity.

THE ARGUMENT FROM EXISTENCE

If our criticism of the ontological argument is sound, then the lesson that argument has for us is that we cannot go from our idea of existence, even our idea of necessary existence, to the fact of existence. If the existence of God is to be shown by argument then it must be shown to follow from the fact that something else exists. Such is the method of the cosmological argument. The world exists, and there is nothing in the world to account for its own existence, therefore God exists. The cosmological argument has many forms, for there are many aspects of the world which seem to show the world's dependence for its existence on something beyond itself. The best known formulation of these arguments is by Thomas Aquinas, and we shall look at these briefly.

Thomas' first argument, which he considers the "more manifest," is based on the fact of change. The argument assumes that some things in the world are in process of change. Anything that changes, however, must be changed by something else, for nothing can change unless first it is capable of becoming something different from what it already is. Change actually is, in Thomas' words, "the reduction from potentiality to actuality." But no thing's potentiality can bring about the change; for if a thing is to be changed from a state of potentiality to a state of actuality, only something actual can bring about that change. The potential, as potential, can *do* nothing; the potential is only what *can* be, not what is actual. A mere can-be cannot act. So a thing cannot be in the same respect that which is changed and that which brings about the change, hence whatever is changed must be changed by something else. If this something else undergoes change then it, in turn, must be changed by something other than itself. But this cannot go on indefinitely. There must be a first agency of change, as Thomas says, a "first mover." Without a first agency of change, that is, one which does not itself change and thus need another agent to bring about that change, there would be no agency of change at all. This first mover "everyone understands to be God." [13]

[13] The statement of this and the other of Thomas Aquinas' five arguments are paraphrased and parts are quoted by permission from *The Summa Theologica*, Part I, Q. 2, Art. 3, *The Basic Writings of Saint Thomas Aquinas*, edited by Anton C. Pegis (copyright 1945 by Random House, Inc., New York, 1945), Volume I, pp. 20-24.

This argument does not make it entirely clear as to whether the "first mover" is first in time or first in some other sense. If first in time only, then this argument would suggest a deistic conception of the relation of God to the world. Even if Thomas did not so intend his argument, his statement of it here is exposed to this interpretation if we take that statement by itself. The dependence of a thing which changes upon something else to change it, he says, "cannot go on to infinity." We might supplement this by saying that even if the relation of dependence did go on to infinity there would be nothing in that infinite series of "movers" to make any of them actual; they would all be potential only. No mere possibility can account for the existence of an actual world. The world must receive its existence from something that does not depend on something else for its own existence, that is, from something that is self-existent. This supplementation of Thomas' first argument is suggested in the other arguments. The first argument, then, is not complete in itself; it needs the second and third to complete it.

The second argument is from the nature of efficient cause. We find nothing in the world of nature which is the efficient cause of itself, for if a thing were to be its own cause it would have to be prior to itself, and this is impossible. But no series of efficient causes can be an infinite series. If we take any specific cause as the last cause of some specific change we are considering, then it must be itself the effect of a preceding cause, and the preceding cause of one prior to it. The preceding cause Thomas calls an "intermediate cause." The intermediate cause, however, must have a first cause, for if in any series of causes you take away a cause you take away its effect. Without a first cause there would be no intermediate cause and without the intermediate cause there would not be the cause whose operation we are aware of, that is, the last cause. All the causes in nature are dependent on other causes; none of them accounts for itself. So there must be a first cause, "to which everyone gives the name of God."

Thomas' statement of the second argument has seemed to many to beg the question. The heart of the argument he states:

> Now in efficient causes it is not possible to go on to infinity, because in all efficient causes following in order, the first is the cause of the intermediate cause, and the intermediate is the cause of the ultimate cause, whether the intermediate cause be several, or one only. Now to take away the cause is to take away the effect. Therefore, if there be

no first cause among efficient causes, there will be no ultimate, nor any intermediate, cause.[14]

The apparent begging of the question may perhaps be avoided if we understand this to mean that no system of causes composed solely of causes which themselves depend on other causes can be in operation without a first cause, that is, a cause that does not itself depend on other causes. For no one of a system of dependent causes can initiate causal action by itself. So where all causes are dependent causes, no action would occur.

The third argument is based on the distinction between possibility and necessity. We find in nature things which might not have been, since they are things which come into existence and go out of existence. Now if anything that exists is something that comes into existence and passes out of existence, then there was a time when it did not exist; if this were true of everything, and if the existence of things extended back into an infinite past, then there would have been a time when nothing existed. For in an infinite past time all possible contingencies and all possible combinations of contingencies must have occurred. In a world in which everything comes into and goes out of existence, one possible combination of contingencies would be for all things in existence to pass out of existence simultaneously. But if there had been such a time then nothing would exist now, for nothing could have begun to exist. Therefore, something does exist whose existence is necessary and not merely possible. This necessary existence must have its necessity in itself and not from some other being, for, as we saw in the second proof, it is impossible for a causal series to go back to infinity. This being which has necessary self-existence "all men speak of as God."

The force of the third argument becomes much more apparent with the recognition that the world is in process of evolution, a conception quite foreign to Thomas' thinking. The more advanced stages of evolution, such as living organisms and conscious selves, were potential in even the earliest stages. Now we may ask, whence did nature receive these potentialities? What was then potential was not a part of nature itself. How can a thing bring from itself something it is not? Yet its power to become something else is a part of what a thing actually is, and so what a thing is at any one stage of its existence is only a part of the nature which belongs to it. So it would

14 *Ibid*, p. 22.

seem that to take evolution seriously as a basic fact of natural existence leads to the conclusion that the ultimate cause of existence in nature must be a cause capable of giving to a natural existent not only the nature it actually has at a specific time, but capable of giving to it a potential nature. Such a cause would seem to have to be in some sense intelligent, and thus would have to exist beyond the limits of nature itself.

According to the fourth argument the value differences and relationships we find in things imply the existence of God. We distinguish between the more and less good, true, noble, and the like.

> But *more* and *less* are predicated of different things according as they resemble in their different ways something which is the maximum, as a thing is said to be hotter according as it more nearly resembles that which is hottest.[15]

Thus if things show an order of perfection, there must be a being which is the maximum of perfection. In other words, unless there is an absolute standard of value which is really existent, then the value distinctions we make in our judgments of things are purely arbitrary and subjective. They are, at best, only expressions of our likes and dislikes.

The fifth argument is based on the fact that nature seems to show design. Although natural bodies lack awareness they still act for an end. "Now whatever lacks knowledge cannot move towards an end, unless it be directed by some being endowed with knowledge and intelligence." So there must be some intelligent being "by whom all natural things are directed to their end; and this being we call God." [16] In more modern terms this argument could be stated as the improbability that the order of nature is fortuitous, the result of chance. The fifth argument has obvious relations with the third.

Thomas' five arguments may be summarized or interpreted as the contention that the world of nature is a contingent world. Its contingency is apparent in the fact that it is a world of change, and in the fact that the change which occurs is orderly change. From our modern perspective this may be reinforced by our recognition that the natural order is one in which latent potentialities of the earlier stages become actual in a process of evolution. For those who see the world as contingent, for whom everything in nature is something

[15] *Ibid*, p. 23.
[16] Ibid.

which might not have been and whose basic impression of the world is of something transitory and precarious in its existence, the reality of God as a self-existent creative being upon whom depends the whole order of nature seems a most evident truth. This is particularly the case with one who is unwilling to rest with an ultimate unintelligibility and who is convinced that the existence of the actual world is something which somehow must make sense. For those who see no mystery in the fact that there is a world, for whom its existence seems self-explanatory, such argument appears to be empty of meaning.

EXAMINATION OF THE ARGUMENT FROM EXISTENCE

The traditional cosmological argument has been attacked from many sides. One of the most influential criticisms was that of Kant, who contended that the cosmological argument depends on the ontological. It is curious that Kant's criticism, although it rests on his own general philosophical position, has been eagerly accepted and endorsed by many who have little else in common with Kant's philosophy. Another frequent criticism is based on the rejection of causality, and a more moderate version of this rejects the concept of a First Cause. To argue back to God as the Cause that made the world leaves unanswered the question of who made God. If things in nature need causes to explain their existence then why does not the "first" cause need a cause also?

Concerning the objections to the argument from existence we may say, first of all, that this argument in any of its traditional forms does not by itself establish the existence of God with certainty. To demand that any such type argument should do so is to misunderstand the nature of proof. Rational proof of existence must always assume some existence. We do not discover existence originally by reasoning but by experience, first in sense perception and then in our experience of our own processes of awareness. Thus the cosmological proof may not be cogent as against philosophical idealism, subjectivism, philosophical skepticism, positivism, or pragmatism. For these all deny that we have rational assurance of the existence of a real temporal world which has its own existence and is not in some sense a construct of our knowing processes or adaptive functions. Neither does the argument hold against those who deny that existence is intelligible, that anything whose existence is not self explanatory must be accounted for by something else.

The criticism that the cosmological argument misuses the causal principle is a grave one and must be carefully considered in any defense of that argument. If the cosmological argument is sound in principle it must distinguish the causal principle to which it appeals from that of natural science. A natural cause is a cause of change, but the kind of cause required by the cosmological argument is a cause of existence. This is a metaphysical, not a scientific principle. A cause of change is what Thomas Aquinas calls an "intermediate" cause; only a cause of existence could be a first cause.

With these considerations in mind, we may say that the cosmological argument makes certain definite assumptions:

(1) The world which we know and in which we act really exists as temporal fact.
(2) The existence of the world is not only fact but also intelligible fact.

The basic logic of the cosmological argument may be analyzed into the following steps:

(1) A temporal world is contingent.
(2) As something intelligible the existence of the temporal world presupposes a non-contingent existence as its cause.
(3) The non-contingent cause of nature is a cause of existence, not a cause of change.
(4) Any cause of existence must be a self-existing being; there can be only one such being, and this is what traditional theism has understood by God.

If the assumptions of this argument are to be defended rationally, that defense would appear to have to be along the lines of an existential dialectic.[17] Concerning such an enterprise as this we may say with some assurance that philosophers who are intent upon establishing the existence of God by rational argument are dealing with a matter of first importance. Their temptation, however, is to allow their desire for success to make them uncritical of the arguments they use. But the same considerations apply to those who are intent upon discrediting the attempt to prove the existence of God.

[17] For an analysis and development of each of these steps, see Thompson, *op. cit.*, Chapters 18-21.

The difficulty which faces anyone who makes a study of this problem is, first, that of finding rational theists who are willing to face and expose their own assumptions, and, secondly, to find critics of the traditional arguments who are aware of the attempts which have been made to meet the criticisms usually encountered.

SUMMARY

A religion is the set of beliefs and practices which express for a group its ideas of what is of final significance in life and existence and by which that group maintains itself in effective relationship with those ultimates. In earlier stages of society the religious permeates all life and action; the distinction between the religious and the secular appears only where man attributes to nature existence and powers of its own. The emergence of a secular interpretation of nature has been a source of conflict and dissension in Western culture. This makes imperative the problem of whether the two kinds of attitude toward existence can be reconciled with each other. One attempt to accomplish this has been by a distinction and division of existence into two realms, the natural and the supernatural. The effectiveness of this approach has weakened as our scientific knowledge of the natural has extended its range and come to include much of what was earlier assigned to the supernatural. Another and more fruitful approach may be found in the concept of the religious and the scientific as different perspectives of existence. This raises the question, however, of just what kind of truth is available to us from the religious perspective.

We may approach the question of truth in religion by considering the basis upon which religions may be significantly compared. We find two ways of distinguishing religions, the distinction between higher and lower and the distinction between the true and the false. The basis of such comparisons is in the values expressed in different religions. Higher religions are those which embody the higher values, and true religions are those whose values are genuine values, not disvalues. The application of these standards to religions, and the consideration of the issues between a religious and a nonreligious outlook involve serious difficulties. The character of these difficulties raises the question of how religious truth is apprehended and communicated.

The problem of the communication of religious truth is clarified by the distinction between descriptive truth and existential truth. Religion is concerned with existential truth; the discovery and appreciation of values comes only by encounter. Such encounter is either in direct experience or by means of a mode of communication which enables us to grasp something individual. Such a means of communication we find in art and poetry, and these are the instruments by means of which religious truth is communicated.

Since religion is concerned with man's relation to the ultimate, a religious perspective understands the ultimate as in some sense personal. In polytheism there are many such beings, while in monotheism only one is recognized. Pantheism, deism, and theism are different ways of understanding the relation of God and the world. Of these, polytheism and theism have been of central importance in Western culture.

Polytheism is the personification of the forces of nature, and the polytheist finds the meaning of existence and life in the relationships of these gods to each other. In many advanced polytheisms, however, there has been a tendency to seek something more basic than the plurality of divinities, and this has been conceived frequently as a single ultimate impersonal principle of fate, or destiny, or justice which is inherent in the world and to which even the gods are subject. Such a world, however, is a finished world in which nothing that man does can make any difference. This leads to an impression of the meaningless of existence. Man's only role is to submit and to accept what comes; he cannot in any way change the course of events.

Monotheism breaks the rigid finality of the world by finding the ultimate explanation of the world's existence in a being which transcends the world. A Creator who is in some sense personal takes the place of the impersonal and immanent principle of necessity. The development from polytheism to theism, and the transformation of theism from a local and historical version to a universal and transcendent conception of the basic drama of existence can be traced in the Hebrew-Christian tradition.

A test of truth of the advanced forms of theism may be found in their success in contributing to a kind of advance in knowledge and organization of life which requires both that man be convinced of his own freedom and of his possession of potentialities which reach beyond all that has ever been achieved or even imagined. A test of truth may be found also in the success with which the higher theistic religions have survived the cataclysmic changes in human institutions and human knowledge.

Although religion provides no answer to the philosophical problem of the existence of God, the considerations which lead to skepticism concerning God's existence are of importance to religion. No proof of the existence of God can be final by itself, for the same reason that no proof by itself can establish the existence of anything. The strength of a proof for the existence of God, provided the proof is logically sound, is in the force of its assumptions concerning existence.

Questions for Study and Discussion

1. *Terms:* cosmological proof, deism, existential truth, First Mover, Humanism, immanence, Manichaeism, monotheism, moral proof, ontological proof, pantheism, perspective, teleological proof, theism, theology, transcendence, Zoroastrianism.

2. Soviet Communism and Hitler's National Socialism have sometimes been referred to as religions. Can such a characterization be justified?

3. (a) Is Confucianism a religion? Examine the difference between an ethical system and a religion.

   (b) What is the meaning of the statement one sometimes hears concerning a person that business is his religion?

4. Does the theist's idea of Providence differ in any essential respect from the polytheist's notion of causes in nature?

5. Distinguish between the idea of perspectives of truth and Pompanazzi's doctrine of a two-fold truth. Is the theory of perspectives itself a perspective?

6. Can a religion be adequately grasped and its appeal appreciated by one who is not born into it? If not, then how can any comparison of different religions be significant? If so, then how does the outsider manage to remain outside?

7. (a) Adherents of a religion sometimes argue that its basic claims of truth cannot be understood except by an act of faith, hence those who do not already accept those truth claims are not competent to judge whether they are true. Examine this argument.

(b) Would it be a pertinent reply to the argument in (a) to say that the argument itself cannot be understood except by those who accept it, and hence it makes no sense when addressed to those who are not already believers?

8. Distinguish belief, faith, and knowledge.

9. Is theism necessarily anthropomorphic?

10. Compare magic and religious ritual.

11. How can God be thought of as both immanent and transcendent? Can you find any parallel between this and the relation of the power of the State to the local community?

12. Compare the Hebrew and Greek components of Western culture. Are these influences in mutual conflict or are they complementary?

13. Examine Thomas' third argument for the existence of God. Do the alternatives he proposes exhaust the possibilities?

14. Examine: The problem of the existence of God is primarily the problem of the relation of the potential to the actual.

15. If God does not exist in time how can God be referred to as "First Cause"? What does "first" mean in this context?

16. Which of the assumptions of the cosmological argument would you be able to deny, not merely in thought but in practice as well?

Selected Bibliography

The following will be helpful in providing background and opening up special phases of topics discussed in this book. With a few exceptions, books referred to in the text and notes are not included here. Paperback books are identified in parentheses.

THE BACKGROUND AND HISTORY OF PHILOSOPHY

GREEK RELIGION: Edith Hamilton, *Mythology* (Mentor); F. M. Cornford, *Greek Religious Thought*, E. P. Dutton, New York, 1923.

GENERAL BACKGROUND AND CULTURE: Henri Frankfort and others, *Before Philosophy* (Pelican); G. L. Dickinson, *The Greek View of Life*, Methuen and Company, Ltd., London, 1932; W. C. Greene, *Moira—Fate, Good, and Evil in Greek Thought*, Harvard University Press, Cambridge, 1944; Werner Jaeger, *Paideia: The Ideals of Greek Culture*, 2 vol., Oxford University Press, New York, 1939; *The Legacy of Greece*, edited by R. W. Livingstone, Clarendon Press, Oxford, 1921, includes material on Greek science and mathematics. In this connection see also S. Sambursky, *The Physical World of the Greeks*, The Macmillan Company, New York, 1956; and for an interesting interpretation of the import of early Greek philosophy for physical science, Erwin Schrödinger, *Nature and the Greeks,* Cambridge University Press, 1954. For a discussion of the unrecognized assumptions in philosophy, with special reference to Greek thought, see F. M. Cornford, *The Unwritten Philosophy and Other Essays,* Cambridge University Press, Cambridge, 1950.

EARLY GREEK PHILOSOPHY: C. M. Bakewell, *Source Book in Ancient Philosophy,* Charles Scribner's Sons, New York, 1907; F. M. Cornford, *Before and After Socrates,* Cambridge University Press, Cambridge, 1932; M. T. McClure, *The Early Philosophers of Greece,* Appleton-Century, New York, 1935.

HISTORIES OF PHILOSOPHY: Frank Thilly and Ledger Wood, *History of Philosophy,* Third Edition, Henry Holt and Company, New York, 1957; W. T. Jones, *A History of Western Philosophy,* Harcourt, Brace and Company, New York, 1952, includes many quotations from the philosophers discussed. Crane Brinton, *Ideas and Men,* Prentice-Hall, New York, 1950, is an intellectual history of Western culture written by an historian. A standard history of modern philosophy is the two-volume work by H. Hoffding, *A History of Modern Philosophy,* Humanities Press, New York, 1950; and representative selections from present day philosophers will be found in James L. Jarrett and Sterling M. McMurrin, *Contemporary Philosophy,* Henry Holt and Company, New York, 1954.

Selections from the works of important philosophers will be found in the Everyman's Library series, E. P. Dutton and Company, New York; in the Scribner series of *Selections;* and in the six volumes of the Mentor *Philosophers* series. The latter may be supplemented with Rex Warner, *The Greek Philosophers* (Mentor). A comprehensive set of selections will be found in the four volumes of *The World's Great Thinkers,* edited by Saxe Commins and Robert N. Linscott, Random House, New York, 1947.

In addition to general dictionaries and encyclopedias, a *Dictionary of Philosophy,* edited by Dagobert D. Runes (Students Outline Series), is available.

THE FIELD AND METHOD OF
PHILOSOPHY

William Oliver Martin, *The Order and Integration of Knowledge*,
The University of Michigan Press, Ann Arbor, 1957, is an
analysis of the fundamental kinds of knowledge and their interrelations, with special reference to the nature and limitations of
each. Karl Jaspers, *The Perennial Scope of Philosophy*, Philosophical Library, New York, 1949, attempts to redefine the
position of philosophy in the world today; an earlier and widely
influential attempt to do the same thing for an earlier day is
John Dewey, *Reconstruction in Philosophy*, Henry Holt and
Company, New York, 1920.

THE NATURE AND PROCESS OF THINKING: C. J. Keyser, *Thinking
About Thinking*, E. P. Dutton, New York, 1926; John Dewey,
How We Think, D. C. Heath and Company, Boston and New
York, 1933, and *Logic: The Theory of Inquiry*, Henry Holt
and Company, New York, 1938; Brand Blanshard, *The Nature
of Thought*, 2 vol., Allen and Unwin, Ltd., London, 1939;
Henry B. Veatch, *Intentional Logic*, Yale University Press,
New Haven, 1952; Arthur E. Murphy, *The Uses of Reason*,
The Macmillan Company, New York, 1943; Stephen Toulmin,
The Uses of Argument, Cambridge University Press, Cam-
bridge, 1958.

THE METHODS OF PHILOSOPHY: R. G. Collingwood, *An Essay on
Philosophical Method*, The Clarendon Press, Oxford, 1933;
Mortimer J. Adler, *Dialectic*, Harcourt, Brace and Company,
New York, 1927; Julius Stenzel, *Plato's Method of Dialectic*,
The Clarendon Press, Oxford, 1940; Richard Robinson, *Plato's
Early Dialectic*, The Clarendon Press, Oxford, 1953. Recent
developments in philosophical analysis are reflected in *Readings
in Philosophical Analysis*, edited by Herbert Feigl and Wilfred
Sellars, Appleton-Century-Crofts, New York, 1949.

MATHEMATICS AND SCIENCE

THE NATURE AND METHOD OF SCIENCE: A. N. Whitehead, *Science
and the Modern World*, The Macmillan Company, 1925, in-

cludes an excellent chapter on mathematics as well as an interpretation of science in the setting of its historical development. *What Is Science?* edited by James R. Newman has articles on the major scientific fields by authorities in those fields; Jacob Bronowski, *The Common Sense of Science* (Modern Library Paperback); James B. Conant, *On Understanding Science* (Mentor) and *Harvard Case Histories in Experimental Science*, 2 vol., Harvard University Press, Cambridge, 1957; Ernest Nagel, *Sovereign Reason and Other Studies in the Philosophy of Science*, The Free Press, Glencoe, Illinois, 1954. One of the most illuminating expositions of the kind of knowledge science provides is in Stephen Toulmin, *The Philosophy of Science*, Hutchinson's University Library, London, 1953. A lucid and lively introduction to the philosophy of science is the recent book by John G. Kemeny, *A Philosopher Looks at Science*, D. Van Nostrand Company, Princeton, 1959.

HISTORY OF SCIENCE: George Sarton, *A Guide to the History of Science*, Chronica Botanica, Waltham, Mass., 1952; A. d'Abro, *The Evolution of Scientific Thought from Newton to Einstein*, Dover, New York, 1950; *Scientific Thought in the Twentieth Century*, edited by A. E. Heath, F. Ungar, New York, 1953. On earlier periods: A. C. Crombie, *Augustine to Galileo;* the History of Science, A.D. 400-1650; Herbert Butterfield, *The Origins of Modern Science*, The Macmillan Company, New York, 1951; Hermann Kesten, *Copernicus and His World*, Roy Publishers, New York, 1945; Galilei Galileo, *Dialogues Concerning Two New Sciences* (Dover).

MATHEMATICS: A. N. Whitehead, *Introduction to Mathematics*, Oxford University Press, New York, 1948; Max Black, *The Nature of Mathematics* (Littlefield, Adams). James R. Newman has edited a four volume work which contains a wealth of material about mathematics, *World of Mathematics*, Simon and Schuster, New York, 1955; and E. T. Bell, *The Development of Mathematics* is a valuable historical study (McGraw-Hill, New York, 1940).

POPULAR INTRODUCTIONS TO THE NEW PHYSICS: Leopold Infeld, *Albert Einstein, His Work and Its Influence in Our World*, Charles Scribner's Sons, New York, 1950; Lincoln Barnett, *The Universe and Dr. Einstein*, W. Sloane Associates, New York, 1949;

Max Planck, *Scientific Autobiography and Other Papers*, Philosophical Library, New York, 1949.

BIOLOGY AND EVOLUTION: Morton Beckner, *The Biological Way of Thought*, Columbia University Press, New York, 1951, describes the special methods of concept formation and explanation that distinguish biology from other natural sciences; G. G. Simpson, *The Meaning of Evolution* (Mentor); Julian S. Huxley, *Evolution as a Process*, Allen and Unwin, London, 1954; Harold F. Blum, *Time's Arrow and Evolution*, Princeton University Press, Princeton, 1951, examines the relationships between organic evolution and the second law of thermodynamics; William S. Beck, *Modern Science and the Nature of Life*, Harcourt, Brace and Company, New York, 1957.

THE CULTURAL AND PHILOSOPHICAL SIGNIFICANCE OF SCIENCE: J. W. N. Sullivan, *The Limitations of Science* (Mentor); Everett W. Hall, *Modern Science and Human Values*, D. Van Nostrand Company, Princeton, 1956; Erwin Schrödinger, *Science and Humanism*, Cambridge University Press, New York, 1951; Robert C. Stauffer (editor), *Science and Civilization*, University of Wisconsin Press, Madison, 1949; C. F. von Weizsäcker, *The History of Nature*, University of Chicago Press, Chicago, 1949, and *The World View of Physics*, published also by the University of Chicago Press, 1952; Werner Heisenberg, *Physics and Philosophy*, Harper and Brothers, New York, 1958.

MAN AND HIS PLACE IN NATURE

Ernst Cassirer, *An Essay on Man*, Oxford University Press, London, 1944; Karl Jaspers, *Man in the Modern Age* (Anchor); Paul Weiss, *Nature and Man*, Henry Holt and Company, 1947; Ralph Tyler Flewelling, *The Person, or the Significance of Man*, Anderson and Ritchie, Los Angeles, 1952; Pierre Teilhard de Chardin, *The Phenomenon of Man*, Harper and Brothers, New York, 1959; David Bidney, *Theoretical Anthropology*, Columbia University Press, 1953; Paul Weiss, *Modes of Being*, Southern Illinois University Press, Carbondale, 1958; and Ralph Harper, *Existentialism: A Theory of Man*, Harvard University Press, Cambridge, 1948. Important books on human freedom are Paul Weiss, *Man's Freedom*, Yale University Press, New

Haven, 1950, and Austin Farrer, *The Freedom of the Will,* Charles Scribner's Sons, New York, 1958.

THE WORLD OF VALUES

R. B. Perry, *General Theory of Value,* Longmans, Green and Company, New York, 1926; Stephen C. Pepper, *A Digest of Purposive Values,* University of California Press, Berkeley, 1947; Wolfgang Köhler, *The Place of Values in a World of Facts,* Liveright, New York, 1938.

ETHICS: Eliseo Vivas, *The Moral Life and the Ethical Life,* University of Chicago Press, Chicago, 1950; Philip Rice Blair, *On the Knowledge of Good and Evil,* Random House, New York, 1955; C. I. Lewis, *The Ground and Nature of the Right,* Columbia University Press, New York, 1955; Nicolai Hartmann, *Ethics,* 3 vol., The Macmillan Company, New York, 1932; Thomas E. Hill, *Contemporary Ethical Theories,* The Macmillan Company, New York, 1950; Henri Bergson, *The Two Sources of Morality and Religion,* Henry Holt and Company, New York, 1935.

ESTHETICS AND THE ARTS: Eliseo Vivas, *Creation and Discovery,* The Noonday Press, New York, 1955; Milton C. Nahm, *The Artist as Creator,* The Johns Hopkins Press, Baltimore, 1956; Jacques Maritain, *Creative Intuition in Art and Poetry,* Pantheon Books, New York, 1953; Pepita Haezrahi, *The Contemplative Activity,* Abelard-Schuman, New York, 1956; T. M. Greene, *The Arts and the Art of Criticism,* Princeton University Press, Princeton, 1940; D. W. Gotshalk, *Art and the Social Order,* University of Chicago Press, Chicago, 1947; Roger Fry, *Vision and Design,* Peter Smith, New York, 1947. ON MUSIC: Aaron Copland, *Music and Imagination* (Mentor), and a more advanced analysis, Donald F. Tovey, *The Forms of Music,* Meridian Books, New York, 1956. ON THE COGNITIVE FUNCTION OF ART AND THE RELATION OF ART TO RELIGION: E. L. Mascall, *Words and Images,* Ronald Press, New York, 1957; Philip Wheelwright, *The Burning Fountain,* Indiana University Press, Bloomington, 1954; Herbert Read, *Icon and Idea,* Harvard University Press, Cambridge, 1955; Henry Alonzo Taylor, *Tragedy: A View of Life,* Cornell University Press, Ithaca,

1956; Geddes MacGregor, *Aesthetic Experience in Religion*, St. Martin's Press, New York, 1947; Martin Foss, *Symbol and Metaphor in Human Experience*, Princeton University Press, Princeton, 1949; James Baird, *Ishmael*, The Johns Hopkins University Press, Baltimore, 1956.

NATURE AND PHILOSOPHY OF RELIGION: Samuel M. Thompson, *A Modern Philosophy of Religion*, Henry Regnery Company, Chicago, 1955; Edwin A. Burtt, *Man Seeks the Divine*, Harper and Brothers, New York, 1957; Alban G. Widgery, *What Is Religion?* Harper and Brothers, New York, 1953; Joachim Wach, *Types of Religious Experience*, University of Chicago Press, 1951; William Temple, *Nature, Man and God*, Macmillan and Company, Ltd., London, 1951; John Herman Randall, Jr., *The Role of Knowledge in Western Religion*, Starr King Press, Boston, 1958; *Christianity and Reason*, edited by Edward P. Myers, Oxford University Press, New York, 1951; Erich Frank, *Philosophical Understanding and Religious Truth*, Oxford University Press, New York, 1945, and *Knowledge, Will, and Belief*, Henry Regnery Company, Chicago, 1956; Wilbur M. Urban, *Humanity and Deity*, Allen and Unwin, London, 1951; James Collins, *God in Modern Philosophy*, Henry Regnery Company, Chicago, 1959; Walter Kaufmann, *Critique of Religion and Philosophy*, Harper and Brothers, New York, 1958.

Glossary

In this glossary terms are defined briefly and these definitions are not intended to take the place of dictionaries of philosophy, encyclopedias, and other works of reference. The definitions are intended primarily to indicate the usage of terms in this book, and students are urged to consult more complete discussions of these terms in standard works of reference.

ABSTRACT ART: Composition for esthetic enjoyment which represents or refers to nothing beyond itself; a composition with no subject-matter; non-representative art.

ABSTRACTION: Taken apart from its own context; the direction of attention upon some single aspect of something, leaving other aspects out of account; formation of a concept. *Abstraction in art* may be understood by analogy with conceptual abstraction as the reproduction in a physical medium of sensory qualities or structural features of an object.

ACCIDENT: In traditional logic, something which can be asserted of an object without being essential to that object; something which exists not in itself but in something else, as a shape or size; a change or occurrence which does not flow from the nature of the thing affected but from some cause beyond the thing itself.

ACTUAL: Literally the condition of being in act; that which is, as distinguished from the merely possible and from what no longer is; real, as opposed to unreal; factual, as opposed to imaginary or apparent.

AFTER-IMAGE: Visual sensation which persists after the eyes are closed.

ANALYSIS: Differentiation of the parts of a structure or of a whole and of distinguishable relations among parts.

APPEARANCE: Qualities or characteristics as experienced; presentation to an observer. Often used to differentiate the apparent properties of things from the qualities they have in themselves.

ARGUMENT: The enumeration of propositions which include, or by which there is suggested, the relation of premises to conclusion; reasoned support of a conclusion; the expression of an inference; presentation of reasons for a conclusion.

ART: Broadly, any process of making under the control of the maker, as distinguished from knowing and from following a design already provided, or product of such process. *Fine Art:* composition in which every part or detail is for the sake of the form of the whole, and which, as a composition is intended to be an object of esthetic experience.

ASSUMPTION: A belief accepted as true without question or examination. (cf. *Presupposition, Postulate.*)

ASSYMMETRICAL: Never symmetrical; an irreversible order. See *Symmetrical relation.*

ATOM: An indivisible, unanalyzable, irreducible, separate unit. *Atom* is usually used with reference to physical units, but theories of mind, of logical propositions, of society, etc., are called *atomistic* when they are conceived as reducible to separate and ultimate units.

ATOMISM: The doctrine that all existence may be analyzed into and explained in terms of ultimate, indivisible, and unanalyzable entities and their interrelationships.

ATTRIBUTE: A part of the nature of something, a quality or characteristic; in traditional logic, that which is affirmed or denied of the subject of a proposition.

AUTHORITY: A source of information recognized to be competent and definitive; or some one who specifies or directs a course of action and is recognized as having the competence and right so to do.

AXIOM: An unproved proposition accepted without question as true. Sometimes used in a wider sense to include *postulate.*

BEHAVIORISM: A school of psychology which restricts psychology to the study of behavior and excludes all reference to mind or consciousness. Behaviorism becomes a philosophy of metaphysical materialism when it carries this principle beyond its methodological application to the point of denying the existence of conscious functions.

BEING: That which in some sense is a determinate nature.

CAUSE, CAUSATION: A *cause* is that which brings about or contributes to a change in something, and *causation* is the process of changing something. In the Aristotelian tradition four causes were distinguished: the material cause, or that from which something comes or out of which it is made; the efficient cause, or the activity producing the effect; the formal cause, or the pattern or structure the effect is to have; and the final cause, or the purpose for the sake of which the effect is produced.

CHARACTER: The relatively stable system of attitudes, habits, moral principles and evaluations in accordance with which a person makes his choices and decisions. Strength and goodness of character are relatively independent; a person may have a strong and good character or a strong and evil character.

CHOICE: The selection of one of two or more recognized alternatives. Choice may fall short of decision. See *Decision.*

CLASSIFICATION: A grouping of items according to some common feature.

COMMITMENT: The acceptance of an obligation, or a goal, as final; a pledge. Usually carries a stronger meaning than *promise* and has less strength than *vow.*

COMMON SENSE: Beliefs accepted without question by a culture group or society. *Common sense* has a special technical meaning in Aristotle's philosophy as the faculty by which we apprehend those qualities of objects common to several senses, such as size, shape, motion, etc.

CONCEPT: An awareness, made possible by abstraction, of identities among the natures of things; an awareness of some aspect of the nature of something which can be identified and grasped in thought; a thought, as distinguished from a percept or image.

CONCLUSION, LOGICAL: An inferred proposition; a proposition asserted as following logically from other propositions.

CONFIRMATION: Verification, specifically by finding substantiating cases.

CONSCIENCE: A direct, unreasoned judgment concerning the rightness or wrongness of an act contemplated or carried out by oneself, usually including a feeling of aversion aroused by the idea of acting contrary to what is judged right.

CONTINGENT: Dependent on something other than itself, for existence or action or change; that which may or may not be, may or may not happen; not necessary.

CONTRADICTION, LOGICAL: A relationship of two propositions such that of the two one must be true and the other false.

COSMOLOGICAL PROOF: The argument that God's existence is necessary in order to account for the existence of the world.

COSMOLOGY: The study of the general structures of existence, including basic laws and relationships; the study of existence as constituting a universe. (Compare *Ontology.*)

DECISION: The adoption of a course of action as that one which is to be carried out.

DEDUCTION: Formal reasoning; exhibition of necessary logical relations between premises and conclusions.

DEFINITION: A determination or specification of the meaning of a term. Strict or formal definition includes the general class (genus) to which the subject belongs, and the features which distinguish it from other things belonging to the same more general class (differentia).

DEISM: The doctrine that God exists as the original cause of the world, the giver of moral law, and the rewarder of good and the punisher of evil in a future life. Deism denies the immanence of God and all direct relation to man and the world.

DESCRIPTIVE JUDGMENT: A judgment about the actual nature of something, in distinction from judgments of worth or of possibility.

DESIGNATION: Reference of a word or expression to some object; the function of being about an object.

DETERMINISM: The doctrine that every occurrence or fact is governed by causes beyond itself. The term is used almost exclusively in this universal sense. (Cf. *Fatalism.*)

DIALECTIC: Originally a method of inquiry or persuasion using questions and answers; more specifically in its traditional Platonic sense, inquiry which proceeds by uncovering assumptions and testing them by following out their implications. *Existential dialectic* as used in this book refers to the examination of the relation between what a statement means and what must be recognized as existing in order to make the occurrence of the statement itself possible.

DISVALUE: See *Value.*

DIVINATION: To obtain a supposed knowledge of divine things or knowledge like to that of divinities by some ritual or ceremony; foreseeing future events.

DOUBLE-ASPECT THEORY: The doctrine that mind and body are distinguishable aspects of the self but not separate in existences.

DOUBT: Refusal to acknowledge a claim of truth which has been made in behalf of a statement, or refusal to make such a claim; the questioning or withdrawing of belief.

DRAMATIC PATTERN: A temporal pattern, or a non-temporal structure grasped in a time experience, the awareness of which involves a felt development, suspense, contrast or conflict, and resolution.

DUALISM: Any theory of two separate existences which may be related but neither of which is a property, phase, or aspect of the other. *Mind-body dualism* attributes to mind and body each its own existence, neither one depending on the other for its own existence. *Moral dualism* not only distinguishes between good and evil but considers them distinct in existence, so that good, in so far as it is good, excludes evil; evil, in so far as it is evil, excludes good.

DURATION: The extension of an existence beyond any single present moment; the actual going on of change.

DUTY: See *Obligation.*

EMPIRICISM: The doctrine that knowledge has its source and derives all its content from experience, which is composed either of the products of sensation alone or together with some kind of direct awareness of mental acts.

ENERGY: The power to act on and change other things; physical capacity to do work.

ENTELECHY: For Aristotle, actuality, form or essence, as distinguished from potentiality. For Driesch, the organizing principle of a living being which must be postulated to account for the distinctive functions of life.

ENTROPY: The transformation of kinetic energy into heat, approaching a state in which differences between energy potentials are absent.

EPIPHENOMENALISM: The doctrine that mind exists only as a by-product of the processes of the nervous system, having no influence upon those processes or anything else.

EPISTEMOLOGY: The study of the nature of knowledge, including problems of what can be known, the limits of knowledge, and the processes of knowing.

ESSENCE: In its broadest sense, the nature or *what* of something; more specifically, the basic nature of something or that by virtue of which a thing is
what it is.

ESSENTIAL SELF-EVIDENCE: See *Self-Evident.*

ESTHETIC EXPERIENCE: Awareness of sensory qualities and of the presented
form of something perceived, as distinguished from an understanding of
what it is or means or of how it is related to other things and other
interests of the observer.

ESTHETIC FORM: Relationship of the parts of a composition; the arrangement
of sensory materials which constitutes a unified composition.

ESTHETIC SURFACE: The sensory content of perception as it is immediately
presented, in distinction from what it is recognized to mean.

ESTHETICS: The study of values as grasped in sense experience; particularly
the study of beauty, especially in art, and including the nature of beauty,
taste, and standards of esthetic value.

ETHICS: The study which attempts to determine what is good for man and
what it is right for him to do; examination of the ultimate ends of human
life, the relation of subordinate to ultimate ends, and nature and limits of
obligation.

EVIDENCE: That which supports the truth of a proposition or helps to show the
existence of something.

EVIL: The opposite of good; that which would better not exist; destructive of
good.

EVOLUTION: In its broader sense, development, increase in complexity of organization involving the acquisition of new functions. More specifically, in
biology, the modification of a living species by selective environmental
influences and/or genetic mutation, as opposed to the theory that living
species are fixed and unchanging. Biological evolution includes the concept
of the gradual descent of more complex or "higher" species from less
complex or "lower" species.

EXISTENCE: To have being as such; to be actual, and in interaction with other
things. Distinguished from the merely possible or ideal, and from essence.

EXISTENTIAL DIALECTIC: See *Dialectic.*

EXISTENTIAL SELF-EVIDENCE: See *Self-Evident.*

EXISTENTIAL TRUTH: See *Truth.*

EXPLANATION: That which accounts for or renders intelligible something already known to be true or to be a fact; a demonstration that some occurrence is in accordance with a known law or principle.

FATALISM: The belief that the outcome of life, or of some action or series of
events, is fixed ahead of time. Fatalism is thus distinguished from universal
determinism as only a partial determinism. To the extent that everything
is conceived as fated, this distinction disappears.

FICTION: Unreal, imaginary; a conceptual construct which is referred to as if
it were a real existent, as: "The average family has two children," or "The
company changed its mind about bringing out a model this year."

FINAL CAUSE: The end toward which a thing tends in its existence; that for the
sake of which something takes place or exists.

FIRST MOVER: In Aristotle and Thomas Aquinas, the First Cause, i.e., God.

FORM: Arrangement, pattern, shape, relationships of parts. Generally distinguished from content or material.

FORMALISM: In ethics, the doctrine that the rightness of an act lies in its conformity to a rule and that the ethical good is the attainment of such conformity.

FORMALIZED THINKING: Thinking which makes use of technical concepts already defined and fixed in meaning, so that those meanings are not sought as goals of inquiry but stipulated as instruments of inquiry.

FREEDOM: Negatively, the absence of restraint, particularly external restraint; positively, the power to act in accordance with one's own choice.

GENERALIZATION: The extension of a uniformity to make it inclusive of some class of occurrences; formation of a general concept from the examination of individual cases.

GOD: In monotheism, ultimate existence which is also the source of all other existence and of all value. Ordinarily the term is used only by those who consider ultimate existence to be in some sense personal or supra-personal.

GOOD: The appropriate object of desire; that which fulfills a genuine need; worth, value; existence which ought to be. *Intrinsic good:* That which is good in and of itself. *Extrinsic good:* That which serves or contributes to something else which is good in itself.

HAPPINESS: For hedonism and utilitarianism, the condition of maximum pleasure with the least pain. Some other ethical theories distinguish happiness from pleasure as a condition of satisfaction and fulfillment.

HEDONISM: Psychological hedonism is the doctrine that man always seeks his own pleasure. Ethical hedonism is the doctrine that man ought always to seek his own pleasure, that the highest good for man is the most pleasure together with the least amount of pain or unpleasantness.

HUMANISM, RELIGIOUS: Religion centered upon man and recognizing no need for belief in deity, with emphasis on social justice and the improvement of the conditions of human life.

HYLOMORPHISM: The doctrine that physical things exist as processes of the realization of form in matter. The universe is thus considered to be a hierarchy of levels, from prime matter, which is pure potentiality, to the highest form which is its own matter. On this theory mind and body have the relation of form to matter.

HYPOTHESIS: A proposition the truth of which is under inquiry, or which is tentatively accepted as a basis of inquiry; a conjecture; a possible or probable explanation.

IDEA: In its broadest sense, a specific thought or awareness, including percept, image, and concept. In Platonism, the timeless essences or universals which are the ultimate realities both as the patterns of which particular existents in the world of space and time are imitations or particular embodiments and as the objects of desire.

IDEALISM: The doctrine which affirms that mind, or the spiritual and ideal, is basic to reality and denies that the non-mental or non-ideal has any real existence in its own right.

IDENTITY: Sameness, exclusion of otherness; being something that is what it is and not something else.

IDEOLOGY: A system or set of ideas accepted as the basis of action or belief on grounds other than evidence of truth.

IMMANENCE: As applied to God, the presence and activity of God within the world.

IMMANENT MEANINGS AND VALUES: In art, meanings and values found within the work itself, in the interrelations of its parts and in the form of the composition, in distinction from the meaning a work may have in relation to other things and from all extrinsic values.

INTEGRATION THEORIES: Theories of mind and body which deny their existence as parts of the human self. Integration theories thus are in opposition to dualism and also to theories which reduce either mind or body to the other.

INTELLECT: The faculty or power of conceptual thought, including judging and reasoning.

INTELLIGIBILITY: Being open to explanation, being understandable or capable of rational explanation.

INTENTIONAL, INTENTIONALITY: Direction of the mind toward an object. A concept or a proposition has logical or cognitive intentionality as an awareness of the nature of the object to which it refers; reference to an object.

INTERACTION: Causal or responsive influence of mind on body or of body on mind.

INTRANSITIVE APPREHENSION: Awareness of an object for what it is in itself rather than for what it means with reference to something else.

INTROSPECTION: Direction of attention toward mental acts and content, such as the awareness of the process of perceiving, the examination of visual images, etc. Often confused with reverie, brooding, or morbid preoccupation with oneself.

INTUITION: A direct awareness not mediated by any other awareness; insight.

KINETIC: In motion (used in physics in contrast with *potential*). *Kinetic theory in physics:* that matter is composed of minute particles in constant motion.

KNOWLEDGE: Awareness of truth as truth, that is, of truth together with the grounds which warrant the claim of truth. *Knowledge* refers also to the content of such awareness.

LAW: A general principle; a uniformity of broad scope which, in the case of natural law, is discovered, and in the case of civil or statute law is imposed.

LOGIC: The study of the structure of concepts, propositions, and arguments, and the formulation and application of tests of validity. Logic is concerned with the form of thought rather than with the content.

MANICHAEISM: A synthesis of Zoroastrianism and Christianity founded in Persia by Mani, a Magian. Influential in Europe during the third and seventh centuries. See *Zoroastrianism*.

MASS: A measure of the quantity of matter, determined by dividing the weight of a body by the acceleration due to gravity.

MATERIAL: As distinguished from formal, that which may receive or possess form; e.g. wood is the material of a table, and the shape or design given to the wood in making the table is the form.

MATERIALISM: The doctrine that all real existence is material, i.e. composed of matter and the functions of matter, the latter traditionally conceived as motion in space.

MATHEMATICS: The science of quantity, abstract structure, and order, in which conclusions (theorems) are derived by formal logic from unproved propositions (axioms or postulates) and certain undefined elements.

MATTER: In ordinary usage, stuff, whatever fills space. More specifically in philosophy, content as distinguished from form, the correlate of form; potentiality for taking on form; relatively stable physical structure as distinguished from processes.

MEANING: What is referred to, designated, intended; or the relation itself by which one thing refers to or designates or intends something else.

MECHANISM: A complex structure of moving parts externally connected and correlated for the performance of some specific function. Mechanism as a philosophical theory is the theory that all existence is to be understood in terms of mechanical principles.

MIND: That which performs conscious and intellectual functions, which perceives, remembers, imagines, conceives, judges, reasons, feels, wills, etc.

MODE OF BEING: *How* something is as distinguished from the fact *that* it is, e.g., an idea and a tree both are, but they have different ways of being; being considered under a limited condition.

MONADS: In Leibniz, the indivisible, indestructible, self-contained, spiritual substances related in a preestablished harmony as the ultimate constituents of reality.

MONOTHEISM: The doctrine that there is only one God.

MORAL, MORALITY: In accordance with a generally accepted code of conduct, violation of which arouses judgments of disapproval and condemnation; such a code of conduct. See *ethics*.

MORAL PROOF: The argument that human freedom and the existence of God are necessary in order to account for the fact that man is a moral being and the world is a moral order, and to guarantee the fulfillment of moral requirements in existence.

MORES: Practices and attitudes common to the members of a society or a social group.

MYTH: An expression of evaluations and interpretations of the meaning of existence in the form of a narrative or pseudo-history; originally, a story in which forces of nature are personified, as in the gods and semi-divine personages of polytheism.

NATURAL HISTORY: More or less systematic description of various objects of nature, especially those of plant and animal life. Distinguished from natural science in being primarily descriptive rather than explanatory.

NATURALISM: In philosophy, the view that there is no existence except what is contained in the world of nature. In art, the attempt to portray objects as those objects appear to us in our ordinary experience of them; faithfulness to detail as it is observed; the restriction of art to the portrayal of nature as it is found.

NATURAL LAW: In ethical and political thought, rules of conduct which hold universally by virtue of being implicated in and expressive of the basic nature of man and of human society, the violation of which is a contradiction of man's nature as human. See *Law*.

NECESSITY, LOGICAL: A relation between propositions such that the truth or falsity of one is impossible without the truth or falsity, as the case may be, of the other. Where the truth of one proposition necessitates the truth of a second, the first cannot be asserted together with the denial of the second without logical contradiction.

NIRVANA: Loss of one's separate personal identity by the merging of consciousness with the One of ultimate being in which all pain, suffering, and desire are extinguished.

OBJECTIVISM: The doctrine that things or qualities or values exist in their own right independently of the knower and of the conditions of knowledge; realism; the assertion of the universal validity of principles, values, etc., as opposed to relativism and subjectivism.

OBLIGATION: In ethics, a claim against oneself; a course of action to which one is morally committed, which it would be morally wrong to fail to carry out, i.e. a morally necessary action; a promise of future action upon which promise another has relied.

ONTOLOGICAL PROOF: The argument for the existence of God, first formulated by Anselm, based on the contention that the idea of God includes necessary existence.

ONTOLOGY: The study of being simply as being; of the modes of being and their relationships. Sometimes used interchangeably with *metaphysics;* sometimes denoting a particular branch of metaphysics, coordinate with epistemology and cosmology.

ORGANISM: In the broadest sense, having organs, having internal organization, a system of internally correlated parts and functions; specifically, an individual plant or animal.

OUGHT: Obligation, moral necessity; a demand upon existence or upon a moral agent that some state of affairs shall be.

PANTHEISM: The doctrine that God is All, or that All is God. There are two emphases: that only God, the Absolute One, exists and that all apparent multiplicity and differences are limited manifestations of the One Reality; and the view that nature is divine or a divinity, that God exists only as immanent in the world.

PARALLELISM: The theory that the correlation of mental and physical functions is not the result of any causal connection between the two. The causal relations within each realm are such that there is a correspondence between the two realms, so that for every physical change there is a mental change and for every mental a physical, but no influence passes from the mental to the physical or from the physical to the mental.

PERSPECTIVE: A stand or position from which something is viewed and, by extension, a set of concepts in terms of which something is understood.

PHILOSOPHY: Literally, the love of wisdom; more specifically as a discipline, the rational organization of all knowledge, the attempt to make explicit and examine its basic assumptions and to discover its meaning for man.

PHYSICAL: Something which exists with both spatial and temporal properties, or having to do with such an existent.

PLURALISM: The doctrine that ultimate existence is many rather than one, or only two, as dualism asserts.

POSSIBLE, POTENTIAL: In its broadest sense, that which can be as distinguished from that which is; not excluded as an impossibility. A possibility in the sense of a potentiality refers to a positive capacity to do or to become something.

POSTULATE: A proposition set up as a premise without consideration of its truth or falsity but solely in order to find what follows from it. A *postulate system:* a logical system of propositions the basic premises of which are postulates.

PRAGMATIC, PRAGMATISM: Concerned with action, practice. Pragmatism is the doctrine that the tests of truth and criteria of value are to be found in the practical consequences of ideas rather than in prior principles.

PRE-ESTABLISHED HARMONY: The synchronization of the activities of unconnected entities; specifically with reference to the mind-body relation, a correlation of mental with physical functions resulting from the original constitution of the mind and body and involving no interaction of the two.

PREHENSION: In Whitehead, the grasping of aspects of other things, from a specific perspective, into a distinctive unity of feeling.

PREJUDICE: Literally pre-judgment. A judgment or conclusion which is formed without adequate consideration of the relevant evidence, usually based on emotional attitudes. Sometimes, and in a broader sense, as by Edmund Burke, to refer to those judgments we form intuitively as products of long experience on the part both of the individual and of his society.

PREMISE: Something stated to begin with; more specifically, a proposition from which an inference is drawn, usually in combination with one or more other premises.

PRESENTATIONAL IMMEDIACY: Direct presence in awareness; what is presented directly is seen for what it is *as presented*, not in terms of other meanings it may have or in terms of its relations to anything beyond the direct presentation.

PRESUPPOSITION: An unexpressed assumption or implication; a proposition the truth of which is required for the truth of another proposition.

PROOF: Test, demonstration, establishment of truth by showing that it is implied by other truth. *Formal proof* establishes validity only; i.e. shows only that if the premises of the proof are true the conclusion is true and that if the conclusion is false one at least of the premises is false.

PROPERTY: A quality or character belonging to the nature of something; traditionally used in the more precise sense of an attribute common to and peculiar to all members of a species or one which follows necessarily from such an attribute.

PURPOSE: An end in view and intended to be realized.

QUALITY: A part of the nature of something; a part of *what* something is; attribute; characteristic.

QUANTITY: A property in which differences or variations in degree may be discerned; capable of being identified as an amount or a portion; something capable of increase or decrease.

RATIONALISM: The doctrine that reason or pure thought is the only source of genuine knowledge.

REAL: Actual as distinguished from the merely possible; to be a nature or an essence which has its own existence.

? REASONING: The process of following logical relationships from one thought to another and thus discovering, when reasoning is performed correctly, what else must be true if the premises are true.

REFLECTION: Sometimes used as equivalent to introspection; but more basically the awareness which comes from directing attention upon other awareness.

REIFICATION: To treat something imaginary or abstract as if it were real.

RELATION: A linkage between items, or the status of one item from the standpoint of another.

RELATIVISM: The doctrine that things are what they are only by virtue of relations to other things; variation of truth from individual to individual; denial of absolute standards.

REPRESENTATIONAL ART: Art created with the primary intention of exhibiting some aspect of the nature of the object portrayed; art that is primarily descriptive.

REVELATION: The opening up of knowledge or meanings to those who have failed to discover such meanings from their own experience or by the use of their own powers. In religion, revelation is understood as one means by which divinity communicates with man.

RIGHT: In ethics, an act in accordance with moral law, not contrary to what ought to be done. In its legal sense, an enforceable claim against another. Political rights are liberties and opportunities to exercise certain political functions which ought to be recognized by governments.

RITUAL: A fixed pattern of symbolic acts, usually religious in significance and intended to express man's relationship to hidden powers of existence and to seek or enlist their aid; or any act which, by virtue of its fixed form, is supposed to make accessible some power or influence beyond itself. Many superstitions involve ritual in the latter sense.

SANCTIONS: Rewards or punishments or other influences which encourage or discourage the performance of certain actions, as distinguished from the intrinsic values involved and respect for the inherent rightness or wrongness of the action.

SCIENCE: In its broadest sense, systematic knowledge; in the stricter modern sense, a science is a body of organized knowledge resting upon and finding its confirmation in sense-perception, and depending upon its own established procedures for its tests of truth.

SELF-CONTRADICTORY: A statement or argument is self-contradictory when the contradiction is between parts of itself rather than between it and another statement or argument. See *contradiction.*

SELF-EVIDENT: Truth which is apparent as soon as the meaning of its statement is understood. In this book *existential self-evidence* is distinguished from *essential* self-evidence: *existential* self-evidence is found where the understanding of the meaning of a statement discloses directly the existence of something, while *essential self-evidence* refers to statements which cannot be denied without self-contradiction. See *Evidence.*

SELF-REALIZATION: The ethical doctrine that man's highest good is the most complete possible harmonious fulfillment of his potentialities.

SENSE, SENSATION: Response to physical stimuli; experience resulting from the presence of an object to the senses. The term may refer to the process of sensing or to the content of sensation, such as color, sound qualities, etc.

*SOUL: In Aristotle, the vital principle. Aristotle distinguished between vegetable, animal, and rational souls. The *soul-substance theory* holds that the distinctive and permanent part of the human individual is a simple, indivisible spiritual entity.

SPIRITUALISM: The doctrine that existence is composed exclusively of spirit or of a plurality of spirits and their acts and functions. By *spirit* is meant an immaterial being possessing intelligence and will and capable of acting upon other beings.

SPONTANEITY: Uncaused and unhindered action; self-initiated action; action from internal impulse or energy.

STANDARD: An ideal or a criterion by which certain things are judged or evaluated; a fixed value against which other values are identified or their status determined.

STIPULATION: Something set forth; agreement upon a condition set down to be observed.

SUBJECTIVISM: The doctrine that all things which exist are knowing and experiencing beings or states of such beings; that the world exists only for mind, and thus that all existence is composed of minds and ideas; dependence on mind or on consciousness.

SUBSTANCE: What exists in its own right, not as attribute of something else or as a relation of one thing to another. The *substance of* something is its essential nature, and *substance* is sometimes used to denote a substratum upon which other aspects of the nature of a thing depend.

SUPPOSITION: Something considered provisionally to be true or treated provisionally as true. In its technical sense the supposition of a term indicates the mode of being of that term. In "That tree is dropping its leaves," "tree" indicates real existence and has real supposition; in the phrase "tree of life" the term has mental supposition; in " 'Tree' has four letters," verbal supposition.

SYLLOGISM: Premises and conclusion stated in such a way as to make explicit the logical relationship they have to each other by virtue of their formal properties as propositions.

SYMMETRICAL RELATION: One which, when it holds between terms in one order, holds also when the order is changed, e.g., if A is equal to B, B is equal to A.

SYNTHESIS: A harmonizing or reconciling of differences, or the combining of one thing with something else to constitute a single whole.

TECHNOLOGY: The application of knowledge or a set of principles to practical problems; knowledge for the sake of doing or making.

TELEOLOGICAL PROOF: The argument that God's existence is necessary in order to account for the supposed fact that the world exists with a purposive nature, that there are real relationships of means and ends in nature.

TELIC: Having to do with an end or goal, tending toward an end; purposive.

THEISM: The theory that God exists both as immanent within the world and as transcendent of the world, as creator who not only gives to the world its original existence but sustains it in existence, and as the ultimate end with reference to which all existence has its meaning and in which it has its end.

THEOLOGY: Knowledge or theory concerning God and/or sacred things. In its strict sense as a learned discipline, theology is the conceptual interpretation and understanding of the content of a religion. Theology in this sense is distinguishable from other theoretical disciplines in the fact that its concepts are not obtained by abstraction from direct experience of the world and of ourselves, but by abstraction from a supposed revelation which is accepted as normative.

THEOREM: A conclusion obtained deductively from basic propositions.

THEORY: An attempt to formulate general relationships and to see the structure of an area of knowledge, as distinguished from a concern for specific facts as such and for the practical applications of knowledge.

THOUGHT: In its most general sense, any awareness. More specifically, conceptual awareness and awareness of logical relationships.

TIME: Measured duration; a span of succession in which past, present, and future are distinguishable from positions within the span.

TRANSCENDENCE: Literally, a going beyond. As applied to God, to be beyond imperfection, limitation, comprehension, and to exist beyond nature.

TRANSITIVE RELATION: One which when it holds between a first and a second term and between the second and a third term also holds between the first and third terms, such as *smaller than* or *subsequent to*.

TRUTH: A property of propositions by virtue of which what the proposition says or shows to be the case is the case. Essential and existential truth may be distinguished as (a) the conformity of what is asserted of something to the nature of that thing, and (b) the effective disclosure of the existence of something.

ULTIMATE: Literally that which is last; more generally, a level or step of analysis or mode of existence which is final. This may be an absolute priority or an absolute end, or it may refer to entities incapable of being explained in terms of anything else.

UNIFORMITY: Regularity; preservation of a fixed sequence; sameness of parts and of the relationship of parts.

UNITY: One-ness, being single; in a more restricted sense a condition in which parts or distinguishable entities form one whole.

UTILITARIANISM: The ethical doctrine that the measure of right action is the principle of utility, i.e., that the better act is the one which will produce the greater amount of happiness or pleasure for the greater number of people.

VALIDITY, LOGICAL: The relation of premises and conclusion such that the truth of the premises requires the truth of the conclusion, and the falsity of the conclusion requires the falsity of at least one premise; logical necessity.

VALUE: Worth, desirability, what ought to be, good; or their opposites. When used in the positive sense alone, *disvalue* is used to denote negative values.

VALUE JUDGMENT: A specific evaluation, a judgment that something has or lacks worth of some kind. The term is applied to judgments of disvalue as well as to judgments which attribute positive worth to something.

VIRTUE: Strength or excellence, especially of character; the ability of something to perform its function well; the power to act in accordance with reason; the habitual choice of the right.

VITALISM: The theory that living organisms contain a non-physical agent the existence of which is necessary to account for the performance of the vital functions.

ZOROASTRIANISM: An ancient Indo-Iranian religion and surviving today in some communities in Persia and India, characterized by veneration of fire and sun worship, and a doctrine of ethical dualism of ultimate personal powers of good and evil between which man must choose in the cosmic struggle of light and darkness, of good and evil, of truth and falsehood, and of right and wrong.

Index

certainty, mathematical, 143 ff.
change, 173
Chapman, Harmon M., 250
Chesterton, Gilbert, 58
Christian tradition. *See* Hebrew-Christian tradition
classification, scientific, 116
common sense, 53, 54 ff., 171 ff., 174 ff.
  and language, 174
  and science, 122, 177
  see also philosophy
communication, art as, 340 ff.
Comte, Auguste, 109
Condon, Edward U., 192
conceptual knowledge, 153 f.
concepts, 21, 33 ff., 135
  as intentional, 140 ff.
  see also abstraction
confirmation, scientific, 114
Conrad, Joseph, 18 f.
Constant de Rebeque, Henri Benjamin, 322 f.
contingency, factual, 123 ff.
Copi, Irving M., 175 f.
cosmological argument. *See* God, existence of
creation and discovery in art, 354

D'Arcy, M. C., 268 f.
Darrow, Clarence, 197
Darwin, Charles, 202
Darwinism, social, 199
definitions and science, 156
deism, 378
Democritus, 134
Descartes, René, 224 ff., 229
description, scientific, 114 ff.
desire, pleasure and, 313 f.
determinism, 260, 261 ff., 265 f., 271 ff.
Deutsch, Karl W., 204 f., 209
dialectic, existential, 91 f.
discovery, method of, 79 ff.
double aspect theory. *See* mind and body
Driesch, Hans, 210 ff.
dualism, 220 ff., 223 ff., 238
  and hylomorphism, 239 ff.
DuBois-Reymond, Emil, 209

duty, ethics of, 317 ff.
  and good, 327 ff.

Ecclesiastes, 381 f.
Einstein, Albert, 55, 164, 166, 184
Eliot, T. S., 340 f.
entelechy, 211
entropy, 188
Epictetus, 17 f., 60 f.
Epicurus, 311 f., 314, 316
epiphenomenalism, 228
essence and existence, 97
esthetic experience, 335 ff.
  form, 337 ff.
  level of art, 357
  surface, 336
ethics, 304 ff.
  of duty, 317 ff.
  problem of, 304 f.
ethical formalism, 321 ff.
  situation, 305 ff.
evolution, 196 f., 214 ff.
existence, essence and, 97
  of God. *See* God, existence of
  mathematics and, 142 f., 150 ff., 164 ff.
  thought and, 90 f.
  see also self
existential dialectic, 91 f., 268 ff.
  truth. *See* truth
experience, esthetic, 335 ff.
  sense, 82 ff.
explanation, generalization and, 155 ff.
  logical and psychological, 120 f.
  scientific, 114 ff.

fact and theory, 45 f.
fatalism, 261 f.
Fermi, Enrico, 184
Ferrier, J. F., 66 f.
form, esthetic, 337 ff.
  and matter, 233 ff.
formalism, ethical, 321 ff.
Fourier, Joseph, 187
freedom, 265 ff.
  problem of, 259 ff.
  see also self and freedom, the

mathematics, 105 ff.
  and existence, 142 f., 150 ff., 164
  and quantity, 142 f.
  and science, 110 ff., 157, 165 f.
  and validity, 144 f.
  see also art and mathematics
matter and form, 233 ff.
Maxwell, Clerk, 186
meaning, search for, 10 ff.
meanings, immanent, 336
mechanism, 203 ff., 206 ff., 262 f.
  and vitalism, 201 f., 210 ff.
medicine and science, 109
Mill, James, 263n, 316
Mill, John Stuart, 316
mind-body theories as postulates,
  235 ff.
mind and body, 220 ff.
  double aspect theory of, 231 f., 236,
  238
  integration theories of, 225
  see also dualism and hylomorphism
monotheism, 377 f.
Moore, G. E., 283 f.
Morgan, Charles, 348 f.
Munitz, Milton K., 188
music, 353 f.
myth, 106 ff.
  see also polytheism

National Socialism, 199
natural history, science and, 155
  selection, 215
  see also evolution
nature, the free self and, 271 ff.
Needham, Joseph, 217
neo-Platonism, 229
Newton, Isaac, 184
Newtonian physics, 188 f.
Niebuhr, Reinhold, 374 f.
Nietzsche, Friedrich, 300

obligation, pleasure and, 314 ff.
observation, 112
  in science, 112 ff., 118
ontological argument. *See* God, existence of

pantheism, 377 f.
parallelism, 225, 236
past, awareness of the, 252 ff.
perspectives, religious and secular,
  363 f.
philosophical argument, 84 ff., 89 ff.
  test of, 89 ff.
philosophies, value of false, 65 ff.
philosophy, 105 ff.
  appeal of, 3 ff.
  and common sense, 58 ff.
  competence of, 68 ff.
  having a, 31 ff.
  importance of, 40 ff.
  method of, 77, 92 ff.
  origin of, 51
  and other fields of knowledge, 22 ff.
  and other quests for meaning, 25 ff.
  our introduction to, 29 ff.
  progress of, 71 ff.
  as reflective inquiry, 14 ff.
  and science, 77 f., 111 f., 179 f.
  as a search for truth, 19 ff.
  as a search for ultimates, 62 ff.
  subject matter of, 7 ff.
  as unformalized rational inquiry,
  110 f.
  using a, 35 ff.
physics, 187 ff.
  and biology, 201 ff.
  Newtonian, 188 f.
Planck, Max, 184
Planck's constant, 124, 190
Plato, 30, 71 f., 181, 224, 229, 231,
  291
pleasure and desire, 313 f.
  and obligation, 314 ff.
Plotinus, 229
poetry, 340 ff.
political thought and biology, 199 ff.
polytheism, 377, 379 ff., 384
postulates, assumptions and, 144
potentiality, 214 ff., 292 ff.
Psalms, The, 384
purpose, 174
Pythagoreans, 134
Prall, D. W., 336n
pre-scientific thought, 180 ff.

truth, existential, 373 f., 388 f.
  religious, 374 ff., 386 ff.
  scientific, 163 ff.
  see also art and truth
  see also philosophy as a search for
    truth

ultimates, 12 ff., 68 f. *See also* philosophy as a search for ultimates
Urban, Wilbur Marshall, 292, 299
utilitarianism, 310, 316 f.

validity, logical, 59, 90
  mathematics and, 144 f.
value, 98 f., 279 ff.
  relativity of, 296, 299n
  relations, 300 f.
  standards, 295 ff.
  subjectivist theory of, 284 ff., 287 ff.,
    299n
  theory, 283 ff.
Veatch, Henry B., 83, 97n

vitalism, 210 ff., 216
  and mechanism, 201 ff., 210 ff.
Vivas, Eliseo, 298, 336, 345 f., 354

Watson, John B., 228
Weiss, Paul, 253n
Westermarck, Edward, 284 f., 286n,
  288 f.
Wheelwright, Philip, 184 f., 301, 343
White, Leslie, 228
Whitehead, Alfred North, 8, 174, 193,
  230, 232 f., 376
Whittaker, Edmund Taylor, 133 f.,
  141
Wiener, Norbert, 179
Wild, John, 350 f., 253 f., 272
Wilder, Raymond L., 141
Wordsworth, William, 343
Wright, G. Ernest, 380 f.

Zoroastrianism, 386